MW01034297

EFFECTIVE DOMESTIC REMEDIES AND THE EUROPEAN COURT OF HUMAN RIGHTS

In Malone v. UK (Plenary 1984), the right to an effective domestic remedy in the European Convention on Human Rights Article 13 was famously described as one of the most obscure clauses in the Convention. Since then, the European Court of Human Rights has reinforced the scope and application of the right. Through an analysis of virtually all of the Court's judgments concerning Article 13, the book exhaustively accounts for the development and current scope and content of the right. The book also provides normative recommendations on how the Court could further develop the right, most notably how it could be a tool to regulate the relationship between domestic and international protection of human rights. In doing so, the book situates itself within larger debates on the enforcement of the entire Convention such as the principle of subsidiarity and the procedural turn in the Court's case law.

Michael Reiertsen is judge in Borgarting Court of Appeals, Oslo, Norway. He is a former researcher and lecturer at the Faculty of Law, University of Oslo, and adviser in the Legislation department of the Norwegian Ministry of Justice. He served as expert in the Council of Europe Committee of Experts for the improvement of procedures of the protection of human rights (DH-PR) (2008 to 2012).

Effective Domestic Remedies and the European Court of Human Rights

APPLICATIONS OF THE EUROPEAN CONVENTION
ON HUMAN RIGHTS ARTICLE 13

MICHAEL REIERTSEN

CAMBRIDGE
UNIVERSITY PRESS

University Printing House, Cambridge CB2 8BS, United Kingdom

One Liberty Plaza, 20th Floor, New York, NY 10006, USA

477 Williamstown Road, Port Melbourne, VIC 3207, Australia

314–321, 3rd Floor, Plot 3, Splendor Forum, Jasola District Centre, New Delhi – 110025, India

103 Penang Road, #05–06/07, Visioncrest Commercial, Singapore 238467

Cambridge University Press is part of the University of Cambridge.

It furthers the University's mission by disseminating knowledge in the pursuit of education, learning, and research at the highest international levels of excellence.

www.cambridge.org
Information on this title: www.cambridge.org/9781009153546
DOI: 10.1017/9781009153539

© Michael Reiertsen 2022

This publication is in copyright. Subject to statutory exception and to the provisions of relevant collective licensing agreements, no reproduction of any part may take place without the written permission of Cambridge University Press.

First published 2022

A catalogue record for this publication is available from the British Library.

ISBN 978-1-009-15354-6 Hardback

Cambridge University Press has no responsibility for the persistence or accuracy of URLs for external or third-party internet websites referred to in this publication and does not guarantee that any content on such websites is, or will remain, accurate or appropriate.

Contents

Figures

Preface

The idea and inspiration for writing this book came to me when I was working in the Legislation Department of the Norwegian Ministry of Justice (2008–2012). I was the Norwegian expert in the Council of Europe Committee of Experts for the improvement of procedures of the protection of human rights (DH-PR) and participated actively in the process of the reform of the European Court of Human Rights and the system for protection of human rights under the European Convention on Human Rights. It struck me that everyone talked about how the key to saving the Court and reforming the system was the improvement of domestic remedies. Yet, no one really knew what was required by the one Article in the Convention that explicitly deals with domestic remedies – Article 13. This was, at least partly, due to the fact that the Court's case law was abundant, but, at the same time, not very illuminating. However, we also knew that something could be in the offing. The Court had slowly started to reinforce the scope of application of Article 13, most notably through the Grand Chamber judgment *Kudla v. Poland* (2000), and the calls for achieving a more subsidiary protection of human rights seemed to be unequivocal and growing steadily. At the same time, we were acutely aware of the fact that whenever there is court-made development in law, questions on limits and legitimacy arise. Was this mysterious provision a sleeping beauty about to awake, or was it better tucked back into sleep?

The Faculty of Law at the University of Oslo granted me the opportunity to write a Ph.D. on this subject matter. This book is a thoroughly updated and revised version of my thesis for the degree of Ph.D., defended at the Faculty of Law, University of Oslo, in March 2017. The book is up to date with case law and literature as of November 1, 2021.

The fundament of the book is an analysis of the Court's judgments in Grand Chamber and Chambers in which the keyword search function of the Hudoc database identifies Article 13 as a keyword. As of November 1, 2021, this amounts to 2,534 judgments (approximately 13 percent of all the Court's judgments rendered in Chambers and Grand Chamber). The analysis shows that, in particular, as from the year 2000, there has been a certain development in the case law. Most notably, the Court, now, actually considers whether Article 13 has been violated in addition to substantive Articles. The Court, also, performs a stricter assessment of many requirements arising under Article 13, for example, how an aggregate of remedies may be effective and how the domestic remedial authority must deal with the substance of the Convention complaint. The Court, also, increasingly specifies the relief required in concrete situations, most notably, compensation for nonpecuniary damages in more and more scenarios. However, although Article 13 is starting to come into age, there is still considerable uncertainty both regarding the role that Article 13 has in the system of protection of human rights under the Convention and the content and scope of specific obligations.

The book concludes by providing normative advice with regard to how the Court's case law could further develop, most notably by illustrating the role that Article 13 could have in regulating the relationship between international and national protection of human rights. In doing so, the book situates Article 13 within larger debates of the Convention system, such as the procedural turn in the Court's case law, the enforcement of the entire Convention, and the interpretation and application of the principle of subsidiarity.

Acknowledgments

This book builds on my thesis for the degree of Ph.D., defended at the Faculty of Law, University of Oslo, in March 2017. I am grateful to the adjudication committee, consisting of Professor Malcolm Langford (University of Oslo), Professor Janneke Gerards (Utrecht University), and Professor Patricia Popelier (University of Antwerp), for their thoughtful and insightful comments and critique, which this book has benefited from. Matti Pellonpää, former Justice at the Supreme Administrative Court of Finland, the ECtHR and the Commission in Strasbourg, commented extensively on a draft at the midway evaluation of the project and firmly installed the belief that I was on the right track. My supervisors, Justice dr. juris Arnfinn Bårdsen, now judge in the European Court of Human Rights, then judge in the Norwegian Supreme Court, Professor Inger-Johanne Sand (University of Oslo), and Professor Andreas Føllesdal (University of Oslo), were a constant and necessary support and safely steered me toward the goal line. During the publication process, three anonymous peer reviewers and my editor, Tom Randall, have provided additional and much appreciated advice. The book has, in addition, profited from numerous discussions, advice, and critique from many others. I hope that you know who you are and that I am grateful. Above all, I am thankful to my wife Bärbel and three sons Peter, Johannes, and Emil. You have made this possible and make it all worthwhile.

Citations of Case Law

The book does not distinguish between case law from the original Court and the current (unique) Court introduced by Protocol 11. In text and footnotes, Chamber judgments are referenced by the name and the year, for example, *Silver a.o. v. the UK* (1983). Other judgments and decisions are marked with Plenary, Grand Chamber, Committee, or decision to identify deviations from judgments in Chamber, for example, *Nada v. Switzerland* (Grand Chamber 2012) and *Mifsud v. France* (Grand Chamber decision 2002). Commission reports and Commission decisions are referenced in a similar manner, but adding that it is a Commission report or decision, for example, *Aydin v. Turkey* (Commission report 1996) and *Luberti v. Italy* (Plenary Commission decision 1981).

Abbreviations

ACHR	American Convention on Human Rights
a.o.	and others
Bogotá Declaration	American Declaration of the Rights and Duties of Man
Brighton Declaration	High-level Conference on the Future of the European Court of Human Rights, Brighton Declaration, April 20, 2012
Brussels Declaration	High-level Conference on the Implementation of the European Convention on Human Rights, our shared responsibility, Brussels Declaration, March 27, 2015
CAT	UN Convention against Torture and Other Cruel, Inhuman or Degrading Treatment or Punishment
CDDH	Steering Committee for Human Rights, Council of Europe
CETP	Collected Editions of the *"Travaux Prépara-toires"* Volumes I–VIII, published by Martinus Nijhoff between 1975 and 1985
Commission	European Commission on Human Rights
Convention	European Convention for the Protection of Human Rights and Fundamental Freedoms
Copenhagen Declaration	High-level Conference on Reform of the Convention System, Copenhagen Declaration, April 12 and 13, 2018
Court	European Court of Human Rights
ECHR	European Convention for the Protection of Human Rights and Fundamental Freedoms

ECtHR	European Court of Human Rights
et al.	*et alia*/and others
HRC	UN Human Rights Committee
IACtHR	Inter-American Court of Human Rights
ibid.	*ibidem*/in the same place
ICCPR	UN International Covenant on Civil and Political Rights
ICJ	International Court of Justice
i.e.	*id est*/that is
ILC	International Law Commission
Interlaken Declaration	High-level Conference on the Future of the European Court of Human Rights, Interlaken Declaration, February 19, 2010
Izmir Declaration	High-level Conference on the Future of the European Court of Human Rights, Izmir Declaration, April 27, 2011
P	Protocol
para.	paragraph
TEU	Treaty of the European Union
UDHR	Universal Declaration of Human Rights
UN	United Nations
VCLT	Vienna Convention on the Law of Treaties
Vol.	Volume

1

Setting the Scene

1.1 GOALS AND LIMITATIONS

This book analyzes the legal content and scope of the right to an effective domestic remedy in Article 13 of the European Convention on Human Rights (hereinafter the Convention or the ECHR),[1] as construed and applied in the case law of the European Court of Human Rights (hereinafter the Court or the ECtHR).[2]

The book not only accounts for the current scope of Article 13, but the development in the Court's case law.[3] These elements are both interconnected and independent. It is, on the one hand, not possible to account for the content of law without having, at the very least, a sense of how law has

---

[1] Convention for the Protection of Human Rights and Fundamental Freedoms, signed in Rome on November 4, 1950, entry into force on September 3, 1953, on the condition of ten ratifications; see Article 59(3) of the ECHR. The Convention has been amended by several Protocols, *inter alia*, Protocols 11 and 14 amending the control system, and several Protocols granting additional rights. These rights are additional to the Convention, with the consequence that all provisions of the Convention apply accordingly; see, for example, Article 6 of Protocol 4. As a consequence, the jurisdiction of the European Court of Human Rights (ECtHR), as foreseen in Section II of the ECHR, applies to the Protocols, and, most importantly in this context, Article 13 of the ECHR applies in combination with substantive rights in the Protocols.

[2] The jurisdiction and competences of the Court are regulated in Section II of the ECHR and the Rules of the Court; see Articles 24(1) and 25 *litra* d ECHR.

[3] The most comprehensive expositions of Article 13 in legal literature, which I am aware of, is Mertens (1968) (in French) and Barkhuysen (1998) (in Dutch). Further, the general legal literature on the Convention deals with Article 13 only briefly (between five and thirty pages). Article 13 has also been dealt with in legal articles, focusing on specific contexts, for example, Vysockiene (2002), or as one of the elements in developing a more "... adequate, theoretical understanding of the Court's practice"; see Christoffersen (2009) 1. Remedies have also been analyzed more generally in international human rights law, most thoroughly in Shelton (2015) and Roach (2021). However, these studies are primarily directed at the remedial powers of international courts (Shelton) or with a comparative and more general perspective (Roach).

developed. The present is always understood in the light of the past. This is not only a realization of general hermeneutics,[4] but is firmly present in the legal method applied by the Court, not least when it considers whether its interpretation should be dynamical or not. On the other hand, knowing the past has independent historical value, and knowing the current content of law, is the primary task of lawyers working in practice.

Given the enormous amount of case law from the Court, it is not possible to give an exhaustive account of every judgment and decision in which the Court has dealt with Article 13, nor is it desirable. Facts, details, and tensions in a rapidly expanding case law would distort the general picture. However, the book provides an exhaustive overview of the requirements stemming from Article 13, as they present themselves in the Court's case law, including how they have been developed. The depth and amount of detail of the analyses are guided by three lines of thought: (1) the need for clarification (e.g. because of unclear, contradicting, or a lack of case law), (2) the development in the case law, and (3) the potential for achieving a more subsidiary and effective protection of human rights. This third element is closely related to the second goal of this book, which I return to shortly.

The focus on clarifying what the Court requires and has required, under Article 13, has several consequences.

First, this book does not analyze ideal practices of remedies at the domestic level. Indeed, the Court sets out minimum standards, not an ideal level of protection.[5] This is reflected in the fact that the Court, also under Article 13, affords States a margin of appreciation (Chapter 8). Consequently, for the search of an ideal remedy, the specific remedial structures of Member States must be taken into account, and the discretion that the Court grants left out. In any case, the judgments of the Court rarely provide examples of best practices, but controversial practices, which, arguably, violate the Convention.[6]

Second, Article 13 deals with legal remedies (legal requirements concerning remedies, according to Article 13). But nonlegal remedies, and various nonlegal measures, may certainly be important for the effectiveness of the remedial task and, implicitly, legal remedies, for instance, measures concerning education and professional training, electronic communication, and general

---

[4] See, for example, Gadamer (1975).

[5] See, as an expression, Article 53 of the ECHR.

[6] *Guide to Good Practice in Respect of Domestic Remedies* (adopted by the Committee of Ministers on September 18, 2013, available at the web page of the Council of Europe) attempts to analyze best practices of remedies.

information.[7] Indeed, such measures may, under other circumstances, constitute legal remedies (*i.e.* if the Court had construed the legal requirements differently) but are not dealt with in this book. That being said, the distinction between legal remedies and nonlegal remedies is not always easy to draw – in particular, because of the (legal) requirement that the remedy be effective not only in theory but also in practice (Section 9.4).

Third, when analyzing the legal content of Article 13, both the past and current scope of Article 13 must be read in context with other rights and principles in the Convention.[8] However, many such relationships would have deserved a more thorough and maybe different treatment than that which I provide in this book. Indeed, the guiding criterion of "need for clarification" mostly only implies that I demonstrate this need. I do not always provide a fully fledged account of how I perceive that the question should be clarified. The relationship between Article 13 and similar procedural and remedial requirements under substantive Articles, in particular the positive obligation to secure substantive rights, is one such area. This limitation, however, leads me to the second and normative goal of this book.

In principle, a normative analysis of every requirement in Article 13, including its relationship with other rights and principles in the Convention, could be undertaken. But the normative goal of this book is primarily to illustrate and provide advice concerning the role Article 13 could have in the system of protection of human rights under the Convention. By that I mean the role Article 13 could have in regulating, more generally, the relationship between international and national protection of human rights. In this respect, the developing notion of subsidiarity is essential. This analysis is chiefly undertaken

---

7 The importance of such measures is increasingly recognized within the Council of Europe; see, for example, Rec(2002)13, December 18, 2002, of the Committee of Ministers on the publication and dissemination in the Member States of the text of the ECHR and of the case law of the ECtHR; Rec(2004)4, May 12, 2004, of the Committee of Ministers to Member States on the ECHR in university education and professional training; Rec(2006)12, September 27, 2006, of the Committee of Ministers to Member States on empowering children in the new information and communications environment; Rec(2007)17, November 21, 2007, of the Committee of Ministers to Member States on gender equality standards and mechanisms; Rec(2008)2, February 6, 2008, of the Committee of Ministers to Member States on efficient domestic capacity for rapid execution of judgments of the ECtHR; Rec(2012)3, April 4, 2012, of the Committee of Ministers to Member States on the protection of human rights with regard to search engines; Rec(2012)9, September 12, 2012, of the Committee of Ministers to Member States on mediation as an effective tool for promoting respect for human rights and social inclusion of Roma.

8 See Section 2.4 and the Vienna Convention on the Law of Treaties (hereinafter the VCLT), done at Vienna on May 23, 1969, entry into force on January 27, 1980, Article 31(1).

in Chapters 12 and 13, whereas the more descriptive analyses of case law are undertaken in Chapters 2 to 11. That being said, Chapters 2 to 11 also contain specific normative considerations, but then mostly only to the extent that they are necessary prerequisites for the global normative recommendations in the concluding Chapter 13. Certainly, many other specific legal questions arising under Article 13 and relationships between Article 13 and other rights and principles would have deserved a more independent normative analysis and evaluation. I can only hope that the descriptive and normative analyses that I have undertaken may serve as a fundament for further study.

In the remainder of this introductory chapter, I provide brief overviews of the content of Article 13 (Section 1.2) and the uncertainty and (evolving) development in the Court's case law (Section 1.3).

1.2 ARTICLE 13 IN BRIEF

Article 13 of the ECHR aims to enforce substantive Convention rights at the domestic level.

The English version reads:

Article 13 – Right to an effective remedy

> Everyone whose rights and freedoms as set forth in this Convention are violated shall have an effective remedy before a national authority notwithstanding that the violation has been committed by persons acting in an official capacity.

The French version reads:

Article 13 – Droit à un recours effectif

> Toute personne dont les droits et libertés reconnus dans la présente Convention ont été violés, a droit à l'octroi d'un recours effectif devant une instance nationale, alors même que la violation aurait été commise par des personnes agissant dans l'exercice de leurs fonctions officielles.

The French wording *"recours"* only includes a right to effective access to a national authority that can determine whether substantive Convention rights have been violated, but the English wording "remedy" also includes a right to redress.[9] In the early legal literature, some claimed that the Court and the former

---

9   See, for example, the definition in the *Webster's Encyclopedic Unabridged Dictionary* of the English Language, which holds that the wording "remedy" encompasses "to cure, relieve or heal ... to restore to the natural or proper condition; put right: to remedy a matter" as well as "legal redress; the legal means of enforcing a right or redressing a wrong."

European Commission on Human Rights (hereinafter the Commission) had opted for an interpretation in line with the French wording,[10] but the subsequent case law confirms that Article 13 contains both a right to access to justice and a right to redress at the national level for violations of Convention rights.[11] The right to redress includes a right to enforcement of any redress awarded.[12]

The French wording "*a droit à l'octroi*" could indicate that the right to an effective remedy needs not to exist *per se* but could be granted or bestowed by a decision in individual cases. However, the English wording "shall have an effective remedy" includes an individual right that must exist *per se*.[13] The case law of the Court confirms that the English wording must be followed and that the inclusion of "*à l'octroi*" was merely stylistic.[14]

The wording further indicates that Article 13 only comes into play when other rights and freedoms in the Convention actually "are violated" ("*ont été violés*").[15] In early case law, Article 13 was understood in this manner. However, subsequent case law makes clear that it suffices that the principal claim – the violation of a substantive right – be arguable.[16] As a result, Article 13 contains a double standard of interference: (1) a substantive right must, arguably, have been violated and (2) the right to an effective remedy must have been violated.

Since Article 13 only comes into play if substantive rights in the Convention have, arguably, been violated, it is often stated that Article 13 is auxiliary to the substantive rights and,[17] in the extension, that Article 13 only provides a procedural right.[18] However, this conception is only fitting with regard to the right to access to justice, which concerns the process and form in which arguable (substantive) claims must be heard and decided at the domestic level.[19] The right to redress, in contrast, is a substantive and independent right, which grants the right to some form of (substantive and not merely procedural) redress.[20]

---

[10] See, for example, Raymond (1980) 166.

[11] See, for example, *Kudla* v. *Poland* (Grand Chamber 2000), para. 152.

[12] See Section 11.9. The UN International Covenant on Civil and Political Rights, adopted by General Assembly resolution 2200 (XXI) of December 16, 1966, entry into force March 23, 1976 (hereinafter the ICCPR), Article 2(3), explicitly distinguishes between access to justice, redress, and enforcement. See, also, for example, Shelton (2015) 16–19.

[13] See, for example, Raymond (1980) 162.

[14] See, for example, Raymond (1980) 165; Grote and Marauhn (2006) 1070.

[15] See, also, the latter part of Article 13: "has been committed" ("*aurait été commise*").

[16] See Chapter 7.

[17] See, for example, Matscher (1988) 319; Frowein and Peukert (2009) 391; Grabenwarter (2014) 329.

[18] See, for example, Mertens (1968) 454; Strasser (1988) 596; Békés (1998) 25; Lorenzen et al. (2011) 944.

[19] See, for example, Buyse (2008) 129; Shelton (2015) 16.

[20] See, for example, Antkowiak (2008) 356; David (2014) 263; Waters (2014) 3; Shelton (2015) 16, 19.

The latter part of the wording, "notwithstanding that the violation has been committed by persons acting in an official capacity," is, at first glance, confusing and seems unnecessary.[21] A violation could usually be traced back to some person or entity acting in an "official capacity": Why is it necessary to spell that out in plain language? However, the aim is to specify that the State must provide an effective remedy even if the individual causing the violation has some form of immunity according to national or international law.[22] Nevertheless, this wording has been used as an argument to exclude the challenging of primary legislation, as such, from the scope of application of Article 13 (Section 10.5.3.3). And some have used it as an argument in support of the view that the Convention must have direct horizontal effect (*Drittwirkung*) between third parties.[23] However, in the case law of the Court, there is no indication that Article 13 goes this far.[24] That being said, there must be a remedy against the State, or organs or persons of the State, when the State has violated positive obligations under the Convention.[25] In this sense, one could speak of an indirect horizontal effect.[26] And, depending on the remedies available at domestic level, Article 13 may require that procedures between private parties be initiated in order to achieve sufficient redress, for instance, sufficient compensation,[27] or because Article 13 requires effective investigations.[28]

However, Article 13 not only grants a right for the individual but is an important expression of the principle of subsidiarity upon which the system for the protection of human rights under the Convention is based.[29] Indeed, the primary responsibility for safeguarding Convention rights lies with the Contracting States and the Convention system is subsidiary to national systems for the safeguarding of human rights. Other important expressions of this principle are found in Articles 1, 35, and 46 of the Convention. In fact, these Articles, including Article 13, are considered to be the "key provisions underlying the Convention's human

---

[21] Similarly, Grote and Marauhn (2006) 1091.
[22] See, for example, Raymond (1980) 169–170; Matscher (1988) 329; White (2000) 195; Sinkondo (2004) 369–372; Pellonpää (2007a) 558; Jacobs et al. (2017) 148; Dijk et al. (2018) 1059.
[23] See, for example, Clapham (1993) 240–244.
[24] Similarly, Grabenwarter and Pabel (2012) 495.
[25] See, for example, Holoubek (1992) 151–155; White (2000) 195; Dijk et al. (2018) 1059.
[26] See, for example, Grote and Marauhn (2006) 1092.
[27] See Section 11.5 and, for example, Somers (2018).
[28] See Section 11.7.
[29] With the entry into force of Protocol no. 15 amending the Convention for the Protection of Human Rights and Fundamental Freedoms (hereinafter Protocol 15), a reference to the principle of subsidiarity was included in the Preamble of the Convention; see Articles 1 and 7 of Protocol 15.

rights protection system."[30] A truly subsidiary protection would be realized if States actually fulfilled their primary obligation to secure Convention rights, as foreseen in Article 1, so that violations do not occur. But even if violations occur, it would not be necessary to turn to Strasbourg if they are remedied at home. To accommodate and allow States to realize this secondary goal, Article 35(1) provides that all domestic remedies must be exhausted before the Court may deal with the matter. Lastly, Article 46 obliges States to abide by the final judgment of the Court in any case to which they are parties and sets out a procedure for the supervision of the execution of the Court's judgment.

But subsidiarity also applies to the Court and other Convention organs. States are, for example, granted a certain leeway in the interpretation and application of the Convention, of which the margin of appreciation doctrine is the most well-known expression. Consequently, the Court's interpretation and application of Article 13, as an expression of subsidiarity, is central to the cooperative relationship between the international level (the Convention, the Court, and the Committee of Ministers) and the national level (in particular, courts, other national remedial authorities, legislators, and the governmental branch). I provide my (normative) answer as to what extent such systemic considerations should influence how the Court construes and applies Article 13 in the concluding chapter (Chapter 13).

1.3 UNCERTAINTY AND DEVELOPMENT

In international law, the right to an effective remedy is a relatively new phenomenon, which only appeared in international treaties in the aftermath of the Second World War.[31]

Ever since the inception of the Convention, there has been considerable doubt concerning the content and scope of the obligations arising from Article 13. The famous and much cited quotation from the dissenting opinion of Judges Matscher and Pinheiros Farinha in *Malone* v. *UK* (Plenary 1984) is illustrative: "We recognise that Article 13 constitutes one of the most obscure clauses in the Convention and that its application raises extremely difficult and complicated problems of interpretation. This is probably the reason why,

---

[30] *Guide to Good Practice in Respect of Domestic Remedies* (adopted by the Committee of Ministers on September 18, 2013) 7. Other expressions of subsidiarity are, for example, Article 34 of the ECHR and the Pilot judgment procedure.

[31] See, for example, Mertens (1973) 1. Also in legal literature, remedies have only recently attained attention at the international level. However, at the domestic level, in particular, in the U.S. Constitutional theory, there is a rich body of scholarship concerning the relationship between rights and remedies; see, for example, Starr (2008) 708 with further references. See, also, Roach (2021).

for approximately two decades, the Convention institutions avoided analysing this provision, for the most part advancing barely convincing reasons."[32]

And even though the Court has dealt with Article 13 in a number of judgments and decisions thereafter, the content and scope remain uncertain.[33] In early years, most monist countries even held that the notion of effectiveness was so imprecise that it did not lend itself to direct applicability. Article 13 was not self-executing.[34]

Initially, the Court adopted a restrictive interpretation and application of Article 13.[35] In recent years, however, the Court has reinforced the scope and application of Article 13.[36] The most prominent example is the use of Article 13 in cases concerning excessive lengths of proceedings violating Article 6(1). Until *Kudla* v. *Poland* (Grand Chamber 2000), the Court held that Article 13 was consumed by Article 6(1), but then reconsidered its case law and found it necessary to examine whether Article 13 had also been violated.[37] The Court acknowledged that an aggregate of several remedies could satisfy Article 13, but found that the Polish Government had not indicated whether, and, if so how, the applicant could obtain relief – either preventive or compensatory – by taking recourse to the remedies proposed by the Polish Government.[38] The Court did not indicate the preventive and/or compensatory measures necessary to obtain appropriate relief, either generally (e.g. compensation is required under the following circumstances …) or concretely (e.g. compensation is required in cases such as this one). The choice of preventive and/or compensatory

[32] See, in a similar manner, the dissenting opinion of Judges Bindschedler-Rober, Gölcüklü, Matscher, and Spielmann in *James a.o.* v. *the UK* (Plenary 1986).
[33] See, as general expressions, for example, White (2000) 191; Pellonpää (2007a) 558; Malinverni (2009) 487. Keller and Sweet (2008) 24 claim that the case law of the Court concerning Article 13 has grown "dense and sophisticated," but they are, as far as I can see, a solitary exception. More generally, the topic of remedies is claimed to be "one of the most undeveloped areas of international law" that "cries out for analysis"; see Posner and Sykes (2011) 244, 245. See, also, Roach (2021) 4.
[34] See, for example, Mertens (1968) 463–464; Mertens (1973) 95. From the 1970s, as the case law of the Court grew more specific, monist countries increasingly held that Article 13 was self-executing; see, for example, Flauss (1991) 328. Thus, even though the case law of the Court is not "dense and sophisticated," it has grown sufficiently clear to render Article 13 self-executing.
[35] See Sections 4.3 and 12.3.2 and, for example, Lester (2011) 102.
[36] See Sections 4.3 and 4.5 and, for example, Helfer (2008) 142, 144–146; Christoffersen (2009) 362; Malinverni (2009) 487; Jacobs et al. (2017) 136. This development has been most significant in conjunction with Articles 2, 3, 5, and 6(1). The right to an effective remedy has also, in later years, been construed and applied more expansively in other international human-rights regimes; see, for example, David (2014).
[37] *Kudla* v. *Poland* (Grand Chamber 2000), paras. 150–156.
[38] Ibid., para. 159.

measures was, therefore, left within the margin of appreciation of the State. However, in *Scordino* v. *Italy* (no. 1) (Grand Chamber 2006), the Court went one step further and held that there is a "strong but rebuttable presumption" that excessively long proceedings occasion nonpecuniary damage.[39]

Judges in the Court have divergent opinions with regard to how this reinforcement should be performed (or not). A few examples from the case law are illustrative. In her dissenting opinion in *Zavoloka* v. *Latvia* (2009), Judge Ziemele, for example, held that whether the potential of Article 13 could be fulfilled in a different manner was debated within the Court, in particular when seen in the light of the Court's case load, which illustrated the necessity of improving domestic remedies in a number of States. In *Grosaru* v. *Romania* (2010), Judge Ziemele was more concrete and held that the Court should have elaborated specifically on what was required of the remedy in the case in hand.[40] In *Maksimov* v. *Russia* (2010), Judges Spielmann and Malinverni found that Russia had not provided an effective remedy to claim compensation for a violation of Article 3. They pointed to the principle of subsidiarity and held that the Court should develop its interpretation of Article 13 by requiring that an effective remedy included an examination based upon criteria set out by the Court so as to force States "to ensure that the Convention is effectively incorporated in the domestic court's application of the law."[41] And, in *Bozkır a.o.* v. *Turkey* (2013), Judge Keller argued that the independent nature and violation of Article 13 should lead to a larger amount of compensation under Article 41.[42]

At the same time, the Court is reinforcing the scope of its own remedial powers,[43] the most notable example being the introduction of the Pilot judgment procedure,[44] and increasingly includes procedural and remedial requirements under substantive Articles.[45]

The Court has provided little justification for reinforcing the scope and application of Article 13. But, when a justification is given, it usually includes a reference to the principle of subsidiarity and the case load of the Court.[46]

---

[39] *Scordino* v. *Italy* (no. 1) (Grand Chamber 2006), para. 204.
[40] Concurring opinion of Judge Ziemele in *Grosaru* v. *Romani* (2010).
[41] Partly dissenting opinion of Judges Spielmann and Malinverni in *Maksimov* v. *Russia* (2010).
[42] Partly dissenting opinion of Judge Keller in *Bozkır a.o.* v. *Turkey* (2013).
[43] See, for example, Flauss (2009); Leach (2013); Jahn (2014).
[44] The Pilot judgment procedure is a response to the proliferation of domestic structural and systemic violations capable of generating large numbers of applications to the Court; see, for example, the Information note on the Pilot judgment procedure issued by the Registrar of the ECtHR in 2009 (available at the website of the Court).
[45] See Section 13.2.
[46] See, for example, *Kudla* v. *Poland* (Grand Chamber 2000), paras. 148–149.

And even if no such reference is provided, the factual background is there for everyone to see: The Court is overwhelmed by applications, both well-founded and ill founded. Between the end of the 1990s and the years 2000–2011, the backlog was increasing rapidly and to an extent which threatened to strangle the Court. Indeed, by the end of 2010, the backlog had reached 139,650 cases, a growth of about 20,000 cases since the end of 2009,[47] and by the end of 2011, the backlog had reached 151,600 cases.[48] However, by the end of 2012, the backlog had been reduced to 128,100 cases, by the end of 2013, to 99,900 cases, by the end of 2014, to 69,900 cases, and by the end of 2015, to 64,850 cases. The main reason for this, however, was not a reduction of incoming applications, but the impact of the Single judge procedure introduced by Protocol 14 (now regulated in Articles 26 and 27 of the ECHR).[49] It is illustrative that in 2011, over 100,000 applications were allocated to a Single judge formation, a number, which by the end of 2015, was at 3,200 cases.[50] In addition, the Pilot judgment procedure has allowed the Court to "dispose of thousands of repetitive applications, either by sending them back to new domestic remedies, or on the basis of mass settle-ments offered by the respondent State."[51] Further, the Court and its Secretariat has initiated several other requirements, procedures, and changes to reduce the backlog and effectively deal with the case load.[52] Notwithstanding this, the number of applications remains extremely high. Thus, even though Court has become more efficient, the case load (and the case law) is evidence that many countries have considerable problems in the protection of human rights at national level. In fact, it seems as though the Court currently is able to deal with the incoming inadmissible and repetitive cases, whereas it still has a hurdle to overcome concerning admissible nonrepetitive cases. It is illustra-tive, that out of the 64,850 cases on the docket at the end of 2015, only 30,500 were repetitive cases, whereas 11,500 were priority cases, and 19,600 were nor-mal nonrepetitive cases.[53] At the end of 2016, the Court's backlog had again

---

[47] The Annual Report 2010 of the ECtHR 147.
[48] The Annual Report 2011 of the ECtHR 153. The backlog peaked in September 2011, exceed-ing 160,000 cases; see the Annual Report 2011 6.
[49] The Annual Report 2012 of the ECtHR 12. See, also, for example, Spielmann (2014) 26; Keller and Marti (2015) 829. Protocol 14 entered into force for all States on June 1, 2010.
[50] The Annual Report 2015 of the ECtHR 5. Most of these cases were declared inadmissible.
[51] Spielmann (2014) 29.
[52] For instance, the adoption of a prioritization policy, under which the Court aims at concen-trating its resources on cases which will have the most impact in securing the goals of the Convention and the cases raising the most serious issues of human-rights violations. The policy is available at the website of the Court. See, also, the Rules of the Court Article 41.
[53] Annual Report 2015 of the ECtHR 5.

increased, from 64,850 to 79,750 pending applications.[54] However, the reason for this was not a drop in efficiency on part of the Court, but the fact that a higher number of incoming cases were allocated to a judicial formation and that the Court focused on adjudicating priority cases.[55] Indeed, at the end of 2017, the Court's backlog was again reduced to 56,250 cases,[56] but has since remained relatively stable at 56,350 cases at the end of 2018, 59,800 cases at the end of 2019, and 62,000 cases at the end of 2020.[57] Consequently, the current challenge for the Convention system is to adjudicate the approximately 23,000 normal nonrepetitive cases and improve the domestic protection and enforcement of human rights.[58]

Clearly, Article 13 could play a crucial role in improving the domestic protection of human rights and, thereby, contribute to a more subsidiary protection of human rights.[59] Indeed, in order to enhance subsidiarity, many have called for a more expansive interpretation and a stricter application of Article 13.[60] However, this is not unproblematical. It may, at least in the short run, increase the case load of the Court and lead to a reduction of sovereignty in fields that States wish to control. Indeed, a perceived conflict between sovereignty and the effective protection of human rights presents itself, in some way, in almost every area of the law and politics of human rights.[61] This conflict is clearly visible in the process of reform of the Convention and the Court,[62] to which the latest additions are the *Interlaken Declaration* (2010),[63] the *Izmir Declaration* (2011),[64] the *Brighton Declaration* (2012),[65] the *Brussels Declaration* (2015),[66] and the *Copenhagen*

---

[54] Annual Report 2016 of the ECtHR 191.

[55] ECHR Analysis of Statistics 2016 4 (available at the web-page of the Court).

[56] Annual Report 2017 of the ECtHR 163.

[57] Annual Report 2020 of the ECtHR 155.

[58] Similarly, the then President of the Court, Guido Raimondi, in his opening speech, Solemn Hearing of the ECtHR, January 26, 2018 (available at the web-page of the Court).

[59] See, for example, the *Guide to Good Practice in Respect of Domestic Remedies* (adopted by the Committee of Ministers on September 18, 2013) 7; Jacobs et al. (2017) 135–136, 149; Harris et al. (2018) 745–746.

[60] See, for example, Ridruejo (2005) 1082; Barkhuysen and Emmerik (2008) 448; Wildhaber (2009) 83; Christoffersen (2009), in particular his Chapter 4.

[61] See, for example, Carozza (2003) 63.

[62] See, for example, Milner (2014).

[63] The High Level Conference on the Future of the ECtHR, Interlaken Declaration, February 19, 2010.

[64] The High Level Conference on the Future of the ECtHR, Izmir Declaration, April 27, 2011.

[65] The High Level Conference on the Future of the ECtHR, Brighton Declaration, April 20, 2012.

[66] The High-level Conference on the Implementation of the ECHR, our shared responsibility, Brussels Declaration, March 27, 2015.

declaration (2018).[67] This process has, *inter alia*, resulted in the adoption of Protocols 15 and 16. At every occasion, the primary responsibility of States to adhere to the obligations arising from the Convention has been underlined, while at the same time emphasizing that the principle of subsidiarity implies a shared responsibility between the Contracting States and the Court (the primary responsibility of States goes hand in hand with a subsidiary review by the Court).[68] Indeed, the Court is called upon to take its subsidiary role in the interpretation and application of the Convention fully into account.[69] But this call is ambiguous. On the one hand, it could be taken as a general plea to show greater restraint in the interpretation and application of the Convention (including Article 13),[70] and, on the other hand, as an invitation for the Court to contribute to the improvement of the national implementation and enforcement of the Convention (by enforcing the primary responsibility of States), to which a stricter interpretation and application of Article 13 may contribute. Similarly, the new references to subsidiarity and margin of appreciation in the Preamble, introduced by Protocol 15, could be taken as arguments for a stricter interpretation and application of specific rights, or as an invitation to apply a more lenient interpretation and application.[71] Independently of the view that one takes on this question, the addition reflects real concern about the jurisdiction of the Court and the way in which it interprets and applies the Convention, at least on the part of some States.[72] Thus, the reform process sheds light on more profound issues, such as, for example, the purpose and content of the right to an individual application to the Court and how the relationship between domestic authorities and the Court should be, including the extent of the Court's review.[73] Article 13 may be a tool to mitigate such systemic concerns. I provide my opinion as to how in the concluding Chapter 13.

---

[67] The High-level Conference on Reform of the Convention System, Copenhagen Declaration, April 13, 2018.

[68] See, for example, the Interlaken Declaration under "The Conference," para. 3.

[69] See, for example, the Interlaken Declaration under "Action Plan," Chapter E para. 9 *litra* b.

[70] See, for instance, Mowbray (2014) 37.

[71] See, for example, Milner (2014) 30, who emphasizes that the introduction was a compromise because of the failed proposal to introduce new (and stricter) admissibility criteria. See, also, for example, Popelier and Van De Heyning (2017) 7–8.

[72] Milner (2014) 50. This is, also, reflected in, for example, the Copenhagen declaration. See, also, Section 12.3.2.

[73] See, for example, Milner (2014) 54.

2

Analysis and Selection of Case Law

2.1 INTRODUCTION

Section 2.2 accounts for the selection of case law that forms the basis of the legal analyses of Article 13. Sections 2.3, 2.4, and 2.5 then expound on building blocks of importance for the analysis. The central purpose is to illustrate why there has been, and still is, considerable uncertainty concerning the content of the case law and why the Court's law-making potential concerning Article 13 (still) is large. This insight is not only important for the clarification of the legal content of Article 13 (Chapters 3 to 11) but, also for the normative analyses and recommendations in Chapters 12 and 13. Sections 2.6 and 2.7 briefly explain how legal literature has been used to clarify the content of Article 13 and why a larger comparative analysis has not been performed.

2.2 SELECTION OF CASE LAW

The primary fundament of this book is an analysis of the Court's judgments in Grand Chamber and Chambers in which the keyword search function of the Hudoc database identifies Article 13 as a keyword. As of November 1, 2021, this amounts to 2,534 judgments (approximately 13 percent of all the Court's judgments rendered in Chambers and Grand Chamber).[1]

The selection implies that I have not systematically analyzed judgments which only concern other rights in the Convention (in which Article 13 has

---

[1] Judgments after this date have not been analyzed or taken into account. The Hudoc keyword search function is not 100 percent reliable. I have randomly come across judgments in which Article 13 has been an important theme, but in which Article 13 is not plotted as a keyword; see, for example, *Aleksandr Nikonenko* v. *Ukraine* (2013) and *Söderman* v. *Sweden* (Grand Chamber 2013). Such judgments have been included in the analyses to the extent they have come to my knowledge.

not been plotted as a keyword in the Hudoc database) and Committee judgments,[2] and any decision, most notably admissibility decisions,[3] even though
they deal with Article 13.

Judgments which only deal with other rights could be important in order
to delineate the scope of Article 13 from such rights, in particular procedural
and remedial obligations arising under substantive Articles. However, a majority of the cases in the selection concern this relationship and should,[4] in this
regard, provide a sufficient basis for clarifying what the Court has required
under Article 13, as such. Committee judgments, for their part, are important
for empirical and statistical purposes, but should not cast additional light on
the legal requirements stemming from Article 13. Hard cases are to be dealt
with in Chambers and Grand Chamber.[5] Admissibility decisions, in particular
decisions concerning the exhaustion of domestic remedies (Article 35(1) of
the ECHR) and decisions concerning Article 13 that are declared manifestly
ill-founded (Article 35(3) of the ECHR), could, on the other hand, shed some
light on Article 13.

There is considerable case law concerning the exhaustion rule which
often contains more detailed reasoning compared to judgments dealing with
Article 13. This is connected to the fact that States often argue the nonex-
haustion of domestic remedies extensively, whereas the applicant often has
less interest in arguing a violation of Article 13. In addition, the Court only
rarely considers whether Article 13 has been violated *ex-officio*, although it has
done so (mostly in cases concerning systemic and structural problems).[6] But
even though the requirements of effectiveness under Articles 35(1) and 13 are,
in many aspects, overlapping, there are, also, many differences (Chapter 5).
It is, therefore, difficult to say whether the requirements, in concrete cases,
are the same, at least to the extent that Article 13 is not explicitly dealt with.
Admissibility decisions declaring applications concerning Article 13 manifestly ill-founded could, for their part, inform us about what is not required
under Article 13. But the justification is mostly limited, and many decisions

---

[2] See Articles 26(1) and 28 of the ECHR. The possibility of ruling in Committee was intro-
     duced by Protocol 14, which entered into force for all States on June 1, 2010. A provisional
     Protocol 14bis made rulings in Committee and Single judge formation possible for some
     States as of various dates in 2009.
[3] See Article 35 of the ECHR.
[4] See Sections 4.3 and 4.5.
[5] See Article 28(1) of the ECHR.
[6] See, for example, *Nsona v. the Netherlands* (1996) para. 116; *Kopp v. Switzerland* (1998) para.
     78 and compare, for example, *Haas v. the Netherlands* (2004) para. 46; *Gorshkov v. Ukraine*
     (2005) para. 47; *Wesołowska v. Poland* (2008) para. 71; *Gubin v. Russia* (2010) para. 41.

are not published in the Hudoc database. Consequently, and since the primary goal is to clarify what the Court actually has required under Article 13, and the normative goal to provide recommendations as to how the Court could use Article 13 for systemic purposes, I have not systematically analyzed such admissibility decisions. However, I describe the relationship between the exhaustion rule, the admissibility criterion "manifestly ill-founded," and Article 13, more generally, in Chapters 5 and 7. Nor have I systematically analyzed Commission reports and decisions concerning Article 13. But I have analyzed all reports which have been transferred to the Court for judgment, and in which the Court has identified differences of opinion between the Commission and the Court.[7]

Further, the Court may set out requirements concerning domestic remedies under the Pilot judgment procedure and Article 46.[8] Such judgments could, also, shed light on the content of Article 13. However, as long as the Court, in the same judgment, does not explicitly consider whether Article 13 has been violated, including its relationship to the remedial prescription under Article 46 and/or the Pilot judgment, it is hard to say whether such judgments promote a general remedial rule that applies for every State, as an obligation stemming from Article 13, or whether the remedial prescription under Article 46 and/or the Pilot judgment is limited to the specific circumstances in the responding State.[9] As a consequence, and in accordance with the primary goal of this book, I have neither analyzed such judgments systematically.

2.3 HOW TO EXTRACT GUIDANCE FROM THE COURT'S CASE LAW?

Judgments are not always couched in general terms, and their use as authoritative guides depends on a somewhat shaky inference from particular decisions. The reliability of this inference "fluctuates both with the skill of the interpreter and the consistency of the judges."[10]

I have read the selection of judgments chronologically, from past to present, with the goal of deducing the content and development of Article 13. The result is presented in Chapters 3 to 11, in particular Chapters 7 to 11.[11]

---

7   See, for example, *Young, James and Webster* v. *the UK* (Plenary 1981) and *Young, James and Webster* v. *the UK* (Plenary Commission report 1979).
8   See, for example, *Torreggiani a.o.* v. *Italy* (2013).
9   See, also, Section 13.2.
10 Hart (2012) 97.
11 I have attached weight to citing the case law which established a requirement or principle and, thereafter, a selection which illustrates content and development. More exhaustive references to case law are found in Reiertsen (2017).

The overall conclusion is that the Court has provided little abstract and principled reasoning concerning the various requirements arising from Article 13. In contrast, the case law is extremely case-specific, inextricably linked to the concrete facts of the case. This has made it difficult to deduce general principles and starting-points that can be applied to new cases.[12] It could, of course, be possible to extract patterns of argumentation that can be generalized into more principled starting-points, either from single judgments or a larger number of judgments. Indeed, any legal order finds its shape during continuous application.[13] However, the specific and fact-centered case law has made that too a difficult task. Indeed, there is a lack of consistency and clarity, not only in the Court's (lacking) interpretation but also application of Article 13. Two examples are illustrative:

(1) The Court uses different abstract wording to explain what the requirement of effective investigations (arising under Article 13) entails. It may refer to that the requirements under Article 13 "are broader," "may be broader," simply not refer to, or that it is not necessary to examine the requirements of effective investigations under Article 13 in addition to procedural requirements under Articles 2 and 3. On the other hand, similar facts may entail violations of Article 13, or no violation. For instance, in one case, the lack of an autopsy or the interrogation of witnesses may cause a violation, whereas, in other cases it is not, without it being clear as to why this should be, just by comparing the facts (at least in the way that the facts are described in the judgments).[14]

(2) The Court has never generally stated that a continuing violation must be ended, with potential (generally phrased) exceptions, in order to satisfy Article 13.[15] But many cases demonstrate ineffective remedies because the violation has not been put to an end. However, in other cases, the Court accepts that continuing violations may be sufficiently redressed through compensation. And even in cases with very similar facts, for instance, in many cases concerning the lack of execution of domestic judgments, there are judgments with contradictory results.[16]

---

[12]   Compare, for example, Harris, O'Boyle *et al.* (2018) 749.
[13]   Bogdandy and Venzke (2012) 14–15. See, also, Venzke (2012) 6.
[14]   See Section 11.7.
[15]   See Section 11.3.4.
[16]   See Section 4.5.2.

Further, both Article 13 and the Convention system, more generally, have distinct features that make it difficult to deduce general principles and requirements from the Court's application of Article 13. Most important is that the Court awards States a wide margin of appreciation in setting up their remedial systems. And this is only natural. The remedial systems of the Member States, including court procedures, are very different. But such differences may distinguish one case from another, and, accordingly, make it difficult to deduce general patterns based upon a number of cases. This is accentuated by the fact that an aggregate of remedies may satisfy Article 13 (Section 9.3) and that the context in which the remedial issue arises, for instance, national security, is of significance (Chapter 8). Thus, even though the facts seem similar, there may be relevant differences in remedial systems and contexts, including remedial possibilities unknown to the Court. In addition comes that the remedial question is mostly pleaded in little detail before the Court, the remedy may potentially be effective or not on a number of grounds, Article 13 is always applied in relation to a specific substantive Article, and the type of violation is of significance for the required remedy (Chapter 8). Consequently, in the lack of principled reasoning, it is difficult to say to what extent the remedial requirements set out in relation to specific substantive Articles, in specific situations, against specific States, are transferable to another.

Justifications may, also, change over time.[17] To the extent that there is a development in the case law, it is, therefore, difficult to say whether principled reasoning deduced from the application of older case law is applicable in the present. Reasons underlying the judgments may also be hidden or camouflaged.[18]

All such factors, seen in conjunction with the number of judgments, have made the identification of principled starting-points difficult. It remains for the reader to judge whether the reason lies more in the skill of the interpreter than in the consistency of judges. That said, because of such factors and because they have made it necessary to apply a certain restraint when deducing and exposing the content of the various requirements arising from Article 13, the following Chapters, in particular Chapters 10 and 11, should be read as a firm floor, but not necessarily the ceiling.

---

[17] An example from another field of law: All societies have penal sanctions, but the justification varies both within and between societies, not least over time. For a Norwegian perspective, see, for example, Hauge (1996), and, from the UK, for example, Ashworth and Horder (2013) in their Chapter 2.

[18] See, for example, Senden (2011) 4–5.

2.4 THE COURT'S METHOD OF INTERPRETATION

The law of the Convention is, to a large extent, the result of the interpretive practice of the Court. The Court is guided by Articles 31 to 33 of the VCLT.[19] The starting-point is thus the ordinary meaning of the terms read in their context and in the light of the object and purpose of the Convention.[20] The context includes not only the relationship between terms in Article 13 as such, but Article 13 and other Articles in the Convention, as well as the Preamble.[21]

In general public international law, there is disagreement as to the relationship between the different elements of Articles 31–33 of the VCLT, in particular the elements of Article 31(1) (ordinary meaning, context, and object and purpose).[22] Originally, the Court gave no explicit priority to the various elements, but preferred a flexible and holistic approach in which the elements of Article 31(1) might be given different weight depending on the circumstances.[23] However, within this flexibility, the "object and purpose" of the Convention has been a key concept, through which the Court, most notably, has developed the doctrine of dynamic interpretation (living instrument).[24] Sometimes, the Court also refers to the Convention as a law-making treaty.[25]

The Court has developed many other (sub-)doctrines and principles relevant for the interpretation of the Convention, such as, by way of nonexhaustive examples, the principle of practical and effective rights,[26] the notion of objective obligations which benefit from a "collective enforcement",[27] the

---

[19]   See, for example, *Golder* v. *the UK* (Plenary 1975) para. 29 and, more generally, Ulfstein (2020).
[20]   Article 31(1) of the VCLT.
[21]   Article 31(2) of the VCLT.
[22]   See, for example, Rietiker (2010) 253.
[23]   See, for example, *Golder* v. *the UK* (Plenary 1975) para. 30.
[24]   See, for example, Matscher (1993) and, as examples, *Tyrer* v. *the UK* (1978) para. 31; *Selmouni* v. *France* (Grand Chamber 1999) para. 101; *Mamatkulov and Askarov* v. *Turkey* (Grand Chamber 2005) para. 121; *Hirsi Jamaa a.o.* v. *Italy* (Grand Chamber 2012) para. 175. The doctrine of dynamic interpretation, and its counterpart, the margin of appreciation, has received considerable criticism. But at least some degree of evolution is foreseen in the Preamble, which refers to the further realization of human rights and principles such as democracy and the rule of law. A purely textual approach, based upon original intent, would clearly conflict with these goals. Today, few deny that some evolution is necessary, not least to keep track of societal changes. The difficulty is rather deciding the limits and finding objective criteria that guide judges when choosing between reasonable alternatives; see, for example, Mahoney (1990) 68.
[25]   See, for example, *Wemhoff* v. *Germany* (1968) para. 8; *Leyla Şahin* v. *Turkey* (Grand Chamber 2005) para. 141.
[26]   See, for example, Callewaert (2000) ; Rietiker (2010), and, as examples, *Airey* v. *Ireland* (1979) para. 24; *del Río Prada* v. *Spain* (Grand Chamber 2013) para. 88.
[27]   See, for example, *Ireland* v. *the UK* (Plenary 1978) para. 239; *Mamatkulov and Askarov* v. *Turkey* (Grand Chamber 2005) para. 100; *Paladi* v. *Moldova* (Grand Chamber 2009) para. 84.

principle of the predictability of the law (legal certainty),[28] broad interpretations of scope – narrow interpretation of exceptions,[29] the margin of appreciation (Section 12.2.6), the principle of subsidiarity (Section 12.2.5), the concept of a common European standard,[30] the principle of internal coherence,[31] autonomous concepts,[32] and, not least, a doctrine of precedent, in which the Court attaches weight to its previous decisions to preserve "legal certainty and the orderly development of the Convention case law."[33] The Court also frequently points to other rules of international law,[34] although it remains unclear to what extent such rules have independent weight in relation to, for example, the doctrine of dynamic interpretation.[35] Further, even though Article 32 of the VCLT considers the preparatory work a supplementary means of interpretation, the Court holds that it "should be slow to adopt an evolutive interpretation which runs counter to the drafters' specific and recorded understanding."[36] Accordingly, the Court has, for instance, with reference to what it held to be the intention of the drafting fathers, excluded the right to challenge primary legislation from the scope of application of Article 13.[37] That being said, the preparatory work has, overall, had little effect on the case law of the Court.[38]

---

[28] See, for example, Mahoney (1990) 77; Pellonpää (2007) 419–420; Popovic (2008) 374.

[29] Most notably when interpreting Article 5; see, for example, *Medvedyev a.o.* v. *France* (Grand Chamber 2010) para. 78; *Assanidze* v. *Georgia* (Grand Chamber 2004) para. 170.

[30] Which, primarily, is a tool to find the correct margin of appreciation. To find consensus, the Court must engage in some form of comparative interpretation and/or empirical analysis, which is difficult. Jonas Christoffersen holds, in this context, that "comparative interpretation is a Trojan horse in which evolutive interpretation is hidden"; see Christoffersen (2009) 57. For a powerful critique of the lack of methodology when establishing "consensus"; see Helfer (1993). In a more positive manner, Keller and Sweet (2008) 6 hold that the Court has developed an overarching comparative methodology. Personally, having read somewhere between 3,000–4,000 judgments in the context of this work, I find it hard to detect any overarching comparative methodology. In any case, difficulties in comparative approaches call for caution when establishing consensus; compare, for example, Tushnet (2009) 5.

[31] See, for example, *Klass a.o.* v. *Germany* (Plenary 1978) para. 68; *Stec a.o.* v. *the UK* (Grand Chamber decision 2005) para. 48; *Austin a.o.* v. *the UK* (Grand Chamber 2012) para. 54.

[32] See, for example, *Allen* v. *the UK* (Grand Chamber 2013) para. 95; *Parrillo* v. *Italy* (Grand Chamber 2015) para. 211.

[33] See, for example, *Cossey* v. *the UK* (Plenary 1990) para. 35; *Scoppola* v. *Italy (no. 3)* (Grand Chamber 2012) para. 94.

[34] Compare Article 31(3) *litra* c of the VCLT.

[35] See, for example, Pellonpää (2007) 414–419; Ulfstein (2020). Forowicz (2015) 213–214, after analyzing factors that may influence the reception of international law in the Court's case law, concludes that the Court is not aiming at reducing the fragmentation of international law, but rather to preserve the Convention system.

[36] *Young, James and Webster* v. *the UK* (Plenary 1981) para. 70.

[37] See Section 10.5.3. But, the Court has, in other cases, gone against the explicit recorded intent of the drafting fathers; see, for example, Mahoney (1990) 70.

[38] See, for example, Harris, O'Boyle *et al.* (2018) 22.

The limits of the method of interpretation are, primarily, that the catalogue of rights and the territorial application of the Convention may not be extended.[39] But this has not prevented the Court from discovering implied rights, which, according to an ordinary understanding of the wording, are difficult to include. Such implied rights have most notably been included through the doctrine of practical and effective rights. The most prominent example is the right of access to a court, which was included in Article 6(1) in *Golder* v. *the UK* (Plenary 1975), and which has had significant consequences for the Court's application of Article 13.[40] This last point illustrates how the legal context in which Article 13 finds itself may impose limits, or at least influence how Article 13 is construed and applied. The relevant legal context also includes general principles under-lying the Convention, such as the notion of positive obligations and the princi-ples of subsidiarity and margin of appreciation. The legal institutional context may also influence how Article 13 is construed and applied, most notably, the interpretation and application of the exhaustion rule, the remedial powers of the Court, including the Pilot judgment procedure, and the surveillance of the execution of the Court's judgments by the Committee of Ministers. However, judges may have very different opinions of the scope and *raison d'être* of such relationships and principles.[41] And their role and significance for Article 13 have not been clarified in the case law. Consequently, such contexts, relationships, and principles do not, as such, impose any absolute limits on the interpretation and application of Article 13.

Further, even though the teleological canon of interpretation may be said to have gained some prevalence, the Court's case law reveals traces of at least four major canons of interpretation of statues: (1) textual, verbal, or grammati-cal; (2) systematic, structural, or contextual; (3) historical; and (4) teleologi-cal or purposive.[42] What remains as an advice to lawyers pleading before the Court, not least in cases concerning Article 13, is thus not much more than "make use of all methods".[43] Some outer limits exist, most notably, the outer

---

[39] These limits are connected to the mandate of the Court; see Article 19 of the ECHR. See, also, for example, Mahoney (1990) 60.

[40] See Section 4.5.2.

[41] See Section 12.2.

[42] See, concretely in the context of the Convention, for example, Dothan (2019) and, more gen-erally, for example, Brugger (1994) 396–398. Koskenniemi (2005) 219 holds that international lawyers are in constant movement from one position to another without being able to stay permanently in any.

[43] Compare Brugger (1994) 400, 407, more generally, with regard to interpreting statutes. In the specific context of the US Constitution, Laurence Tribe similarly held: "I am doubtful that any defensible set of ultimate [interpretive] rules exists. Insights and perspectives, yes; rules, no"; see Tribe (1997) 73.

boundaries of grammatical analysis and the fact that most judges generally place more importance on the "objective" textual, systematic, and teleological methods than on the "subjective" historical method.[44] And even if the judges roughly agree upon the major canon (or canons) of interpretation to be applied in a concrete case, disagreement over concrete interpretive techniques, for instance, the scope of the margin of appreciation, often arises. Indeed, there seems to be no way of ensuring that judges adhere to the same interpretive theory.[45]

If we then turn to the open-ended wording of Article 13, including its legal and institutional context, it becomes clear that the Court's legal method, as such, provides few answers as to how Article 13 must be interpreted.[46] Accordingly, legal method may be used to construe Article 13 in an extensive or restrictive manner, in a principled or nonprincipled manner and by requiring abstract or concrete results. There is, for example, nothing in the legal method that impedes the Court from requiring that domestic remedial authorities always must state how to put an end to continuing violations (Section 11.3.4) or that restitution must be the prime objective of redress (Section 11.4). This does not mean that I normatively hold that the Court should require this – just that the answer is not to be found by a simple reference to legal method. True, when reading the judgments of the Court, the legal answer seems to flow directly from the Court's application of the legal method on the facts of the case. But, mostly, the Court could have bent the method in order to achieve a different result.[47]

This seemingly "limitless" discretion of judges is,[48] within the legal system of the Convention and the legal method of the Court, primarily constrained by the fact that the Court does not depart from its previous case law "without good reason",[49] for example, by responding to evolving convergence regarding

---

[44] Compare Brugger (1994) 400–401.

[45] Compare Tushnet (2009) 84, and, more generally, for example, Vermeule (2004). See, also, for example, Sunstein (2015), who holds that the choice of interpretive theory depends on your constitutional personae (hero, mute, soldier, or minimalist).

[46] Compare, for example, Hart (2012) 136, who holds that the consequences of legal indeterminacy or open-endedness is that a "large and important field is left open for the discretion of courts and other officials" and, more specifically in the context of the Convention, for example, Mahoney (1990) 60.

[47] For a similar perspective on the Norwegian Supreme Court; see, for example, Bernt (2002) 84. Concerning the US Constitution, Learned Hand famously held that the Articles therein were "empty vessels into which [a judge] can pour nearly everything he will", as quoted in, for example, Mahoney (1990) 63.

[48] Koskenniemi (2005) 36.

[49] See, for example, *Scoppola v. Italy (no. 3)* (Grand Chamber 2012) para. 94, and, more generally on precedent as a limiting and stabilizing factor in law, for example, Brugger (1994) 409; Dworkin (2011) 171.

the standards to be achieved.[50] But, at the very least, the case law creates an argumentative burden: In order to deviate from previous case law, the deviation needs to be justified.[51] Well-known techniques for deviating include, *inter alia*, distinguishing the case on the facts and the law and attaching weight to changes in law and society, including teleological aspects, underlying principles, tendencies, and developments.[52]

Hence, the Court is torn between the need for interpretive adjustments, due, for example, to new problems and the evolving values in European societies, and the need for legal certainty.[53] Or, as Joseph Raz puts it, more generally, constitutional interpretation has a Janus-like aspect – it faces both backwards, aiming to elucidate the law as it is, and forwards, aiming to develop and improve it.[54] The Court must, therefore, connect to both the past and the future.[55]

Further, in well-functioning democratic domestic legal systems, the major constraining factor on court development of law is a finely tuned power balance between the legislative, executive, and judicial branches. As a representative of the people (*demos*), it is primarily for the legislative branch to develop law. However, the Council of Europe has no legislator comparable to that in domestic law, and the constraining elements of checks and balances are not present, at least in a manner comparable to domestic systems. This may lead the Court in two different directions: (1) a restrictive interpretive approach, out of respect for the domestic democratic system; and (2) an expansive interpretive approach, because there is no international legislator that can develop Convention law. Over the years, the Court has been both restrictive and expansive. But independently of whether the restrictive or expansive road is taken, the fact remains that the law of the Convention is primarily developed by the Court. The law of the Convention is what the Court finds it to be.[56]

Because the Court has provided little principled reasoning concerning Article 13, and since it is hard to extract principled starting-points from the Court's application of Article 13, even the precedent of the Court provides few limits as to how the Court could and should construe, develop, and apply Article 13. Moreover, in the few cases where the Court has taken a principled stand, it has primarily done so to limit the scope of application, for instance, by linking the

---

[50] See, for example, *Scoppola v. Italy (no. 3)* (Grand Chamber 2012) para. 94.
[51] See, for example, Jacob (2011) 1024.
[52] The possibility of deviating from precedent is a major difference between judge-made law and legislation; see, for example, Raz (2009) 195.
[53] See, for example, Pellonpää (2007) 409, and, more generally, for example, Barak (2016) 31.
[54] Raz (1998) 177.
[55] Compare Venzke (2012) 48–49.
[56] Similarly, for example, Keller and Sweet (2008) 7–8; Venzke (2012) 137.

notion of arguability to the notion of manifestly ill-founded (primarily applying a contextual canon of interpretation),[57] and by excluding the right to challenge legislation as such (primarily applying a historical canon of interpretation – the assumed will of the drafting fathers).[58] But nothing in the legal method, including the legal context and precedent of the Court, prevents the Court from departing from its former case law concerning these questions, which I, in some cases, argue that the Court should do (e.g., in Sections 7.3.3 and 10.5.3).

2.5 THE WIDER PRECEDENTIAL EFFECTS OF THE COURT'S CASE LAW

Even though judgments of the Court, according to Article 46(1) of the ECHR, are only formally binding on the parties and, therefore, have no formal *erga omnes* effect,[59] they function as normative guidance to other Member States and actors affected.[60] And democracies and the Council of Europe are based on a deeply rooted notion of equality, which leads to the expectation that like cases are dealt with alike.[61] States that wish to promote equality and avoid being judged by the Court, therefore, implement and follow the case law of the Court, even if such judgments are not formally binding.[62]

This poses at least three problems concerning how the Court could construe and apply Article 13.

First, to what extent could and should the Court take into account expected compliance, both in the individual case, more generally within the affected State, and in other States, when construing Article 13? To what extent could and should the Court take the wider (precedential) effects of its judgments into account?

Second, and extending this point, whereas many Member States implement the Court's judgments, even though they occasionally and particularly in politically sensitive cases raise their voices in protest,[63] other Member States

---

[57] See Section 7.3.1.
[58] See Section 10.5.3.3.
[59] Some argue that the judgments of the Court should be given formal *erga omnes* effect; see, for example, Klein (2000); Czerner (2008).
[60] See, for example, Papier (2006) 1–2; Czerner (2008) 347; Gerards (2008) 410; Costa (2009a) 12; Voßkuhle (2010) 187; Backer (2011) 193; Bogdandy and Venzke (2014) 507–512. In the process of reform of the Court, all Member States have repeatedly confirmed and accepted the ultimate authority of the Court to interpret the Convention; see, for example, Jagland (2014) 74.
[61] Compare Jacob (2011) 1007.
[62] Compare Scalia (1989) 1177. See, also, for example, Ulfstein (2009) 127; Staden (2012) 1024, and, more generally, in the context of the Convention, for example, Bjorge (2015).
[63] See, more generally, for example, Krisch (2008), and, as an example, Reiertsen (2016).

have serious problems not only in taking judgments against other Member States into account but also in preventing new and similar violations identified in judgments against themselves.[64] Should such differences between States influence how the Court construes and applies Article 13?

Third, such questions are connected to judicial economy. Indeed, without a functioning doctrine of precedent, every legal question could, in principle, be taken to the Court anew. To what extent should the case load of the Court influence how it construes and applies Article 13?

Questions such as these have been at the forefront of the process of the reform of the Court and important rationales for developing, *inter alia*, the Pilot judgment procedure, the Court's prioritization policy, and changes in admissibility criteria. They are, also, important underlying rationales for some developments in the Court's case law concerning Article 13, *inter alia*, the fact that the Court now actually considers whether Article 13 has been violated in addition to substantive Articles (Section 4.3), that domestic reme-dial authorities must scrutinize the substance of the Convention complaint in a stricter manner (Section 10.5.4), and that compensation must be granted in more scenarios (Section 11.5). However, such underlying rationales could be taken further into account when construing and applying Article 13. Indeed, if the Court truly wants to be a "law-maker," it needs to produce law both in the conviction and with the goal that the law is followed, and do so in a way which preserves a well-functioning legal system. This implies *first* that the judgments of the Court concerning Article 13 must provide a minimum of guidance and clarity, not only for the responding State. Seen from a systemic point of view, this is more important than the question of whether the content should be construed in a minimalist or expansive man-ner. *Second*, the manner in which clarity and guidance is provided must take the variety of needs in different Member States into account, including their ability and willingness to take the precedential effect of the Court's judgments into account. These insights all underlie the concluding recom-mendations in Chapter 13.

2.6 LEGAL LITERATURE AND ARTICLE 13

The legal literature concerning the Convention is vast and available in many languages. It is impossible to get an overview of everything.[65] However, the

---

[64] See, more generally, for example, Popelier, Lambrecht *et al.* (2016).

[65] Concerning the margin of appreciation, one author has illustratively held that the literature is a veritable "maze of abstractions"; see Emberland (2006) 163.

legal literature concerning Article 13 is not very large.[66] I have attempted to go through English legal literature systemically and have occasionally consulted German and French legal literature that deals with Article 13. This literature is mainly used to account for disagreement and critique of the Court's case law, not to underscore it.

2.7 COMPARATIVE ANALYSES

There are close to one hundred regional and global human-rights treaties. Most human-rights treaties explicitly recognize the right to an effective remedy.[67] Some even hold that the right to an effective remedy for violations of human rights forms part of customary international law.[68] But there are significant differences with regard to the content and the manner in which the right is protected. For instance, the treaties contain different compliance mechanisms, the ICCPR provides no right for the individual, only an obligation on part of Member States,[69] and Article 47 of the EU Charter of Fundamental Rights is not limited to the fundamental rights in the Charter, but extends to all rights and freedoms guaranteed by the law of the Union, and the obligation is primarily directed at the organs of the EU, and Member States "only when they are implementing Union law."[70]

Further, remedies are not only required by international human rights instruments but are also an essential part of domestic legal systems, other

[66] See, generally, for example, Mertens (1968); Mertens (1973); Matscher (1988); Flauss (1991); Holoubek (1992); Thune (1993); Malinverni (1998); Békés (1998); Bruyn (2000); Frowein (2000); Vospernik (2001); Sinkondo (2004); Vorwerk (2004); Pellonpää (2007a) 558–568; Frowein and Peukert (2009) 391–401; Grabenwarter and Pabel (2012) 483–495; Pollmann and Lohmann (2012) 267–268; Grabenwarter (2014) 327–339; Jacobs, White *et al.* (2017) 135–149; Dijk, Hoof *et al.* (2018) 1036–1083; Harris, O'Boyle *et al.* (2018) 745–763.

[67] See, for example, Article 8 of the Universal Declaration of Human Rights (UDHR); Article 2(3) ICCPR, which also contains specific remedies in case of unlawful arrest in Articles 9(5) and 14(6); Article 25 of the American Convention on Human Rights (hereinafter the ACHR); The EU Charter of Fundamental Rights Article 47; the International Convention on the Elimination of All Forms of Racial Discrimination Article 6; the Convention against Torture and Other Cruel, Inhuman or Degrading Treatment or Punishment (CAT) Article 14; the Convention on the Elimination of All Forms of Discrimination against Women Article 2 *litra* c. Some human rights instruments deal with more specific remedies, for instance, the UN International Convention for the Protection of All Persons from Enforced Disappearance (ICED), in which, for example, Article 6 concerns measures of investigation and access to justice, Articles 4 and 7 criminalization, and Article 24 the right to truth and reparation.

[68] See, for example, Shelton (2005) 28–29 and Shelton (2014) 1201. This is, however, disputed; see, for example, Antkowiak (2008) 355.

[69] See, for example, Grabenwarter (2014) 328.

[70] Article 51(1) of the Treaty of the European Union (TEU).

international legal instruments, and various international soft law instruments.[71] In fact, remedies are part of any discourse of rights, but in different manners. Some countries still apply the old Latin (Roman) phrase *ubi jus ibi remedium* (for the violation of every right, there must be a remedy). And common law countries have long accepted that courts can invent remedies through injunctions for the violations of rights, even though no specific remedy is provided by legislation. The US Supreme Court, for example, held, in the landmark judgment *Marbury* v. *Madison*, that the very essence of civil liberty consists in the right of every individual to claim the protection of the laws, whenever he or she receives an injury. One of the first duties of Government is to afford this protection. If that protection is not afforded, the courts must intervene.[72] In Germany, a right to an effective remedy must be seen in conjunction with the general *Rechtsstaatsprinzip* included in the German Constitution (*Grundgesetz*) Article 19(4).[73] And directive 2008/115/EC (Returns Directive) is an example of an international legal instrument, not classified as a human rights instrument, but which demand effective domestic remedies in cases concerning the return of illegally staying third-country nationals.[74]

If one includes soft law instruments, the international legal remedial discourse is expanded enormously. Two of many examples from the Council of Europe are the Committee of Ministers' "Twenty Guidelines on Forced Return",[75] and the resolution of the Parliamentary Assembly of the Council of Europe on Enforced Disappearances.[76] On a more general level, the van Boven/Bassiouni principles are the most authoritative and elaborate (nonbinding) principles with regard to remedies concerning human rights violations.[77]

---

[71] See, for an overview, for example, Shelton (2015) 32–86.

[72] See Shelton (2005) 29 ff. with further examples.

[73] See, for example, Grote and Marauhn (2006) 1066–1113; Grabenwarter and Pabel (2012) 484–485.

[74] Directive 2008/115/EC of the European Parliament and of the Council of 16 December 2008 on common standards and procedures in Member States for returning illegally staying third-country nationals ("Returns Directive"). See, in particular, Articles 12 and 13.

[75] The Committee of Ministers, Twenty Guidelines on Forced Return, CM(2005)40, adopted on May 4, 2005, in which Articles 2 and 5 concern remedies against a removal order.

[76] The Parliamentary Assembly of the Council of Europe (PACE) Resolution 1463 (2005) on Enforced Disappearances.

[77] Resolution 60/147 by the United Nations General Assembly on "Basic Principles and Guidelines on the Right to a Remedy and Reparation for Victims of Gross Violations of International Human Rights Law and Serious Violations of International Humanitarian Law" (van Boven/Bassiouni principles), adopted on December 16, 2005.

I do not systematically compare the right to an effective remedy in Article 13 with remedies required by such instruments. The very brief account above should have shown that there are many special regimes of remedies, not one universal regime.[78] However, for the sake of illustration, I occasionally refer to such instruments, most notably the soft law instruments of the Council of Europe and the UN instruments of a more general approach.

---

[78] Gray (2014) 873.

3

The Requirement of Effectiveness in Abstract

3.1 INTRODUCTION

Any evaluation of effectiveness requires the measurement of goal realization. For something to be effective, it must do what it is supposed to do. Accordingly, a remedy is "effective" if it accomplishes its aim(s).[1] But, even without an explicit reference to an "effective" remedy, it would be necessary to clarify the purpose(s) of the remedy. All legal rules are designed to promote certain goals and values.[2] Consequently, no rule is more important than the reason for which it exists, and any course of action, including deviation from a clear rule, may be defended by making reference to their underlying reasons.[3] In order to understand what an effective remedy is and could be, it is thus necessary to know what purpose or purposes the "effective remedy" is or are to serve.[4] Indeed, any requirement stemming from Article 13 could be measured against the requirement of effectiveness, and, accordingly, the purposes that the remedy is meant to fulfill.[5]

Any rule and legal system may have a broad specter of purposes. Remedies are no different. Below I account for purposes which may, semantically construed, be considered intrinsic in the wording "effective remedy". Broader purposes underlying Article 13 and Convention law, for instance, the principles of subsidiarity, democracy, and the rule of law, are accounted for in Section 12.2.

The chapters on the various requirements arising from Article 13, in particular Chapters 9 to 11, show that the Court has not taken a firm stand on the purposes Article 13 are to promote – neither in concrete situations nor

---

[1] Compare, for example, Shany (2012) 230 as to what constitutes an effective organization.
[2] See, for example, Feteris (2008) 483; Feteris (2008a) 22; Barak (2016) 36.
[3] Koskenniemi (2005) 591.
[4] See, more generally, on goals that remedies may serve, for example, Shelton (2015) 19–27; the slightly different classification in Shelton (2005) 7–20 and Roach (2021) 73–127.
[5] Compare Raymond (1980) 167; Matscher (1986) 268.

more generally. The overview below, therefore, primarily accounts for potential purposes that Article 13 may have, as these are exposed in existing legal literature. However, I broadly point to what may, more generally, be read out from the case law of the Court. The below thus primarily informs us of the uncertainty that has surrounded Article 13 and points to elements, which merit principled clarification by the Court (see also Section 13.3).

3.2 FUNCTIONS AND PURPOSES

The below accounts for relationships between functions and purposes and between different purposes which, in an abstract framework for analyzing the effectiveness of a remedy, merit clarification in the Court's case law.[6]

First, purposes may serve different functions. Indeed, Article 13 not only functions as an individual right but may also promote the cooperative relationship between the international and national level, third persons, and the general public (Fig. 3.1).

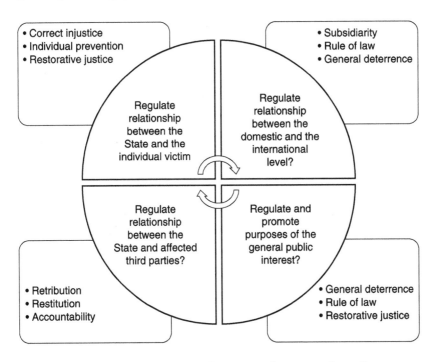

FIGURE 3.1 *Linkages between functions and purposes of remedies*

[6] Compare Greer (2006) 87.

The slices in the inner circle illustrate broader functions that Article 13 may have, whereas the outer connected squares provide nonexhaustive examples of purposes that may promote those functions. Generally, the prime function of Article 13, and remedies in general, has been perceived to regulate the relationship between the State and the individual victim, by correcting injustice through providing redress to the individual victim.[7] However, Article 13 may have other functions and may be required to promote purposes that satisfy also these functions. In the recent case law, the Court has, for instance, required domestic remedial authorities to attach weight to general deterrence in some cases revealing systemic or structural problems, for example when measuring out the compensation required by Article 13 (Section 11.5). Thus, the functions of Article 13 may be to regulate not only the relationship between the State and the individual victim but also the relationship between domestic and international protection of human rights and promote general public interests. These relationships are complicated by the fact that the same purposes may promote different functions.

Second, the rights to access to justice and redress may serve distinct and different purposes, or be more or less interrelated. The right to access to justice may, for instance, aim to promote the rule of law more generally, paying more or less consideration to redress, whereas the right to redress may aim to correct individual injustice, with more or less consideration to promoting the rule of law, more generally. But the right to redress may, also, promote purposes without any consideration of how access to justice is obtained.[8] Indeed, some seem to perceive redress as the ultimate aim of effective remedies,[9] whereas others, including the Court, seem to promote access to justice and relief both as individual goals and as a collective enterprise.[10] However, notwithstanding the normative perspective which one is bound to take, seen from a practical perspective, access to justice and relief are closely linked. Indeed, redress can only be achieved through some form of access to justice, and the required relief may affect the access to justice required to obtain this relief. Against this background, it may be argued that the access to justice must promote, at the very least, the same purposes as redress. On the other hand, it could be claimed that the only goal of the access to justice inherent in Article 13 should be to promote purposes of (individual) redress and that the access to justice, in this context, has no other intrinsic purpose(s), as such.

---

[7] See, for example, Shelton (2015) 19.
[8] Compare, for example, Shelton (2015) 16–27.
[9] See, for example, Shelton (2005) 8–9, 114.
[10] See, for example, *A.D. & O.D. v. the UK* (2010) para. 100.

The Court has provided no clear guidelines as to how this relationship should be. It may, therefore, be difficult to ascribe specific rights and requirements under Article 13 as expressions of access to justice and/or relief. Indeed, the Court mostly does not distinguish strictly and deals with the various requirements arising under Article 13 as a collective exercise – the right to one "effective remedy." However, in order to understand, construe, and apply specific requirements arising under Article 13, it may be necessary to distinguish between access to justice and relief. To what extent, for instance, is the requirement of effective investigations to promote broader purposes of access to justice (for instance the rule of law) and/or potential purposes underlying the right to redress, such as, for example, establish the truth about the violation and facilitate prosecution and punishment (Section 11.7)?

Third, the functions and purposes of Article 13 may be affected by the functions and purposes of substantive Articles. Indeed, several substantive Articles contain remedial requirements, for instance, the requirement of effective investigations in, most notably Articles 2 and 3, which, also, is included under Article 13. Is there overlap in these purposes? Do purposes in substantive Articles exclude the use of Article 13? To what extent does Article 13 serve distinct and separate purposes? In its early case law, the Court avoided such questions completely by holding that it was not necessary to consider whether Article 13 had been violated in addition to substantive Articles.[11] However, as the Court in more recent case law has started to consider whether also Article 13 has been violated, such questions grow pertinent. Yet, the Court avoids answering such questions and typically only finds an additional violation of Article 13 by pointing to the facts and justification under the substantive Article. The most prominent example is the requirement of effective investigations, arising under both substantive Articles and Article 13 (Section 11.7).

Fourth, effectiveness requires a measurement of the extent to which goals are fulfilled.[12] But goals may be conflicting or mutually supportive, and not all goals are equally important.[13] It is, therefore, necessary to establish, at the very least, some loose form of hierarchy between relevant goals, and the extent to which different goals must be realized.[14] This, again, raises questions of threshold and compliance. As the Court, at least in more recent case law, has required domestic remedial authorities to attach weight to other purposes than the correction

---

[11] See Sections 4.3 and 4.5.
[12] Compare, for example, Shany (2012) 248.
[13] See, for example, Gewirtz (1983) 594.
[14] See, for example, Feteris (2008a) 20, 23. The tension between, in particular, the goal of correcting injustice and preventing future violations is central in Roach (2021).

of injustice, most notably deterrence, the question of threshold grows pertinent. How and to what extent should the Court review whether domestic remedial authorities has attached sufficient weight to different purposes? And to what extent should the Court attach weight to actual compliance? Before the goal is actually achieved, the judge is no more than a promoter of remedial effectiveness.[15] Remedies thus embody a tension between the ideal and the real.[16] Franz Matscher has illustratively held that effectiveness under Article 13 is a *rechtssoziologisches Kriterium,* which contains legal and factual elements to which a certain degree of prospect of success (*Erfolgsaussicht*) is necessary.[17] Further, any assessment of performance is difficult and may depend on several factors relating to output, outcome, and impact.[18] These questions are illustrated, and largely remain unanswered, by the Court's application of the requirement that the remedy must be effective in theory and practice seen in conjunction with the fact that the Court holds that Article 13 does not require a remedy bound to succeed (Sections 9.4 and 10.6).

Fifth, the question arises as to whether the evaluation of effectiveness may be affected by assessments of efficiency, for example, the resources (people, time, money, *etc.*) used to achieve the goal. Is it permissible, or even necessary, to consider both the degree of goal realization and the resources used to achieve those goals? The Court has only reluctantly recognized efficiency as a mitigating concern when realizing the minimum standards required by Article 13, in particular, the cost connected to the remedy.[19] However, since States, under the various requirements arising under Article 13, are awarded a wide margin of appreciation, they are, in practice, able to attach weight to a variety of competing interests (Chapter 8).

Sixth, and extending this last point, remedies may have undesired effects, and competing concerns may speak for a lower threshold of goal realization. In this regard, there are two different approaches to remedies. On the one hand, a rights-maximizing approach, in which the only question asked, is what is most effective for victims. On the other hand, an interest-balancing method, in which other interests may reduce the remedial effectiveness (the degree of goal realization).[20] It is illustrative that even though the IACtHR

---

[15] Gewirtz (1983) 596.
[16] Gewirtz (1983) 587.
[17] Matscher (1986) 267. See, also, Sections 10.6 and 9.4.
[18] Compare, for example, Andresen, Boasson *et al.* (2012) 7.
[19] See, for example, the Guide to good practice in respect of domestic remedies (adopted by the Committee of Ministers on September 18, 2013) in note 21 and *Georgia v. Russia (I)* (Grand Chamber 2014) para. 151.
[20] See, for example, Gewirtz (1983) 591–593; Shane (1988) 557; Starr (2008) 698.

and the Court in Strasbourg allow for some balancing when they set out their own remedies, their methods are different. Whereas the IACtHR only allows for social interests to be taken into account, the Court in Strasbourg allows for a broad range of external and internal factors to be taken into account. Accordingly, the IACtHR is victim-centered, the Court in Strasbourg cost centered.[21] Considering the margin of appreciation that States are granted under Article 13, the same could be claimed concerning the Court's approach toward domestic remedies. However, independently of the approach that one may favor, some limits must apply. Uncertainty and disagreement regarding the content of the substantive right may, for example, influence how the remedy can be construed and strong and inflexible remedial rules may lead to remedial deterrence (the cost of the remedy may deter remedial authorities from vindicating substantive rights).[22] And even strict rights-maximizing approaches must take unavoidable remedial imperfection into account. Multiple remedial goals may, for example, conflict or practical issues may make it impossible to achieve the remedial goals. This imperfection must be distributed.[23] That being said, it remains that a balancing approach allows other trade-offs, not only relating to the victim, for instance, financial costs and risks to the health and safety of others, to be taken into account. The fundamental difference between a rights-maximizing approach and a balancing approach is, thus, that the balancing approach, at least at the outset, accepts a gap between the right and the remedy, which, in principle, could have been closed, in contrast to unavoidable remedial imperfection.[24]

Seventh, considering the existence of such difficulties, it could be tempting to hold that an evaluation of effectiveness should only consider actual alternatives and not engage in assessments of goal realization more independently. If access to justice and redress can be performed in one way only, an evaluation of goal realization makes little sense. And if access to justice and redress may be performed in different ways, the evaluation of effectiveness could consist of considering which alternative best satisfies the relevant goals and provides the best balance between competing concerns. The threshold would then be the comparison of alternatives, not an abstract threshold of goal realization. Occasionally, the Court seems to apply such an approach.[25]

---

[21] Antkowiak (2011) 288, 290.
[22] See, for example, Starr (2008) 710–737.
[23] Gewirtz (1983) 595.
[24] Gewirtz (1983) 600.
[25] See, for example, *Klass a.o. v. Germany* (Plenary 1978) para. 70. For an analysis of to what extent the Court requires an assessment of alternatives under the positive obligation; see Stoyanova (2018).

3.3 ACCESS TO JUSTICE

Refusing to grant access to justice, for violations of any right, is a primary manifestation of the concept of denial of justice.[26] Both access to justice and denial of justice are concepts which could have many-faceted meaning. Neither are defined in the Convention nor has the Court defined them in the abstract. Defining access to justice is, furthermore, mostly avoided in academic works.

Access to justice could be approached from a procedural perspective and/ or a substantive perspective. In the procedural perspective, the focus is on the means and the procedures for securing rights and obligations. Consequently, this perspective primarily focuses on the possibility for using courts and tribunals and the procedures thereto connected. The substantive perspective, by contrast, also focuses, to a larger or lesser extent, on whether the outcome is "just and equitable" or helps realize "material justice".[27]

Further, substantive justice can be delivered in a direct or indirect manner. The direct route grants the individual immediate access to institutions with the power to award substantive relief (material justice). The indirect route does not directly improve the individual situation, but allows general measures, which, in a second instance, may lead to the improvement of the individual situation.[28]

Clearly, the access to justice required by Article 13 contains both procedural and substantive elements. Indeed, Article 13 requires the competent domestic remedial authority to be able to deal with the substance of the relevant Convention complaint and to grant appropriate relief.[29] Further, in doing so, the Court has set out a number of procedural requirements that the domestic remedial authority needs to comply with (Chapter 10). The Court has, moreover, held that the right to an effective remedy, at the outset, is a strictly personal right for the individual (Section 9.2). It could, therefore, be argued that the access to justice required by Article 13 primarily aims at providing a specific and direct form of substantive justice (relief). Or, put in another manner, the procedural requirements are not an intrinsic value, but a prerequisite for the domestic remedial authority to be able to deal with the substance of the substantive Convention complaint and provide relief (thus a direct and specific individual substantive justice). But the procedural requirements, and,

---

[26] See, for example, Shelton (2015) 17. See, also, *Golder v. the UK* (Plenary 1975) para. 35. Some even include enforceability in the definition of legal rights; see, for example, Shelton (2015) 17.
[27] Gerards and Glaz (2017) 13.
[28] Ibid. 14.
[29] See, for example, *A.D. & O.D. v. the UK* (2010) para. 100.

accordingly, the access to justice promoted by Article 13, may have a broader intrinsic value for the individual and/or aim to accommodate for broader interest. This tension and linkage between access to justice and redress is illustrated by, most notably, the requirement to perform effective investigations (Section 11.7).

That being said, the case law of the Court indicates that Article 13 has a primary and specific substantive goal – to offer relief. This is not least so because the Court primarily has dealt with purely procedural requirements, as such, under Article 6(1).[30] The relationship between Article 6(1) and Article 13 may, accordingly, offer some guidance concerning the access to justice required by Article 13.

Both articles provide for some form of access to justice, including procedural guarantees which govern the functions and conduct of the authority providing access. But whereas Article 6(1) has a more general scope – all cases concerning the determination of civil rights and obligations and a criminal charge – Article 13 only requires access to justice to remedy alleged and arguable violations of substantive provisions of the Convention.[31] Further, the authority required by Article 13 must not necessarily be judicial, whereas Article 6(1) requires access to justice by independent and impartial tribunals. That being said, both Articles require that access to justice be effective. In Article 13, this is expressed directly in the wording. Under Article 6(1), this follows from consistent case law.[32]

Against this background, it would seem as though Article 6(1) to a considerable degree absorbs the access to justice required by Article 13. Indeed, this was a central consideration in *Golder* v. *the UK* (Plenary 1975). The UK contested that access to justice was included in Article 6(1), *inter alia*, because it would lead to confusing Article 6(1) with Articles 13 and 5(4) and make these provisions superfluous.[33] The majority, however, rejected this argument by pointing to the different authorities required and the difference in scope.[34] But a minority of two judges attached some weight to this argument.[35] They accepted that the access in Article 6(1) would, in principle, provide "all that was needed", but conceded that "mere access does not necessarily entail a remedy". There might be access, but no remedy available upon access. Article 13 would thus

---

[30] See Section 4.5.2.
[31] Vospernik (2001) 361, therefore, holds that the Articles are completely different ("*völlig unterschiedlich*").
[32] See, for example, *Airey* v. *Ireland* (1979) para. 24.
[33] *Golder* v. *the UK* (Plenary 1975) para. 33.
[34] Ibid.
[35] Judges Zeika and Fitzmaurice.

not be completely superfluous.[36] They thus seemingly only pointed to the redress required by Article 13. Taking this to the letter, it could be tempting to conclude that the access to justice in Article 6(1) completely absorbs the right to access in Article 13 and that the sole aim of Article 13 is to provide redress – not to promote and/or enforce other purposes that may underlie access to justice. However, Article 13 has, at the very least, some independent impact on the right to access to justice.

First, with regard to violations of the Convention not considered "civil" or "criminal", in accordance with their autonomous meaning, Article 13 provides an independent right to access to justice.

Second, Article 6(1) requires access to justice to determine civil rights and obligations and a criminal charge, whereas Article 13 requires access to justice to deal with the substance of the Convention complaint and redress human-rights violations. Depending on the domestic legal system, this can be achieved in procedures which determine civil rights and obligations and a criminal charge, but not necessarily. And the procedural guarantees necessary to achieve a determination of civil rights and obligations and a criminal charge may, at least theoretically, be different from the guarantees necessary to achieve sufficient redress. It may, therefore, be important to underline the significance of the access to justice required to deal with the substance of a Convention complaint and to achieve redress for human-rights violations. The required scope of domestic review is, for example, one area where the procedural requirements of Article 13 may have developed beyond those of Article 6(1) (Section 10.5). That being said, although there has been some development in the Court's case law, to the extent that Article 6(1) applies, the Court, still, mostly holds that it is not necessary to consider whether also Article 13 has been violated (Section 4.5.2).

Third, to the extent that violations caused by courts must be redressed, in particular, violations of Article 6, access to justice must be provided by Article 13 (Section 4.5.2).

Fourth, in many cases, it is difficult to distinguish between violations of access to legal institutions, as such, other procedural guarantees, and redress. For instance, the recovery (and the possibility of recovery) of legal costs may influence the effectiveness of access to legal institutions, as such, to procedures and to redress. Depending on, *inter alia*, the pleadings, the facts of the case, and the deliberations of the judges, it may be more or less coincidental

---

[36] The flip side of this argument, according to Fitzmaurice, was that the reasoning of the majority was flawed since they had concluded that a right to a fair trial is of no avail without a trial; see the reasoning of the majority in para. 35.

if the lack of recovery of costs is seen as a violation of access to institutions, procedures, redress, or several of these elements. Such practical difficulties may lead the Court to see the purposes of Articles 6 and 13 more as a collective enterprise. This seems, for example, to be the approach in the EU Charter of Fundamental Rights Article 47.

Similar questions arise in the relationship between Article 13 and other Articles in the Convention that provide for more specific access to justice. The obvious example is Article 5(4), which provides that anyone deprived of his/her liberty by arrest or detention is to be entitled to take proceedings by which the lawfulness of his or her detention is to be decided speedily by a court (Section 4.5.4).

Increasingly, the Court, also, includes remedial requirements of a procedural nature under other substantive Articles, most notably in combination with the positive obligation to secure rights, but also procedural obligations of a more independent nature, such as, for instance, the requirement of effective investigations under, most notably, Articles 2 and 3 (Section 11.7). The Court, also, increasingly attaches weight to how the Convention issue procedurally has been dealt with by domestic remedial authorities when setting out the margin of appreciation under substantive Articles (Section 13.2).

All such relationships may affect how the purpose and nature of the access to justice under Article 13 is perceived, and thus, how the concrete requirements arising therefrom could and should be construed and applied. Indeed, many of the proceeding chapters illustrate an unclear relationship between procedural requirements under substantive Articles and Article 13.

3.4 SUBSTANTIVE REDRESS

3.4.1 *Introduction*

In most legal systems, correction of injustice and deterrence are cited as the foundation of the law of remedies, although restorative justice, retribution, and economic analyses have provided other theoretical models on how to respond to human-rights violations.[37] But even correction of injustice and deterrence may have different underlying reasons and justifications. Rectifying a wrong may, for instance, not only build upon a moral obligation to put things right in the relationship between the State and the individual, but be more or less connected to avoiding, for example, unrest in society, thus aiming at regulating the relationship between the State and society.

---

[37] See, for example, Shelton (2015) 13; Chavez (2017) 373.

Below I account for possible intrinsic purposes of the requirement of redress, but first make the following two overarching introductory remarks.

First, correction of injustice is primarily directed at the past and the present. It seeks to rectify wrongs and put the victim in the same position as if the wrong had not been performed (*restitutio in integrum*). Deterrence, on the other hand, primarily seeks to influence the future, either on an individual level (individual deterrence) or on a general level (general deterrence). However, the same type of remedy may serve several aims. For the assessment of goals and effects, this may be problematic. Providing compensation in the form of money may, for example, seek to rectify the effects of a wrong, but also prevent similar violations, both against the individual victim and others. Lacking authoritative sources, it is difficult to decide what aims, including its underlying reasons, for example, compensation seeks to promote.[38] This, again, makes it hard to set out a correct amount of compensation. Although the Court's case law concerning compensation under Article 13 primarily seems to aim at correcting individual injustice, it remains unclear to what extent other purposes, in particular, deterrence, must be promoted (Section 11.5).

Second, depending on how the wrong (the violation) is perceived, redress may aim at having effects not only for the individual victim, but, for example, the offender, other persons, and society more generally, including, for example, the national executive and legislator. The following chapters make clear that the required redress under Article 13 primarily aims to have effects for the individual victim (including indirect victims). However, increasingly the Court seems to require that the domestic remedy also must promote general deterrence, in particular in cases revealing systemic and/or structural problems.

3.4.2 *Correct Injustice*

The primary aim of remedial justice is to rectify the wrong done to a victim – to correct individual injustice.[39] The Court has not explicitly stated so, under Article 13, in the abstract, but it is illustrated by, in particular, the Court's case law with regard to compensation (Section 11.5). However, how injustice is corrected, depends on the wrong, and, it may be difficult to set out what the harm actually consists of.[40] In human-rights law, the wrong is mainly directed at

---

[38] Similarly, penal sanctions may be directed at the past (retribution) and future (deterrence); see, for example, Wacks (2015) 308.

[39] See, for example, Shelton (2015) 19. This is also a central goal in most systems of tort law; see, for example, Schwartz (1996–1997); Horsey and Rackley (2013) 8–9.

[40] See, for example, Shane (1988) 556.

the individual victim.[41] But, not only may the individual be perceived to have been wronged, but society, or groups in society, more generally.[42] If so, this injustice should, in principle, also be corrected. To what extent such injustice needs to be taken into account under Article 13 remains unclear in the Court's case law.

Further, injustice may be corrected in different ways. In international human-rights law, more generally, the primary remedial goal is achieving *restitutio in integrum*, i.e., placing the victim as far as possible in the same position that he/she was in before the wrong was committed.[43] Restitution is, also, the primary goal under the general rules on State responsibility. Some violations may be restituted, for instance, returning property expropriated in violation of P1 Article 1. But, in many cases, it is not possible to put the victim in exactly the same position he/she was in before the violation. It is, for instance, impossible to undo torture, and it may be impossible or undesirable to return illegally expropriated property because it will violate other rights.[44] In such cases, correcting injustice must consist of some form of compensation for that which cannot be restituted. But even if a wrong may, in principle, be rectified, compensation may be preferred, for instance, because restitution is disproportionate considering other legitimate costs and concerns.[45] Although the primary remedial goal in human rights law, more generally, is achieving *restitutio in integrum*, the Court has never stated so in the abstract in conjunction with Article 13, nor specified what the relationship between restitution and compensation is. That being said, the case law reveals that compensation is the practical rule (Sections 11.4 and 11.5).

Moreover, many hold that any human-rights violation creates a moral imbalance between the victim and the wrongdoer, which must be corrected.[46] But a moral imbalance cannot be corrected, neither in the form of restitution nor compensation, in a precise manner. Some specific forms of redress may come close, for instance, a declaratory judgment or an official excuse. However, it may be argued that something more is needed, or that something else is sufficient, for instance, compensation in the form of money. However, the adequacy of using money as a means to correct moral imbalance is a

---

[41] Article 34 of the ECHR and the protected subject in substantive Articles are evidence of this.
[42] See, for example, Shelton (2005) 146.
[43] See, for example, Shelton (2013) 678.
[44] See, for example, Neuman (2014) 331.
[45] Compare, for example, the International Law Commission Draft Articles on Responsibility of States for Internationally Wrongful Acts Article 55 and Principle 15 first sentence of the van Boven/Bassiouni principles.
[46] See, for example, Shelton (2015) 19–20.

contested phenomenon, both in human-rights law and in other fields of law.[47] Compensation in the form of money must, at the very least, not create an attitude of impunity in the sense that human-rights violations are acceptable as long as you pay for them. Further, in many countries, the lack of money and resources is a contributing factor to human-rights violations. On the other hand, compensation, also in the form of money, may have an important rehabilitative effect, *inter alia*, through alleviating suffering and providing for material needs.[48] Although the Court, in its more recent case law under Article 13, has provided some guidance with regard to when compensation for nonpecuniary damages must be provided, it still remains, in many areas, unclear both when and to what extent (Section 11.5).

3.4.3 *Deterrence*

Deterrence is a central goal in criminal law and most systems of tort law.[49] Also within human-rights law, deterrence is a central goal. In the Convention, avoidance of, and security against, violations are primordial, illustrated most notably through Article 1.[50] Clearly, remedies may deter violations. Indeed, the linkage between the general obligation to secure rights and domestic remedial action was explicitly recognized by the drafting fathers, who originally proposed to include these obligations in the one and same Article.[51] However, in the Court's early case law, deterrence did not appear as a central goal under Article 13. But in more recent case law, the Court has increasingly required that domestic remedial authorities attach weight to deterrence, in particular in cases revealing systemic or structural problems. This is most clearly visible in the Court's case law concerning effective investigations and compensation (Sections 11.5 and 11.7). But the Court has never in the abstract given any guidance as to when domestic remedial authorities need attach weight to deterrence. To what extent Article 13 currently promotes deterrence, and, if so, what kind, thus remains unclear.

Deterrence aims at discouraging certain forms of behavior in the future. In criminal law, it is distinguished between general and individual deterrence.[52] Individual deterrence aims at dissuading the particular offender from committing future crimes, both against the victim and others. General deterrence

---

[47]　See, for example, White (2005–2006).
[48]　See, for example, Shelton (2015) 20 and compare White (2005–2006) in his Chapter 3.
[49]　See, for example, Schwartz (1996–1997); Horsey and Rackley (2013) 8–9.
[50]　Also in the capabilities approach of Martha Nussbaum, security for capabilities is primordial; see, for example, Nussbaum (2011) 145.
[51]　See Section 4.2.
[52]　See, generally, for example, Brooks (2014).

aims at dissuading people and institutions, more generally, from committing crimes.[53] It is contested to what extent deterrence actually works, both more generally,[54] and, specifically, for example within domestic criminal law.[55] Some domestic penal systems have, therefore, directed more of their focus toward maintaining social order and/or retribution.[56] But when deterrence is held to work, it is because it is assumed that rational actors weigh the anticipated costs of transgression against the anticipated benefits.[57] If so, the potential law violator must consider the costs of violating the law to be greater than the advantages of not following the law. Even if one accepts these uncertain starting-points as relevant when seeking to regulate the behavior of individuals, it is highly uncertain if they are appropriate when seeking to regulate the behavior of States, which is the main duty bearer of human rights and, therefore, at least in principle, should be the main subject to be deterred.[58] In any case, the effects of deterrence are based upon uncertain hypothetical situations and conditions. What different actors perceive as benefits and disadvantages may, for example, vary considerably. And, even assuming that all (rational) actors would act in a reasonably similar manner, or, at the very least, with a comparable degree of rationality, it is hard to measure the advantages and disadvantages.

As for domestic remedies in the context of the Convention, the prime recipient for individual deterrence would seem to be the violating State, but specific deterrence may, also, be directed against individual actors or groups of actors within the State. The recipients of general deterrence could, on the one hand, be the State as such and/or other States, but, also, people, actors, or society more generally, both within that State and outside the State. But States and societies within the Council of Europe are different, even though they have a common European heritage. That which deters one State, or people within one State, may not necessarily deter others.[59] These traits of individuality raise difficult challenges, especially if the Court is to determine whether, and, if so, how and when general deterrence must be a factor when setting out remedies within a State.[60] However, the Court could demand, more generally,

---

[53] See, for example, Garner and Black (2009) 514.

[54] See, for example, Hodges (2015) 153–157.

[55] See, for example, Ashworth and Horder (2013) 16; Jareborg (2002) in his Chapter 6.

[56] See, for example, Wacks (2015) 312.

[57] See, for example, Shelton (2015) 22.

[58] Similarly, Fikfak (2019).

[59] Compare Neuman (2014) 330.

[60] In the framework of the Pilot judgment procedure, the Court is better equipped to measure the need for general deterrence within the State because it can consider a larger number of cases in context.

that domestic remedial authorities consider whether the remedy is a sufficient deterrent and specify both what and against whom the deterrent effect must be directed. The Court could then verify whether the domestic authority has sufficiently justified and considered whether and to what extent the domestic remedy has had a sufficient deterrent effect (Chapter 13).[61]

3.4.4 *Accountability and Retribution*

In domestic criminal law, it is contested whether retribution and revenge is the purpose of the condemnation and penalty. In Norwegian criminal law, one has, for example, moved away from considering retribution an official goal. The primary goal is the deterrent effects that the condemnation and penalty are assumed to have, both on general and specific levels. But criminal condemnation and penalties may have retributive effects, both seen from the perspective of individual victims and of society more generally. In many systems of domestic criminal law, retribution seems to gain (new) popularity, in particular, because there is little evidence that deterrence works.[62]

Remedies may have retributive effects. That the wrongdoer is held responsible and must provide redress may be seen, both from the point of view of the victim and of society more generally, as a form of retribution. To the extent that the Convention violation is perceived as creating a moral imbalance between the wrongdoer and the victim, and maybe society more generally, retribution may contribute to restoring this imbalance. If so, retribution is linked with the task of correcting injustice,[63] and thus mainly directed at the past. However, for similar reasons as to why retribution has been abandoned in many systems of criminal law, many find it hard to accept retribution as a remedial goal. That being said, when retribution within criminal law has been abandoned, it is primarily because it is perceived as illegitimate to inflict an evil on another person in order to satisfy another person's or society's need for retribution.[64] However, it may be easier to accept retribution as a legitimate aim when the wrongdoer is a collective entity such as the State. Still, it remains difficult to accept that emotions such as anger, hatred, and revenge are appropriate when determining the remedy for human-rights violations, even though it may be

---

[61] This has similarities with the dialogic approach argued for in Roach (2021).

[62] Wacks (2015) 312.

[63] Compare, for example, Shelton (2015) 20–21.

[64] See, for a Norwegian perspective, for example, the preparatory work to Law no. 25, May 20, 2005 on punishment (straffeloven 2005), for instance, the proposal from Government to Parliament (*Stortinget*) in Ot.prp. no. 90 (2003–2004) Section 6.2.

healing to recognize such emotions.[65] Further, if retribution is accepted as a remedial goal, the remedial authorities must decide the retribution necessary in order for the remedy to be effective. This is no easy task and may lead to questions of legitimacy.

The Court has consistently rejected retribution as a goal of the remedial task, although some dissenting opinions seem to award compensation and just satisfaction for punitive, in the sense of being retributive, purposes.[66] That being said, both within general remedial theory and in the practice of the Court under Article 13, it is a central purpose to identify and express condemnation of the violation and the violator, although not for the purpose of retribution.[67] Accountability is thus a goal and must, in some manner, be established (Section 11.7.5).

3.4.5 *Restorative Justice and Reconciliation*

Restorative justice and reconciliation are gaining momentum in international human-rights and humanitarian law.[68] Reconciliation presupposes a process in which the victim and the offender mend fences. In newer theory of criminal law, it is primarily reconciliation between individual victims and offenders that is discussed. In international human-rights and humanitarian law, reconciliation between groups is, also, discussed, for instance, in the aftermath of conflicts or civil wars between different groups of people. This process is often called restorative justice. The work of many reconciliation and truth commissions are examples of processes aiming at achieving restorative justice on a larger scale.

Restorative justice may be perceived in at least two different ways. *First*, as a process in which all stakeholders affected by an injustice have an opportunity to discuss how they have been affected by the injustice and to decide what should be done to repair the harm. *Second*, as a substantive value in which the goal is to heal (restore) rather than to hurt. The healing is directed at both

---

[65] See, for example, Shelton (2015) 21.

[66] See, for example, *Öneryıldız v. Turkey* (Grand Chamber 2004) para. 147; *Budayeva a.o. v. Russia* (2008) para. 191. However, in some cases, the Court may use arguments pointing in the direction of revenge, as a purpose. The joint partly concurring and joint partly dissenting opinion of Judges Lazarova Trajkovska and Pinto de Albuquerque in *Bljakaj a.o. v. Croatia* (2014) paras. 10 and 11 is illustrative. See, also, for example, Buyse (2008) 151; Shelton (2015) 410–420; Fikfak (2019) 1095–1096. Notice that Chavez (2017) 379–385 claims to have identified several judgments in which a "double aim" is visible, including a punitive (retributive) aim. However, none of these judgments are explicit, and it can easily be argued that the aim was solely to correct injustice and/or deter and establish responsibility.

[67] See, for example, Shelton (2013) 678–679.

[68] See, for example, Antkowiak (2011) 284–286; Wemmers (2014).

the victim (e.g., through redress) and the offender (e.g., through reintegration). But, to achieve this healing, the process is, in any case, of paramount importance.

Remedial processes may promote reconciliation and restorative justice. Remedial procedures may focus both on the healing of victims and achieving reconciliation between victim(s) and offender(s). But the traditional view of reconciliation and restorative justice presupposes that you have two parties that may participate in a process and that both can be reconciled and healed. Offenders and duty bearers in the Convention are States, as such. The traditional perspective of reconciliation and restorative justice does not fit well on such a collective entity.

In the case law of the Court, there is, in any case, little evidence that reconciliation and restorative justice are goals in the remedial process.

4

Historical and Statistical Overview

4.1 INTRODUCTION

This chapter starts out (Section 4.2) by analyzing how Article 13 was dealt with during the drafting of the Convention. A central conclusion is that the drafting does not explain the Court's timid development of Article 13 in early years and that it, rather, may provide support for a further development in the present. Section 4.3 then describes how the number of cases concerning Article 13 has increased in tandem with the general rise in the Court's case law and how, in more recent years, the Court actually considers whether Article 13 has been violated, in addition to substantive Articles. This development makes it difficult to distinguish between remedial requirements under Article 13 and substantive Articles. Section 4.4, therefore, raises the question of how and to what extent the Court could and should apply remedial requirements under substantive Articles and/or Article 13. Section 4.5 provides a more detailed overview of how Article 13 has been dealt with in conjunction with substantive Articles.

4.2 ARTICLE 13 IN THE *TRAVAUX PRÉPARATOIRES*

This overview is primarily based upon the texts of the official *travaux préparatoires* (the Collected Editions of the "*Travaux Préparatoires*" Volumes I–VIII) published by Martinus Nijhoff between 1975 and 1985 (hereinafter CETP).[1]

The *travaux préparatoires* contain few discussions concerning Article 13 directly.[2] In fact, the drafting fathers displayed a rather indifferent attitude

[1] See, also, for example, Partsch (1954); Bates (2010); Bates (2013); Dörr, Grote and Marauhn (2013) 9–56; Demir-Gürsel (2021).
[2] Similarly, Matscher (1988) 317.

toward Article 13, as such.[3] But some of the more general discussions may shed light on how the requirement to provide effective domestic remedies should be understood. Article 13 also went through technical changes which shed some light on its content.

The original Convention proposal, presented by the Preparatory Commission of the Council of Europe (1949) (the Teitgen proposal), did not propose a traditional Convention, but a collective guarantee to be applied and secured through domestic legislation until a Convention could be agreed upon.[4] But the Committee of Ministers wanted a Convention that could be adopted immediately and, therefore, established a Committee of Experts who presented a new proposal in the form of a Convention, albeit in two alternative versions.[5] The Committee of Ministers thereafter established a Conference of Senior Officials who were to decide on some questions of method considered to be of a more political nature.[6] This Conference presented a draft Convention which was close to the final product, but the text went through some minor changes after comments from the Consultative Assembly, the Committee of Ministers, and various subcommittees.[7] The final Convention was signed on November 15, 1950, by thirteen Member States.[8]

The text of the Convention was highly influenced by the Universal Declaration on Human Rights (UDHR) adopted in 1948.[9] In fact, the original proposal incorporated the rights considered to be the most important in the UDHR with a simple reference.[10] The right to an effective remedy was included through a reference to Article 8 UDHR, which reads:[11]

---

3 Mertens (1973) 2.
4 Pierre-Henri Teitgen was a lawyer, law professor and member of the French resistance movement. During the drafting of the Convention, he was a member of the French Parliament and the Consultative Assembly of the Council of Europe. He was appointed judge of the Court in September 1976. His influence on the drafting should not be underestimated; see, for example, Madsen (2007) 141–143.
5 See, in particular, the CETP Volume III.
6 See, in particular, the CETP Volume IV.
7 See, in particular, the CETP Volumes V and VI.
8 See the CETP Volume VII 46. The last two volumes (volume VII and VIII) mainly contain discussions concerning the establishment of the first additional Protocol, which contain rights which, for various reasons, were not included in the original Convention.
9 See, for example, the CETP Volume I 194, 228. Some claim that Article 13 is more influenced by Article 18 of the American Declaration of the Rights and Duties of Man (1948) (the Bogotá Declaration); see, for example, Matscher (1988) 316; Raymond (1980) 165; Grote and Marauhn (2006) 1070. However, in the official *travaux préparatoires*, there are few signs of such an influence. That being said, the UDHR was influenced by the Bogotá Declaration, which again builds on the Latin-American Amparo-complaint; see, for example, Mertens (1968); Matscher (1988) 316. Holoubek (1992) holds that the influence of the Bogotá Declaration on Article 8 UDHR, was limited.
10 See, for example, the CETP Volume III 8.
11 See, for example, the CETP Volume I 228.

Everyone has the right to an effective remedy by the competent national tribunals for acts violating the fundamental rights granted him by the constitution or by law.[12]

More generally, the subsidiary system of protection of human rights under the Convention was strongly influenced by the UDHR. In fact, Article 8 UDHR built on the realization that an all-encompassing and effective international protection was unrealistic.[13] René Cassin, therefore, considered Article 8 UDHR the most important Article in the Declaration.[14]

In contrast to Article 8 UDHR, the adopted Article 13 of the ECHR has a more limited scope in two aspects. *First*, the UDHR grants the right to a remedy by competent "national tribunals" and not just a "national authority." *Second*, the UDHR requires an effective remedy for violations of any "fundamental rights granted him by the Constitution or by the law", not only arguable violations of the Declaration.[15]

In the early stages of the drafting, there were no explicit discussions as to why the content of Article 13 of the ECHR was to be similar to that of Article 8 UDHR,[16] but there were lengthy discussions concerning the need to exhaust domestic remedies before taking a case to international level,[17] and there was a general discussion on the content of the principle of "denial of justice", as understood in international law in relation to the responsibility of States for the acts of their judicial organs.[18]

In time, the references to the UDHR were replaced with independent wording in order to give the Convention a more self-sufficient content.[19]

The right to a domestic remedy was first explicitly discussed in conjunction with the presentation of the extract from the report addressed by the Commission on Human Rights of the United Nations to the Economic and

---

[12] Article 8 UDHR was unanimously adopted; see the *United Nations Yearbook on Human Rights 1948* (1949) 466.

[13] See, for example, Matscher (1988) 317.

[14] See, for example, Mertens (1968) 450; Mertens (1973) 28.

[15] The reason was that the declaration, as such, was not legally binding and that it was considered to make little sense to require an effective remedy against nonbinding rights; see, for example, Grote and Marauhn (2006) 1069.

[16] See, for instance, the list of questions prepared by the Secretariat to the meetings of the Committee of Experts, in the CETP Volume III 32–36. None of the questions concerned Article 13.

[17] See, for example, the documents assembled by the secretary-general relating to the rule on the exhaustion of domestic remedies in public international law in the CETP Volume III 38–74.

[18] See, for example, the documents assembled by the secretary-general in the CETP Volume III 74–155. Against this background, some emphasize, more generally, the relationship between Article 13 and the concept of denial of justice; see, for example, Grote and Marauhn (2006) 1070.

[19] See, for example, the CETP Volume III 190–191, 204.

Social Council, which was among the working papers of the Committee of Experts, prepared by the Secretariat General. The UK proposed, both in the UN and the context of the Convention, a more expansive wording. The UK Convention proposal included the right to an effective remedy in a separate section of the general obligation to secure (ensure) rights (the current Article 1 of the ECHR) and to which the second paragraph had the following wording:

Each State party hereto undertakes to ensure:

a) that any person whose rights or freedom as herein defined are violated shall have an effective remedy notwithstanding that the violation has been committed by persons acting in an official capacity;

b) that any person claiming such a remedy shall have his rights thereto determined by national tribunals whose independence is secured; and

c) that the police and executive authorities shall enforce such remedies when granted.[20]

This was the first time that the scope was limited to violations of Convention rights and reference was made to "notwithstanding that the violation has been committed by persons acting in an official capacity". The proposal also included an element of enforcement which is not contained in the current wording of Article 13.

The official *travaux préparatoires* provide no explicit explanation as to why this proposal was not followed up, and why the final version of Article 13 contain a less stringent wording than Article 8 UDHR. But the final version seems to have been supported by three lines of thought.

First, Article 13 was placed at the back of the Convention because it was considered that "this is not a human right in itself, but a mode to secure these [the foregoing] rights."[21]

Second, during the procedures before the Committee of Experts, two schools of thought as to how specific rights should be formulated emerged. One school, supported, in particular, by the UK and the Netherlands, considered that the rights should be defined in as much detail as possible (the definition method).[22] Another school, supported, in particular, by France, Italy, and Belgium, wanted a more simplistic Convention with general principles and less details (the

---

[20] See the CETP Volume III 188, 222, and compare the proposal in the UN setting at 158 as well as the adopted ICCPR Article 2(3) *litra c*.

[21] See, for example, the CETP Volume III 262, 263 (the French version) and the CETP Volume IV 22. Because of this quotation, which was not justified any further, it was, for some time, questioned whether Article 13 provided the individual with a subjective right; see, for example, Mertens (1973) 55–68; Grote and Marauhn (2006) 1070.

[22] These States were also against the establishment of the Court; see, for example, Bates (2013) 34.

enumeration method).[23] The Committee of Experts, therefore, submitted two texts to the Committee of Ministers which included alternatives in which the creation of the Court was included or not.[24] That being said, a more concrete comparison reveals that Alternative B (the definition method) was only scarcely more detailed than Alternative A (the enumeration method).[25] And with regard to Article 13, both alternatives had an almost identical and limited wording, similar to the original Teitgen proposal, but limited to violations of the Convention.[26] Further, none of the alternatives contained a reference to enforcement, but both alternatives held that the authority needed to be judicial.[27] In fact, Alternative B, which one would expect to be the most detailed, contained a briefer wording, not making explicit reference to a judicial authority, although it was clear that the proposal held that the authority needed be judicial.[28]

The Committee of Ministers did not decide between the alternatives, but convened the Conference of Senior Officials to prepare the ground for the "political decision" to be taken by the Committee of Ministers.[29] The Conference was not able to agree unanimously on the method, but provided the Committee of Ministers with a single draft Convention based upon decisions of the majority. The majority was, however, not the same in all cases.[30] The consolidated text must, therefore, be seen as a compromise between the two methods,[31] although Alternative B (the definition method) served as the basis of the text.[32]

The Conference removed the reference to a judicial authority and replaced it with the reference to a "national authority". The right to an effective remedy was originally placed at the beginning of the Convention, as the second paragraph of Article 1 concerning the general obligations on the part of States,[33] but, in the final proposal, it was, again, moved to the back of the Convention (at the time, Article 15).[34] This proposal was then examined by the Committee

---

[23] See, on the justification for these two schools of thought, for example, the CETP Volume III 252–258, Volume IV 8–14 and Volume IV 102–112.

[24] See, for example, the CETP Volume IV 16.

[25] Compare M. Chaumont (France) at the Conference of Senior Officials in the CETP Volume IV 110.

[26] CETP Volume IV 56 (Article 9 in Alternative A and A/2 and Article I(2) in Alternative B and B/2).

[27] See, for example, the CETP Volume IV 30.

[28] See, for example, ibid.

[29] See, for example, ibid. 92.

[30] See ibid. 208, 246 and the draft convention text at 274–296.

[31] See ibid. 248.

[32] See ibid. 258.

[33] See ibid. 182.

[34] See ibid. 282. The reason, at this point, being that "this is a question of the right to bring cases before national courts in respect of the rights protected by this Convention. This Article should therefore be placed after the Articles defining these rights" (at 260).

of Legal Affairs of the Consultative Assembly and the Committee of Ministers who transmitted it to the second session of the Consultative Assembly for comments.[35] At this point, the requirement was moved to Article 13.

In the second session of the Consultative Assembly, there was a considerable debate as to whether the Convention, in what, more generally, was considered a "weakened" form should be accepted as a whole or not. Several changes were proposed and discussed, in particular concerning rights that had been removed from the original proposal of the Consultative Assembly (most notably, education and property) as well as the weakened competences of the Court. But nothing was said about the weakened content of the requirement of an effective domestic remedy. Indeed, no explicit justification, at any point, was provided for the reduced scope of application. The reason is, therefore, best explained by a *third* line of thought.

The drafting fathers were acutely aware of the parallel process of developing a binding human-rights convention in the UN framework.[36] Indeed, the general opinion was that the drafting had to pay due attention to the work in the UN,[37] that the Convention should not conflict with the UN Convention, and that the more detailed the European Convention was, the greater the chance for conflict would be.[38] The drafting fathers would thus have taken note of the following developments in the UN context.

First, the reference to "notwithstanding that the violation has been committed by persons acting in an official capacity" was included in the UN draft already in 1948.[39]

Second, at the sixth session of the Commission on Human Rights in 1950, it was proposed and discussed whether the reference to "national tribunals" should be replaced with a reference to "competent judicial, administrative or legislative authorities". Some held that all remedies had to be provided by judicial authorities and considered it particularly undesirable that a person whose freedoms had been violated should have to have his/her remedy determined by a political organ, since the very same organ might be the organ which had violated his/her rights. But others held that omitting a reference to political authorities would preclude remedies granted by the legislature and the executive in cases in which they might be the only, or the most effective, agency for that purpose. It was, at the same time, observed that a judicial remedy was

---

[35] See, for example, the CETP Volume V 120–156.

[36] This work, obviously, ended up being more time-consuming and was not finalized before the adoption of the UN International Covenant on Civil and Political Rights (ICCPR) and the International Covenant on Economic, Social and Cultural Rights in 1966.

[37] See, for example, the CETP Volume III 248.

[38] See, for example, M. Chaumont (France) who used this as an argument in favor of Alternative A at the Conference of Senior Officials in the CETP Volume IV 110.

[39] See, for example, Bossuyt (1987) 64.

preferable, but that it might be impossible to impose the immediate obligation to provide such remedies upon States. It was, therefore, proposed that each State should undertake "to develop the possibilities" of a judicial remedy at national level.[40]

The UN negotiations do not, on the other hand, explain the total omission of any reference to enforcement in the ECHR.[41] That being said, the Court has, in time, included an element of enforcement in the general concept of an effective remedy.[42]

Moreover, the different opinions on how to formulate rights cannot be understood without taking into account the resistance, from some States, against the establishment of the Court. Indeed, the idea of international accountability was not met with great enthusiasm,[43] in particular from the UK, the Netherlands, and the Nordic countries. There was no need to establish a Court, in addition to the Commission. In any case, because the rights in the Convention were vaguely formulated, the subjects with access to the Court should be limited and the competences of the Court be kept to a minimum. States needed to know what they signed up for if the rights were to be developed and enforced by an international Court. But other States saw the Court as the cornerstone of the Convention and considered that it should be open for complaint to both individuals and States. Indeed, it was precisely these factors which distinguished and legitimized the establishment of a European system in addition to the UN system. Further, these States wanted to make the Court as effective as possible by providing it with far-reaching powers, most notably, the power to declare domestic legislation null and void. In the end, a compromise was reached. The Court was established, but only through an optional clause concerning jurisdiction and individual complaints,[44] and the powers of the Court were significantly limited compared to the most expansive proposals. The Court was, *inter alia*, not granted the power to declare legislation null and void.[45]

This skepticism toward the Court, seen in combination with the skepticism toward open-ended provisions, at least on part of some States, could

---

[40] See, for example, Bossuyt (1987) 67–68.
[41] The reference to enforcement by the "competent authorities" was present in the draft UN Convention and negotiations from the very beginning in 1948; see, for example, Bossuyt (1987) 70.
[42] See Section 11.9.
[43] Christoffersen and Madsen (2013a) 6.
[44] The optional clause required at least nine States (the number was heavily debated) to accept the jurisdiction of the Court before it could enter into force. This did not happen until 1958, even though the first States signed the Convention in November 1950. Accepting the jurisdiction of the Court is now mandatory under Articles 32–34 of the ECHR; see the Explanatory Report to Protocol 11 paras. 85–86.
[45] On the establishment of the Court and the Commission; see, Bates (2013) 25–27.

have contributed to the Court's reluctance of developing Article 13 in early years. However, most of the drafting fathers believed, on the other hand, that domestic policies would remain the primary site of enforcement and that international control was to serve only as an external signaling device to trigger an appropriate domestic response. The Court was, therefore, by all camps, primarily seen as a tool to strengthen the existing domestic institutions of judicial review, parliamentary legislation, and public action – not to supplant them.[46] Against this background, it could be deemed surprising that Article 13, as a tool to improve the domestic implementation of human rights, received so little attention in the Court's early case law.[47] That being said, before domestic remedial authorities may review the substance of Convention complaints, they need to know a minimum of the substance that they are to review. However, in the current context, in which substantive Convention rights have been considerably developed by the Court, the *travaux préparatoires* could hardly serve as a limitation for improving the domestic protection of human rights, rather the opposite (Section 12.3).

4.3 THE COURT'S APPLICATION OF ARTICLE 13

As of January 1, 2021, the Court had rendered 3,247 judgments in which Article 13 was a theme – 68 in Grand Chamber, 2,437 in Chamber, and 742 in Committee.[48] The judgments are distributed per year as illustrated by Fig. 4.1.

The first case in which the Court considered Article 13 was *de Wilde, Ooms and Versyp v. Belgium* (Plenary 1971). The Court did not deem it necessary to consider whether there had been a violation of Article 13 in addition to Article 5(4).[49]

Between 1971 and 1986, the Court dealt with Article 13 occasionally. In some years, there were no judgments, in 1984 three, and mostly one or two judgments per year.

A slight increase came in 1987, in which the Court dealt with Article 13 in six judgments. Between 1987 and 1995, the number of judgments varies between four and nine. A new slight increase came in 1996, in which the Court dealt with Article 13 in thirteen judgments. The main reasons for the augmentation

---

[46] See, for example, Moravcsik (2000) 238. See, also, Section 10.5.3.3.

[47] See Sections 4.3 and 4.5 and, for example, McGregor (2012) 738.

[48] All statistics in this chapter include judgments up to 1 January 2021. The numbers are established by using the Hudoc keyword search function to which Article 13 is used as keyword. The possibility of ruling in Grand Chamber was introduced with Protocol 11. It replaced the plenary function of the former Court. The first Grand Chamber judgment concerning Article 13 was *Murray v. the UK* (Grand Chamber 1994). The possibility of ruling in committee was introduced by Protocol 14. The first Committee judgment concerning Article 13 was *Wetjen v. Germany* (Committee 2010).

[49] See para. 95. The Court has, thereafter, consistently held, in cases in which it has found a violation of Article 5(4), that it is not necessary to consider whether Article 13 has also been violated; see Section 4.5.3.

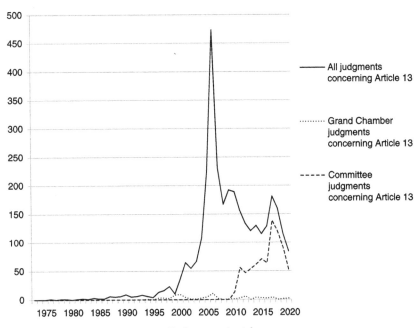

FIGURE 4.1 *Judgments Article 13 per year*

in 1987–1996 were some specific problems in the UK, Sweden, and Austria.[50] Many of the major principles, in particular, many of the major limitations in the scope of Article 13, were developed in cases against these three States. In the cases against the UK, the Court, *inter alia*, dealt with the restricted scope of review by national courts, including the question of whether Article 13 granted a right to challenge legislation as such, for instance, in cases concerning expulsions which could violate Article 3.[51] The judgments against Sweden and Austria concerned, *inter alia*, violations of access to court in cases concerning civil rights and obligations, Article 6(1), in which the Court held that it was not necessary to also examine Article 13,[52] and complaints in which the Court accepted that an aggregate of remedies could satisfy Article 13.[53]

Between 1997 and 2003, the number of judgments concerning Article 13 increased in a steady manner to 67 in 2003. This augmentation is attributable to three main factors. *First*, the Turkish problems of ineffective investigations, which posed a problem under Article 13 in conjunction with arguable violations of, in particular, Articles 2 and 3, but also Articles 5, 8, and P1 Article 1,

---

[50] Of the 68 judgments in which the Court dealt with Article 13 between 1987 and 1996, 43 concerned the UK, Sweden and Austria – the UK 22, Sweden 13, and Austria 8.
[51] See Sections 10.5.3 and 10.5.4.
[52] See Section 4.5.2.
[53] See Section 9.3.

for deaths, disappearances, inhuman treatment, and the destruction of homes and property, inflicted by State agents or unknown perpetrators in southeast Turkey, which suffered from serious disturbances between Turkish security forces and the PKK (Worker's Party of Kurdistan).[54] *Second*, there were still many judgments against the UK,[55] particularly concerning the scope of domestic court review, *inter alia*, in cases concerning expulsion and secret surveillance which, arguably, violated Article 8.[56] *Third*, the Convention entered into force for many new Member States, in particular from Eastern Europe, in which the Court increasingly had to deal with alleged violations of Article 13.[57]

These early signs of an increasing case load concerning Article 13 from the new Member States were to be confirmed in the coming years.[58] Indeed, between 2004 and 2006, the judgments concerning Article 13 increased exceptionally to 108 in 2004, 224 in 2005, and 473 in 2006,[59] which still is the year in which the Court has dealt with the most cases concerning Article 13. The main reasons are: *First*, the impact of some repetitive problems in many new Member States, most notably excessive length of proceedings, nonenforcement of judgments, conditions of detention, and lack of effective investigations.[60] *Second*, the problem of ineffective investigations in southeast Turkey persisted.[61] *Third*, the Italian problem of excessive length of proceedings, which violates Article 6(1), started having an effect on Article 13.[62] Indeed, until the

---

[54] See Section 11.7. Out of the 272 judgments concerning Article 13 in this period, 91 were against Turkey (33.5%). The basic principles concerning effective investigations were developed in these cases and still apply today.

[55] Out of the 272 judgments concerning Article 13 in this period, 51 were against the UK (18.75%).

[56] See Section 10.5.4.

[57] Between 1989 and 1999 the Convention entered into force for the following countries: San Marino (1989); Finland (1990); Bulgaria (1992); Hungary (1992); the Czech Republic (1993); Slovakia (1993); Poland (1993); Slovenia (1994); Romania (1994); Lithuania (1995); Estonia (1996); Albania (1996); Andorra (1996); the former Yugoslav Republic of Macedonia (1997); Latvia (1997); Croatia (1997); Ukraine (1997); Moldova (1997); Russia (1998); Georgia (1999). Out of the 272 judgments between 1997 and 2003, 38 were against the following new Member States (approximately 14%): Finland (5); Bulgaria (8); the Czech Republic (2); Slovakia (8); Poland (5); Romania (8); Lithuania (1); Estonia (1).

[58] After the year 2000, the Convention has also entered into force for the following Member States: Armenia (2002); Azerbaijan (2002); Bosnia and Herzegovina (2002); Serbia (2004); Monaco (2005); Montenegro (2006).

[59] The major rise in 2006, and the drop thereafter, is, primarily, due to the fact that the Court, exceptionally, dealt with a number of cases concerning excessive length of proceedings in Slovenia (approximately 170 cases) in ordinary Chambers, and not by using the Pilot judgment procedure.

[60] Out of the 805 judgments concerning Article 13 in this period, 432 (53.7%) came from these nine Member States: Bulgaria (33); Croatia (38); the Czech Republic (15); Hungary (10); Romania (12); Russia (40); Slovakia (28); Slovenia (171); Ukraine (85).

[61] Out of the 805 judgments concerning Article 13 in this period, 162 were against Turkey (approximately 20.12%), of which the majority were cases concerning ineffective investigations.

[62] Out of the 805 judgments concerning Article 13 in this period, 46 were against Italy (approximately 5.71%). Most of these cases concerned excessive length of proceedings violating Article 6(1).

landmark judgment *Kudla* v. *Poland* (Grand Chamber 2000), the Court had more or less consistently held that it was not necessary to consider whether Article 13 had been violated in cases of excessive length of proceedings. But in *Kudla* the Court parted from its previous case law and found it necessary to consider whether Article 13 had also been violated. Because of the number of cases concerning excessive length of proceedings, in particular from Italy and many of the new Member States from Eastern Europe, this change had a significant impact on the number of judgments concerning Article 13. The most stunning example is the cases against Slovenia in 2006. Out of 473 judgments concerning Article 13 in 2006, 170 were against Slovenia (approximately 35.9 percent), out of which most concerned violations of Article 6(1) because of excessive length of proceedings.[63]

On a positive side, the problems concerning the restricted scope of review by UK courts disappeared – at least to judge by the cases arriving at the Court. Out of the 805 judgments concerning Article 13 between 2004 and 2006, only 10 were against the UK. This change may be traced back to the incorporation of the Convention in UK law through the UK Human Rights Act 1998 (which entered into force on October 2, 2000).[64]

As from 2007, the number of judgments concerning Article 13 dropped considerably compared to the peak in 2006 and decreased in a relative stable manner until 2015. The following factors contributed to this reduction: *First*, the Court introduced the Pilot judgment procedure in *Broniowski* v. *Poland* *(Merits)* (Grand Chamber 2004), which started to have an effect, in particular as from 2006. The procedure allows the Court to adjourn similar cases, which, in the end, through successful implementation of the Pilot judgment and friendly settlements, may remove the case from the docket of the Court without a judgment. This has, *inter alia*, led to a significant reduction of judgments concerning Article 13 and excessive length of proceedings. *Second*, the first part of the conflict in southeast Turkey ended with a ceasefire, which again reduced the complaints concerning lack of effective investigations.[65]

On the other hand, the number of judgments concerning Article 13 remains high, in particular because of the identification of new structural and repetitive problems in some Eastern European Member States, in particular, Russia,

---

[63] Some of these cases concerned lack of execution/enforcement of judgments, which may be perceived as a violation of excessive length of proceedings or a separate violation of the requirement to enforce binding decisions, which both are violations of Article 6(1).

[64] Article 13 is not incorporated in UK law; see the Human Rights Act 1998 Article 1(1). However, Articles 8 and 10 of the Human Rights Act contain provisions on judicial remedies and power to take remedial action.

[65] On the number of judgments from the Court, this can, in particular, be seen from 2008 onwards. Between 2008 and the end of 2012, for example, the Court only dealt with 15 cases concerning effective investigations in Turkey.

Ukraine, Bulgaria, Hungary, and Moldova, but also Turkey, Greece, and Italy.[66] The main problems are lack of remedies concerning conditions of detention which, arguably, violate Article 3, to which Russia and Ukraine are the main contributors, the lack of effective investigations in new Member States, most notably Russia, delay or total lack of enforcement of domestic judgments (Article 6), most notably Russia and Ukraine,[67] expulsion/deportation procedures (possible violations of Articles 2, 3, and 8), most notably Bulgaria, secret surveillance procedures (Article 8), most notably Bulgaria, and some specific problems in conjunction with Articles 10, 11, and P1 Article 1, most notably Greece. The number of judgments concerning effective remedies in cases of excessive length of proceedings also remains high, in particular, due to the identification of the problem in new Member States, most notably Bulgaria, Greece, Russia, Turkey, and Ukraine. The relatively higher numbers in 2017 and 2018, and the following reduction in 2019 and 2020, must be seen in conjunction with the fact that the Court in the two previous years had focused on adjudicating priority cases.[68]

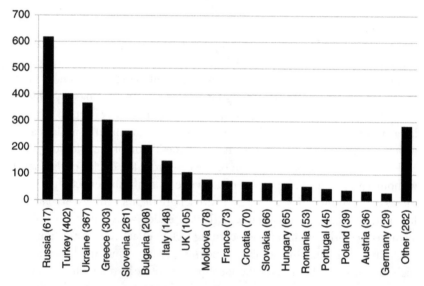

FIGURE 4.2 *Judgments Article 13 per Member State as of December 31, 2020*

---

[66] Out of the 1,452 judgments concerning Article 13 rendered between 2007 and the end of 2015, 1,061 were against these seven Member States (approximately 73.1%): Bulgaria (139); Greece (159); Italy (81); Russia (325); Slovenia (89); Turkey (136); Ukraine (132).

[67] The most striking illustration of the scope of this "new" problem is *Burmych a.o. v. Ukraine* (Grand Chamber 2017) in which the Court struck out 12,143 applications against Ukraine because they were to be dealt with by the Committee of Ministers in compliance with the obligation deriving from the Pilot judgment *Yuriy Nikolayevich Ivanov v. Ukraine* (2009), which found a structural problem giving rise to violations of Articles 6(1) and 13 due to the lack of non-enforcement of domestic judgments, including remedies against the non-enforcement.

[68] See the ECHR Analysis of Statistics 2016 4.

Since the first judgment concerning Article 13 in 1971 and until 31 December 2020, the Court has rendered 23,396 judgments concerning all articles. Fig. 4.3 illustrates how the total number of judgments relates to the judgments in which the Court has dealt with Article 13.

The overall percentage of judgments in which the Court has dealt with Article 13 is high. In the whole period, Article 13 was a theme in 3,247 out of 23,396 judgments – approximately 14 percent of all judgments. The numbers vary some per year, for instance, approximately 30 percent in 1990, 7 percent in 1995, 5.2 percent in 2000, 20.3 percent in 2005, 30.3 percent in the top year 2006, and 12.6 percent in 2010. But the number increases and decreases in relative correlation with the total number of judgments. Thus, between 1971 and the end of 1999, Article 13 was a theme in 132 out of 1,002 judgments (approximately 13.2 percent) and between the year 2000 and the end of 2020 in 3,126 out of 22,394 (approximately 14 percent). There may be several reasons for this: *First*, any alleged violation of substantive Articles could, in principle, be accompanied with a complaint under Article 13. *Second*, and in connection with the foregoing, as the content of substantive Articles expands through dynamic interpretation, the scope of Article 13 expands: More arguable claims could, in principle, be brought before domestic authorities and the Court. *Third*, the Court has, in some areas, taken a more active role when construing and applying Article 13.[69] The pivotal example is *Kudla* v. *Poland* (Grand Chamber 2000).

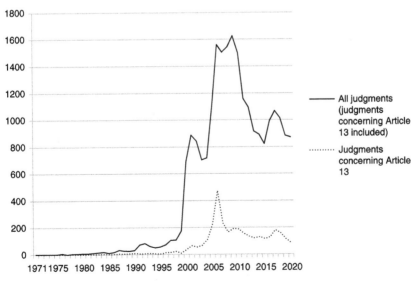

FIGURE 4.3 *Relationship between all judgments and Article 13 judgments*

---

[69] See Sections 4.5 and 12.3.2.

The relationship deviates slightly in time – and with reverse signs when the overall number of judgments are increasing and decreasing. On the one hand, the sharp rise in all judgments commences at the end of the 1990s, whereas the sharp rise in Article 13 judgments commences in the early 2000s. The sharp rise in all judgments is due to the identification of systemic and structural problems in some Member States, for example, excessive length of proceedings and the lack of effective investigations. The lag in judgments concerning Article 13 may indicate that the Court and the applicants are more willing to use Article 13 when the existence of a systemic problem has been established. On the other hand, with regard to the successive decline, the judgments concerning Article 13 precede the decline in the total number of judgments. This may indicate that the remedial problem could be fixed before the substantive problem. The applicant may, for instance, still be a victim of a substantive violation, even though the domestic remedy has been improved to the extent that it is rendered effective. For instance, in cases concerning excessive length of proceedings, the applicant may be considered a victim at the international level because he/she has not been awarded sufficient compensation at domestic level, even though the domestic remedy was effective.[70]

Further, the relationship – over time – between judgments in which Article 13 was violated, not violated, or, for various reasons, not considered necessary to examine is illustrated by the following graphs (Fig. 4.4).[71]

---

[70] See, for example, Section 11.5.

[71] These graphs are not entirely correct due to the following uncertainties in the data provided by the Hudoc database: *First*, in the same case, Article 13 may be claimed violated for several reasons and in conjunction with different substantive Articles. In most cases, the database then only indicates one violation and one non-violation, but, in some cases, one or both of the additional violations or non-violations are included. That being said, the majority of cases concern only one alleged violation of Article 13, and, in cases in which several violations of Article 13 are claimed, the result is mostly either violation or non-violation on all or several grounds, and that the Court considers it not necessary to examine Article 13 on remaining grounds. Accordingly, the data concerning violations and non-violations should be close to correct. *Second*, the Hudoc database does not contain data on the judgments in which the Court did not consider it necessary to examine Article 13. I have, therefore, extracted these data by subtracting the joint number of violations and non-violations from the total number of judgments concerning Article 13 in each year. These data are, therefore, only correct as long as Article 13 is allegedly violated on only one ground. However, if several violations of Article 13 are alleged, the data are not correct, to the extent that at least one violation or non-violation of Article 13 is found. To reduce uncertainty in this respect, I have gone through the conclusions in all judgments in the years 2008–2020. This does neither provide 100 per cent accuracy, but the graphs, at the very least, provide a clear indication of a trend that corresponds with my impression after analyzing the judgments accounted for in Section 2.2.

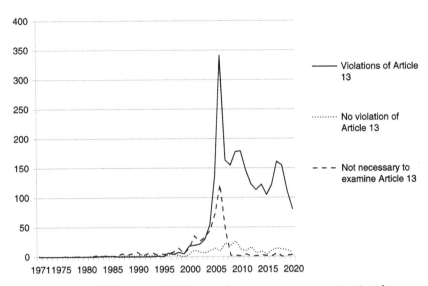

FIGURE 4.4 *Violation, no violation, and not necessary to examine Article 13*

The first case, in which the Court found a violation of Article 13, was *Silver a.o. v. the UK* (1983). It thus took 12 years between the first judgment in which the Court considered whether Article 13 had been violated (the *Vagrancy* case in 1971) before the Court found a violation.[72] Indeed, in early years, the Court found few violations of Article 13. Before the year 2000, Article 13 was violated in 42 out of 132 judgments – approximately 31.8 percent. However, between the year 2000 and the end of 2020, Article 13 was violated in 2,535 out of 3,126 judgments – approximately 81.1 percent.

Until 1996, Article 13 was violated in fewer cases than not. But, as from 1997, the violations increasingly started to supersede nonviolations. As from 2007, the relative number of violations compared to nonviolations diminished some, with the exception of the years 2017 and 2018, which must be seen in conjunction with the fact that the Court in the two previous years had focused on adjudicating priority cases. Still, the number of violations compared to nonviolations remains high.

Further, until the year 2000, the judgments in which the Court did not consider it necessary to examine Article 13 remained higher than both the judgments in which Article 13 was violated and the judgments in which it was not. This practice of not considering Article 13 was criticized, in particular,

---

[72] The *Silver* case was the eighth judgment in which the Court considered whether Article 13 had been violated.

because the Court provided no justification for the refusal.[73] Franz Matscher held that the only justification was judicial economy.[74]

As from around the year 2000, the relationship between not necessary judgments and violations and nonviolations depart. Until 2004, the not necessary judgments increased approximately at the same rate as violations, but considerably more than nonviolations. The not necessary judgments increased further in 2005, but thereafter the number of not necessary judgments has decreased drastically compared to both violations and nonviolations, to the point where the Court now only rarely considers it not necessary to examine whether Article 13 has been violated. Accordingly, the Court is making more active use of Article 13, not only by declaring more violations of Article 13 compared to nonviolations but also by actually considering whether Article 13 has been violated, instead of holding that it is not necessary to examine Article 13 in addition to substantive Articles.

The underlying reasons for this development may be complex, but are, clearly, related to the number of repetitive violations. To the extent that the Court finds it necessary to consider whether Article 13 has been violated in cases revealing repetitive problems, the number of violations will increase. The shift in the *Kudla* case is illustrative. The same development can be seen, for example, in cases concerning lack of effective investigations, lack of nonenforcement of judgments, and conditions of detention. Indeed, the Court has, in recent years, had a particular focus on tackling structural problems in repetitive cases. However, the case law and the statistics reveal that at least from around 2006, the Court has been more willing to consider whether Article 13 has been violated in addition to substantive Articles, more generally, not just in cases revealing structural problems.

The reasoning and justification for declaring a violation of Article 13 are, however, still limited.[75] Indeed, the Court mostly only reiterates the basic facts of the case, and repeats or refers to the justification under the substantive Articles with little additional reasoning concerning the content of Article 13. It is, therefore, difficult to deduce the purposes that Article 13 is to serve more generally (Chapter 3), the specific requirements of access to justice (Chapter 10), and what forms of redress the domestic remedy must include (Chapter 11).[76] Thus, even though the Court makes more active use of Article 13, it still awards States a wide margin of appreciation (Chapter 8). This is probably, at least partly, connected to the fact that the Court's

---

[73] See, for example, Vospernik (2001).
[74] Matscher (1988) 315.
[75] Compare McGregor (2012) specifically with regard to remedies against torture.
[76] See, also, Section 2.3.

possibility to issue specific requirements under Article 13 often is inhibited because the rule of the exhaustion of domestic remedies does not require every domestic remedy to be exhausted (Chapter 5). As a consequence, the Court may be reluctant to examine all remedies at international level under Article 13 because the remedial *problématique* has not been truly exhausted, only the substantive.[77] For instance, in torture cases, litigants are mostly able to fulfill the requirement of the exhaustion of domestic remedies without having exhausted the possibility of obtaining compensation.[78] However, the Court could issue more principled and abstract reasoning concerning both purposes in general and specific requirements and procedurally test how domestic remedial authorities have considered such purposes and requirements (Chapter 13).

4.4 A CHOICE BETWEEN NORM COMPLEXES?

The development toward more active use of Article 13 raises the question what the relationship between remedial requirements under Article 13 and substantive Articles is, could, and should be. The prime example is the overlap between the access to justice required by Articles 6 and 13 and Articles 5 and 13. But there are many other examples. Under Articles 2 and 3, for instance, the Court includes a procedural obligation that aims at ensuring that the right to life and the prohibition of torture and other inhuman and degrading treatment are not theoretical or illusory, but practical and effective.[79] Under Article 2, the Court has, since the landmark judgment *Šilih* v. *Slovenia* (Grand Chamber 2009), even explicitly recognized that the procedural obligation to carry out an effective investigation has evolved into a "separate and autonomous duty".[80] Further, for interferences to be in accordance with law and to be necessary in a democratic society in order to achieve a legitimate aim under Articles 8 to 11, various procedural requirements must be satisfied. For instance, a system of secret surveillance must have "adequate and effective guarantees against abuse" to be in accordance with Article 8.[81] This implies, *inter alia*, that the applicant must have "effective control" to challenge an arguable allegation of unlawful telephone tapping,[82] be able to seek recognition in law of a *de facto*

---

[77] Compare McGregor (2012) 739, 743–745.
[78] McGregor (2012) 744.
[79] See, for example, *İlhan* v. *Turkey* (Grand Chamber 2000) para. 91; *Mesut Deniz* v. *Turkey* (2013) para. 56.
[80] *Šilih* v. *Slovenia* (Grand Chamber 2009) para. 159.
[81] See, for example, *Leander* v. *Sweden* (1987) paras. 60–67.
[82] See, for example, *Lambert* v. *France* (1998) paras. 30–41.

separation,[83] establish or challenge paternity,[84] or regain access to family life with a child.[85] It is rarer that substantive Articles require redress, either in a general or a specific form.[86] But some requirements may be perceived from the angles of both access to justice and redress, for instance, the requirement to perform effective investigations.[87]

A direct conflict between requirements under Article 13 and substantive Articles can hardly be imagined. Stricter remedial requirements under the one or the other Article do not provide incompatible solutions, only a higher level of protection. But the question may arise as to whether parallel violations of Article 13 and the substantive Article should be declared, or a violation of either the substantive Article and/or Article 13 and/or a nonviolation or a finding that it is not necessary to examine the issue under the one or the other Article.

As Section 4.3 shows, in early years, the Court did mostly not deem it necessary to examine whether Article 13 had been violated in addition to substantive Articles. This is the main reason why Article 13 for a long time played a marginal role in the Court's case law.[88] But even though the Court now more often declares a violation of Article 13, it rarely explains why.[89] The *Kudla* case, which justifies the new use of Article 13 with reference to the Court's case load and some reflections on subsidiarity, is an exception.

When, then, should Article 13 be applied in addition to or instead of (remedial) requirements in substantive Articles?

The simple answer is that Article 13 needs to be applied to the extent that it is necessary to satisfy the requirements of access to justice and redress in Article 13 (Sections 3, 10 and 11). To the extent that similar requirements under substantive Articles offer the same level of protection, it is immediately tempting to conclude, in accordance with the principle of *lex specialis*, that it is not necessary to examine Article 13. However, this temptation should be moderated by at least four objections, which are further elaborated on in the concluding Chapter 13.

First, similar requirements may play different roles and serve different purposes under different Articles.[90] For instance, effective investigations may promote purposes underlying access to justice and redress, as such, but also

[83] See, for example, *Airey* v. *Ireland* (1979) paras. 31–33.
[84] See, for example, *Mikulić* v. *Croatia* (2002) paras. 60–66; *Paulik* v. *Slovakia* (2006) paras. 47 and 50.
[85] See, for example, *Mincheva* v. *Bulgaria* (2010) paras. 83 and 112.
[86] Article 5(5) of the ECHR is, however, an example.
[87] See Section 11.7.
[88] Similarly Kilpatrick (2000) 24.
[89] See, also, for example, Pollmann and Lohmann (2012) 268 and, as an example, *Mugemangango* v. *Belgium* (Grand Chamber 2020) para. 135.
[90] Similarly, Vospernik (2001) 367, specifically on the relationship between Articles 6(1) and 13. See, also, for example, *Iatridis* v. *Greece* (Grand Chamber 1999) para. 65. See, also, Chapter 3.

purposes underlying, for example, the positive obligation to secure rights. Even though the requirements are similar, it may be of significance to underline differences in purpose by considering whether both Articles have been violated.

Second, under substantive Articles, remedial requirements tend to be part of broader assessments, for instance, the positive obligation to protect life or considerations as to whether an interference is necessary in a democratic society. Such broader assessments may undercommunicate remedial goals and requirements. For instance, to what extent is it necessary to perform effective investigations to correct injustice, promote deterrence, and establish the truth?[91]

Third, remedial requirements under substantive Articles are mostly of a procedural nature, similar to the requirements of access to justice under Article 13. The element of redress is rarely dealt with.

Fourth, and connected to the foregoing, in the case law of the Court, there is a trend toward a proceduralization of substantive rights.[92] For all its merits, this proceduralization may hamper the further development and clarification of what is required by Article 13, in particular, the element of redress. Indeed, when the Court, in its more recent case law, also finds breaches of Article 13, it mostly does so with a simple reference to the finding under the substantive Article, which only deals with procedural issues, but without any principled reasoning as to why it is necessary to declare a violation of Article 13, for instance, by elaborating on the required redress (Section 13.3). But also applying purely procedural elements under Article 13 in addition to or instead of substantive Articles may have additional advantages compared to the approaches under substantive Articles (Section 13.2).

4.5 ARTICLE 13 AND SUBSTANTIVE ARTICLES

4.5.1 *Introduction*

Fig. 4.5 illustrates that in the Court's case law, Article 13 has primarily been a theme in conjunction with violations of Articles 6, 3, 5, 8, 2, 14, 10, 11, and P1 Article 1.

The lower column displays all judgments in which Article 13 has been dealt with by the Court as of December 31, 2020. The following columns show the substantive Articles that have been considered in conjunction with Article 13 in the same judgments. In many of these judgments, several substantive Articles have been alleged violated in conjunction with Article 13.[93]

---

[91] See Chapter 3 and, as a concrete example, Section 11.7.3.
[92] See Section 13.2.
[93] The judgments in the lower column (all judgments concerning Article 13) have been extracted by using Article 13 as a keyword in the keyword search function of the Hudoc database. The other columns have been extracted by using the filter function in the Hudoc database.

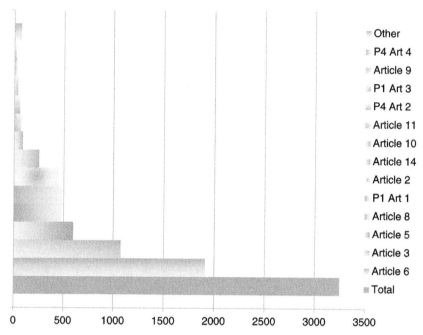

FIGURE 4.5 *Alleged violations of Article 13 in conjunction with substantive articles*

4.5.2 *Article 6*

In the case law of the Court, Article 13 has, above all, been a theme in conjunction with Article 6 (as of December 31, 2020, 1,911 out of 3,247 judgments).

The first case was *Airey* v. *Ireland* (1979). Article 6(1) was violated because the applicant was denied the possibility of instituting effective judicial proceedings for separation because she was not able to use legal assistance.[94] A majority of four judges simply stated that the requirements of Article 13 were "less strict" than Article 6(1) and "in this case", "entirely absorbed" by Article 6(1).[95] The only additional justification was a *mutatis mutandis* reference to *de Wilde, Ooms and Versyp* v. *Belgium* (Plenary 1971), the first case in which the Court dealt with Article 13, and in which the Court concluded that, because of the finding of a violation of Article 5(4), it was not necessary to consider whether Article 13 had been violated, but without any justification.[96] The minority of three judges found that the Court should have examined whether Article 13 had been violated. Two judges found that the Court should have concluded that Article 13 had not been violated.[97]

---

[94] Para. 28. For similar reasons, Article 8 was violated.
[95] Para. 35.
[96] *de Wilde, Ooms and Versyp* v. *Belgium* (Plenary 1971) para. 95.
[97] Judge O'Donoghue held that since Article 6(1) had not been violated, nor was Article 13. Judge Vilhjálmsson added that neither the Government nor the Commission had expanded on

One judge (Judge Evrigenis) did not conclude on the question of violation, but held that whereas the judicial proceedings in Article 6(1) concerned "civil rights", the remedy in Article 13 concerned fundamental rights protected by the Convention. He could, therefore, not see how there was any overlap or absorption between Articles 6(1) and 13.

On one occasion, a Commission majority found a violation of Article 13, but without elaborating on the relationship with Article 6(1).[98]

On a few occasions, dissenting and concurring opinions demanded further justification as to why it was not necessary to examine Article 13. In W v. *the UK* (Plenary 1987), Article 6(1) was violated under its civil head because the domestic tribunal could not determine the case sufficiently in all its aspects. The majority of the Court referred to the doctrine of less strict and absorbed, and concluded that it was not necessary to examine Article 13.[99] Judges Pinheiro Farinha and de Meyer, on the other hand, held that the relationship needed to be considered more thoroughly before concluding that it was not necessary to examine Article 13.[100] In their dissenting opinion in *Putz* v. *Austria* (1996), the judges de Meyer and Jungwiert, on the other hand, simply concluded that, because the applicant had no access to court in a criminal case and since Article 6(1), therefore, had been violated, the applicant had, also, been deprived of an effective remedy under Article 13. In *Pizzetti* v. *Italy* (Plenary Commission report 1991), the minority held that Article 13 was, in principle, applicable against violations committed by courts, irrespectively of the substantive Article affected. But some complaints under Article 6(1) (*"certains griefs"*) had to be considered *lex specialis*, with the consequence that the requirements of Article 13 were absorbed. However, in other cases, such a relationship did not exist, such as, for example, complaints concerning excessive length of proceedings.[101]

---

the arguments concerning Article 13. He thus had problems understanding what the alleged violation of Article 13 could consist of, but pointed to two possible grounds. On the one hand, the lack of an alternative remedy to compensate for the absence of a system of legal aid. But this ground pre-supposed a violation of Articles 6(1), 8 or 14, which, in his opinion, were not violated. Another ground could have been the possibility of testing whether the applicant had the right to legal aid before domestic courts. But this argument had not been pursued before the Court, and there was no evidence that this possibility had not been open to the applicant.

98 *Sporrong and Lönnroth* v. *Sweden* (Plenary Commission report 1980). The Court, however, concluded that it was not necessary to examine Article 13 by referring to the doctrine of "less strict" and "absorbed"; see *Sporrong and Lönnroth* v. *Sweden* (Plenary 1982) para. 88.

99 *W* v. *the UK* (Plenary 1987) para. 86. See, also, *B* v. *the UK* (Plenary 1987); *O* v. *the UK* (Plenary 1987); *R* v. *the UK* (Plenary 1987), which are almost identical cases from the same day with the same majority and separate opinions.

100 See, in this regard, also, the dissenting opinion by Mr. Fawcett and Mr. Kellberg in *Sporrong and Lönnroth* v. *Sweden* (Plenary Commission report 1980).

101 See the dissenting opinion of A. Weizel, H. Danelius, G.H. Thune, Sir Basil Hall, C.L. Rozakis and M.P. Pellonpää in *Pizzetti* v. *Italy* (Plenary Commission report 1991). See, also, Sir Basil Hall in *Goisis* v. *Italy* (Commission report 1992).

However, apart from a few dissenting and concurring opinions, the practice of referring to Article 13 as "less strict" and "absorbed" was repeated in a string of judgments, mostly without any further justification.[102]

On a few occasions, the justification for not examining Article 13 was linked to the fact that the Convention, including Article 13, does not include a general right to appeal against court proceedings.[103] Indeed, a right to appeal is only explicitly foreseen in Article 2 of Protocol 7 in criminal proceedings. However, the consequence of the argument is that Article 13 is not applicable on any violation caused by domestic courts.[104]

Moreover, on some occasions, the Court simply held that it was not necessary to examine Article 13,[105] or simply stated that no separate issue arose,[106] but without any reference to less strict and absorbed.

In a few cases, the Court explicitly emphasized that it was a civil case and that, in such cases, Article 6(1) was *lex specialis* – thus seemingly holding that Article 13 might need examination in criminal cases.[107] However, even though the doctrine of less strict and absorbed was mainly emphasized in civil cases, it was, also, referred to in criminal cases.[108] Further, in some cases, the Court referred to less strict and absorbed, but underlined, in "this case" or "here" absorbed.[109]

The now well-known shift concerning excessive length of proceedings was firmly established in *Kudla v. Poland* (Grand Chamber 2000), but was prepared by *Mikulski v. Poland* (Plenary Commission report 1999). A majority of 17 against 10 Commission members found no violation of Article 6(1), but that the claim was arguable under Article 13. They then held, more generally, that Article 13 made no exception where a violation of the Convention was the result of acts by domestic courts, but, "in some respects," Article 6 was *lex specialis* so that the guarantees of Article 13 where absorbed by those of Article 6. This was the case, in particular, "when the issue under Article 6 is one of access to court, since the right to such access in cases falling under Article 6 must be seen as a special way of ensuring the right to an

---

[102] See, for a few examples, *Sporrong and Lönnroth* v. *Sweden* (Plenary 1982) para. 88; *Silver a.o.* v. *the UK* (1983) para. 110; *Mason and van Zon* v. *the Netherlands* (Plenary Commission report 1994) para. 76; *Cordova* v. *Italy (no. 1)* (2003) para. 70. See, also, Vospernik (2001) 361.

[103] See, for example, *Pizzetti* v. *Italy* (Plenary Commission report 1991) para. 41; *Kremzov* v. *Austria* (Commission report 1992) para. 139; *Goisis* v. *Italy* (Commission report 1992) para. 27.

[104] Compare the dissenting opinion of A. Weizel, H. Danelius, G.H. Thune, Sir Basil Hall, C.L. Rozakis and M.P. Pellonpää in *Pizzetti* v. *Italy* (Plenary Commission report 1991).

[105] See, for example, *Papageorgiou* v. *Greece* (1997) para. 51; *Zielinski and Pradal & Gonzalez a.o.* v. *France* (Grand Chamber 1999) para. 74; *Komanický* v. *Slovakia* (2002) para. 60.

[106] See, for example, *Escoubet* v. *Belgium* (Grand Chamber 1999) para. 40.

[107] See, for example, *Brualla Gómez de la Torre* v. *Spain* (1997) para. 41; *Vasilescu* v. *Romania* (1998) para. 43.

[108] See, for example, *Lauko* v. *Slovakia* (1998) para. 68; *Kadubec* v. *Slovakia* (1998) para. 64.

[109] See, for example, *Osman* v. *the UK* (Grand Chamber 1998) para. 158; *Coëme a.o.* v. *Belgium* (2000) para. 117.

effective legal remedy."[110] However, the right to a court determination within a reasonable time was not *lex specialis*. That being said, one majority fraction, in accordance with, *inter alia*, the *Pizzetti* case, held that, if a violation of Article 6(1) was found, it was not necessary to examine Article 13,[111] whereas another majority fraction deviated more expressly from the former practice of the Court and Commission by holding that a finding that it was not necessary to examine Article 13 only applied when Article 6, in fact, "offers stronger guarantees compared to Article 13." However, when a claim under Article 13 concerned the absence of a remedy against an alleged violation of precisely Article 6, it "would be outright illogical and inconsistent with the purpose of that Article to decide that there is no need to consider Article 13."[112]

The majority added, seemingly more as an afterthought than as a decisive argument, that the slowness of court proceedings was a general problem in a number of Convention States:

> which is demonstrated by the very large number of complaints about such matters which have continuously been brought before the Convention organs and by the numerous judgments of the Court and reports of the Commission in which violations of Article 6 have been found in those cases. It is therefore highly desirable that States should feel responsible for creating effective domestic remedies so as to ensure that the obligation to provide justice within a reasonable time is respected without the necessity of having recourse to the complaints procedure under the Convention. The applicability of Article 13 in this respect may therefore be of considerable practical importance in giving effect, already at the domestic level, to one of the fundamental procedural guarantees included in Article 6.[113]

One Commission member still held that a "tribunal" within the meaning of Article 6(1) could only be "supervised" by another court. Consequently, Article 13 would mean nothing less than a right to appeal. Therefore, "whenever Article 6 is at issue, there is no room for the application of Article 13, whatever the particular aspect of the right of access to a court and to fair proceedings."[114]

In *Kudla v. Poland* (Grand Chamber 2000), the Court then took the full leap concerning excessive length of proceedings. The Court recognized that, in numerous previous cases, it had not considered it necessary to rule on Article 13 when Article 6(1) had been violated. But the Court reconsidered its previous case law and confirmed, *first*, that, when the case concerned the safeguards of Article 6(1) implying the full panoply of a judicial procedure (access to justice

---

[110] *Mikulski v. Poland* (Plenary Commission report 1999) para. 98.

[111] Ibid., para. 99.

[112] Concurring opinion of M.A. Nowicki joined by J.-C. Soyer, G.H. Thune, C. Rozakis, E. Alkema and M. Vila Amigó.

[113] *Mikulski v. Poland* (Plenary Commission report 1999) para. 100.

[114] Dissenting opinion of M. Trechsel in *Mikulski v. Poland* (Plenary Commission report 1999).

as such), and, *second*, when the applicant's grievance is directed at the adequacy of an existing appellate or cassation procedure, the requirements of Article 13 are less strict and absorbed by Article 6(1). There would thus be no legal interest in reexamining the same subject matter of the complaint under the less stringent requirements of Article 13.[115] However, when the alleged violation was the right to trial within a reasonable time, there was "no overlap and hence no absorption". This applied both in criminal and civil cases.[116] Even though the Court had, in previous cases, found that Article 13 was absorbed, it was time:

> to review its case law in the light of the continuing accumulation of applications before it in which the only, or principal, allegation is that of a failure to ensure a hearing within a reasonable time in breach of Article 6 § 1.[117]

The Court added that the growing frequency with which violations in this regard were found had led the Court to draw attention to the important danger that existed for the rule of law within national legal orders when excessive delays in the administration of justice occurred and to which litigants had no domestic remedy.[118] Against this background, it was necessary to consider the complaint under Article 13 separately, in addition to Article 6(1).[119]

Based upon this general reasoning, one could argue that had it not been for the situation of judicial need (the number of excessive length of proceedings cases), the Court would not have reconsidered its practice. But, in the analysis of the concrete applicability of Article 13, the Court referred to some additional and principled arguments concerning the relationship between Articles 13 and 6(1):

- There was nothing in the wording or drafting history of Article 13 which limited the scope of application in relation to any of the aspects of the "right to a court" embodied in Article 6(1);[120]
- The place of Article 13 in the scheme of human-rights protection set up by the Convention argued in favor of keeping the implied restrictions of Article 13 to a minimum, most notably because the primary responsibility for implementing and enforcing the guaranteed rights and freedoms is on the national authorities;[121]
- A remedy against unreasonable length of proceedings does not, as such, involve an appeal against the "determination" of any criminal charge or of civil rights and obligations;[122]

[115] *Kudla v. Poland* (Grand Chamber 2000) para. 146.
[116] Ibid., para. 147.
[117] Ibid., para. 148.
[118] Ibid.
[119] Ibid., para. 149.
[120] Ibid., para. 151.
[121] Ibid., para. 152.
[122] Ibid., para. 154.

- A remedy against excessive length of proceedings could be construed so that domestic proceedings were not made more cumbersome;[123]
- To hold that Article 13 is not applicable in cases of excessive length of proceedings would force applicants to turn to Strasbourg for complaints that, more appropriately, should be addressed within national legal systems. In the long term, this would threaten the effective functioning of the system for protection of human rights set up by the Convention, both at national and international levels.[124]

One out of 17 judges, Judge Casadevall, held that it was not necessary to depart from the Court's former precedent. He admitted that nothing in the wording prevented Article 13 from being applied to the various aspects of the "right to a court" embodied in Article 6(1). However, this interpretation was going to cause complications. Most notably, the cure might be worse than the disease because an additional finding of a violation would not necessarily reduce the Court's case load, nor fix the root problem of excessive length of proceedings. Further, the justification in judicial need was of "no legal interest" and "smacks … more of expediency than of law."

With regard to excessive length of proceedings, the *Kudla* judgment has been consistently followed. With a few exceptions, the Court has, thereafter, always considered whether Article 13 has also been violated, mostly declaring parallel violations of Articles 6(1) and 13.[125] The Court even holds that there must be some form of remedy against undue delays caused by the highest courts at domestic level.[126]

Of the few cases concerning excessive length of proceedings, in which the Court has not considered it necessary to examine whether Article 13 has also been violated, *Žiačik v. Slovakia* (2003) is one example. A new constitutional complaint was claimed to be effective for the purposes of both Articles 35(1) and 13. However, at the time when the applicant could have made use of the complaint, it was not considered sufficiently effective for the purposes of Article 35(1) as no case law confirmed that the remedy was effective in practice.[127] However, under Article 13, the Court stated, contrary to the ruling in *Kudla*, that:

> In the light of its above finding under Article 6 of the Convention and having regard to the fact that a new remedy under Article 127 of the

---

[123] Ibid.

[124] Ibid., para. 155.

[125] See, as a few examples, *Horvat v. Croatia* (2001); *Konti-Arvaniti v. Greece* (2003); *Todorov v. Bulgaria* (2005); *Jovićević v. Serbia* (2007); *Kaemena and Thönebohn v. Germany* (2009); *Radvák and Radváková v. Slovakia* (2011); *Pašić v. Slovenia* (2013); *Yagnina v. Bulgaria* (2015); *Xenos v. Greece* (2017); *Fil LLC v. Armenia* (2019); *Galea and Pavia v. Malta* (2020).

[126] See, for example, *Kirsten v. Germany* (2007) paras. 56–57; *Schneider v. Austria* (2008) para. 46.

[127] *Žiačik v. Slovakia* (2003) para. 34. See, also, Sections 9.4 and 10.6.

Constitution has been available in Slovakia since 1 January 2002 in similar cases, the Court finds that it is not necessary to examine the applicant's complaint under Article 13 of the Convention.[128]

This could indicate that the main purpose of examining Article 13 in addition to Article 6(1), at least in cases of excessive length of proceedings, is systemic – not to provide individual relief. However, the following case law, both in cases against Slovakia and other States, reveals a broken picture. In some cases, which are more or less identical on the facts, the Court has considered whether Article 13 has also been violated,[129] whereas in other cases, it has applied the same reasoning as in *Žiačik*.[130]

Considering the justification in *Kudla*, one might have expected the Court to reconsider, more generally, to what extent it is necessary to examine Article 13 in addition to Article 6(1). But, to date, the Court has more or less consistently refused to consider whether Article 13 has been violated in conjunction with other types of violations of Article 6(1), mostly without any additional justification or consideration.[131] In some cases, the Court has even held, more generally, that Article 6(1) is *lex specialis* in relation to Article 13, that the requirements of Article 13 are less strict than those of Article 6(1), that Article 13 is not applicable "as a rule" in cases where the alleged violation of the Convention has taken place in the context of judicial proceedings and that the only exception to this are complaints concerning excessive length of proceedings.[132] In other cases, the Court simply holds that the same facts have already been examined and that no different question arises,[133] that, in view of the findings above, it is not necessary to consider Article 13,[134] or that, for the same reasons as under Article 6(1), there has been no violation of Article 13.[135]

---

[128] *Žiačik v. Slovakia* (2003) para. 50.

[129] See, for example, *Laidin v. France (no. 2)* (2003) paras. 101–102; *Číž v. Slovakia* (2003) paras. 74–75; *Macková v. Slovakia* (2005) para. 62.

[130] See, for example, *Vujčík v. Slovakia* (2005) paras. 59–60; *Shcherbakov v. Russia (no. 2)* (2013) paras. 118–123; *Tychko v. Russia* (2015) paras. 74–80.

[131] See, for example, *Anagnostopoulos a.o. v. Greece* (2000) (Civil case. Unreasonable interference by legislature and excessive length of proceedings); *A.B. v. Slovakia* (2003) (Civil case. Equality of arms); *Assanidze v. Georgia* (Grand Chamber 2004) (Civil case. Failure to comply with domestic judgment); *Indra v. Slovakia* (2005) (Civil case. No impartial tribunal); *Vanyan v. Russia* (2005) (Penal case. Use of evidence provoked by the Police); *Díaz Ochoa v. Spain* (2006) (Civil case. Applicant not able to defend himself properly); *Sace Elektrik Ticaret ve Sanayi A.Ş. v. Turkey* (2013) (Access to court); *Xenos v. Greece* (2017) (Access to court).

[132] *Menesheva v. Russia* (2006) para. 105. See, also, for example, Pellonpää (2007a) 561 and Frowein and Peukert (2009) 398–399, both of whom define excessive length of proceedings as an exception to a general rule of absorption.

[133] For example, *Boldea v. Romania* (2007) para. 64.

[134] For example, *Straisteanu a.o. v. Moldova* (2009) para. 99.

[135] For example, *Muscat v. Malta* (2012) para. 62.

However, Article 13 has been applied in addition to, or instead of, Article 6(1) in cases which, in addition to Article 6(1), concern violations of other substantive Convention rights. The Court then often, but not always, considers the remedial question solely under Article 13, even though it could have been considered under Article 6(1). The Court mostly offers no justification as to why.[136] But based upon the facts of the cases, at least two categories may be deduced: (1) cases with broader and more composite questions including both elements of access to justice and redress; and (2) cases in which the possibility of achieving sufficient redress is totally lacking, mostly compensation in the form of money.

The most prominent example is effective investigations that pose broader questions of access to justice and redress (Section 11.7). This practice was initiated in *Aksoy* v. *Turkey* (1996), approximately four years before *Kudla* v. *Poland* (Grand Chamber 2000). The *Aksoy* case concerned primary violations of Article 3 (torture by State agents) and Article 5(3) (detention incommunicado). Under Article 6(1), the applicant claimed that he had been denied access to civil proceedings to claim compensation. The crux of his claim was that any civil proceedings for compensation would be ineffective until the facts had been established by criminal proceedings and investigations. The Court recognized that the right to access to court in Article 6(1) encompassed a civil right to claim compensation. However, as the crux of the complaint was related to the alleged lack of investigation, and as the applicant claimed that compensation was not sufficient to redress the violations, the Court did not deem it necessary to consider the complaint under Article 6, but exclusively and more appropriately under Article 13.[137] This practice has been upheld in a string of later cases.[138]

More generally, in *Z a.o.* v. *the UK* (Grand Chamber 2001) the fact that the applicants could not sue local authorities in negligence for compensation, in relation to complaints that they had violated Article 3, was an issue to be considered under Article 13. It was fundamental that the national systems provided redress for breaches of the Convention – the supervisory role of the Court being subject to the "principle of subsidiarity". In this context, Article 13

---

[136] See, for example, *Tüzel* v. *Turkey* (2006) (Primary violation of Article 10); *Ceni* v. *Italy* (2014) (Primary violations of Articles 10 and 8); *Mursaliyev a.o.* v. *Azerbaijan* (2018) (Primary violation of P4 Article 2).

[137] *Aksoy* v. *Turkey* (1996) paras. 93–94. A minority, Judge de Meyer, found that a violation of both Article 6(1) and Article 13 should have been declared.

[138] See Section 11.7, and, with regard to Articles 13 and 3, and Article 6(1), for example, *Aydin* v. *Turkey* (Grand Chamber 1997) paras. 101–102 and *Yavuz* v. *Turkey* (2006) para. 46; with regard to Articles 13 and 2, and Article 6(1), for example, *Kaya* v. *Turkey* (1998) paras. 104–105 and *Dündar* v. *Turkey* (2005) para. 96; and, with regard to Article 13 and Articles 8, 3, and P1 Article 1, for example, *Menteş a.o.* v. *Turkey* (Grand Chamber 1997) paras. 87–88 and *Nuri Kurt* v. *Turkey* (2005) para. 111.

played a crucial function. To the extent that the applicants' complaints were essentially that they had not been afforded a remedy against the Article 3 violation, it was "under Article 13 that the applicants' right to a remedy should be examined and, if appropriate, vindicated."[139]

Yankov v. Bulgaria (2003) concerned violations of Articles 3 and 10 because of the forced removal of hair in prison and a punishment for the writing of a manuscript. Domestic disciplinary proceedings were instigated against the prison guards who had shaved the applicant's hair. It was not necessary to decide whether the disciplinary proceedings were determining a "criminal charge" within the meaning of Article 6 of the Convention because the complaint concerned a broader set of events which was to be examined under Article 13 in conjunction with Articles 3 and 10.[140]

Iatridis v. Greece (Grand Chamber 1999) concerned the availability of a remedy to enforce a national judgment. National courts quashed an eviction order, but the judgment was not complied with by the responsible domestic authorities. This refusal violated both P1 Article 1 and Article 13.[141] The Court held, without any further justification, that the requirements of Article 6(1) were subsumed by P1 Article 1 and Article 13.[142]

Karamitrov a.o. v. Bulgaria (2008) concerned lack of effective remedies against the unlawful seizure of a vehicle. The complaint was examined under P1 Article 1 and Article 13, instead of Article 6(1), because the case concerned "lack of a substantive right of action under domestic law rather than of the existence of procedural bars preventing or limiting the possibilities of bringing potential claims to court."[143] But the distinction between procedural bars and substantive rights is not easy to draw. In *Slavcho Kostov v. Bulgaria* (2008), for instance, Article 3 was violated because of conditions of detention. The applicant had received compensation for pecuniary and nonpecuniary damages but had been obliged to pay court fees which, in reality, rendered the compensation insufficient (approximately 63 percent of the compensation awarded). The Court admitted that the question of court fees in other cases had been treated under Article 6(1) (as a question of disproportionate requirements to access court),[144] but still found that the question was to be dealt with under Article 13 and that no separate issue arose under

---

[139] *Z a.o. v. the UK* (Grand Chamber 2001) paras. 102–103. Notice that two judges found that Article 6(1) had been violated and that it, therefore, was not necessary to examine Article 13 because Article 6(1) was *lex specialis*; see the partly dissenting opinion of Judge Rozakis joined by Judge Palm.

[140] *Yankov v. Bulgaria* (2003) para. 152. See, also, for example, *Ivan Vasilev v. Bulgaria* (2007) para. 73.

[141] *Iatridis v. Greece* (Grand Chamber 1999) para. 65.

[142] Ibid., para. 69.

[143] *Karamitrov a.o. v. Bulgaria* (2008) para. 62. Similarly, for example, *Atanasov and Ovcharov v. Bulgaria* (2008) para. 63.

[144] *Slavcho Kostov v. Bulgaria* (2008) para. 62.

Article 6(1).[145] And, in *Kochetkov v. Estonia* (2009), which concerned a primary violation of conditions of detention, the applicant alleged that the lack of impartiality and the wrongly assessed evidence by national courts violated Article 6(1). The Court, however, only considered the complaint under Article 13 because the central element was that national law could not award compensation (thus no effective redress) for the violation of Article 3.[146]

Halis Doğan a.o. v. Turkey (2005) concerned a prohibition of distributing a newspaper. Article 10 was violated, *inter alia*, because there was no legal control against abuse.[147] For similar reasons, and simply by pointing to the considerations under Article 10, Article 13 was violated.[148] But under Article 6(1), the Court simply stated, without any further explanation, that it had decided to examine the complaint under Article 13.[149]

Further, in some cases concerning excessive length of proceedings, in which the case primarily concerns violations of substantive Convention rights, and not just arguable violations of Article 6(1), because of the excessive length of proceedings, the Court may consider the remedial question more globally only under Article 13, not also Article 6(1).[150]

Moreover, Article 13 has been applied in addition to, or instead of, Article 6(1), in cases concerning nonenforcement or delay in the execution of judgments violating Article 6(1). In such cases, the Court has, in the majority of cases, found violations of both Articles 6(1) and 13, mostly without any justification,[151] but, in a few cases, with a simple reference to the *Kudla* case.[152] However, in many such cases, the Court considers that it is not necessary to examine Article 13, even though it is alleged violated.[153] But at least in one case, the Court has only considered that Article 13 has been violated, without any justification as to why Article 6(1) was not considered.[154]

However, when no other substantive Article of the Convention has been violated, the Court only declares an additional violation of Article 13 in cases of

---

[145] Ibid., para. 66. See, also, for example, *Sabev v. Bulgaria* (2013) para. 102.

[146] *Kochetkov v. Estonia* (2009) paras. 57–59.

[147] *Halis Doğan a.o. v. Turkey* (2006) para. 27.

[148] Ibid., para. 35.

[149] Ibid., para. 31. See, also, for example, *Saygılı et Seyman v. Turkey* (2006) paras. 29–30.

[150] See, for example, *Iovchev v. Bulgaria* (2006) para. 154 (primary violation of Article 3). Under Article 13, the length of proceedings was one of several elements rendering the remedy ineffective in practice. See, also, for example, *Stoycheva v. Bulgaria* (2011) (primary violation of P1 Article 1).

[151] See, for a few examples, *Voytenko v. Ukraine* (2004); *Cravcenco v. Moldova* (2008); *Ventouris v. Greece* (2012); *Kopnin a.o. v. Russia* (2014); *Arbačiauskienė v. Lithuania* (2016); *Pialopoulos a.o. v. Greece (no. 2)* (2017); *Cristea v. the Republic of Moldova* (2019).

[152] See, for example, *Zazanis a.o. v. Greece* (2004) para. 43; *Svintitskiy and Goncharov v. Ukraine* (2005) para. 27.

[153] See, for a few examples, *Derkach and Palek v. Ukraine* (2004); *Öçkan v. Turkey* (2006); *Hajiyeva a.o. v. Azerbaijan* (2010); *Marinković v. Serbia* (2013).

[154] *Koshchavets v. Ukraine* (2006) para. 21 (only violation of P1 Article 1 and Article 13).

excessive length of proceedings and lack of, or delayed, enforcement of judgments.[155] The consequence is that Article 13 has had limited effect for other
violations of Article 6(1).[156] The justification has been a simple reference to the
fact that the procedural guarantees in Article 13 are less strict and absorbed by
Article 6(1).[157] However, this also absorbs any right to redress under Article 13 for
other procedural violations of Article 6(1). It is, therefore, difficult to conceive
how Article 6(1) should totally absorb Article 13.[158] That being said, granting
remedies and redress to enforce procedural guarantees may require the introduction of multistage proceedings, which could conflict with the position that
Article 13 does not grant a right to appeal against court decisions.[159] Indeed,
intuitively it seems to pose a conflict between the principle that the Convention
contains no general right to appeal and the right to an effective remedy against
violations of the Convention, including violations of Article 6(1). But it is one
thing to hold that there is no right to appeal against court decisions as such,
and another to hold that there must be a remedy (including redress) against
specific flaws by courts when these flaws violate human rights. As a minimum,
it is important to recognize that courts may commit human-rights violations.
Article 13 should, therefore, at the very least, require some form of remedy
against procedural court decisions which violate Article 6(1) and which do not
form part of the main complaint as such.[160] But some hold that even such a limited remedy would undermine the independence of judges and that it is fundamentally (*"grundsätzlich"*) not possible to have a remedy against violations
of judges by any other remedial authority than a court.[161] Against this position,

---

[155] See, also, for example, Grabenwarter (2008).

[156] See, also, for example, Grabenwarter and Pabel (2012) 487. See, however, *Baratta v. Italy*
(2015) paras. 87–95, in which the Court considered whether the applicant had an effective
remedy under Article 13 against a condemnation *in absentia*, which could constitute a violation of Article 6(1). There, also, needs be a remedy against violations of Article 6(2) not caused
by domestic courts; see, for example, *Maslarova v. Bulgaria* (2019) paras. 51–53.

[157] Conversely, the procedural safeguards under Article 6(1) may be absorbed by procedural safeguards under other Articles, most notably Article 5, which are then considered *lex specialis*,
but also other Articles; see, for example, *Metropolitan Church of Bessarabia a.o. v. Moldova*
(2001) para. 142 (Article 6 absorbed by Article 9) and *Covezzi and Morselli v. Italy* (2003) para.
144 (Article 6(1) absorbed by Article 8). This absorption may also concern excessive length of
proceedings; see, for example, *Vajagić v. Croatia* (2006) paras. 50 and 55, in which the excessive length of proceedings was taken into account both under P1 Article 1 and Article 13, but
not Article 6(1).

[158] Compare Vospernik (2001) 367.

[159] See, for example, Frowein and Peukert (2009) 396–398; Grabenwarter (2014) 331.

[160] Compare, for example, Grote and Marauhn (2006) 1092–1093. See, also, for example,
Schilling (2014).

[161] Frowein and Peukert (2009) 398–399. However, the same authors accept excessive length of
proceedings as an exception, without any further justification than the subsidiary nature of
the Convention.

it could of course be argued that the remedy need not necessarily require the reopening of proceedings or remedies equivalent to appeal proceedings, but only a specific remedy against the particular procedural flaw. If so, it is difficult to understand how the independence of judges should be overly threatened. Such specific remedies could, also, be implemented in a manner that avoids "endless remedies". Such considerations may underlie *Hammerton v. the UK* (2016), which could indicate a change in the Court's practice.[162] The case concerned a violation of Articles 6(1) and 6(3) *litra* c because the applicant did not have legal representation during domestic county court hearings. The lack of representation led to imprisonment of the applicant for a period of six weeks, instead of one. This violation was recognized by the domestic High Court, but the applicant was not awarded any further redress, in particular, financial compensation. The Court, therefore, concluded that the applicant was still a victim under the Convention and found that Article 13 had been violated.[163] The Court did not provide any further explanation as to how this result relates to its former practice in which Article 6(1) has been held to be *lex specialis* and, therefore, absorbs Article 13.

Concerning the redress required for excessive length of proceedings and nonenforcement of judgments, the Court has, in a number of cases, held that compensation for both pecuniary and nonpecuniary damages needs to be provided.[164]

4.5.3 *Articles 2 and 3*

As of December 31, 2020, Article 13 had been a theme in conjunction with Article 2 in 441 judgments and Article 3 in 1075.

The majority of the cases concerns lack of effective investigations.[165] Many of these cases concern remedies which must be made available to the next of kin of disappeared persons.[166] The requirement to perform effective investigations under Article 13 has a particular difficult relationship to the similar requirement arising under substantive Articles (Section 11.7).

Many of the cases concerning Article 13, seen in conjunction with Article 2, concern alleged violations of the positive obligations to secure life. Indeed, the first case concerning Article 13 in conjunction with Article 2 was *D v. the UK* (1997) in which the Court found that the applicant had received

---

[162] A referral to the Grand Chamber was requested, but rejected.
[163] *Hammerton v. the UK* (2016) paras. 150–152.
[164] See Section 11.5.
[165] See Section 11.7.
[166] See, more generally, Jötten (2010).

an effective remedy against a claim that the authorities had endangered life by removing a patient from a hospital. Also in such cases it is, in the Court's case law, difficult to distinguish between what is required as positive action under Article 2 and remedial action under Article 13.[167]

Several cases concerning both Articles 2 and 3 seen in conjunction with Article 13 concern the lack of the possibility of obtaining compensation at domestic level, both for pecuniary and nonpecuniary damages (Section 11.5).

Many cases concern the competences remedial authorities need have when examining complaints that expulsion or extradition will violate Articles 2 and 3.[168] Indeed, the first case concerning Article 13 seen in conjunction with Article 3, *Soering v. the UK* (1989), concerned the question whether judicial review by UK courts of administrative decisions of expulsion, which could lead to inhumane and degrading treatment, was sufficient to satisfy Article 13.

Article 13 has, also, played a major role in conjunction with Article 3 in cases concerning conditions of detention. Many of these cases concern administrative measures with no possibility of judicial review.[169] Other cases concern the form of redress that the remedial authority must provide. In such cases, the remedy must be both preventive and compensatory.[170]

4.5.4 *Article 5*

As of December 31, 2020, Article 13 had been a theme in conjunction with Article 5 in 597 judgments.

The first case was *de Wilde, Ooms and Versyp v. Belgium* (Plenary 1971) (the *Vagrancy* case), in which the Court did not deem it necessary to examine Article 13 in addition to Article 5(4). In *de Jong, Baljet and van den Brink v. the Netherlands* (1984), the Court added that the requirements under Article 13 were less strict than those of Article 5(4), which were *lex specialis*.[171] The same practice has, thereafter, been consistently upheld.[172]

---

[167] See Section 11.7.3 and, as an example, *Centre for Legal Resources on behalf of Valentin Câmpeanu v. Romania* (Grand Chamber 2014).

[168] See, in particular, Section 10.5.4.

[169] For example, *Ramirez Sanchez v. France* (Grand Chamber 2006) para. 166; *Onoufriou v. Cyprus* (2010) para. 123.

[170] See Section 11.3.4.

[171] *de Jong, Baljet and van den Brink v. the Netherlands* (1984) para. 60.

[172] See, for a few examples, *Brogan a.o. v. the UK* (Plenary 1988); *Chahal v. the UK* (Grand Chamber 1996); *Herz v. Germany* (2003); *Yuldashev v. Russia* (2010); *Khlaifia a.o. v. Italy* (Grand Chamber 2016); *Mangîr a.o. v. the Republic of Moldova and Russia* (2018). One dissenting opinion is found in *Brannigan and Mcbride v. the UK* (Plenary 1993).

Most of the judgments only refer to Articles 5(4) and 5(5) being *lex specialis*, but in some judgments, it is unclear whether all of Article 5 is considered *lex specialis*. The Court may, for instance, hold that "the more specific guarantees of Article 5" are *lex specialis* and thus absorb the requirements of Article 13.[173] However, with regard to Article 5(3), the Court has, at least in one case, considered whether Article 13 had also been violated, instead of referring to the doctrine of less strict and absorbed.[174]

In some cases in which other substantive Convention rights were also violated, the Court has considered more globally under Article 13 whether the applicant had an effective remedy in conjunction with several Articles, without specifying why Article 13 had also been violated in conjunction with Article 5, or, to the contrary, why Article 13 had not been violated in conjunction with Article 5, but in conjunction with other Articles. The most prominent example is lack of effective investigations, which may violate, *inter alia*, Articles 2, 3, 5, 8, and P1 Article 1. Most notably, in some cases concerning lack of effective investigations in connection with enforced disappearances, violating Articles 2, 3, and 5, the Court concludes that Article 13 has also been violated in conjunction with Article 5, whereas, in other cases, Article 13 has only been violated in conjunction with Articles 2 and 3.[175]

In a few newer cases, the Court has found violations of Article 13 in conjunction with only Article 5. The first example is *Ivanțoc a.o. v. Moldova and Russia* (2011), in which the violation of Article 13 was explicitly seen in conjunction with the lack of any remedy against an arbitrary detention in violation of Article 5(1).[176] No justification was given as to why this was necessary compared to previous cases in which it was not necessary. One justification may be that there was, in principle, no remedy at all, no remedial authority, nor redress, against the violation of Article 5(1), in contrast to cases in which there was a remedial authority, but one which did not satisfy the requirements of Articles 5(3) and 5(4). Such a distinction may, for example, underlie the view of the majority in *Georgia v. Russia (I)* (Grand Chamber 2014), in which a violation of Article 13 in relation to Article 5(1) was found, but in which it was not necessary to consider Article 13 in relation to 5(4), even though both Articles 5(1) and 5(4) were violated.[177] The minority, on the other hand, held that once

---

[173] See, for example, *Garabayev v. Russia* (2007) para. 108.

[174] *Ryckie v. Poland* (2007) paras. 48–55.

[175] See Section 11.7.2. See, also, *Venken a.o. v. Belgium* (2021) (conditions of detention).

[176] *Ivanțoc a.o. v. Moldova and Russia* (2011) paras. 132–135. See, also, *Iustin Robertino Micu v. Romania* (2015) paras. 97 and 111 and compare the concurring opinion of Judge Silvis.

[177] *Georgia v. Russia (I)* (Grand Chamber 2014) paras. 211–214.

a violation of Article 5(4) was found, there was no need to examine Article 13 in conjunction with Article 5(1) because that complaint was subsumed by the finding under Article 5(4).[178]

4.5.5 Article 8

As of December 31, 2020, Article 13 had been a theme in conjunction with Article 8 in 479 judgments. The first was the Belgian *Vagrancy* case.[179]

Article 13 has a difficult relationship with procedural requirements arising under Article 8. Most notably, Article 8 includes a positive obligation to secure private and family life, which includes an obligation to make the means of protection effectively accessible, when appropriate, to anyone who may wish to have recourse thereto. For instance, in *Airey v. Ireland* (1979), the applicant was unable to seek effective recognition in law because of a *de facto* separation from her husband. Article 8 had therefore been violated,[180] but the Court did not examine whether Article 13 seen in conjunction with Article 8 had been violated.[181]

In *Silver a.o. v. the UK* (1983), however, which concerned safeguards against abuse of powers to control prisoners' correspondence, both Article 8 and Article 13 had been violated, but without any additional justification as to why.[182] However, this development was reversed in *Malone v. the UK* (Plenary 1984), in which a majority of sixteen to two judges found that it was not necessary to examine Article 13 in addition to Article 8.[183]

The practice of not considering Article 13 has been more or less consistently upheld in cases which concern the scope of procedural guarantees against abuse (Article 8) and effective access to justice (Article 13).[184] Although there

---

[178] Partly dissenting opinion of Judge López Guerra joined by Judge Bratza.

[179] *de Wilde, Ooms and Versyp v. Belgium* (Plenary 1971).

[180] *Airey v. Ireland* (1979) para. 33. For similar reasons, Article 6(1) was violated.

[181] Ibid., paras. 34–35.

[182] An almost identical case with the same reasoning and conclusion was *Campbell and Fell v. the UK* (1984).

[183] *Malone v. the UK* (Plenary 1984) para. 91.

[184] See, for example, *Lambert v. France* (1998) (Tapping of telephone conversations); *Mikulić v. Croatia* (2002) (No effective procedures to establish paternity); *Monory v. Hungary and Romania* (2005) (No effective procedures to challenge the lack of access to child); *Paulík v. Slovakia* (2006) (No effective procedures to challenge paternity); *Tysiąc v. Poland* (2007) (No effective mechanism to determine conditions for abortions); *Berková v. Slovakia* (2009) (No effective procedures to restore legal capacity); *Mincheva v. Bulgaria* (2010) (No effective procedures to re-establish family life); *Davydov a.o. v. Ukraine* (2010) (No effective procedures against interference in correspondence).

are some newer judgments to the contrary, in which more or less the same procedural issues are analyzed under both Articles,[185] without any justification as to why, the Court still seems to hold, more generally, that, even if procedural guarantees are part of Article 13, it is sufficient to consider purely procedural issues under Article 8.[186] However, at least in cases in which the question is whether a remedy at all is available,[187] or in which the complaint is more directed against the lack of possibility of achieving redress, even though this is related to procedural issues concerning access to justice, the Court more often than not also declares a violation of Article 13,[188] or may even consider the issue solely or primarily under Article 13.[189]

In some specific areas, the Court also considers procedural issues more broadly and in depth under both Article 13 and Article 8, seemingly because of their significance for the effectiveness of the remedy overall, for instance, effective investigations in cases of the destruction of homes and possessions,[190] and deportation procedures.[191]

Secret surveillance cases raise difficult issues both under Article 8 read in isolation and Article 13 seen in conjunction with Article 8. As long as the surveillance is legitimately kept secret, the potential applicant has no practical possibility of obtaining a remedy. The Court has accepted that such surveillance, as long as it does not violate Article 8, cannot violate Article 13.[192] But both Article 8 and Article 13 demand safeguards against abuse, which must be effective and

---

[185] See, for example, *Riener v. Bulgaria* (2006) para. 138; *Golovan v. Ukraine* (2012) para. 75; *Arkhestov v. Russia* (2014) paras. 110–111; *B.A.C v. Greece* (2016) para. 47.

[186] See, for example, *Nicklinson and Lamb v. the UK* (Decision 2015) para. 81 with further references.

[187] See, for example, *Keegan v. the UK* (2006) (No means to achieve redress against search of home); *Iordache v. Romania* (2008) (No remedy against removal of parental rights); *Zaurbekova and Zaurbekova v. Russia* (2009) (No remedy against intrusion in flat); *Konstantin Moskalev v. Russia* (2017) (No remedy against interception of telephone communication); *Voykin a.o. v. Ukraine* (2018) (no remedy against police searches).

[188] See, for example, *Halford v. the UK* (1997) (No redress against interception of phone), but compare *Copland v. the UK* (2007); *Panteleyenko v. Ukraine* (2006) (No redress against unlawful search); *Krasimir Yordanov v. Bulgaria* (2007) (No redress against seizure of correspondence); *R.K. and A.K. v. the UK* (2008), *A.D. & O.D. v. the UK* (2010) and *M.A.K. and R.K. v. the UK* (2010) (No possibility to obtain compensation for interference in family life).

[189] See, for example, *Abuhmaid v. Ukraine* (2017) paras. 116–124; *Voynov v. Russia* (2018) paras. 38–52.

[190] See, Section 11.7.2.

[191] See, for example, *Al-Nashif v. Bulgaria* (2002); *C.G. a.o. v. Bulgaria* (2008); *Asalya v. Turkey* (2014).

[192] See, for example, *Leander v. Sweden* (1987) para. 78.

there must be some review of the surveillance after it has been terminated.[193] The applicant must be informed and have the possibility of complaint about the legality of the procedures.[194] The same goes for the holding and use of information, including the possibility of refuting the truth about such information.[195] The cases concerning secret surveillance and interference with correspondence further illustrate the difficulty in determining when a remedy must be able to prevent and determine violations and not only redress past violations.[196]

In several cases, the Court has, in concrete, but not in the abstract, specified the form of redress required to repair violations of Article 8 at domestic level. Data may, for example, have to be destroyed,[197] unlawfully registers deleted,[198] and disclosure of information ended.[199] Further, in many cases, a simple finding of unlawfulness is not deemed sufficient.[200]

4.5.6 Article 9

As of December 31, 2020, Article 13 had been a theme in conjunction with Article 9 in twenty-six judgments. In most of these cases, Article 13 was not violated, or deemed not necessary to examine. The cases in which Article 13 is found to have been violated, primarily concern cases in which no remedy at all was available.[201] But, strikingly, in many cases in which there was no remedy at all available, Article 13 has been deemed not applicable because legislation, as such, was challenged.[202] In some cases, the domestic remedial authority has not been able to deal with the substance of the complaint,[203] or the lack of compliance with a final judgment caused by structural problems has violated Article 13.[204]

---

[193] See Section 10.5.4. Similarly, when it comes to searches and seizures, the applicant must, in some manner, be able to vindicate his or her rights afterwards, but not necessarily prevent the searches and seizures beforehand; see, for example, *Iliya Stefanov v. Bulgaria* (2008) para. 59; *Lindstrand Partners Advokatbyrå AB v. Sweden* (2016) para. 124.
[194] See, for example, *Volokhy v. Ukraine* (2006) para. 59.
[195] See, for example, *Rotaru v. Romania* (Grand Chamber 2000) paras. 71–72.
[196] See Sections 3.3 and 11.3.4.
[197] See, for example, *Segerstedt-Wiberg a.o. v. Sweden* (2006) paras. 120–121.
[198] See, for example, *Dimitrov-Kazakov v. Bulgaria* (2011) para. 37.
[199] See, for example, *Panteleyenko v. Ukraine* (2006) para. 83.
[200] See, for example, *Goranova-Karaeneva v. Bulgaria* (2011) paras. 58–64.
[201] See, for example, *Efstratiou v. Greece* (1996); *Boychev a.o. v. Bulgaria* (2011); *Dimitrova v. Bulgaria* (2015); *Mozer v. the Republic of Moldova and Russia* (Grand Chamber 2016).
[202] See Section 10.5.3 and, for example, *Holy Monasteries v. Greece* (1994); *Supreme Holy Council of the Muslim Community v. Bulgaria* (2004); *Holy Synod of the Bulgarian Orthodox Church (Metropolitan Inokentiy) a.o. v. Bulgaria* (2009).
[203] See Section 10.5.4 and, for example, *Hasan and Chaush v. Bulgaria* (Grand Chamber 2000); *Metropolitan Church of Bessarabia a.o. v. Moldova* (2001); *Glas Nadezhda EOOD and Elenkov v. Bulgaria* (2007).
[204] See Section 11.9.

4.5.7 *Article 10*

As of December 31, 2020, Article 13 had been a theme in conjunction with Article 10 in eighty-five judgments. In many cases, it has not been considered necessary to examine Article 13.[205] But such cases are growing rare, even though the Court, under Article 13, mostly only refers to the finding under Article 10.[206]

In some cases, the Court has refused to consider Article 13 because legislation, as such, is challenged.[207]

In most of the cases in which Article 13 has been violated, there has been no remedy at all, or there is clearly no effective remedy available.[208] Some cases concern lack of procedural guarantees.[209] Other cases concern the lack of enforcement,[210] and justification,[211] of domestic decisions. And some cases concern the lack of the ability of the remedial authority to deal with the substance of the complaint.[212]

In one case, the Court has demanded that the remedial authority be able to come to a decision before a planned action is executed.[213]

4.5.8 *Article 11*

As of December 31, 2020, Article 13 had been a theme in conjunction with Article 11 in sixty-eight judgments.

The first case was *Swedish Engine Drivers' Union v. Sweden* (1976). This was also the first case in which the Court explicitly held that neither Article 13, nor the Convention in general, lay down for the Contracting States any given manner for ensuring within their internal law the effective implementation of any of the provisions of the Convention.[214]

---

[205] See, for example, *Young, James and Webster v. the UK* (Plenary 1981); *Amann v. Switzerland* (Grand Chamber 2000); *Zarakolu et Belge Uluslararası Yayıncılık v. Turkey* (2004); *Segerstedt-Wiberg a.o. v. Sweden* (2006); *Bucur and Toma v. Romania* (2013).

[206] See, for example, *Guseva v. Bulgaria* (2015).

[207] See Section 10.5.3 and, for example, *Sunday Times v. the UK (no. 1)* (Plenary 1979); *Observer and Guardian v. the UK* (Plenary 1991); *Steel a.o. v. the UK* (Commission report 1997); *Appleby a.o. v. the UK* (2003).

[208] See, for example, *Vereinigung demokratischer Soldaten Österreichs and Gubi v. Austria* (1994); *Willie v. Liechtenstein* (Grand Chamber 1999); *Halis Doğan a.o. v. Turkey* (2006); *Mackay & BBC Scotland v. the UK* (2010); *Szél a.o. v. Hungary* (2014).

[209] For example *Yankov v. Bulgaria* (2003) and *Kayasu v. Turkey (no. 1)* (2008).

[210] For example *Kenedi v. Hungary* (2009).

[211] For example *Eusko Abertzale Ekintza – Acción Nacionalista Vasca (EAE-ANV) v. Spain* (2010).

[212] See Section 10.5.4 and, for example, *VgT Verein gegen Tierfabriken v. Switzerland* (2001); *Peev v. Bulgaria* (2007).

[213] *Mackay & BBC Scotland v. the UK* (2010).

[214] See Section 10.5.2.

In many cases, the Court has not found it necessary to consider Article 11 in addition to other substantive Articles, most notably Articles, 8, 9, and 10, and thus neither Article 13 in conjunction with Article 11.[215]

More generally, in early years, the Court did not find it necessary to consider Article 13 because of the finding under Article 11,[216] but, in later years, the Court has more or less consistently considered Article 13, although mostly with a simple reference to the analysis under Article 11.[217]

In other cases, the Court has excluded using Article 13 with reference to legislation, as such, being challenged.[218]

Most of the cases in which a violation of Article 13 has been found, concern cases in which the applicant had no remedy at all, or in which the remedy clearly was not effective in practice.[219] In some cases, the Court has identified required forms of redress, for instance, the need for a binding decision before a planned event takes place,[220] or the need to erase documents from a register.[221]

4.5.9 Article 14

As of December 31, 2020, Article 13 had been a theme in 248 judgments in which Article 14 was also claimed violated. In most of these cases, Article 14 was eclipsed by other substantive Articles, with the consequence that Article 13 was not considered in conjunction with Article 14, but other substantive Articles.[222] In other cases, the Article 13 issue is solely considered in relation to other substantive Articles,[223] without making any explicit reference as to why Article 14 is not included under Article 13. In many

[215] See, for example, *Hasan and Chaush v. Bulgaria* (Grand Chamber 2000); *Biserica Adevărat Ortodoxă din Moldova a.o. v. Moldova* (2007); *Grande Oriente d'Italia di Palazzo Giustiniani v. Italy (no. 2)* (2007).
[216] See, for example, *Young, James and Webster v. the UK* (Plenary 1981); *Grande Oriente d'Italia di Palazzo Giustiniani v. Italy* (2001); *Linkov v. the Czech Republic* (2006).
[217] See, for example, *Helsinki Committee of Armenia v. Armenia* (2015).
[218] See Section 10.5.3 and, for example, *Holy Monasteries v. Greece* (1994); *Gustafsson v. Sweden* (Grand Chamber 1996); *Appleby a.o. v. the UK* (2003).
[219] See Section 9.4 and, for example, *Djavit An v. Turkey* (2003); *Promo Lex a.o. v. the Republic of Moldova* (2015); *Sadrettin Güler v. Turkey* (2018).
[220] See Section 11.3.3 and, for example, *Ivanov a.o. v. Bulgaria* (2005); *Bączkowski a.o. v. Poland* (2007); *Alekseyev a.o. v. Russia* (2018).
[221] For example *Segerstedt-Wiberg a.o. v. Sweden* (2006).
[222] See, for example, *Airey v. Ireland* (1979); *Halford v. the UK* (1997); *Carabulea v. Romania* (2010).
[223] See, for example, *Kamasinski v. Austria* (1989); *Tanrikulu v. Turkey* (Grand Chamber 1999); *Sabanchiyeva a.o. v. Russia* (2013).

cases, Article 14 is not found to have been violated.[224] Moreover, some cases are excluded from examination because legislation, as such, is considered challenged.[225]

The very few cases, in which Article 13 seen in conjunction with Article 14 has had some independent value, are cases in which domestic remedial authorities have not been able to deal with the substance of the discrimination complaint.[226] Further, in one case, the Court found a violation of Article 13 because of insufficient investigations into the discrimination issue.[227]

4.5.10 *P1 Article 1*

As of December 31, 2020, Article 13 had been a theme in 477 judgments in conjunction with P1 Article 1.

The first case was *Sporrong and Lönnroth v. Sweden* (1982). The applicants claimed that they had no remedy which could put an end to long-term expropriation permits and prohibitions on construction violating P1 Article 1. The Court did not deem it necessary to determine whether there had been a violation of Article 13 since it had found a violation of Article 6(1).[228] Similarly, in a number of cases concerning access to justice when determining whether P1 Article 1 had been violated, the Court has only considered Article 6(1), without finding it necessary to consider Article 13.[229] But in the aftermath of *Kudla v. Poland* (Grand Chamber 2000), a string of cases concerning nonenforcement or delayed enforcement of domestic judgments concerning awards of compensation for expropriation of property reveals a broken picture. In some cases, the Court finds a violation of Article 13 in addition to Article 6 and/or P1 Article 1, but without any additional justification, whereas, in others, it holds that it is not necessary to examine Article 13.[230]

---

[224] See, for example, *Sporrong and Lönnroth v. Sweden* (Plenary 1982); *Kurt v. Turkey* (1998); *McShane v. the UK* (2002); *Maskhadova a.o. v. Russia* (2013).

[225] See Section 10.5.3 and, for example, *Willis v. the UK* (2002); *Christine Goodwin v. the UK* (Grand Chamber 2002); *A. v. the UK* (2002); *P.M. v. the UK* (2005).

[226] See Section 10.5.4 and, for example, *Abdulaziz, Cabales and Balkandali v. the UK* (Plenary 1985); *VgT Verein gegen Tierfabriken v. Switzerland* (2001); *Religionsgemeinschaft der Zeugen Jehovas a.o. v. Austria* (2008); *E.B. a.o. v. Austria* (2013).

[227] *Cobzaru v. Romania* (2007).

[228] *Sporrong and Lönnroth v. Sweden* (Plenary 1982) para. 88.

[229] See, for example, *Pudas v. Sweden* (1987); *Hentrich v. France* (1994); *Tripodi v. Italy* (2000); *Tărbăşanu v. Romania* (2003).

[230] See Section 4.5.2.

In cases concerning investigations into the destruction of homes and property, the Court has mostly considered Article 13 in conjunction with both
Article 8 and P1 Article 1.[231]

In a few cases, the Court has attempted to distinguish between the purpose of examining procedural issues under P1 Article 1 and Article 13, holding that, whereas Article 13 affords a procedural safeguard (the right to
an effective remedy), the procedural requirement in P1 Article 1 is ancil-
lary to the wider purpose of ensuring respect for the right to the peaceful
enjoyment of possessions. With reference to this difference in purpose, the
Court has then deemed it necessary to examine the same facts under both
Articles.[232]

Many of the cases in which the Court finds a violation of Article 13
in conjunction with P1 Article 1 are cases in which the applicant had no
remedy at all,[233] or in which the domestic remedial authority was not able
to deal with the substance of the complaint.[234] Some cases have been
excluded from examination because legislation, as such, is considered to
be challenged.[235]

The question of whether a particular form of redress has to be provided has
rarely arisen, which is understandable as P1 Article 1, to a large extent, regulates the question of redress explicitly. Indeed, to the extent that compensation
must be offered and is deemed sufficient under P1 Article 1, no separate question seems to arise under Article 13. However, domestic decisions of both compensation and return of property must be effectively enforced, and the lack of
such enforcement may violate Article 13.[236] Further, if the return of property is
required by a final domestic decision, that decision cannot be substituted by
an administrative decision awarding compensation.[237] Moreover, the unlawful expropriation of property may occasion nonpecuniary damages. In this

---

[231] See Section 11.7.2.

[232] See, for example, *Iatridis v. Greece* (Grand Chamber 1999) para. 65; *Karamitrov a.o. v. Bulgaria* (2008) para. 75; *Borzhonov v. Russia* (2009) para. 50.

[233] For example *Saggio v. Italy* (2001); *Georgi Marinov v. Bulgaria* (2011); *Sandu a.o. v. the Republic of Moldova and Russia* (2018).

[234] See Section 10.5.4 and, for example, *James a.o. v. the UK* (Plenary 1986); *Pine Valley Developments Ltd. a.o. v. Ireland* (1991); *Matos e Silva, Lda., a.o. v. Portugal* (1996); *Cyprus v. Turkey* (Grand Chamber 2001); *Stockholms Försäkrings- och Skadeståndsjuridik AB v. Sweden* (2003).

[235] See Section 10.5.3 and, for example, *Lithgow a.o. v. the UK* (Plenary 1986); *Holy Monasteries v. Greece* (1994); *Gustafsson v. Sweden* (Grand Chamber 1996); *Connors v. the UK* (2004); *Draon v. France* (Grand Chamber 2005); *Roche v. the UK* (Grand Chamber 2005).

[236] See Section 11.9 and, for example, *Karamitrov a.o. v. Bulgaria* (2008); *Pialopoulos a.o. v. Greece (no. 2)* (2017).

[237] *Vasilev and Doycheva v. Bulgaria* (2012) paras. 59, 30, and 69.

regard, domestic remedial authorities must not take a too formalistic approach to the question of whether any damage has been sustained.[238] Further, in *Bartolo Parnis a.o.* v. *Malta* (2021), Article 13 was violated in conjunction with P1 Article 1 because domestic courts did not award the applicants a higher rent or evicted tenants and, thereby, stopped a continuous violation, even though domestic courts had awarded compensation for damages already incurred.[239]

---

[238] See Section 10.3.3 and, for example, *Georgi Marinov* v. *Bulgaria* (2011) paras. 46–49.
[239] *Bartolo Parnis a.o.* v. *Malta* (2021) paras. 60–70. See, also, Section 11.3.4.

5

Relationship with the Rule on Exhaustion of Domestic Remedies

The Court may only deal with alleged violations of the Convention after all domestic remedies have been exhausted, according to the generally recognized rules of international law, and within a period of four months from the date on which the final decision was taken.[1]

The exhaustion rule grants States the opportunity to prevent or repair a violation before the case is brought to the Court. If the opportunity is taken, the violation is dealt with domestically and the work of the Court becomes truly subsidiary. If the violation is not sufficiently remedied (after the exhaustion of domestic remedies) and the applicant is still a victim,[2] he/she may turn to the Court.

Article 35(1) has close affinity with Article 13.[3] Under both Articles, the Court has adopted a flexible approach in which it decides upon a case-by-case basis if the remedies are effective.[4] Both Articles thus contain relative standards. The relativity of Article 13 is analyzed in Chapter 8, more generally, and Chapters 9 to 11, more specifically. In the case of Article 35(1), realistic account must, for example, be taken not only of the existence of formal remedies, but of the general legal and political context in which they operate as well as the personal circumstances of the applicant.[5]

---

[1] Article 35(1) of the ECHR. The period was changed from six to four months with the entry into force of Protocol 15 on August 1, 2021. See on the exhaustion rule in the Convention, for example, Bårdsen (1999) 307–390; Harris, O'Boyle *et al.* (2018) 49–62; Dijk, Hoof *et al.* (2018) 105–138. Concerning the more general requirement in public international law; see, for example, Trindade (1983); Amerasinghe (2004); Romano (2013).
[2] Article 34 of the ECHR.
[3] See, for example, *Kudla* v. *Poland* (Grand Chamber 2000) para. 152.
[4] See Chapter 8 and, in the case of Article 35(1), for example, *Strategies and Communications and Dumoulin* v. *Belgium* (2002) para. 54.
[5] See, for example, *Akdivar a.o.* v. *Turkey* (Grand Chamber 1996) para. 69; *Kuric a.o.* v. *Slovenia* (Grand Chamber 2012) para. 286.

Moreover, under both Articles, the remedy may, in principle, consist of either preventing or redressing the violation.[6] And also Article 35(1) requires, more generally, the remedy to be effective.[7] Indeed, the applicant must only exhaust remedies that "relate to the alleged breaches" and are "available and sufficient". The existence of such remedies must be sufficiently certain not only in theory, but also in practice, and offer "reasonable prospects of success". It falls upon the respondent State, at least as a starting-point, to establish that these conditions are satisfied.[8] Theoretically, all such criteria could be included in a more general requirement of effectiveness, in a similar manner as under Article 13.[9] The question then arises, is the effectiveness required by Article 35(1) the same as that under Article 13?

Even though the Court, at least in some cases, seems to hold that the effectiveness must essentially be the same,[10] it is not given that the requirements should correspond in all aspects.[11] Indeed, several factors speak for a different threshold and evaluation of the required effectiveness:

First, the main purpose of Article 35(1) is to afford States the opportunity to prevent or redress the alleged violations, before they are submitted to the Court.[12] The central consideration is, therefore, whether the applicant provided the competent remedial authority with the opportunity to consider the substance of the appeal (in the sense that the appeal is presented to the Court).[13] Article 13, on the other hand, requires States to provide effective remedies, including redress, in cases of arguable violations of substantive Convention rights. Seen from the point of view of States, Article 13 thus imposes an obligation, Article 35(1) an opportunity. On the other hand, seen from the point of view of the applicant, Article 35(1) imposes an obligation, Article 13 a right.

---

[6]   See, for example, *Mifsud* v. *France* (Grand Chamber decision 2002) para. 17 and Section 11.1.

[7]   See, for example, Matscher (1986) 267; Bårdsen (1999) 334–360; Harris, O'Boyle *et al.* (2018) 54–55; Dijk, Hoof *et al.* (2018) 116–123.

[8]   See, for example, *Akdivar a.o.* v. *Turkey* (Grand Chamber 1996) paras. 66–67; *Mifsud* v. *France* (Grand Chamber decision 2002) para. 15; *Nada* v. *Switzerland* (Grand Chamber 2012) para. 141. But the burden of proof may shift according to the circumstances; see, for example, Harris, O'Boyle *et al.* (2018) 53–54; *Akdivar a.o.* v. *Turkey* (Grand Chamber 1996) para. 68; *Reshetnyak* v. *Russia* (2013) para. 57.

[9]   See, for instance, Dijk, Hoof *et al.* (2018) 115–123.

[10]   See, for example, *Kadikis* v. *Latvia* (No. 2) (2006) para. 59; *Apap Bologna* v. *Malta* (2016) para. 79.

[11]   Similarly, Strasser (1988) 600. Some seem to hold that there is full correlation and interdependence, for example, Matscher (1986) 265; Matscher (1988) 327; Grabenwarter and Pabel (2012) 484. However, they do not point to differences or consider the consequences that such differences could have, although Matscher points to a few "exceptions" in which different notions must apply; see Matscher (1988) 327–328.

[12]   See, for example, *Gäfgen* v. *Germany* (Grand Chamber decision 2010) para. 142.

[13]   Ibid., para. 143.

This entails, *inter alia*, that the applicant may have to exhaust remedies which are not fully effective within the meaning of Article 13. The remedial authority may, for instance, be able to deal with the substance of the complaint, which is the primary aim of the requirement under Article 35(1), but not be in a position to offer adequate relief, which seems to be the primary aim of Article 13. On the other hand, an applicant who has availed himself of a remedy that is effective and sufficient within the meaning of Article 35(1) is not required to try other remedies that are available but no more likely to be successful.[14] However, under Article 13, an aggregate of remedies may be sufficient.[15] Somewhat imprecisely put: Under Article 35(1), the applicant may chose the remedy which (independently) has to be sufficient, whereas no such choice pertains under Article 13, as an aggregate may be sufficient, regardless of whether the applicant actually made use of the remedies.[16] A remedy may, therefore, be ineffective (admissible) for the purposes of Article 35(1), whereas the aggregate of remedies may be effective for the purposes of Article 13.

Against this background, it could be argued, more generally, that the Court should apply a more lenient evaluation of effectiveness under Article 35(1). If not, substantive violations of Article 13 could be declared inadmissible. That being said, in some cases, it may be more important to grant States the opportunity to redress the violation at home, whereas in others more important for the Court to clarify the remedies required by Article 13. The Articles so applied could thus complement each other in order to achieve a practicable and reasonable application of the principle of subsidiarity. A distinction could, for instance, be made between cases that reveal systemic remedial problems and little prospect of success when applying other remedies, and cases which reveal single or individual mistakes and which, in principle, could be remedied when using other remedies.

Second, when the Court considers the effectiveness of remedies under Article 35(1), it must assume that the substantive application is well founded. Based upon this assumption, the question is whether the nonexhausted remedy could have provided the applicant with sufficient redress, which builds upon the prognosis "reasonable prospect of success".[17] Accordingly, the assessment under Article 35(1) builds upon an assumption (well-founded application) and a prognosis (the success of the remedy).[18] Article 13, on the other

[14] See, for example, *Nada v. Switzerland* (Grand Chamber 2012) para. 142.
[15] See Section 9.3.
[16] See, for example, Bårdsen (1999) 360–361.
[17] See Section 10.6.
[18] See, for example, Bårdsen (1999) 335–336.

hand, grants the right to an effective remedy in cases of arguable claims, but only so that actual violations must be repaired. These different premises for the assessments may lead to concrete differences in result, in particular concerning what is to be considered effective redress. Some cases may, therefore, overcome the hurdle of Article 35(1) more easily than that of Article 13.

Third, special circumstances may absolve the applicant from exhausting domestic remedies, even though they are effective.[19]

Fourth, Article 35 contains other requirements that may lead to inadmissibility, without a consideration of the effectiveness of the remedy for the purposes of Article 35(1).[20]

Fifth, the Court only partly considers the exhaustion rule *ex officio*. Before an application is communicated to the respondent State, the applicant must provide the Court with a concise and legible statement on the compliance with the exhaustion rule.[21] At this stage, the Court considers the exhaustion of domestic remedies at its own motion upon the basis of the information from the applicant and rejects the case if it appears that an appropriate remedy has not been resorted to.[22] However, both the scope and degree of the Court's assessment may vary, depending on, *inter alia*, the alleged violation and how well the Court knows the remedies in the respondent State.[23] If the application is formally communicated to the responding State, the burden of proof

---

[19] See, for example, Bårdsen (1999) 372–390; Dijk, Hoof *et al.* (2018) 129–132; *Akdivar a.o. v. Turkey* (Grand Chamber 1996) para. 77; *Selçuk and Asker v. Turkey* (1998) para. 71. That being said, the existence of such circumstances are only exceptionally recognized, for instance, in cases of severe civil strife in the responding State, as, for example, in *Akdivar a.o. v. Turkey* (Grand Chamber 1996) para. 68.

[20] There is no formal hierarchy between admissibility criteria; see, for example, Bårdsen (1999) 127. However, the new *de minimis* rule in Article 35(3) *litra* b does not apply if respect for human rights as defined in the Convention and the Protocols thereto requires an examination of the application on the merits and that no case may be rejected on this ground which has not been duly considered by a domestic tribunal. The latter indicates that an application could not be declared inadmissible if domestic remedies are not sufficiently effective for the purposes of Article 35(1); see, in a similar manner, Christoffersen (2013) 192. But, to date, this admissibility criterion has not been put much to use; see, for example, Buyse (2014) 121; Vogiatzis (2016).

[21] See the Rules of Court Article 47(1) *litra* g (individual applications) and Article 46 *litra* d (inter-State applications), which, however, only requires a "statement" from the complaining State, not a "concise and legible statement".

[22] See, for example, Harris, O'Boyle *et al.* (2018) 52.

[23] See, for example, the Rules of the Court Article 47 para. 5.1, which provides that failure on part of the applicant to provide information on the exhaustion of domestic remedies "will result in the application not being examined by the Court" unless the applicant has provided an adequate explanation for the failure to comply, the application concerns a request for an interim measure or the Court otherwise directs of its own motion or at the request of an applicant.

shifts, and it falls upon the responding State to prove that the remedy is (not) exhausted, including its effectiveness. At this stage, the Court will not consider the effectiveness of remedies that are not presented by the responding States. Accordingly, the State may wave the right to rely on the exhaustion rule, even though domestic remedies could have proved effective.[24]

Sixth, under both Articles, the moment of time at which remedies have to be effective must be established. Under Article 35(1), the starting-point is the date at which the application was lodged at the Court. But this rule is subject to exceptions, which may be justified by the particular circumstances of each case.[25] Also under Article 13, it normally suffices to show that the remedy was not effective at the time of the introduction of the application at the Court.[26] But the Court has, in some cases, taken into account developments, which occurred after the date of introduction of the application.[27] And if new facts come to light, for instance, evidence that a person may be subjected to torture if he/she is expelled, the applicant needs to be provided an effective remedy against these new facts, at domestic level, even though the expulsion case already has been dealt with by national authorities.[28] In *refoulement* cases, these new facts need to be subject to "close and rigorous" scrutiny, and (also) the new remedy must have automatic suspensive effect.[29] And the remedial authority must – as a minimum – explain convincingly why the new facts are not relevant.[30]

Seventh, the Convention contains no rules on the burden of proof and evidence concerning procedures before the Court. Neither has the Court

---

[24] See, for example, Bårdsen (1999) 316; Harris, O'Boyle *et al.* (2018) 54. Note that Harris, O'Boyle *et al.* (2018) 54 in note 67 hold that the Court on one occasion, *Laidin* v. *France* (Final decision admissibility 2002), has applied the rule on exhaustion of domestic remedies *ex officio* (no request from the responding State) after communication to the responding State, but that "this ruling has not been followed and it is to be queried whether the case is still good law." Seen from the point of view of the responding State, there may be good reasons for not pleading lack of exhaustion of domestic remedies. It may, for instance, be of value to get a decision from the Court on the substantive issue, even though domestic remedies have not been used. Recall, in this regard, that the purpose of the exhaustion rules is to grant States the opportunity to fix things at home. Seen from the point of view of the Court, the argument against is that it may increase the case load.

[25] See, for example, *Giacometti and 5 others* v. *Italy* (Final decision 2001) and compare Rule 47(6) *litra* b of the Rules of the Court.

[26] See, for example, *Lutz* v. *France* (2002) para. 20; *E.O. and V.P.* v. *Slovakia* (2004) paras. 97 and 77; *Barillon* v. *France* (2006) para. 27; *Vlad a.o.* v. *Romania* (2013) para. 111.

[27] See, for example, *Strategies and Communications and Dumoulin* v. *Belgium* (2002) para. 54; *Žiačik* v. *Slovakia* (2003) para. 50; *Malejčík* v. *Slovakia* (2006) para. 59. But, seemingly to the contrary, for example, *Číž* v. *Slovakia* (2003) paras. 74–75; *Macková* v. *Slovakia* (2005) para. 62; *Z.M. and K.P.* v. *Slovakia* (2005) para. 76.

[28] See, for example, *Budrevich* v. *the Czech Republic* (2013) paras. 106–107.

[29] See Section 11.3.2.

[30] See, for example, *Budrevich* v. *the Czech Republic* (2013) para. 117.

developed a coherent and exhaustive practice in this regard. Indeed, the burden of proof and the required evidence may shift and vary depending on the violation and situation, including whether the Court is dealing with admissibility conditions or substantive rights. It is not clear whether the burden of proof and required evidence under the two Articles are the same. But, at least as a starting-point, the burden of proof and the degree of evidence required under Article 35(1) cannot be higher than when considering whether Article 13 has been violated. Otherwise, applications that amount to violations of Article 13 could be declared inadmissible in proceedings before the Court.

Notwithstanding such differences, many cases reveal a form of parallelism. Indeed, in many cases, the Court joins the examination of admissibility and merits,[31] and proceeds with the examination without any separate assessment under Article 35(1) or Article 13. In some cases, the analysis is performed under the heading of Article 35(1) and the Court under Article 13 only takes note of its conclusion under Article 35(1).[32] In other cases, the analysis is performed under the heading of Article 13 and the Court under Article 35(1) only refers to the assessment under Article 13.[33] Sometimes, the analysis is merged under the same heading, and it may be difficult to identify to what extent the analysis is relevant for both Article 35(1) and Article 13.[34] Because of potential differences between the Articles, such as those mentioned above, the Court should, as a minimum, explicitly make clear whether the assessment under Article 35(1) is directly transferable to Article 13 and *vice versa*.

---

[31] See Rule 54A of the Rules of Court.

[32] See, for example, *A.B. v. the Netherlands* (2002) para. 98; *Merit v. Ukraine* (2004) para. 78; *Kurić a.o. v. Slovenia* (Grand Chamber 2012) paras. 371–372; *Mitrofan v. the Republic of Moldova* (2013) para. 61; *Igbo a.o. v. Greece* (2017) para. 51; *Maslarova v. Bulgaria* (2019) para. 52.

[33] See, for example, *Kienast v. Austria* (2003) paras. 57 and 32; *Sürmeli v. Germany* (Grand Chamber 2006) para. 78; *McFarlane v. Ireland* (Grand Chamber 2010) para. 75; *Piskunov v. Russia* (2016) paras. 42 and 46; *X a.o. v. Russia* (2020) para. 66.

[34] See, for example, *Gorbulya v. Russia* (2014); *Voynov v. Russia* (2018); *Fil LLC v. Armenia* (2019).

6

Scope of Application

6.1 INTRODUCTION

This chapter provides an overview of the material, personal, territorial, and temporal scope of Article 13. The material (substantive) scope is dealt with in more detail in Chapters 7 to 11.

6.2 MATERIAL SCOPE

The material scope of Article 13 compromises two elements: (1) an arguable claim that substantive rights in the Convention are violated (Chapter 7) and (2) if an arguable claim exists, the right to an effective remedy, which consists of access to justice (Chapter 10) and redress (Chapter 11). Further, as a negative delimitation of the material scope, the Court excludes the challenging of primary legislation from Article 13 (Section 10.5.3). But Article 13 cannot be derogated from in emergency situations.[1] However, to the extent that substantive rights may be derogated from, Article 13 cannot apply.[2]

Article 13 does not contain explicit clauses that stipulate limitations in the right, such as, for example, Articles 8(2) to 11(2).[3] But, Article 13 has "inherent limitations".[4] This implies, in particular, that the context, in which an alleged violation occurs, may entail inherent limitations on the conceivable remedy.[5] The concept of inherent limitations may lead to think of an exception in

---

[1] Article 15 of the ECHR.
[2] Similarly, for example, David (2014) 261.
[3] See, also, Article 2(1) second sentence, Article 2(2) *litra* a-c, Article 5(1) *litra* a-f, and Article 6(1) second sentence.
[4] See, for example, *Leander* v. *Sweden* (1987) para. 79; *Kudla* v. *Poland* (Grand Chamber 2000) para. 151.
[5] See Chapter 8, and, for example, *Kudla* v. *Poland* (Grand Chamber 2000) para. 151.

an already established scope, in a similar manner as under Articles 8 to 11. However, the Court establishes in one and the same exercise whether the remedy, in the context of the case in hand, is effective. Accordingly, the finding of inherent limitations, in concrete cases, does not lead to inapplicability. It only means that the requirement is "a remedy that is as effective as can be having regard to the restricted scope for recourse inherent in [the particular context of the case in hand]."[6]

6.3 PERSONAL SCOPE

Article 13 applies to "everyone" (*"toute personne"*) with an arguable claim that his/her Convention rights have been or are being violated. The same wording is applied in several other Articles.

The English "everyone" encompasses both individuals and legal entities claiming that their Convention rights have been or are being violated. The French wording *"toute personne"* could indicate that legal entities are excluded from the scope. This finds support in the fact that some Articles explicitly refer to legal entities, for instance, P1 Article 1 which refers to natural and "legal persons" ("personne morale") and Article 10(1) which refers to "enterprises" (*"entreprises"*). However, Article 34 presupposes, more generally, that nongovernmental organizations or groups of individuals may be victims at international level. Moreover, the Commission and the Court have, on several occasions, considered whether Article 13 has been violated in cases concerning legal entities.[7] This corresponds with Article 6(1), which, at least as a starting-point, applies to legal entities. On the other hand, to the extent that an organization falls outside the scope of Article 34, it cannot be protected by Article 13.

Private organizations, without any connection to central Government, are clearly encompassed by Article 34 and, accordingly, Article 13. Central organs of the State are, on the other hand, unmistakably considered to be governmental organizations. But also decentralized authorities that exercise public functions, notwithstanding the extent of their autonomy vis-à-vis the central organs, are considered governmental. This is the case even if, for instance, a municipality claims that, in this particular situation, it is acting as a private organ.[8] In addition, legal entities other than decentralized authorities are

---

[6] See, for example, *Klass a.o.* v. *Germany* (Plenary 1978) para. 69; *Kudla* v. *Poland* (Grand Chamber 2000) para. 151.

[7] See, for example, WASA *Ömsesidigt, Försäkringsbolaget Valands Pensionsstiftelse, a group of approximately 15000 individuals* v. *Sweden* (Plenary Commission report 1988); *Agrotexim a.o.* v. *Greece* (1995).

[8] See, for example, *Danderyds Kommun* v. *Sweden* (Decision 2001).

considered governmental organizations if they participate in the exercise of governmental powers or run a public service under Government control. In order to determine whether legal entities other than a territorial authority fall within this category, account must be taken of "its legal status and, where appropriate, the rights that status gives it, the nature of the activity it carries out and the context in which it is carried out, and the degree of its independence from the political authorities."[9]

Even though the requirement of an effective remedy apply for individuals and private legal entities, it must not necessarily apply in the same way. Moral injustice, for instance, must not necessarily be redressed in the same manner for persons and legal entities. However, there is little guidance in the case law of the Court as to whether, and, if so, how it could and should be distinguished.[10] The Court has neither given any guidance as to who may claim the right on behalf of entities.[11]

Any person, or legal entity covered by the scope of Article 13, within the jurisdiction of the State, is, in principle, covered by the scope of Article 13. During the drafting, Article 1 originally contained the wording "all persons residing within the territories of the signatory states". The current wording "everyone within their jurisdiction" was introduced by the Committee of Experts because it "was felt that there were good grounds for extending the benefits of the Convention to all persons in the territory of the signatory States, even those who could not be considered as residing there in the legal sense of the word."[12] That being said, nationality or residence may affect how the requirement of an effective remedy plays out in concrete cases.[13] But there is little principled guidance in the case law of the Court as to whether and, if so, how it could and should be distinguished.[14]

More generally, the question arises as to whether the "victim" at international level, as understood under Article 34, must be considered a victim at national level, in the sense that Article 13, at the very least, requires that the same persons and entities who can enforce Convention rights at international level have the right to an effective remedy at national level.

Under Article 34, the Court distinguishes between directly (personally) affected victims, potential victims, future victims, and indirect victims.[15]

---

[9]   *Islamic Republic of Iran Shipping Lines* v. *Turkey* (2007) para. 79.
[10] See, however, Chapter 8 for general factors that may speak for a distinction.
[11] But see *Hasan and Chaush* v. *Bulgaria* (Grand Chamber 2000) paras. 98–99.
[12] The CETP Volume IV 20.
[13] See, as an illustration, *M.S.S.* v. *Belgium and Greece* (Grand Chamber 2011).
[14] See, however, Chapter 8 for factors that may speak for a distinction.
[15] See, for example, Dijk, Hoof *et al.* (2018) 50–60.

Under Article 13, however, the question, at the outset, seems to be regulated exclusively by the material scope of Article 13. On the one hand, both the requirement of arguability and the exclusion of the challenging of legislation as such from the scope of application of Article 13,[16] may lead to situations in which the applicant has no right to an effective remedy at national level, whereas he could be considered a "victim" under substantive Articles at international level. On the other hand, a claim could be arguable under Article 13, although the applicant is not considered a victim under substantive Articles.[17]

With regard to indirect victims, the Court has, under Article 34, in a number of situations, for example, acknowledged that the applicant's heirs and next of kin, in particular, parents, partners, and children, may claim rights on behalf of deceased persons.[18] Under Article 13, however, the Court has not answered this question in a principled manner, although it has, in some situations, required that indirect victims must be able to invoke Article 13 rights, most notably have arguable substantive violations effectively investigated.[19] Two perspectives may, in this regard, be taken. On the one hand, it could be claimed that Article 13 primarily aims at providing redress to the persons or entities whose personal rights actually have been violated, and, accordingly, that only these persons or entities may claim the right to an effective domestic remedy at national level. If so, it could be argued that indirect victims who are encompassed by Article 34 at international level, primarily with the goal of securing not only the individual interest, but the more general public interest, should not be encompassed by Article 13. On the other hand, it could be argued that if these persons or entities may claim substantive rights on behalf of the direct victims at international level, they should be able to do the same at national level. If not, the Court would, in these cases, turn into a court of first instance, which, indeed, does not chime well with the principle of subsidiarity.

6.4 TERRITORIAL SCOPE

The Contracting States are obliged to secure effective remedies to everyone "within their jurisdiction".[20]

---

[16] See Chapter 7 and Section 10.5.3.
[17] See Section 7.1 and, as an example, *Kebe a.o.* v. *Ukraine* (2017) para. 89.
[18] See, more generally, for example, Dijk, Hoof *et al.* (2018) 59–61, and, as examples, *Kaya* v. *Turkey* (1998) para. 122; *Centre for Legal Resources on behalf of Valentin Câmpeanu* v. *Romania* (Grand Chamber 2014) paras. 96–100; *Syltogov a.o.* v. *Russia* (2014) paras. 384–386.
[19] See Section 11.7.
[20] Article 1 of the ECHR.

As a general rule, the concept of "jurisdiction" under Article 1 of the ECHR reflects the position under general public international law. This notion is "primarily" or "essentially" territorial.[21] However, in exceptional cases, jurisdiction may be assumed outside the boundaries of the State. Extraterritorial jurisdiction has, *inter alia,* been declared in cases of acts of public authority performed by diplomatic and consular representatives of the State abroad, and when a contracting State exercises effective control of an area outside its national territory.[22] In such cases, States are obliged to provide effective remedies to persons residing outside the territory of the State, and for acts committed outside the territory of the State.[23] The scope of the obligation to provide effective remedies in such cases may, however, differ from the remedy which is provided both for residents and for acts committed within the territory of the State. But, there is little principled guidance in the case law of the Court as to whether, and, if so, how it could and should be distinguished.

In cases of State succession, the question arises of against which States a claim can or must be enforced, both at domestic and at international level. Or, to put it another way, what new and/or old States are obliged to provide remedies?[24] In this situation, the personally affected victim must, at the very least, have the same right to access to justice at domestic level, which he/she would have had at international level.

6.5 TEMPORAL SCOPE

It is a general principle of public international law that a treaty is not binding upon a party in relation to any act or fact which took place, or any situation which ceased to exist, before the date of entry into force of the treaty with respect to that party.[25] The principle applies to the Convention.[26] As a consequence, if substantive rights in the Convention are violated before ratification, Article 13 is not applicable, either. However, violations initiated by an act at a given time, but which continues to violate the Convention as a consequence of the original act, may fall within the temporal scope of the Convention. Occupation or

---

[21] See, for example, *Bankovic a.o. v. the UK* (Grand Chamber decision 2001) paras. 59–61; *Nada v. Switzerland* (Grand Chamber 2012) para. 119.

[22] See, for example, *Al-Skeini a.o. v. the UK* (Grand Chamber 2011) paras. 130–150.

[23] See, for example, *Issa a.o. v. Turkey* (2004).

[24] See, for example, *Ališić a.o. v. Bosnia and Herzegovina, Croatia, Serbia, Slovenia and FYROM* (Grand Chamber 2014).

[25] Article 28 of the VCLT.

[26] See, for example, *Ilascu a.o. v. Moldova and Russia* (Grand Chamber 2004) para. 400; *Janowiec a.o. v. Russia* (Grand Chamber 2013) para. 128.

other restrictions on land may, for instance, amount to continuing violations of P1 Article 1. Even if the original act starts before the entry into force of the Convention, the Court has jurisdiction to try the continuous violation for the period following the entry into force.[27] In such cases, the Court has jurisdiction to try if the substantive right is accompanied with an effective domestic remedy, but the State has no obligation to provide redress for wrongs caused prior to the date of entry into force.[28] In some cases, such as, for example, occupations continuously violating P1 Article 1, or detention continuously violating Article 5, it may, depending on the form of redress required, be hard, or may not even be necessary, to distinguish on the date – for instance, if the appropriate redress is the return of property or the cessation of detention. On the other hand, with regard to generic redress, in particular, compensation for moral damages, it may be distinguished. Further, in some cases, it is difficult to determine the exact time or time frame of the violation. For instance, when does a procedural obligation to perform effective investigations begin, and for how long does it continue?[29]

The Convention may be denounced in accordance with Article 58(1) of the ECHR, but is applicable to that State for another six months, if the alleged violation is "capable" of constituting a violation of the Convention.[30]

---

[27] See, for example, *Papamichalopoulos a.o. v. Greece* (1993) para. 40; *Ilascu a.o. v. Moldova and Russia* (Grand Chamber 2004) paras. 401–402.

[28] See, for example, *Janowiec a.o. v. Russia* (Grand Chamber 2013) para. 130.

[29] See, for example, the joint partly dissenting opinion of Judges Ziemele, de Gaetano, Laffranque and Keller in *Janowiec a.o. v. Russia* (Grand Chamber 2013).

[30] Article 58(2) of the ECHR.

7

The Arguability Test

7.1 INTRODUCTION

Article 13 provides that the right to an effective remedy only comes into play if other rights in the Convention or its Protocols "are violated" ("*ont été violés*").[1] The wording implies that the applicability of Article 13 depends on the actual finding of a violation of substantive rights. In the Court's earliest case law, this also seemed to be the opinion of the Court.[2] However, in *Klass a.o. v. Germany* (Plenary 1978), the Court held that Article 13 had to be interpreted as guaranteeing an effective remedy "to *everyone who claims* that his rights and freedoms under the Convention have been violated."[3] But later practice clarifies that the principal claim – the violation of a substantive right – must, at the very least, be "arguable".[4]

Clearly, Article 13 would have lost much of its effect at domestic level if it were to come into play only after the finding of actual violations.[5] Indeed, if rights are to be effectively recognized and repaired domestically, the question of whether substantive rights have been violated must actually be decided upon.[6] The extension of the scope of application to arguable claims,

---

[1]   See, also, the latter part of the wording: "has been committed" ("*aurait été commise*").
[2]   See, for example, *Swedish Engine Drivers' Union v. Sweden* (1976) para. 50.
[3]   Para. 64 (my emphasis).
[4]   See, for example, *Silver a.o. v. the UK* (1983) para. 113; *Leander v. Sweden* (1987) para. 77; *Kudla v. Poland* (Grand Chamber 2000) para. 157. But notice that the introduction of "arguable" in *Silver* was made with reference to *Klass a.o.* (Plenary 1978) in which the Court only stated that the applicant had to claim a violation. Arguability was thus introduced without any additional justification or reasoning as to where the threshold should lie.
[5]   At international level, it could, however, still have effect; see, for example, Holoubek (1992) 139–140.
[6]   Compare Matscher (1988) 320; Holoubek (1992) 146; Frowein and Peukert (2009) 392.

98

therefore, confirmed that Article 13 is an individual and autonomous right which places concrete obligations on States.[7]

The arguability of the claim is particularly important for the required access to justice. Indeed, because Article 13 does not guarantee a successful outcome (Section 10.6), Article 13 is not necessarily violated even though the Court finds that substantive rights were violated and affords redress. Somewhat imprecisely put: Article 13 only requires redress when the national authority actually finds a violation of substantive rights.[8] On the other hand, Article 13 may be violated because sufficient access to justice was not provided, even though the substantive right was not violated. At international level, redress must then be provided for the violation of Article 13.[9] Further, in proceedings before the Court, the applicant may no longer be a victim in relation to substantive Articles, but a victim with respect to Article 13.[10]

In order for the claim to be arguable, it must be presented to the domestic remedial authority with some degree of certainty as to both facts and law. The applicant must thus establish a *prima facie* case that substantive rights have been violated. It follows, on the one hand, that it is not sufficient to simply claim that a substantive right has been violated, and, on the other hand, that it is not necessary to fully establish a violation of substantive rights. Between these two extremes, the Court has emphasized few general guiding criteria as to what is necessary to establish the *prima facie* case (the arguable claim). In contrast, the Court underlines that it will not give an abstract definition of arguability and determines, on a case-by-case basis, whether each individual claim forming the basis of a complaint is arguable, in the light of the particular facts and of the nature of the legal issues raised.[11] Arguability, therefore, does not express one common threshold that applies in all cases. That being said, the Court has linked the notion of arguability to the international admissibility criterion "manifestly ill-founded" in Article 35(3) *litra* a of the ECHR. This linkage provides important pointers as to where the threshold lies, but is not unproblematical (Section 7.3). The question also arises as to what the

---

7 Compare Matscher (1988) 320.
8 Similarly, the Court only awards just satisfaction under Article 41 if the Court finds that rights are violated; see, for example, Buyse (2008) 149. The applicant also only has a right to compensation under Article 5(5) if a violation of one of the other paragraphs in Article 5 is established, either by the Court or a domestic authority; see, for example, N.C. v. *Italy* (Grand Chamber 2002) para. 49.
9 *Valsamis* v. *Greece* (1996) was the first case in which the Court found a violation of Article 13 without also finding a violation of the substantive Article.
10 See, as one example, *Gebremedhin [Gaberamadhien]* v. *France* (2007).
11 See, for example, *Boyle and Rice* v. *the UK* (Plenary 1988) para. 55.

relationship between arguability and the scope of application of substantive rights is (Section 7.2).

7.2 ARGUABILITY AND THE SCOPE OF APPLICATION OF SUBSTANTIVE RIGHTS

The scope of application of substantive rights may concern their personal, territorial, temporal, and material scope.[12]

If an application falls outside the scope of application of substantive rights, the Court normally declares it inadmissible as incompatible with the provisions of the Convention or the Protocols thereto according to Article 35(3) first alternative.[13] But even though the principal complaint does not fall within the scope of a substantive Convention right, it may, at least conceptually, be arguably within the scope of the right. The following analysis is, in the first hand, limited to the relationship between arguability and the material scope of application of substantive rights.

The scope of application *ratione materiae* concerns questions such as whether one is within the concept of "civil rights and obligations" or that of a "criminal charge" in Article 6(1), within "private life", "family life" or "home", and "correspondence" in Article 8(1), or within the concept of "possessions" in P1 Article 1. The Court has never considered the relationship between arguability and the material scope of application of substantive rights on a principled level. However, in most cases in which the Court finds that the principal claim falls outside the Convention *ratione materiae*, even after considerable and thorough considerations, which may contain serious doubts, the Court mostly concludes, without any further reasoning and without commenting on the question of arguability, that having regard to its decisions with regard to, most notably, Article 6(1), Article 13 is not applicable,[14] or that no separate issue appears to arise under Article 13.[15]

---

[12]   See, for example, Dijk, Hoof *et al.* (2018) 4–7, 11–23.

[13]   See, for example, Bårdsen (1999) 117–118 and the Council of Europe/European Court of Human Rights (ECtHR), *Practical Guide on Admissibility Criteria* (2014) paras. 220–225.

[14]   See, for example, *Kaukonen v. Finland* (Plenary Commission decision 1997); *Zubko a.o. v. Ukraine* (2006) para. 59; *Smiljan Pervan v. Croatia* (Decision 2014) para. 40. However, the Court's justification in these cases often goes back to the period in which the Commission held that for Article 13 to apply, it was sufficient that the applicant claimed that a substantive right had been violated, that is, before the criterion arguable claim was introduced; see, for example, *Dzhidzheva-Trendafilova v. Bulgaria* (Decision 2012) para. 38, which refers to *Kaplan v. the UK* (Plenary Commission report 1980) para. 173.

[15]   See, for example, *Escoubet v. Belgium* (Grand Chamber 1999) para. 40; *Dexter a.o. v. Cyprus* (Decision 2013) para. 79.

On the other hand, in some cases, the Court concludes that, for example, Article 6(1) does not apply in its civil or penal aspect and that Article 6(1), therefore, is not violated (thus a decision on the merits), and, at the same time, that the applicant therefore has no arguable claim, and that Article 13 has not been violated (thus a decision on the merits also concerning Article 13).[16] The Court may also conclude that the substantive Article is not applicable *ratione materiae*, that the complaint is not arguable (which then should not be necessary to consider), and that Article 13, therefore, is not applicable.[17] Further, in some cases in which, Article 6(1), for example, is found to be inadmissible *ratione materiae*, the Court, under Article 13, only refers to the doctrine of "less strict and absorbed" and that the complaint under Article 13, therefore, is manifestly ill-founded.[18] However, even though such references may indicate that the Court actually considers the arguability of a claim when it finds the principal claim inadmissible *ratione materiae*, it is hard pressed to say that the current understanding is so. Indeed, the reference to arguability seems to be included automatically and without any underlying reasoning, thus indicating that the inapplicability of Article 13 is a direct consequence of the principal claim being outside the scope of application of substantive rights, not an actual assessment of arguability.

This result, however, is not unproblematical. In some cases, the scope of application of substantive rights is construed broadly, but with exceptions that limit the scope significantly. In other cases, the scope is construed narrowly and with a small and rather negligible number of exceptions. Further, from the point of view of the applicant, it is of little significance if the claim is denied because he/she is outside the scope of application or because an exception to that right applies. His/her need for a remedy and protection against abuse and denial of justice is just as important in both situations. But, there is an obvious loss of effectiveness if the scope of application is excluded from the arguability test. Indeed, outside the scope, he/she then has no right to an effective remedy. Further, from a systemic perspective, it would make sense to demand that national authorities actually deal with arguable complaints concerning the material scope of application of substantive rights. If not, the Court must deal with the question in the first hand, which does not chime well with the principle of subsidiarity.

---

[16] For example *Kienast* v. *Austria* (2003) paras. 54–57.

[17] See, for example, *Kervoëlen* v. *France* (2001) paras. 30 and 33; *Herold Tele Media, s.r.o. a.o.* v. *Slovakia* (Decision 2010) para. 94; *Petropavlovskis* v. *Latvia* (2015) para. 92.

[18] See, for example, *Wendenburg a.o.* v. *Germany* (Decision 2003); *Panjeheighalehei* v. *Denmark* (Decision 2009).

With regard to the personal, territorial, and temporal scope of substantive Articles, excluding the arguability test seems less problematical. Indeed, there are fewer borderline cases and one is to a larger extent either clearly within or outside the scope. Concerning the temporal and territorial scope, I have not seen such questions analyzed in the Court's case law, but in some cases, the Court has considered claims arguable under Article 13 even though the applicant is outside the personal scope of substantive Articles.[19]

7.3 ARGUABILITY AND THE NOTION OF "MANIFESTLY ILL-FOUNDED"

7.3.1 *Same or Different Threshold?*

Manifestly ill-founded concerns the admissibility of a case at international level,[20] whereas arguability concerns the applicability of Article 13 at domestic level. Accordingly, the operational spheres of the tests differ. But both tests require some form of examination of the merits of the principal claim, both as to facts and law.

In *Boyle and Rice* v. *the UK* (Plenary 1988), the Commission had rejected most of the substantive complaints as "manifestly ill-founded". Before the Court, the Government maintained that claims declared "manifestly ill-founded" by the Commission could not be arguable under Article 13. The delegate of the Commission, however, held that when deciding whether a complaint is manifestly ill-founded, the Commission "applied a spectrum of standards that encompassed, but ranged beyond, the absence of arguability." Indeed, an arguable claim "only needs to raise a Convention issue which merits further examination", whereas a conclusion that a complaint is manifestly ill-founded "may be reached after considerable written and oral argument". The Court, however, held that when a complaint is rejected as manifestly ill-founded, "there is not even a prima facie case against the respondent State" and that, based upon the ordinary meaning of the words, "it is difficult to conceive how a claim that is 'manifestly ill-founded' can nevertheless be 'arguable', and *vice versa*."[21] But even though the Court was precluded from reviewing the merits of a complaint rejected as manifestly ill-founded, it was competent to take cognizance of all questions of fact and of law arising in the context of the complaint under Article 13, "including the arguability or not of the claims of violation of the substantive provisions."

---

[19]   See, for example, *A.D. a.o.* v. *Turkey* (2014).
[20]   Article 35(3) *litra* a second alternative of the ECHR.
[21]   *Boyle and Rice* v. *the UK* (Plenary 1988) paras. 53 and 54.

When doing so, the Commission's decision on the admissibility of the underlying claims, "whilst not being decisive, provide significant pointers as to the arguable character of the claims for the purposes of Article 13."[22] Although the latter sentence could indicate that the threshold of the tests could differ, it must be read in context with the fact that (at the time) the Court was not procedurally competent to deal with a question declared inadmissible by the Commission. However, if a question concerning Article 13 was referred to the Court, no such procedural hindrance concerning the arguability of the claim existed.

The relationship between the tests was again considered in *Powell and Rayner v. the UK* (1990). The Commission had found the principal complaints manifestly ill-founded, but a majority still found the complaint under Article 13 admissible and argued that there was a distinction between manifestly ill-founded and arguability.[23] The Court, however, repeated its statements from *Boyle and Rice* and added that the coherence of the "dual system of enforcement is at risk of being undermined" if Article 13 was interpreted as requiring national law to make available an effective remedy for a grievance "so weak as not to warrant examination on its merits at international level." Therefore, "whatever threshold the Commission has set in its case law for declaring claims manifestly ill-founded", "in principle," the Court should "set the same threshold in regard to the parallel notion of 'arguability' under Article 13."[24]

Although the reference to "in principle" could be taken as holding the door open for a different threshold, I am not aware of successive judgments in which the Court has found a claim arguable under Article 13 when the principal claim has been declared manifestly ill-founded. On the contrary, in newer judgments in which the question of admissibility is dealt with in the same procedure as the substantive questions, in accordance with Rule 54A of the Rules of the Court,[25] and in which the principal complaint is declared manifestly ill-founded, the Court has consistently denied the arguability of a claim under Article 13 with a simple reference to the decision on admissibility, even though the admissibility of the principal claim has been thoroughly scrutinized.[26]

---

[22] Ibid.
[23] *Powell and Rayner v. the UK* (1990) para. 32.
[24] Ibid., para. 33.
[25] Rule 54A of the Rules of the Court was inserted on June 17 and July 8, 2002, and amended on December 13, 2004, and November 13, 2006.
[26] See, for example, *Čonka v. Belgium* (2002) para. 76; *A, B and C v. Ireland* (Grand Chamber 2010) para. 159; *H.S. a.o. v. Cyprus* (2015) para. 282; *Shalyavski a.o v. Bulgaria* (2017) paras. 85–86. Notice that Grabenwarter (2014) 332 claims that the threshold is not identical in the practice of the Court, but only with reference to the older case law *Boyle and Rice v. the UK* (Plenary 1988) and *Plattform "Ärzte für das Leben" v. Austria* (1988).

In order to determine the threshold of arguability, it is thus necessary to establish the threshold for declaring a case manifestly ill-founded.

7.3.2 *Threshold for Declaring a Case "Manifestly Ill-Founded"*

The purpose of the Court's assessment of the merits of a claim is to conclude whether or not provisions of the Convention have been violated. It is, therefore, tempting to conclude that any assessment of merits should be excluded at the admissibility stage. Indeed, a strict distinction between form (admissibility) and content (merits) is normal in many domestic legal systems,[27] and in other parts of public international law.[28]

From the point of view of the applicant, a fully fledged review of the merits provides the greatest security for a correct result. However, considering the number of cases, it is impossible for the Court to provide this in all cases. The manifestly ill-founded criterion enables the Court to look into the merits and dispense with a case at the admissibility stage, but without giving the merits its full consideration.

During the drafting of the Convention, the understanding of the manifestly ill-founded criterion was closely related to the understanding of the roles of the Commission and the Court. Indeed, the Commission was to form a "kind of barrier – a practical necessity well known to all jurists – which would weed out frivolous or mischievous petitions" so that the Court only dealt with petitions "worthy of serious considerations".[29] Reference was also made to complaints that are "fantastic or obviously ill-founded".[30] Indeed, the wording "manifestly ill-founded" indicates a claim to which it is "immediately obvious to the average reader that it is far-fetched and lacks foundation."[31] However, the practice of both the Court and the Commission shows that manifestly ill-founded encompasses a spectrum of standards that goes far beyond applications that clearly lack a foundation or are frivolous or mischievous.[32] In many cases, the decision on admissibility then turns into an alternative form of deciding upon the merits of the case.[33]

---

[27] In Norwegian civil law, at the stage of admissibility, it is, for example, sufficient for the plaintiff to claim the existence of a fact. The courts do not enter into an assessment of the merits of the claimed fact; see, for example, Skoghøy (2017) 393.

[28] See, for example, Bårdsen (1999) 449.

[29] The CETP Volume I 48.

[30] See, for example, Pierre-Henri Teitgen in the CETP Volume I 282, 284.

[31] The Council of Europe/ ECtHR, *Practical Guide on Admissibility Criteria* (2014) para. 375.

[32] See, for example, Pellonpää (2007a) 159, 560; Wildhaber (2013) 211; Harris, O'Boyle *et al.* (2018) 75.

[33] Compare Bårdsen (1999) 458–459; Lorenzen, Christoffersen *et al.* (2011) 946; Gerards (2014a) 156.

Further, with the entry into force of Protocol 11 on November 1, 1998, and Protocol 14 on January 1, 2010, the Court's system for handling applications was amended significantly. Protocol 11 replaced the Commission with the unique Court, which decides on both admissibility and merits, and Protocol 14 introduced the division of work between Single judge formations, Committees, Chambers, and the Grand Chamber.[34] Currently, the majority of cases declared manifestly ill-founded are decided by a Single judge or a Committee of three judges.[35] The reasoning in these cases is very limited.[36] Accordingly, such decisions provide little information concerning the actual threshold of manifestly ill-founded.[37] Further, the guidance from the decisions of the former Commission is uncertain in the present, and the cases decided in Chambers and Grand Chamber only indicate the tip of the iceberg.

Further, when deciding on the merits, the Court applies a range of tools and principles, which may vary, depending, *inter alia*, on the context and the type of violation.[38] The Court also uses different methods for appreciating facts, under which the burden of proof may shift, depending on the circumstances. In principle, although not explicitly underlined by the Court, the same tools and principles are available when considering whether an application is manifestly ill-founded.[39] This clearly illustrates the difficulty in pinpointing one common threshold for declaring a case to be manifestly ill-founded.[40]

In addition, with the number of cases arriving at the Court, the notion of manifestly ill-founded has become an important technique in the selection process that is essential to the Court's survival. Since 1999, the relationship between applications allocated to judicial formation, inadmissibility decisions, judgments, and pending applications has been as follows (Fig. 7.1).[41]

---

[34] Article 26 of the ECHR.

[35] See Articles 27 and 28 of the ECHR. But some questions of admissibility are examined by a Chamber or, in exceptional cases, the Grand Chamber; see Articles 29 and 31 of the ECHR and the Council of Europe/ECtHR, *Practical Guide on Admissibility Criteria* (2014) para. 377.

[36] See, for example, Keller, Fischer *et al.* (2010) 1046; Lester (2013) 107.

[37] For a critique of the practice of not providing reasoning in such admissibility decisions; see Gerards (2014a). As from 2016 and onward, the Court has, however, provided reasoned Single judge decisions; see, for example, the Annual Report 2015 of the ECtHR 5–6. However, the reasoning is and must, in most cases, be very limited.

[38] See Section 2.4.

[39] The practical guide on admissibility criteria published by the Court (prepared by the research division of the Court) indicates that this is the case; see the Council of Europe/ECtHR, *Practical Guide on Admissibility Criteria* (2014) paras. 375–404.

[40] See, also, for example, Gerards (2014a); Dijk, Hoof *et al.* (2018) 165–169.

[41] These numbers have been extracted from the statistics and annual reports of the Court, available at the website of the Court. Pending cases await a legal decision, either in the form of a decision on admissibility or a judgment on the merits. Inadmissibility decisions include

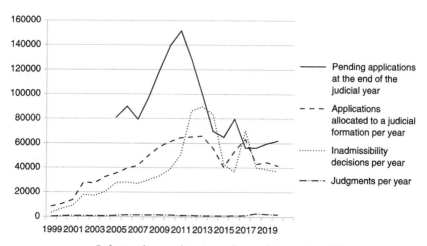

FIGURE 7.1 *Relationship applications allocated to a judicial formation, inadmissibility decisions, judgments, and pending applications*

The number of allocated applications has increased rapidly from 1999. At the same time, the Court's case-handling capacity, judged, in particular, from cases declared inadmissible and the reduced backlog, has increased steadily. Notice in particular how the renewed income of applications allocated to judicial formations in 2016 and 2017 primarily was disposed of through inadmissibility decisions. Indeed, judgments only amount to a small part of the Court's work.[42] The majority of cases are rejected as inadmissible.[43] The available statistics contain no information on the grounds upon which applications are declared inadmissible, but it is assumed that the majority are declared manifestly ill-founded.[44] Accordingly, the threshold of manifestly ill-founded will, at least in practice, vary over time.[45]

Moreover, the content and threshold of the manifestly ill-founded criterion is unclear and under pressure for additional reasons.

First, there is no formal hierarchy between different admissibility criteria. A case may, for instance, be declared manifestly ill-founded even though

cases struck out of the list for other reasons than being inadmissible, for example, because a friendly settlement has been reached or because of a unilateral declaration. However, the preponderant number of cases, in this category, are decisions on inadmissibility.

[42] Already in 1994, Schermers (1994) 370 referred to the workload of the Strasbourg institutions as an iceberg where "[o]nly a little top is visible to the outside world; the great mass remains hidden under water."

[43] Presently between 90–96 percent of the examined cases are rejected as inadmissible or struck out of the list for other reasons.

[44] See, for example, Keller, Fischer *et al.* (2010) 1028.

[45] Compare, for example, Bårdsen (1999) 459.

domestic remedies have not been exhausted or the application is presented too late.[46] This relationship is further complicated with the introduction of the *de minimis* rule by Protocol 14, under which an application is to be declared inadmissible if the applicant has not suffered a significant disadvantage.[47] The criterion was introduced to allow the Court to "devote more time to cases which warrant examination on the merits, whether seen from the perspective of the legal interest of the individual applicant or considered from the broader perspective of the law of the Convention and the European public order to which it contributes."[48] Consequently, if this criterion is actually put to use, it may increase the threshold of "manifestly ill-founded".

Second, the manifestly ill-founded criterion may be used as a last resort for disposing of cases for reasons other than an evaluation of certainty with regard to facts and law, for example, political undertones or controversial questions which the Court does not consider ripe for deciding.[49] Indeed, in the current climate of reform proposals and critique, the Court may be tempted to use "manifestly ill-founded" not only to regulate its case load, but to accommodate critical voices and increase its legitimacy.[50] Further, the Brighton declaration, for example, assumes that the Court declares an application inadmissible if a domestic court has duly considered the complaint, unless the Court finds that the application raises a serious question affecting the interpretation or application of the Convention.[51] And many perceive the introduction of the references to subsidiarity and margin of appreciation in the Preamble as a substitute for the failure to introduce new and stricter admissibility criteria.[52]

For all such reasons, the threshold of manifestly ill-founded is uncertain and may vary not only depending on the circumstances of the case,[53] but also the context and case load of the Court. Indeed, manifestly ill-founded "resembles an empty black box" which necessarily leaves the Court a "wide measure of discretion in giving substance to it."[54]

---

[46] Compare, for example, Bårdsen (1999) 127–128.

[47] Article 35(3) *litra* b of the ECHR.

[48] Explanatory Report to Protocol 14 paras. 77–78.

[49] See, already, Bårdsen (1999) 454–455 and, more recently, Graham (2020).

[50] See, for example, Ichim (2014) 237.

[51] The Brighton Declaration para. 15 *litra* d. In his opening address at the Brighton Conference, the then presiding President of the Court, Nicolas Bratza, confirmed that "it is indeed the Court's practice to reject a case as inadmissible where it finds that the complaint has been fully and properly examined in Convention terms by the domestic courts"; see Bratza (2014a) 82.

[52] See, for example, Milner (2014) 30.

[53] Similarly, for example, Greer and Wildhaber (2012) 665.

[54] Keller, Fischer *et al.* (2010) 1046. See, also, for example, Parish (2011) 201. It has, for these and other reasons, been argued that more definitional criteria of the "manifestly ill-founded" criterion are needed; see, for example, Keller, Fischer *et al.* (2010) 1047–1048.

7.3.3 A New Start

Because the threshold of manifestly ill-founded and arguability is to be the same, the uncertainty and, at least in practice, high threshold of manifestly ill-founded adversely affects the arguability test and, consequently, how Convention complaints are required to be dealt with domestically. Clearly, this does not chime well with the calls for subsidiarity and improvement of domestic remedies (Section 12.3.3). Further, the Court's arguments when introducing the linkage in *Boyle and Rice* v. *the UK* (Plenary 1988) and *Powell and Rayner* v. *the UK* (1990) seem difficult to uphold in present day circumstances. Recall that the Court presented two main arguments for upholding the linkage.

First, "on the ordinary meaning of the words", it was "difficult to conceive how a claim that is 'manifestly ill-founded' can, nevertheless, be 'arguable', and *vice versa.*" But whereas manifestly ill-founded has its basis in the Convention and must be interpreted in the light of Articles 31–33 of the VCLT and the method developed by the Court, the notion of arguability was introduced and developed in the case law of the Commission. Hence, "manifestly ill-founded" is the starting-point of a legal analysis, whereas arguability the result. Comparing and using the wording of the terms as an argument *per se* for concurrence in threshold thus seems flawed. In any case, the Court currently applies the criterion "manifestly ill-founded" so as to encompass cases that clearly go beyond the ordinary meaning of manifestly. At least in the current context, a comparison of the wording thus provides little support for upholding the linkage.

Second, the "coherence" of the "dual system of enforcement" risked being undermined if Article 13 was interpreted as requiring national law to make available an effective remedy for a grievance classified "as being so weak as not to warrant examination on its merits at international level." However, as we have seen above, in the present, many cases are rejected as manifestly ill-founded after considerable analysis that contain serious doubts as to both facts and law. At least in these cases, it cannot be the "weakness" of the international case that supports the linkage. Further, there is nothing in the context, object, or purpose of the current Convention system, more generally, or Articles 13 and 35(3), more specifically, that demand an identical threshold. On the contrary, the main object and purpose of the Convention system is to secure the effective enforcement of human rights at home,[55] and the object and purpose of Article 13 and the international admissibility criterion are partly divergent. Indeed, whereas Article 13 seeks to provide effective means for individuals to obtain relief for violation of the Convention at

---

[55] See, for example, Paraskeva (2008) 422.

national level, the manifestly ill-founded criterion seeks to ensure the effectiveness of the Court. To achieve this, the Convention must, at the very least, demand a threshold of arguability that actually requires and encourages national authorities to deal with alleged human-rights violations that deserve serious consideration. Therefore, although the argument of coherence had a certain logic in 1990, when the Court had few problems in dealing with its case load, it is not appropriate in the present. Indeed, what is currently needed is not coherence, but tools that allow the Court to deal with its case load and improve domestic remedies.[56]

If the linkage between manifestly ill-founded and arguability was to be removed, the threshold for arguability needs to be set anew.

Currently, and with reference to the manifestly ill-founded test, the Court determines the threshold of arguability on a case-by-case basis, in the light of the particular facts and the very nature of the legal issue or issues raised. In doing so, the Court may use a spectrum of standards. The current arguability test, therefore, does not express one single threshold that applies in all cases. Given the range of different complaints that may arise, this flexibility should be transferred to the national level. But the new starting-point must emphasize that the threshold cannot be too high. The guiding criterion must be whether the Convention issue merits examination, so that Article 13 may actually become effective in practice.[57] This could, in the abstract, be expressed by using similar wording to that in the *travaux préparatoires* concerning the "manifestly ill-founded" criterion, for instance, by referring to frivolous or mischievous complaints, or wholly unsubstantiated facts or legal issues. Guidance may, also, be taken from the Court's case law concerning "civil rights and obligations" under Article 6(1), which requires the dispute to be "genuine and serious",[58] and under which the Court assesses whether the applicant's arguments are "sufficiently tenable".[59] But, it cannot be more difficult to raise an issue under Article 13 than under Article 6(1).[60] Further, in a similar manner as under Article 6(1), the Court should not exclude the applicability of the arguability test because the question falls outside the scope of application of substantive Convention rights, as long as one is arguably within the scope of application (Section 7.2).

---

[56] Similarly, for example, Frowein and Peukert (2009) 392–393. See, also, Frowein (2000) 549, who holds that the Court "links two completely different notions".

[57] Compare the opinion of the Commission referred to by the Court in *Boyle and Rice v. the UK* (Plenary 1988) para. 53.

[58] See, for example, *Benthem v. the Netherlands* (Plenary 1985) paras. 32–33; *Berger-Krall a.o. v. Slovenia* (2014) para. 313. Indeed, some claim, more generally, that this requirement may shed light on the arguability test; see, for example, Matscher (1988) 320; Dijk, Hoof *et al.* (2018) 1040–1041.

[59] See, for example, *Neves e Silva v. Portugal* (1989) para. 37; *Yanakiev v. Bulgaria* (2006) para. 58.

[60] Similarly, for example, Dijk, Hoof *et al.* (2018) 1041.

8

A Relative Standard

Article 13 only requires a remedy that is as effective as can be having regard to the restricted scope for recourse inherent in the particular context of the case.[1] Article 13 thus contains a relative standard of effectiveness. This relativity could play itself out differently under the various requirements arising under Article 13, and the threshold in concrete cases could be influenced by a string of more general factors. I do not here account for uncertainty in purposes (Chapter 3) or more general normative and contextual factors which may affect the relative standard (Chapter 12). The goal is neither to exhaustively account for how the relativity plays itself out under the different requirements, which should become clearer in the subsequent Chapters 9 to 11, but to provide an overview of the most important factors that have been explicitly emphasized in the Court's case law.

Notice in the first hand that the relativity provides for different possibilities for assuring effective remedies in practice. As a consequence, States have a margin of appreciation or discretion when implementing the requirements in their domestic systems.[2] Sometimes the Court also holds that Article 13 must be applied with a certain *"souplesse"*.[3] Accordingly, Article 13 does not *per se* require any particular form of remedy.[4] The remedy must not, for example, be granted in specific forms of proceedings. But the remedial proceedings, be they penal, civil, disciplinary, constitutional, or administrative, must either

---

[1] See, for example, *Klass a.o. v. Germany* (Plenary 1978) para. 69; *Kudla v. Poland* (Grand Chamber 2000) para. 151.

[2] Under Article 13, the Court mostly refers to discretion or margin of discretion; see, for example, *de Souza Ribeiro v. France* (Grand Chamber 2012) para. 85; *Bastys v. Lithuania* (2020) para. 65, although it sometimes refers to "margin of appreciation"; see, for example, *Smith and Grady v. the UK* (1999) para. 135; *İrfan Güzel v. Turkey* (2017) para. 92.

[3] See, for example, *Strategies and Communications and Dumoulin v. Belgium* (2002) para. 54.

[4] See, for example, *Budayeva a.o. v. Russia* (2008) para. 190.

alone or in aggregate (Section 9.3) satisfy the minimum requirements of access to justice (Chapter 10) and redress (Chapter 11). Whether, in a given case, Article 13 is satisfied will, therefore, depend upon the manner in which States have chosen to discharge their obligation to secure to anyone within their jurisdiction the substantive Convention rights.[5] Consequently, the choice of system has implications for the discretion and the type of remedy required.[6] Indeed, in a given situation, concerning a given right, in a given State, only a limited selection of remedies, or even only one remedy, may be effective. For instance, if a State, in a specific situation, only provides a penal remedy, and this penal remedy does not grant the possibility for the victim to achieve the required redress, for instance, compensation, Article 13 is violated because the State has chosen only to provide the penal remedy. And, if domestic administrative proceedings do not satisfy the requirements of independence and impartiality, Article 13 is violated if this lack of independence and impartiality is not remedied by another authority, even though the administrative authority is authorized to grant sufficient relief. Notice that in most domestic systems, State liability is primarily built upon the framework of tort law, even for human-rights violations.[7] However, some States have introduced general remedies that are intended to redress any violations of the Convention without being limited to particular factual or legal contexts, be they, for example, penal, civil, disciplinary, or administrative.[8] However, even though such general domestic remedies intuitively may seem preferable, it is not given that they can, in all cases, satisfy all requirements of Article 13. And, specific remedies directed against specific problems and situations may, at least in given situations, be more effective.

The most important general factor emphasized by the Court is the character and degree of the violation. Indeed, the scope of obligations arising from Article 13 varies according to the nature of the right and the complaint.[9] To put it bluntly, more important rights require more stringent remedies.[10] The requirements of Article 13 are, most notably, applied stricter in conjunction with arguable violations of Articles 2 and 3, for instance, stricter requirements of effective investigations (Section 11.7), stricter procedural guarantees of the domestic authority (Section 10.2), stricter requirements concerning the

---

[5] See, for example, *Silver a.o. v. the UK* (1983) para. 113.
[6] See, for example, *Budayeva a.o. v. Russia* (2008) paras. 190–191.
[7] Shelton (2005) 22; Roach (2021) 239.
[8] See, for an overview, the Guide to good practice in respect of domestic remedies (adopted by the Committee of Ministers on September 18, 2013) 45–53.
[9] See, for example, *Al-Nashif v. Bulgaria* (2002) para. 136.
[10] Similarly, for example, Harris, O'Boyle *et al.* (2018) 747.

manner in which the authority deals with the substance of the complaint (Section 10.5.4), nonpecuniary damages always being required (Section 11.5.2), speedier remedies (Section 10.7), and more important to put an end to continuing violations (Section 11.3.4). Accordingly, both the required access to justice and redress must be proportional to the gravity of the violation and the harm suffered.[11] Further, under substantive Articles, the gravity of the violation is considered more severe if the very essence of the right is threatened. Similarly, some requirements under Article 13 are more absolute than others and have an essence that cannot be limited with reference to proportionality,[12] for instance, the requirement that Article 13 must provide the applicant with a personal right (Section 9.2). Such proportionality assessments raise many difficult questions which have not been dealt with by the Court, for instance, to what extent must alternatives be supported by empirical evidence, measures be able to fulfill the pursued aim, and evidence of causation be present.[13]

Further, the context and situation may influence how the requirements are applied. The most notable examples are cases that raise issues of national security, which may, for instance, affect the required scope of domestic review (Section 10.5.4). More generally, the political context under which remedies operate may affect how the remedy has to be applied in concrete.[14] And, more concretely, by way of a few examples, a climate of precipitation and intimation, in which the applicant fears retaliation, may lead to stricter application of the requirements,[15] the nature and degree of scrutiny which satisfies the minimum threshold of a required investigation "depends on the circumstances of the particular case",[16] the special situation of asylum-seekers may necessitate giving them the benefit of the doubt when assessing the credibility of their statements and the supporting documents they have submitted,[17] and the danger of irreversible damage may lead to stricter requirements of, for

---

[11] Compare Principle 15 first sentence of the van Boven/Bassiouni principles. More generally, the fact that the van Boven/Bassiouni principles only apply to "gross violations of international human rights law" indicates that the modalities of reparation with regard to "minor violations" can be "left to the discretion of individual States"; see, for example, Principle 11 of the van Boven/Bassiouni principles and Tomuschat (2007) 572.

[12] Similarly, under EU law, the ECJ has accepted that, in the periphery, limitations on the right to an effective remedy may be permissible if they pursue a legitimate objective and are proportionate, but, in the very essence, the right is more absolute; see, for example, Hoffman (2014) 1225.

[13] Compare, for example, Christoffersen (2009) 166, 717. See, also, Roach (2021) 61–71.

[14] See, for example, *Georgia v. Russia (I)* (Grand Chamber 2014) para. 151.

[15] See, for example, *Georgia v. Russia (I)* (Grand Chamber 2014) para. 154.

[16] See, for example, *Velikova v. Bulgaria* (2000) para. 80.

[17] See, for example, *A.A. v. Switzerland* (2014) paras. 59–63.

instance, the need to put an end to continuing violations and the need for access to documents and information.[18] On the other hand, the Court has never accepted scarcity of funds as an excuse for not providing an effective remedy.[19]

Moreover, the personal situation of the applicant is of significance.[20] Mentally unsound patients,[21] disabled persons,[22] and children,[23] may, for instance, need special assistance and particular procedural safeguards. *Keenan* v. *the UK* (2001) illustrates, more generally, how more assistance is required when the applicant is in a vulnerable situation or state of mind (in concrete, automatic review was necessary).[24] Conversely, the attitude of the applicant may affect what is required, for instance, when considering whether investigations have been effective.[25] In extreme cases, the conduct of the applicant may even deprive him/her of the right to an effective remedy altogether.[26] This indicates, more generally, that the right to an effective remedy may be waived, although the Court has not explicitly considered it.[27] The Court has not, in the abstract, considered if it matters whether the applicant is a company in contrast to a physical person, but the general weight attached to the personal situation of the applicant indicates that this is relevant.[28]

More generally, what is necessary in one State is not necessarily the same as in another. Most notably, the Court increasingly seems to attach weight to whether the remedial problem stems from a systemic mistake. If so, the

---

[18] See, for example, M.S.S. v. *Belgium and Greece* (Grand Chamber 2011) paras. 304 and 318; *Rupa* v. *Romania (no. 2)* (2011) paras. 38–39; *Rahimi* v. *Greece* (2011) paras. 96 and 77. Compare, also, Chapter V of the International Law Commission Draft Articles on the Responsibility of States for Internationally Wrongful Acts.

[19] See, for example, *Reshetnyak* v. *Russia* (2013) para. 70.

[20] See, for example, the Guide to good practice in respect of domestic remedies (adopted by the Committee of Ministers on September 18, 2013) in note 21 and *Georgia* v. *Russia (I)* (Grand Chamber 2014) para. 151.

[21] See, for example, the Guide to good practice in respect of domestic remedies (adopted by the Committee of Ministers on September 18, 2013) 19.

[22] See, for example, *Centre for Legal Resources on behalf of Valentin Câmpeanu* v. *Romania* (Grand Chamber 2014) para. 153; *Kalandia* v. *Greece* (2016) para. 96.

[23] See, for example, *Margareta and Roger Andersson* v. *Sweden* (1992) para. 101.

[24] *Keenan* v. *the UK* (2001) paras. 126–127.

[25] See, for example, *Goygova* v. *Russia* (2007) paras. 102–104.

[26] See N.D. and N.T. v. *Spain* (Grand Chamber 2020) para. 242, in which the applicants did not use existing and proportional official entry procedures. This not only deprived them of their protection under P4 Article 4, but the right to an effective remedy under Article 13.

[27] Under Article 6, this may to a certain extent be done; see, for example, Christoffersen *et al.* (2011) 371–374.

[28] Similarly, the fact that the applicant is a company may affect the requirements of Article 6; see, for example, *Agrotexim a.o.* v. *Greece* (1995) para. 73.

requirements of Article 13 are applied stricter, most notably with regard to the requirement that the remedy must be effective not only in theory, but in practice (Section 9.4). This is not least so when the State does not conform to a Pilot judgment and the reason relates to the lack of effective remedies.[29] Indeed, the areas in which the Court increasingly has put Article 13 into effect mostly concern subject-matters in which the existence of systemic human-rights violations, in some manner, has been established.[30] This raises the question as to what extent the systemic nature of the violation is and should be of relevance under Article 13.[31]

Changes in the Court's case law may create new law. This, again, may necessitate access to justice and redress in situations which were not necessary at an earlier stage. In such cases, the applicant has the right to an effective remedy, including redress, from the point of time at which the case law changed.[32]

---

[29] See Section 9.4 and, for example, *Burmych a.o. v. Ukraine* (Grand Chamber 2017).

[30] See, in particular, Sections 4.3, 4.5 and 9.4, and compare, for example, Jötten (2010) 111.

[31] See, in particular, Section 9.4 and compare, for example, the dissenting opinion of Judge Pettiti in *Higgins a.o. v. France* (1998) as regards Article 6 of the ECHR.

[32] See Christoffersen (2009) 435–438.

9

General Requirements and Principles

9.1 INTRODUCTION

This chapter analyzes three requirements and principles that are overarching to both access to justice (Chapter 10) and redress (Chapter 11).

9.2 A PERSONAL RIGHT

The remedy must provide the applicant with a personal right to access to justice and redress.[1] It does not suffice that the national authority has supervisory or discretionary powers to look at a case and provide redress. The remedy must, as a minimum, compel the authority to exercise its supervisory or discretionary powers.[2] Many judgments concerning the lack of a personal right to a remedy concern hierarchical complaints to higher domestic public administrative authorities with supervisory and discretionary powers, but which are not obligated to deal with the complaint from the applicant.[3] However, the requirement applies to any type of national authority. For instance, it does not suffice that a court has discretionary power to verify whether an act or decision is legal. It must be obliged to do so.[4]

---

[1] See, for example, *Hartman v. the Czech Republic* (2003) para. 66; *Sürmeli v. Germany* (Grand Chamber 2006) para. 109; *Dirdizov v. Russia* (2012) para. 77; *Neshkov a.o. v. Bulgaria* (2015) para. 212; *Sukachov v. Ukraine* (2020) para. 120.

[2] See, for example, *Kadikis v. Latvia (no. 2)* (2006) para. 61; *V.A.M. v. Serbia* (2007) paras. 154 and 85; *Petridis v. Greece* (2010) para. 34.

[3] See, for example, *Reshetnyak v. Russia* (2013) para. 64 and *Neshkov a.o. v. Bulgaria* (2015) para. 212 (no personal right compelling public prosecutors to use their supervisory powers).

[4] See, for example, *Kadikis v. Latvia (no. 2)* (2006) para. 61; *Panzari v. Moldova* (2009) para. 41; *Mackay & BBC Scotland v. the UK* (2010) paras. 32–34.

Further, it cannot be left solely in the hands of the State or its officials to set the remedy in motion.[5] It must be a right for the applicant to set the remedy in motion. In some cases, the Court links this aspect to the accessibility of the remedy and states that the remedy must be independent of discretionary action taken by the authorities and directly available to those concerned.[6]

The Court particularly insists on the importance of the personal right to a remedy when the violation is committed by the same authority or branch of Government which is supposed to rectify the situation. For instance, in the event of a failure to enforce judgments against the State, which are violations of Article 6(1), it goes without saying that the enforcement cannot be left to the discretion of the administrative authorities and that it must be obligatory and able to compel the authority(ies) to remedy the situation.[7]

The requirement also implies that the proceedings must involve the applicant in a sufficiently effective manner.[8] To this end, the authority must be obliged to involve the applicant.[9]

Further, the personal right must compel the State and its authorities to do what they should. A remedy only compelling third persons, for instance, neighbors in a case concerning an administrative decision to demolish a building possibly violating Protocol 1 Article 1, is not sufficient for the purposes of Article 13.[10]

It remains uncertain whether the establishment of some form of personal responsibility of a public official may be sufficient. Such cases may be combined with more direct responsibility and compelling obligations on part of the State, and the case against the public official may have more or less direct consequences on the personal situation of the applicant. However, if the case only concerns the personal responsibility of a public official, for instance, in disciplinary proceedings, and even if it improves the situation of the applicant, the Court has been reluctant to recognize the proceedings as a personal remedy (right) for the applicant. For instance, in cases concerning the lack of execution of judgments, the Court has refused to recognize proceedings against the public official responsible for the execution as a personal remedy, even

---

[5] See, for example, the *Russian Conservative Party of Entrepreneurs a.o.* v. *Russia* (2007) paras. 87–88; *Bastys* v. *Lithuania* (2020) para. 69.

[6] See, for example, *Efimenko* v. *Ukraine* (2006) paras. 64 and 49; *Mandić and Jović* v. *Slovenia* (2011) para. 110.

[7] See, for example, *Kanellopoulos* v. *Greece* (2008) paras. 33 and 21.

[8] See, for example, *Donner* v. *Austria* (2007) para. 45; *Stoyanov and Tabakov* v. *Bulgaria* (2013) para. 99.

[9] See, for example, *Ananyev a.o.* v. *Russia* (2012) para. 104.

[10] See, for example, *Fotopoulou* v. *Greece* (2004) paras. 45–46.

though the proceedings may indirectly affect the execution of the judgment.[11] Similarly, in cases of excessive length of proceedings, the remedy must be aimed at speeding up the case or providing the applicant with personal redress. Proceedings that only engage the personal responsibility of the judge responsible for the delay are not effective.[12] This is the case even if the judge is ultimately dismissed.[13] Similarly, at least in cases concerning excessive length of proceedings, proceedings resulting in other forms of disciplinary punishment are not sufficient.[14] Neither is the possibility of demanding that the expert who slowed down the case is replaced nor the filing of a complaint for damages against the expert, at least as long as the measures do not redress the personal situation of the applicant, but limit themselves to sanctioning the actions and the behavior of the expert.[15]

9.3 AGGREGATE OF REMEDIES

The Court has, since its early case law, held that an aggregate of remedies may satisfy Article 13.[16] The applicant may, therefore, have to turn to several authorities in order to obtain relief. From the point of view of the applicant, this may be a significant loss of effectiveness, in particular, if processes are repetitive and overlapping. And even if authorities have exclusive competences to deal with separate issues, it is usually more time-consuming and cumbersome to turn to two or more authorities. Some, therefore, argue that the Court should be reluctant to allow for an aggregate of remedies,[17] or even that the whole concept is mistaken.[18]

However, an aggregate of remedies may, at least under given circumstances, enhance the effectiveness of the remedial task. For instance, in some cases, it may be necessary to act with extreme speed in an early phase, for example, to stop continuing violations. An administrative authority not

---

[11] See, for example, *Zazanis a.o. v. Greece* (2004) para. 46.
[12] See, for example, *Ebru and Tayfun Engin Çolak v. Turkey* (2006) para. 106.
[13] See, for example, *Olshannikova v. Russia* (2006) para. 44.
[14] See, for example, *Benyaminson v. Ukraine* (2007) para. 118.
[15] See, for example, *Konti-Arvaniti v. Greece* (2003) para. 29, followed by a string of almost identical cases against Greece over many years.
[16] The first case was *Klass a.o. v. Germany* (Plenary 1978) para. 72. See, subsequently, for example, *Silver a.o. v. the UK* (1983) para. 113; *Chahal v. the UK* (Grand Chamber 1996) para. 145; *Kudla v. Poland* (Grand Chamber 2000) para. 157; *Sürmeli v. Germany* (Grand Chamber 2006) para. 98; *Nada v. Switzerland* (Grand Chamber 2012) para. 207; *Nicolae Virgiliu Tănase v. Romania* (Grand Chamber 2019) para. 218.
[17] See, for example, Harris, O'Boyle *et al.* (2018) 754.
[18] See, for example, Frowein and Peukert (2009) 395.

satisfying, for example, the requirements of independence and impartiality, and not offering necessary procedural guarantees, may then improve the initial effectiveness of the remedial task, before the decision is left in the hands of a court.[19] Splitting up the responsibility to provide access to justice, redress, and enforce the redress may also enhance the effectiveness of the remedy. Indeed, the enforcement of remedies is usually always performed by a different authority than the authority determining the substance of the complaint. It may, also, be more effective to split up the task of determining the substance of the complaint and providing redress. Initial proceedings may then concentrate on the question of whether there has been a violation of substance, without complicating the proceedings with a difficult question of (potential) redress.[20]

The first case in which the Court dealt with this principle in some detail was *Leander* v. *Sweden* (1987). The storing and release of personal information, coupled with no possibility to refute the information, violated Article 8. A majority of four against three judges found that an aggregate of four remedies satisfied Article 13: (1) an application for the information, including appeal to the Government; (2) an application to the National Police Board upon the basis of the Freedom of the Press Act, and, if refused, an appeal to the administrative courts; (3) a complaint to the Chancellor of Justice; and (4) a complaint to the Parliamentary Ombudsman. The Parliamentary Ombudsman and the Chancellor of Justice lacked the power to issue legally binding decisions. The Government, on the other hand, could issue a legally binding decision, but was not sufficiently independent. Nonetheless, the Court found the aggregate of remedies effective.[21] Consequently, in order to obtain an effective remedy not only in theory but also in practice, the applicant first had to resort to the Ombudsman or the Chancellor and then, in a second instance, complain to the Government, maybe upon the basis of the decisions taken by the Ombudsman or the Chancellor.[22]

The principle was more strictly applied in *Chahal* v. *the UK* (Grand Chamber 1996). The question was whether judicial review by UK courts in deportation procedures, which could violate Article 3, seen in conjunction

---

[19] See, for example, *Tomov a.o.* v. *Russia* (2019) para. 150.

[20] In a similar manner, many systems of tort law allow for splitting up tort proceedings, for example by first deciding on the question of accountability and, thereafter, if necessary, the question of compensation; see, for example, the Norwegian Act on Civil Procedure 2005 (*tvisteloven*) §§ 1–3 and 16–1(2).

[21] *Leander* v. *Sweden* (1987) paras. 80–84.

[22] Harris, O'Boyle *et al.* (2018) 754 criticize the judgment because the majority did not elaborate on how these four remedies on aggregate would be effective.

with the powers of an advisory panel on aggregate satisfied Article 13. The judicial review was limited to balancing the risk of ill-treatment contrary to Article 3 against interests of national security. However, under Article 3, interests of national security are not a material consideration. Thus, the review did not allow UK courts to deal with the substance of the Convention complaint (Section 10.5.4).[23] And, at the advisory panel, the applicant was not entitled, *inter alia*, to legal representation and only given an outline of the grounds for the notice of intention to deport. Further, the panel had no power of decision, and its advice to the Home Secretary was not binding and not disclosed. Consequently, these remedies did not satisfy the requirements of Article 13 on aggregate.[24]

In *Kudla* v. *Poland* (Grand Chamber 2000), the Court then required the Government to show, in concrete, how the remedies/authorities worked together in order to provide relief. The Government did not indicate whether and, if so, how the applicant could obtain relief – either preventive or compensatory – by having recourse to the remedies, and the Court stressed that the Government did not supply any example from domestic practice, which showed that, by using the means in question, it was possible for the applicant to obtain sufficient relief.[25] Accordingly, the State must now substantiate how the remedies satisfy the requirements of Article 13 on aggregate. Uncertainty, in this regard, is the responsibility of the State.[26]

In more recent case law, the Court has, also, voiced a general skepticism toward two proceedings being employed to determine the substance of a claim (Section 10.5.4). Not only is this less effective, but runs the risk of making the combined duration of the proceedings excessive, especially in cases which already concern excessive length of proceedings. Particular attention should, therefore, be paid to the speediness of the remedial action itself (Section 10.7), so as not to "put an unreasonable burden on the applicant to require him to make use of both remedies." To find the aggregate of the remedies effective in such circumstances would "run counter to the principles and spirit of the Convention."[27] The Court, therefore, mostly considers the flaws of each

---

[23] *Chahal* v. *the UK* (Grand Chamber 1996) paras. 149–153.
[24] Ibid., paras. 154–155.
[25] *Kudla* v. *Poland* (Grand Chamber 2000) para. 158. See, subsequently, concerning excessive length of proceedings, for example, *Lukenda* v. *Slovenia* (2005) paras. 87 and 69; *Sürmeli* v. *Germany* (Grand Chamber 2006) para. 113; *Štokalo a.o.* v. *Croatia* (2008) para. 65, and, more generally, for example, *Bazjaks* v. *Latvia* (2010) para. 129; *M.S.S.* v. *Belgium and Greece* (Grand Chamber 2011) para. 289; *de Souza Ribeiro* v. *France* (Grand Chamber 2012) para. 79.
[26] Compare Harris, O'Boyle *et al.* (2018) 754.
[27] *Lukenda* v. *Slovenia* (2005) paras. 87 and 70.

remedy separately, and, if no explanation is given as to how the aggregate could repair the flaws, Article 13 has been violated.[28]

Further, in cases concerning ineffective investigations in criminal proceedings, the Court has considered whether criminal investigations in combination with new civil proceedings could satisfy Article 13 (Section 11.7). While not excluding that the aggregate may be effective, the Court has, in many cases, held that the civil proceedings are ineffective because the outcome is too dependent on flawed criminal investigations.[29] And *Čonka v. Belgium* (2002), for example, illustrates how an aggregate of remedies could not provide the required automatic suspensive effect (Section 11.3.2).

In short, even though an aggregate of proceedings, in principle, still may satisfy Article 13, the Court looks at the cumulative effect more strictly.[30] That being said, there are still cases in which the Court may find an aggregate of procedures justified.[31] And, at least in one case, the Court has accepted that the applicant's choices may influence the assessment.[32]

9.4 EFFECTIVE IN PRACTICE AS WELL AS IN LAW

The Convention shall "guarantee rights that are not theoretical or illusory, but practical and effective".[33] This general principle is applied to every right in the Convention, but with slightly different expressions in different contexts. For instance, effective investigations under Article 2 must "secure accountability in practice as well as theory",[34] and the existence of remedies to be exhausted under Article 35(1) "must be sufficiently certain not only in theory but also in practice",[35] or "available in theory and practice at the relevant time".[36]

---

[28] See, for example, *Hartman v. the Czech Republic* (2003) paras. 81–84; *Bazjaks v. Latvia* (2010) para. 136; *Ananyev a.o. v. Russia* (2012) paras. 100–119; *A.K. v. Liechtenstein (no. 2)* (2016) paras. 89–102; *Balogh a.o. v. Slovakia* (2018) para. 57.

[29] See, for example, *Menesheva v. Russia* (2006) paras. 74–76; *Cobzaru v. Romania* (2007) para. 83.

[30] Similarly, Mowbray (2004) 208. Harris, O'Boyle *et al.* (2018) 754 hold that the concept made sense in earlier years, when not all States had incorporated the Convention, but is harder to justify today.

[31] See, for example, *Grzinčič v. Slovenia* (2007) para. 98; *Giuliani and Gaggio v. Italy* (Grand Chamber 2011) paras. 336–337.

[32] *Maksimov v. Russia* (2010) para. 67. But compare the dissenting opinion of Judges Spielmann and Malinverni.

[33] See, for example, *Airey v. Ireland* (1979) para. 24; *Scordino v. Italy (no. 1)* (Grand Chamber 2006) para. 192; *Nada v. Switzerland* (Grand Chamber 2012) para. 195.

[34] See, for example, *Shanaghan v. the UK* (2001) para. 92.

[35] See, for example, *Assanidze v. Georgia* (Grand Chamber 2004) para. 127.

[36] See, for example, *Akdivar a.o. v. Turkey* (Grand Chamber 1996) para. 68.

Also under Article 13, the Court uses different expressions to breathe life into the general principle. The expression most commonly used, and the one first applied directly under Article 13, is that the remedy "must be effective in practice as well as in law".[37] More often than not, albeit not always, the Court adds that this implies, in particular, that the remedy must "not be unjustifiably hindered by acts or omissions of the authorities". However, sometimes, the Court simply refers to the assessment under Article 35(1),[38] the application under Article 35(1),[39] or repeats the same wording as under Article 35(1), for instance, that the remedies must be sufficiently certain not only in theory but also in practice.[40] Occasionally, the Court uses slightly different expressions, for instance, that the effect of the law "appears to be limited in practice",[41] that "the absence of any case-law does indicate the uncertainty of this remedy in practice",[42] that the remedy must be effective and accessible both in theory and in practice,[43] that the remedy cannot be considered effective both in theory and in practice,[44] or simply that the remedy must be effective in practice as well as in theory.[45] Even though different expressions are used, there seems to be no difference in substance. The point is that the remedy must not only be effective in theory but also in practice.

The requirement was established directly under Article 13 in *Aksoy v. Turkey* (1996), which was the first of a string of cases against Turkey concerning ineffective investigations. Investigations that are not effective in practice have, thereafter, revealed itself as a problem in cases against many different States (Section 11.7). Indeed, ineffective investigations often render any remedy ineffective. Without effective investigations (performed by the authorities), it may, for example, be virtually impossible to establish the facts necessary to make other remedies effective.[46]

Many remedies against conditions of detention have, also, in recent years, been found ineffective in practice, *inter alia*, in many cases against Russia,[47]

---

[37] See, for example, *Aksoy v. Turkey* (1996) para. 95; *Kudla v. Poland* (Grand Chamber 2000) para. 157; *Vilho Eskelinen a.o. v. Finland* (Grand Chamber 2007) para. 80; *Nada v. Switzerland* (Grand Chamber 2012) para. 207; *Khlaifia a.o. v. Italy* (Grand Chamber 2016) para. 268.

[38] For example, *Horvat v. Croatia* (2001) para. 65.

[39] For example, *Rodić and 3 Others v. Bosnia and Herzegovina* (2008) para. 85.

[40] For example, *Cyprus v. Turkey* (Grand Chamber 2001) para. 323.

[41] For example, *Volokhy v. Ukraine* (2006) para. 59.

[42] For example, *Gjonbocari a.o. v. Albania* (2007) para. 80.

[43] For example, *Vlasov v. Russia* (2008) para. 153.

[44] For example, *Burdov v. Russia (no. 2)* (2009) para. 116.

[45] For example, *Yepishin v. Russia* (2013) para. 56.

[46] *Aksoy v. Turkey* (1996) para. 99 is illustrative.

[47] For example, *Gubin v. Russia* (2010).

Moldova,[48] Slovenia (in particular, overcrowding),[49] Bulgaria,[50] Greece,[51] and Turkey.[52] In several of these cases, the remedies were effective in theory, but rendered ineffective by various acts and omissions of the authorities.[53]

The requirement has, also, been applied in a number of cases concerning excessive length of proceedings which, arguably, violate Article 6(1), in which *Kudla* v. *Poland* (Grand Chamber 2000) was the first. A remedy is ineffective in practice if excessively lengthy proceedings simply are pending without any decision or possibility of speeding up the case.[54] And if the reason for the excessive length of proceedings lies in procedural steps awaiting decision, the fact that these procedural steps may be challenged is not decisive if such challenges lead to further delays and the overall delay is never acknowledged or compensated.[55] Further, if the remedial authority is not able to take all periods into account,[56] the remedy is not effective in practice. Nor is a separate claim for damages effective if these proceedings are excessively long, or if the Government is not able to show that such proceedings could have been speedier.[57] Similarly, if an action to speed up proceedings is taken too late, the remedy is not effective in practice.[58]

In cases concerning nonenforcement or excessively long enforcement of judgments which, arguably, violate Article 6(1),[59] and also in many cases concerning P1 Article 1,[60] a compensatory remedy is not effective in practice if the State blatantly ignores or chooses not to pay the compensation awarded by domestic courts,[61] or omits to complement the remedy with the necessary budgetary measures.[62] More generally, if the State refuses to take the necessary steps to enforce the binding decision of the remedial authority, the remedy is not effective in practice.[63] And even though a specific procedure to

---

[48] For example, *Rotaru* v. *Moldova* (2011).
[49] For example, *Mandić and Jović* v. *Slovenia* (2011).
[50] For example, *Iordan Petrov* v. *Bulgaria* (2012).
[51] For example, *Mahmundi a.o.* v. *Greece* (2012).
[52] For example, *Yarashonen* v. *Turkey* (2014).
[53] For example, *Keenan* v. *the UK* (2001); *Dankevich* v. *Ukraine* (2003); *Ramirez Sanchez* v. *France* (Grand Chamber 2006).
[54] See, for example, *Rajak* v. *Croatia* (2001); *Dimitrov* v. *Bulgaria* (2004).
[55] See, for example, *Efimenko* v. *Ukraine* (2006) para. 64.
[56] See, for example, *Rutkowski a.o.* v. *Poland* (2015) paras. 180–181.
[57] See, for example, *V.A.M.* v. *Serbia* (2007) paras. 154 and 86.
[58] See, for example, *Vilho Eskelinen a.o.* v. *Finland* (Grand Chamber 2007) para. 82.
[59] See, for example, *Iza Ltd and Makrakhidze* v. *Georgia* (2005).
[60] See, for example, *Driza* v. *Albania* (2007).
[61] See, for example, *Iatridis* v. *Greece* (Grand Chamber 1999) para. 66.
[62] See, for example, *Voytenko* v. *Ukraine* (2004) paras. 48 and 30.
[63] See, for example, *Hasan and Chaush* v. *Bulgaria* (Grand Chamber 2000) para. 101.

enforce judgments against the State exists, the procedure may be ineffective if it is unclear who is responsible for the execution and enforcement of the judgment. This uncertainty may, for instance, be caused by a lack of clear jurisprudence in combination with a lack of administrative bodies which can determine who is responsible for the execution.[64]

A number of remedies have been found ineffective in practice in cases concerning expulsions and extraditions which, arguably, violate Article 2,[65] Article 3,[66] and Article 8.[67] *I.M.* v. *France* (2012), for example, illustrates how several different acts and omissions by the authorities may render the remedy ineffective in practice, for instance, automatic classification in procedures dealing with the complaint in a more summary and speedy manner than usual, the time available for making complaints, and the practical difficulties in presenting and collecting evidence due to the fact that the applicant was in detention facilities. *M.E.* v. *France* (2013) further illustrates that the assessment of the Court is very concrete. The same asylum procedures as in *I.M.* v. *France* (2012) were now effective in practice, in particular, because the behavior of the applicant was taken into account, most notably, his delayed complaint and the fact that he actually received the possibility of presenting evidence.[68]

In cases concerning interference with correspondence, which, arguably, violate Article 8, in particular, that of a prisoner,[69] a remedy granting the possibility of demanding the return of seized correspondence is ineffective in practice if the items have disappeared.[70] And if every complaint of censorship of prisoner correspondence has to be sent through prison authorities, the applicant may have legitimate fears of repercussions or sanctions that render an otherwise effective remedy ineffective.[71] *Messina* v. *Italy (no. 2)* (2000) illustrates that judicial review of decisions restricting correspondence and family visits which, arguably, violate Article 8 may be effective, but is ineffective in practice if new administrative decisions are always being introduced and administrative authorities are not bound by court decisions with regard to the previous measures.[72]

If compensation for nonpecuniary damage is required in order to achieve sufficient redress (Section 11.5.2), domestic courts cannot exclude evidence that

---

[64] See, for example, *Stoyanov and Tabakov* v. *Bulgaria* (2013) paras. 96–98.
[65] See, for example, *A.D. a.o.* v. *Turkey* (2014).
[66] See, for example, *Čonka* v. *Belgium* (2002).
[67] See, for example, *de Souza Ribeiro* v. *France* (Grand Chamber 2012).
[68] See, also, *M.V. and M.T.* v. *France* (2014) and *R.D.* v. *France* (2016).
[69] See, for example, *A.B.* v. *the Netherlands* (2002).
[70] See, for example, *Krasimir Yordanov* v. *Bulgaria* (2007) para. 52.
[71] See, for example, *Mikadze* v. *Russia* (2007) paras. 84–86.
[72] *Messina* v. *Italy (no. 2)* (2000) paras. 84–97.

is clearly relevant in determining the extent of nonpecuniary compensation.[73] A claim for compensation may, also, be rendered ineffective in practice through the destruction of evidence by the authorities, for instance, a case file.[74] And even if the substance is tried (Section 10.5.4) and sufficient compensation or redress is, in principle, provided, the remedy may be ineffective in practice, through, for instance, excessive court fees.[75]

A remedy is also ineffective in practice if the applicant is not properly informed of the remedy or prerequisites for making use of the remedy (Section 10.3.4), in particular, if the applicant is in a vulnerable position, if, for other reasons, it cannot be expected that he/she will collect the information himself/herself,[76] if he/she is misguided by the authorities concerning the use of the remedy,[77] or if there is not sufficient transparency in the procedures or time to avail oneself of the procedures, and, if necessary, to summon lawyers.[78]

Further, if a change of practice by, for example, a Constitutional Court is not taken into account by lower courts, the remedy may be rendered ineffective in practice.[79] Jurisdictional conflicts may, also, render a remedy ineffective in practice, in particular, if all jurisdictions refuse to deal with the case.[80] But there need not be a general conflict of jurisdiction. The fact that the domestic court which is clearly competent to deal with the case declines jurisdiction may, for example, render the remedy ineffective in practice.[81]

Many of the areas mentioned above, and in which the Court mostly has applied this requirement, concern domestic structural and repetitive problems, which produce many applications to the Court. This, and the manner in which the Court, in concrete, applies the requirement raises the question whether it is relevant that the acts or omissions are systemic and repetitive? Must the remedy be generally ineffective, or may more isolated acts or omissions render the remedy ineffective in practice? This question is, also, of significance for the relationship between the requirement that the remedy be effective in practice (this chapter) and the principle that the prospect of success is not decisive, as long as the remedial authority is able to deal with

---

[73] See, for example, *Iovchev v. Bulgaria* (2006) para. 146.
[74] See, for example, *Tastan v. Turkey* (2008) paras. 33 and 20.
[75] See, for example, *Slavcho Kostov v. Bulgaria* (2008) paras. 62–66.
[76] See, for example, *Mikadze v. Russia* (2007) para. 78.
[77] See, for example, *Dankevich v. Ukraine* (2003) paras. 170 and 109–110.
[78] See, for example, *Shamayev a.o. v. Georgia and Russia* (2005) para. 459.
[79] See, for example, *Vlasov v. Russia* (2008) paras. 52–55.
[80] See, for example, *Mosendz v. Ukraine* (2013) para. 124.
[81] See, for example, *Štitić v. Croatia* (2007) para. 86.

the substance of the complaint and grant appropriate relief (Section 10.6). A general expression of this relationship is found in *Onoufriou v. Cyprus* (2010):

> Although a remedy, in order to be considered "effective," is not required to lead to a favourable outcome for the applicant, it is necessary that the authorities take the positive measures required in the circumstances to ensure that the applicant's complaints are properly dealt with and that the remedy is effective in practice ... .[82]

The stricter the application of the requirement that the remedy must be effective in practice, the more the Court goes in the direction of demanding certainty of success. That, again, has the consequences that the review of domestic remedial authorities must be more similar to that of the Court and that redress actually must be provided for the remedy to be effective (Sections 10.5.4 and 10.6).

The reasoning of the Court concerning these relationships is not very explicit. It is, therefore, difficult to establish how and where to draw the line and balance between these requirements and principles.

In my opinion, the prospect of success must be one of the several elements when considering whether the remedy is effective in practice. In such an assessment, weight could be attached to whether acts or omissions are systemic and/or repetitive. But many of the cases cited above do not concern systemic and repetitive mistakes. And, in several cases, the remedy is considered effective in practice even though the Court identifies practices which cause many cases to arrive at the Court. The most prominent example is cases in which the amount of compensation awarded at domestic level for excessive length of proceedings is insufficient as redress (Section 11.5),[83] but in which the domestic remedial authority could, in principle, have awarded a sufficient amount.[84] By contrast, in a string of cases against, for example, Poland, in which domestic legislation governing the excessive length of proceedings was, in theory, effective, the practice of domestic courts rendered the remedy ineffective because, for instance, the totality of the excessive length of proceedings was not taken into account,[85] no compensation for nonpecuniary

---

[82] See, for example, *Onoufriou v. Cyprus* (2010) para. 129.

[83] Similarly, in many repetitive cases requiring compensation for violations of P1 Article 1, it has been deemed sufficient that the remedial authority could, in theory, provide an adequate amount of compensation; see, for example, *Gera de Petri Testaferrata Bonici Ghaxaq v. Malta* (2011) paras. 68–69.

[84] See, however, in contrast, for example, *Velkova v. Bulgaria* (2017) paras. 50–53; *Balogh a.o. v. Slovakia* (2018) para. 66; *Galea and Pavia v. Malta* (2020) paras. 62–64.

[85] See, for example, *Tur v. Poland* (2007) para. 67 and *Krawczak v. Poland* (2008) para. 39 and compare, for example, *Christensen v. Denmark* (2009) para. 104, which concerned a more isolated incident.

damage was given (in combination with no justification by domestic courts as to why),[86] because domestic courts clearly made a wrong judgment with regard to whether the proceedings were excessive or not,[87] or because it was not clear which periods were taken into account and what method of calculation the domestic courts had used.[88] Similarly, with regard to the possibility of speeding up administrative proceedings which may become excessively long, the Polish Supreme Administrative Court was, in principle, an effective remedy, but because its judgments were not followed in practice, the remedy was not effective.[89] In addition, the case of *Sorvisto* v. *Finland* (2009) shows how the reduction of a sentence in one set of criminal proceedings may render a remedy effective, whereas the refusal to reduce the sentence in another renders the remedy ineffective in practice.[90]

Moreover, concerning the level of compensation awarded because of conditions of detention which violate Article 3 (Section 11.5.3), the fact that sufficient compensation was not awarded, even though the remedial authority in principle could award it, has led to violations of Article 13. In several cases against Estonia, for example, the Court has recognized that domestic courts could have awarded sufficient compensation, but that the interpretation of domestic law in individual cases, for instance, by demanding fault on the part of the authorities, has excluded the possibility with the consequence that Article 13 was not effective in practice.[91]

Further, in cases concerning whether the remedial authority is able to deal with the substance of the complaint (Section 10.5.4), the remedy may not be effective in practice, for instance, because a complaint has been declared inadmissible or because domestic courts blatantly refuse to examine the allegations of, for example, the risk of torture,[92] even though the authority could, in theory, deal with the complaint.[93] However, in other cases, even though the domestic complaint is declared inadmissible, and the substance is not dealt with, the remedy is considered effective, since the domestic remedial authority was, in principle, able to deal with the complaint.[94]

---

[86] See, for example, *Zwoźniak* v. *Poland* (2007) para. 53.
[87] See, for example, *Swat* v. *Poland* (2007) para. 44.
[88] See, for example, *Wasserman* v. *Russia (no. 2)* (2008) para. 56.
[89] See, for example, *Wesołowska* v. *Poland* (2008) para. 81. Similarly, for example, *Bara and Kola* v. *Albania* (2021) para. 123.
[90] See, for example, *Sorvisto* v. *Finland* (2009) paras. 6–14, 33–43 and 89.
[91] See, for example, *Kochetkov* v. *Estonia* (2009) para. 59.
[92] See, for example, *Tershiyev* v. *Azerbaijan* (2014) para. 72.
[93] See, for example, *Debelić* v. *Croatia* (2005) paras. 45–46; *Dikaiou a.o.* v. *Greece* (2020) para. 69.
[94] See, for example, *Peter* v. *Germany* (2014) para. 57.

Although the case law reveals an unclear picture, *Aslakhanova* v. *Russia* (2012), concerning effective investigations, at the very least, shows that the systemic nature and repeated practice of acts and omissions serve as evidence for the ineffectiveness of the remedy (in practice) in new cases.[95] More generally, in case of ambiguity with regard to the effectiveness of the remedy in practice, be it because of a systemic problem or other reasons, the Court may demand more evidence regarding the effectiveness of the remedy.[96] On the other hand, the Court generally underlines that its role is not to analyze practices and legislation in the abstract. But, to the extent that legislation and practices shed light on and serve as evidence for the individual violation in question, such practices and legislation will be examined.[97]

M.S.S. v. *Belgium and Greece* (Grand Chamber 2011) further illustrates how the Court attaches weight to both systemic concerns and individual problems in concrete cases when determining whether the remedy is effective in practice.[98] The case concerned expulsions which, arguably, violated Articles 2 and 3. The Greek legislation on asylum procedures was, in theory, effective, but the procedure was marked by "major structural deficiencies". Asylum-seekers, therefore, generally had very little chance, in practice, of having their applications and their complaints under the Convention seriously examined. Such concerns related, *inter alia*, to insufficient information, difficult access to the Attica police headquarters, no reliable system of communication between the authorities and the asylum-seekers, shortage of interpreters and lack of training for the staff responsible for conducting the individual interviews, lack of legal aid, effectively depriving the asylum-seekers of legal counsel, and excessively lengthy delays in receiving a decision. The Court also pointed out that almost all first-instance decisions were negative and drafted in a stereotyped manner without any details of the reasons for the decisions being given. The Court then considered the individual case, under which it attached more weight to the applicant's version, *inter alia*, due to the fact that it was supported by the evidence of the systemic errors.[99]

Nonetheless, to what extent systemic mistakes (a practice) are required, or to what extent more isolated mistakes may render the remedy ineffective in practice is difficult to say, based upon the Court's case law, and would benefit from clarification.

---

[95] *Aslakhanova* v. *Russia* (2012) paras. 153–154.
[96] See, for example, *Yarashonen* v. *Turkey* (2014) paras. 64–65.
[97] See, for example, *Etxeberria a.o.* v. *Spain* (2009) para. 81.
[98] See, also, for example, *Beizaras and Levickas* v. *Lithuania* (2020) paras. 151–156.
[99] M.S.S. v. *Belgium and Greece* (Grand Chamber 2011) paras. 299–320.

10

Access to Justice

10.1 INTRODUCTION

To what extent the requirements arising from Article 13 are analyzed from the angle of access to justice, redress, or as collective and overarching requirements may depend on the subject matter which one seeks to underline. Many questions analyzed in the next chapter on redress could have been dealt with in this chapter on access to justice and *vice versa*. The most notable examples are the requirements of effective investigations (Section 11.7) and requirements that seek to prevent violations (Section 11.3), which are analyzed in the chapter on redress because I wish to underline their function as redress, as such. This, however, must not detract from the fact that such requirements promote both access to justice and redress, as part of the collective enterprise to achieve one effective remedy.

10.2 THE NATIONAL AUTHORITY

The national remedial authorities need not necessarily be judicial authorities or courts, but, if not, the powers and procedural guarantees that the authorities possess are relevant in determining whether the remedy is effective.[1]

---

[1] See, for example, *Klass a.o. v. Germany* (Plenary 1978) para. 67; *Silver a.o. v. the UK* (1983) para. 113; *Rotaru v. Romania* (Grand Chamber 2000) para. 69; *Mugemangango v. Belgium* (Grand Chamber 2020) para. 137. In contrast, Article 8 of the UDHR, Article 25 of the ACHR, the EU Charter on fundamental rights Article 47, and Principle 12 of the Van Boven/Bassiouni principles, all require remedies by domestic courts and/or tribunals. Article 2(3) of the ICCPR, however, only requires an effective remedy "by competent judicial, administrative or legislative authorities, or by any other competent authority provided for by the legal system of the State", but obliges States "to develop the possibilities of judicial remedy". See, also, Section 4.2.

Some claim that the further the procedures and practices of a nonjudicial authority depart from those of a court, the more likely it is that the authority does not satisfy the requirements of an effective remedy.[2] However, what works in one situation is not necessarily adequate in another, and the remedial task in relation to different violations and situations may vary greatly. An administrative authority, which works close to the possible violations, for instance, an independent prison authority set up to deal with surveillance and complaints about conditions of detention, may, in practice, work better than a court, at least as an authority that can deal speedily with an initial complaint to which it is possible to appeal to a court.[3] If this is so, an aggregate of remedies may best satisfy Article 13 (Section 9.3). That being said, the procedural guarantees and powers offered by courts and tribunals are usually best suited to deal with the determination of both civil rights and obligations and penal cases.[4] Further, depending on the violation and the situation, a judicial remedy may be necessary. For instance, in cases concerning solitary confinement and disciplinary isolation, an effective remedy before a judicial body is essential due to the serious consequences which such isolation may have on the applicant.[5] In other cases, the Court leaves the question open,[6] or it remains unclear if a judicial remedy actually is required.[7] But, the authority or authorities, in any event, need to provide the necessary procedural safeguards (Section 10.3), possess the powers to grant sufficient relief (Sections 10.4 and 11), and deal with the substance of the relevant Convention complaint with sufficient speed (Sections 10.5 and 10.7). Depending on the domestic circumstances, such requirements may, in practice, only be fulfilled by domestic courts or tribunals, in particular because the Court looks at the aggregate of remedies in a stricter manner (Section 9.3).

Further, even if a judicial remedy is required, something more, or something else, may be needed. Depending on the circumstances, a court may, for instance, not be able to deliver the required redress. Domestic courts may, for example, only be empowered to declare an administrative act illegal, even though additional redress, for example compensation, is required.

---

2 See, for example, Mowbray (2004) 207.
3 The authority must, however, be independent from the prison authority that makes the decisions on detention; see, for example, *Ananyev a.o. v. Russia* (2012) paras. 100–101; *Dikaiou a.o. v. Greece* (2020) para. 66.
4 This, also, underlies Article 6(1) of the ECHR. See, also, for example, David (2014) 264.
5 See, for example, *Ramirez Sanchez v. France* (Grand Chamber 2006) para. 165.
6 See, for example, *Z a.o. v. the UK* (Grand Chamber 2001) para. 110; *İrfan Güzel v. Turkey* (2017) para. 96.
7 See, for example, *Sabanchiyeva a.o. v. Russia* (2013) paras. 154–155; *Arkhestov v. Russia* (2014) paras. 110–111; *de Tommaso v. Italy* (Grand Chamber 2017) para. 182.

10.3 PROCEDURAL SAFEGUARDS

10.3.1 *Article 13 and Procedural Safeguards under Substantive Articles*

In recent years, a proceduralization of substantive Convention rights has taken place in the Court's case law.[8] This chapter provides an overview of the explicit procedural safeguards arising from Article 13, including their relationship to procedural safeguards under substantive Articles, in particular Article 6(1).[9] The domestic review required by Article 13 is analyzed in Section 10.5.

The procedural requirements arising under substantive Articles, most notably Article 6, may point to what is required under Article 13. The fact that, in many cases, the Court considers it unnecessary to examine whether Article 13 has been violated (Sections 4.3 and 4.5.2) does not mean that Article 13 was not violated, only that, under the circumstances, it was not necessary to consider whether Article 13 also was violated. Indeed, under Article 13, the Court holds, more generally, that the requirements of Article 6 "may be relevant" and, as a general rule, that "the fundamental criterion of fairness, including the equality of arms, is a constituent element of an effective remedy".[10] That being said, the Court's assessment under Article 13, as such, is rarely linked to general and abstract criteria such as fairness and equality of arms, the reasoning mostly being very case-specific. On the other hand, when the Court holds that Article 6 is *lex specialis*, it mostly adds that the procedural guarantees provided by Article 13 are less stringent (Section 4.5.2) or that Article 13 does not impose the same obligations because to hold otherwise would be tantamount to extending the scope of Article 6 beyond disputes concerning civil rights and obligations and a criminal charge.[11] Accordingly, not every procedural shortcoming that violates Article 6(1) should result in the ineffectiveness of a remedy under Article 13. But based upon the case law, it is difficult to say where the differences lie. Indeed, procedural concerns are mostly only dealt with under Article 13 in cases which fall outside the scope of Article 6(1), typically certain administrative proceedings, for example, asylum, immigration, and expulsion.[12] And when the Court deals with procedural safeguards under Article 13, it does not compare and contrast them with the safeguards arising under Article 6(1), or other

---

[8] See Section 13.2.
[9] See, also, Sections 3.3, 4.4, 4.5, and 13.2.
[10] See, for example, *Csüllög* v. *Hungary* (2011) para. 46; *G.R.* v. *the Netherlands* (2012) para. 50.
[11] See, for example, *Communist Party of Russia a.o.* v. *Russia* (2012) paras. 84–85.
[12] See, for example, *Maaouia* v. *France* (Grand Chamber 2000) paras. 36–38.

substantive Articles for that sake. Further, a comparison based on the facts of cases would only shed light on how procedural requirements under Article 13 are "less strict" when the Court actually finds no violation of Article 13 and at the same time a violation of Article 6(1) – an exercise which the Court currently does not perform (Section 4.5.2).

Moreover, even though the Court generally underlines that the requirements of Article 13 are "less strict", the procedural requirements under Article 13 may, in some cases, need be stricter, or, at least, different. Indeed, the procedures and guarantees necessary to achieve redress may need to be different and/or stricter than procedures that only aim to provide access to justice. Lack of speed may, for instance, undermine the necessary redress although access to justice is, in principle, provided. Further, some procedural requirements may be necessary not only to achieve access to justice, but as a form of redress, as such. The most notable examples are the requirements of effective investigations and various requirements aiming at preventing substantive violations (Sections 11.5 and 11.7). In these cases, the relationship between Article 13 and similar requirements arising under substantive Articles becomes particularly difficult. Indeed, although the requirements are similar, they may serve different purposes (Section 4.4). This may be important to underline, as such, but, also, lead to differences in the concrete application of the requirements. To what extent, for instance, is it necessary to investigate in order to protect the right to life as part of the positive obligation arising under Article 2 and/or to correct injustice and establish the truth about the violation?

The subchapters below provide examples of areas and cases in which procedural safeguards have been decisive under Article 13, as such. These cases demonstrate that procedural requirements and safeguards have independent and autonomous meaning under Article 13.[13] For such autonomous procedural requirements, which may be more difficult to perceive as a form of redress, as such, it may be of lesser importance whether the requirements are set out only under substantive Articles and/or under Article 13 in conjunction with substantive Articles. The added value in finding a violation of also Article 13, in such cases, consists in underlining requirements which are specifically important for providing redress, but which could, in principle, be stricter or different than similar requirements arising under substantive Articles.

Against this background, the examples below must not be read as an exhaustive list, but considered in light of the procedural requirements under

[13] See, more generally, for example, *Stamose* v. *Bulgaria* (2012) para. 49; *de Souza Ribeiro* v. *France* (Grand Chamber 2012) para. 83; *Reshetnyak* v. *Russia* (2013) para. 63.

substantive Articles, most notably Article 6(1), and the fact that the Court now more often actually considers whether Article 13 has been violated in addition to substantive Articles (Section 4.3).

10.3.2 *Impartiality and Independence*

In Article 6(1), independence and impartiality are explicitly required by the wording of the first sentence. Also under Article 13, the Court has found several violations because the domestic authority did not possess sufficient impartiality and/or independence.[14]

Independence and impartiality are different, but interrelated concepts. Independence primarily refers to the lack of connection, in particular, freedom of influence, from some other person or entity. It is particularly important that the national authority be independent from other powers of State, in particular, the Government and the legislator.[15] Impartiality implies that the decisions of the authority are not biased or prejudiced by irrelevant concerns or interests, both private and public.[16] Thus, whereas independence is more directed at the lack of a formal connection between the authority and other entities, impartiality is more directed at the actual influence on decisions. Accordingly, there may be a lack of independence, even though the actual decision is not affected by irrelevant concerns or unduly influenced by other actors.

Under the heading of independence, the Court has, under Article 6(1), considered, *inter alia*, the manner of the appointment of the members of the authority and their term of office, the existence of guarantees against outside pressure, and whether the body presents an appearance of independence.[17] With regard to impartiality, the Court has, under Article 6(1), distinguished between a subjective test, which seeks to establish the personal conviction of a judge in a given case, and an objective test, which aims at ascertaining whether the judge offers guarantees sufficient to exclude any legitimate doubt as to his/her impartiality.[18] Elements considered under the heading of impartiality include, *inter alia*, whether the members of the court in question have been employed by the parties or have had similar connection to the parties or

[14] The importance of impartiality in relation to Article 13 was emphasized during the drafting; see, for example, the CETP Volume IV 30.
[15] See, for example, Harris, O'Boyle *et al.* (2018) 448–451.
[16] See, for example, Harris, O'Boyle *et al.* (2018) 451; Dijk, Hoof *et al.* (2018) 602.
[17] See, for example, *Langborger v. Sweden* (Plenary 1989) para. 32.
[18] See, for example, *Langborger v. Sweden* (Plenary 1989) para. 32; Harris, O'Boyle *et al.* (2018) 451–456; Dijk, Hoof *et al.* (2018) 603–604.

other interests in the process, have previously participated in the process, for instance, as a member of the prosecuting authority or as a *juge d'instruction*, or have previously made decisions that can be understood as saying that they have taken a stand on the actual question in hand.[19] The rationale behind the requirements of independence and impartiality is that the authority must base its opinion on objective arguments and not be biased by the influence of other actors. Both independence and impartiality thus require "sufficient protection against the abuse of authority".[20] The borderline between independence and impartiality may, therefore, be unclear.[21] Indeed, often, the Court does not distinguish explicitly between the concepts and engages in a more collective evaluation under which it is difficult to affiliate the different elements to one concept or the other.[22]

Most of the cases under Article 13 have been analyzed under the heading of independence. The first case was *Silver* v. *the UK* (1983). Stopping of the correspondence of prisoners violated Article 8. A complaint to the Home Secretary would, in some circumstances, satisfy the independence required by Article 13, but, in others, not.[23] The judgment illustrates two aspects of the independence required by Article 13.

First, the authority cannot be judge in its own cause. But there is a fine line between being judge in its own cause and being independent. Indeed, the Home Secretary was the author of the directives under which the control of correspondence was carried out by the prison authorities. In a complaint against the legality of the directives, the Home Secretary was the judge in his/her own cause. But, in a complaint against the misapplication of these directives, the Home Secretary was not the judge in his/her own cause. However, many cases of application could, in principle, concern questions of the scope and validity of the directives, as such. Indeed, in many later cases, Article 13 was violated because the remedial authority in reality was the judge in its own cause.[24] An example can be found in *Domenichini* v. *Italy* (1996). The decisions to inspect and censor prisoners' letters were taken by the judge responsible for the execution of judgments, which took place in administrative proceedings. The possibility of applying to the same judge responsible for the execution of sentences was not an effective remedy, since the judge

---

[19] See, for example, Harris, O'Boyle *et al.* (2018) 451–458.
[20] See, for example, *Khan* v. *the UK* (2000) para. 47.
[21] Compare, for example, Dijk, Hoof *et al.* (2018) 599.
[22] See, for example, *Langborger* v. *Sweden* (Plenary 1989) paras. 32–36.
[23] *Silver a.o.* v. *the UK* (1983) para. 116.
[24] See, for example, *Khan* v. *the UK* (2000) paras. 45–47; *P.G. and J.H.* v. *the UK* (2001) paras. 87–88; *Kayasu* v. *Turkey (no. 1)* (2008) para. 121; *Özpınar* v. *Turkey* (2010) para. 85.

was required to reconsider the merits of his/her previous decision without any adversarial proceedings.[25] Further, in cases concerning effective remedies against excessive length of proceedings, the complaint cannot be dealt with by the same court which caused the excessive length of the proceedings.[26] And, in cases concerning conditions of detention, prison authorities are often not sufficiently independent from the entities which directly decide upon the conditions of detention.[27]

Second, whereas independence under Article 6(1) requires strict institutional independence, the authority required by Article 13 may be institutionally linked to the Government and/or the legislator, such as the complaint to the Home Secretary, without necessarily rendering the remedy ineffective. But the authority must not be judge in its own cause, and there can be no institutional linkages to the branch or entity actually causing the violation, or to other directly interested parties.[28]

One of few examples in which the Court refers explicitly to impartiality, under Article 13, can be found in a number of cases against Ukraine concerning excessive length of proceedings in criminal cases. The leading case is *Merit* v. *Ukraine* (2004). The main question was whether a complaint to a superior prosecutor was an effective remedy. Ukraine had different prosecutorial levels, and the superior prosecutor did not participate directly in the proceedings in hand. But although the prosecutor acted as a guardian of public interests, he was also a party to the criminal proceedings. Recourse to the superior prosecutor was, therefore, not an effective remedy, since he did not offer adequate safeguards for an independent and impartial review of the applicant's complaints.[29]

10.3.3 *Burden of Proof, Facts, and Evidence*

This subchapter analyzes what Article 13 requires with regard to the examination of facts by domestic remedial authorities. However, this question cannot be completely separated from how the Court examines questions of facts and evidence in their own cases. Seen from the point of view of subsidiarity, domestic remedial authorities, at the very least, need to have the same competences

---

[25] *Domenichini* v. *Italy* (1996) paras. 40–42.
[26] See, for example, *Klyakhin* v. *Russia* (2004) para. 101.
[27] See, for example, *Ananyev a.o.* v. *Russia* (2012) paras. 100–101.
[28] See, for example, *Khan* v. *the UK* (2000) paras. 45–47; *P.G. and J.H.* v. *the UK* (2001) paras. 87–88.
[29] *Merit* v. *Ukraine* (2004) paras. 78 and 62–63.

to examine facts and evidences as the Court. I, therefore, first look at how the Court examines facts and evidence both more generally and specifically with regard to alleged violations of Article 13, before I analyze what the Court has required by domestic remedial authorities under Article 13.

When the Court considers whether the Convention has been violated, States are usually afforded a wide margin of appreciation in the selection and assessment of evidence. Indeed, the Court applies a standard of proof beyond reasonable doubt, under which departure from factual findings in domestic procedures has to be proved beyond reasonable doubt. This starting-point is an expression of subsidiarity and the fourth instance doctrine.[30] However, the Court may reconsider facts, and the burden of proof may shift, depending on the circumstances. There are, for instance, no procedural barriers to the admissibility of new evidence. But the circumstances of the case must render it "unavoidable". Therefore, under normal circumstances, the Court requires "cogent elements to lead it to depart from the findings of fact reached by the domestic courts".[31] However, it has not been the purpose to borrow the approach of proof beyond reasonable doubt in national penal systems. In fact,

> the level of persuasion necessary for reaching a particular conclusion and the distribution of the burden of proof, are intrinsically linked to the specificity of the facts, the nature of the allegation made and the Convention right at stake. The Court is also attentive to the seriousness that attaches to a ruling that a Contracting State has violated fundamental rights.[32]

As a consequence, particularly in cases concerning Articles 2, 3, and 5, the Court has given detailed considerations of the facts of the case, shifted the burden of proof, and reached different factual conclusions than in the domestic proceedings.[33]

More generally, where the events at issue lie wholly, or in large part, within the exclusive knowledge of the authorities, the burden of proof may be placed on the authorities. For instance, in the case of persons in their custody, strong presumptions of fact will arise in respect of injuries and death occurring during such detention. The burden of proof may, then, be said to rest on the authorities to provide a satisfactory and convincing explanation.[34]

---

[30] See, for example, *Varnava a.o.* v. *Turkey* (Grand Chamber 2009) para. 164.
[31] *Austin a.o.* v. *the* UK (Grand Chamber 2012) para. 61.
[32] *El-Masri* v. *FYROM* (Grand Chamber 2012) para. 151.
[33] See, for an overview, for example, *El-Masri* v. *FYROM* (Grand Chamber 2012) paras. 152–167, and, as more recent examples, *Abu Zubaydah* v. *Lithuania* (2018) and *Al Nashiri* v. *Romania* (2018).
[34] See, for example, *Avşar* v. *Turkey* (2001) para. 392; *Zelilof* v. *Greece* (2007) paras. 44 and 45.

With regard to the Court's examination of facts of relevance for the assessment of whether Article 13, specifically, is violated, the Court sometimes refers to the same starting-points as under Article 35(1).[35] For instance, the Court may hold that the Government must convince the Court that the complaint is effective and accessible not only in theory but also in practice. However, once this is done, it is for the applicant to establish that the remedy has been applied, that the remedy is not effective in the particular circumstances of the case, and that the applicant is dispensed from exhausting the remedy. That being said, the latter requirements are set out to dispense the applicant from exhausting a remedy and serve purposes other than that of Article 13 (Chapter 5).[36] Consequently, these starting-points are not necessarily well-suited to shed light on the Court's consideration of evidence with regard to Article 13. Indeed, the Court's general reluctance to reexamine the facts considered in domestic proceedings has been reiterated directly under Article 13. Illustrative of this is *A.D. & O.D.* v. *the UK* (2010), which concerned a violation of Article 8 because of the removal of a child from care. The main question, under Article 13, was whether a procedure existed in which the applicants could obtain compensation for damages. One of the applicant's claims was not successful because domestic courts had found no evidence that the applicant had suffered from a psychiatric disorder caused by the period of separation. The Court considered this a finding of fact by the domestic courts and held that it is not normally within its province to substitute its own assessment of the facts for that of the domestic courts because, as a general rule, it is for the domestic courts to assess the evidence before them.[37]

But, more importantly, what does the Court require with regard to the examination of facts by domestic remedial authorities, as a requirement arising under Article 13?

Notice first, by the way of comparison, that Article 6(1) does not demand that specific rules of evidence be followed by national courts and tribunals.[38] This implies, *inter alia*, that Article 6 does not lay down any rules on the placement of the burden of proof in civil matters.[39] However, for example,

---

[35] See, for example, *Marcu* v. *Romania* (2010) para. 70.

[36] Notice that when this starting-point was set out in *Marcu* v. *Romania* (2010), directly under Article 13, it was done with reference to *Selmouni* v. *France* (Grand Chamber 1999) para. 76; see *Marcu* v. *Romania* (2010) para. 70. However, in *Selmouni* v. *France* (Grand Chamber 1999), this issue was only considered under Article 35(1), not Article 13.

[37] *A.D. & O.D.* v. *the UK* (2010) paras. 103 and 104. See, also, for example, *Kalandia* v. *Greece* (2016) paras. 93–94.

[38] See, for example, Settem (2015), more generally in his Chapter 9, and explicitly at 338.

[39] See, for example, *Hämäläinen a.o.* v. *Finland* (Partial decision 2004) in para. 2 under "the law".

the principles of equality of arms and adversarial proceedings affect the applicant's right to present his/her case, including evidence, even in civil cases.[40] And even though Article 6 does not contain any specific requirement concerning standards of proof, the kind of evidence which may be relied on, and the assessment of evidence, the Court examines such issues "if there is reason to believe that the domestic courts drew arbitrary or grossly unfair conclusions from the facts submitted to them."[41] Further, in criminal cases, Article 6(2) guarantees the presumption of innocence, and Article 6(3) *litra* d the right to call and cross-examine witnesses.

Nor has the Court under Article 13 demanded that specific rules of evidence be followed by domestic remedial authorities. But the domestic assessment of facts and evidence may be of significance under several of the more general requirements arising under Article 13. For instance, the national authority must be able to deal with the questions of law and fact which are decisive for the determination of the substance of the complaint (Section 10.5.4),[42] and elements of facts and evidence are of significance when considering whether proceedings have been adversarial, equality of arms protected and sufficient access to documents, and information provided (Sections 10.3.7 and 10.3.4). Further, when the Government puts forward alternative remedies, their effectiveness has to be proved in practice by providing an example which shows their application in a similar case, or that the remedy exists with sufficient certainty (Sections 9.4 and 10.6). Also under the requirement that the remedy be effective not only in theory but also in practice, evaluations and assessments of fact are often of significance (Section 9.4). The national authority cannot, for instance, take a too formalistic approach to the assessment of evidence, for instance, by excluding evidence that is clearly relevant for the assessment under Article 3,[43] or in a too formalistic manner require and only attach weight to a specific type of evidence,[44] and, a father may have to be compelled to take a DNA test in proceedings involving a paternity claim.[45] Further, if facts are systemically dealt with in a wrongful manner, the Court considers the remedy to be ineffective in practice.[46] And, in some areas, most notably violations of Articles 2 and 3 and excessive length of proceedings violating Article 6(1), the

---

[40] See, for example, *Storck v. Germany* (2005) para. 161.
[41] See, for example, *Waldberg v. Turkey* (Commission decision 1995) under "the law" para. 2; *Firkins v. the UK* (Decision 2011) para. 26.
[42] See, as an example, *Liseytseva and Maslov v. Russia* (2014) para. 177.
[43] See, for example, *Iovchev v. Bulgaria* (2006) para. 146.
[44] See, for example, *Georgi Marinov v. Bulgaria* (2011) paras. 46–49.
[45] See, for example, *Mikulić v. Croatia* (2002) para. 64.
[46] See Section 9.4.

Court has held that there is a strong presumption that the violations occasion compensation for nonpecuniary damages (Section 11.5.2). In such cases, the remedy must reflect that presumption, rather than make the award of compensation dependent on, for example, a detainee's ability to prove the existence of nonpecuniary damage in the form of emotional distress.[47]

More generally, if applicants are obliged to provide impossible or disproportionate amounts of evidence, the effectiveness of the remedy, and the effectiveness of the Convention system more globally, is threatened. It is particularly difficult for the applicant to produce evidence when the evidence is in the hands of the State, or when positive action on part of the State is necessary to shed light on the facts. In a similar manner as the burden of proof may shift in procedures before the Court, one could have expected that the Court demanded that the burden of proof and the assessment of evidence must shift domestically. However, the Court has not set out any general requirement or principle of this sort under Article 13. For instance, in cases concerning secret information or surveillance, it is primarily the State that can shed light on facts, but the Court holds, for instance, in cases of interception of telephone calls, which may violate Article 8, that the applicant must satisfy the Court that there was a "reasonable likelihood" of interception. This may, without some aid from the State, be virtually impossible. As a consequence, the applicant has, in reality, no remedy against such violations.[48] That being said, the authorities may have to provide the applicant with a minimum of information concerning the decisions the applicant wants to contest, for example, the date of its adoption and the name and jurisdiction of the authority who required the surveillance.[49]

However, at the very least, in cases concerning extradition which may violate Articles 2 and 3, the burden of proof with regard to negative facts, such as the lack of a State guarantee in Afghanistan, cannot be placed on the applicant because this would deprive the applicant of any meaningful examination of his claim under Articles 2 and 3.[50] Similarly, if it is not specified where the applicant is to be deported, any examination under Article 13 is rendered meaningless.[51] The Court sees this as an aspect of the requirement that the national authority must be able to deal with the substance of the complaint (Section 10.5). This requirement may, with regard to both the questions of law and fact, vary, depending on the type of violation. Indeed, in cases of

---

[47] See, for example, *Sukachov v. Ukraine* (2020) para. 117; *Dikaiou a.o. v. Greece* (2020) para. 67.
[48] See, for example, *Halford v. the UK* (1997) paras. 69–70; *Kennedy v. the UK* (2010) para. 123.
[49] See, for example, *İrfan Güzel v. Turkey* (2017) para. 105.
[50] See, for example, *M. a.o. v. Bulgaria* (2011) para. 127.
[51] See, for example, *Asalya v. Turkey* (2014) para. 113.

extradition which may, arguably, violate Articles 2 and 3, Article 13 requires independent and rigorous scrutiny by a national authority of any claim that substantial grounds exist for fearing a real risk of treatment contrary to Articles 2 and 3. This also includes rigorous examination of evidence.[52]

Particularly problematical is the extent to which Article 13 allows for secret assessment of evidence, which the applicant has not seen, due to reasons of national security.[53] Article 13 cannot be interpreted as placing an absolute bar on domestic courts receiving closed evidence, but the applicant's interests must be protected at all times before the courts.[54] To this end, the remedial authority has an independent responsibility of shedding light on the arguable violation.[55] Further, even though, as a starting-point, it is for the applicant to cite evidence capable of proving that there are substantial grounds for believing that he/she would be exposed to a real risk of being subjected to treatment prohibited by Article 3, it is for the Government to dispel any doubts about it. The Court has thereto recognized that asylum-seekers are in a special situation, which frequently necessitates giving them the benefit of the doubt when assessing the credibility of their statements and the supporting documents that they have submitted.[56] The Court has, also, found that Article 13 was violated in conjunction with Articles 3, 5, and 8 because secret agents were not obliged to testify in criminal proceedings.[57]

In cases of certain violations of, in particular, Articles 2, 3, 5, P1 Article 1, and, in some instances, Article 8, the Court has partly remedied the difficulties for the applicant to produce sufficient evidence by demanding that the State performs effective investigations (Section 11.7). These requirements may be very specific. For instance, in their joint partly concurring and joint partly dissenting opinion in *Blakaj a.o.* v. *Croatia* (2014), Judges Lazarova Trajkovska and Pinto de Albuquerque voted to find a violation of Article 13 explicitly by reference to false and illogical judgments of facts during the investigation.

10.3.4 *Publication, Transparency, and Access to Documents and Information*

Publication, transparency, and access to documents and information are often part of more global assessments when considering whether a remedy is

---

[52] See, for example, *Singh a.o.* v. *Belgium* (2012) para. 104.
[53] See, for example, *Othman (Abu Qatada)* v. *the UK* (2012) paras. 222–224.
[54] See, for example, ibid. para. 219.
[55] See, for example, *M.S.S.* v. *Belgium and Greece* (Grand Chamber 2011) para. 389.
[56] See, for example, *A.A.* v. *Switzerland* (2014) paras. 59–63.
[57] *Nasr and Ghali* v. *Italy* (2016) paras. 335–336.

effective, for instance, an integral element of effective investigations (Section 11.7), part of the requirement that the remedy is effective not only in theory but also in practice (Section 9.4), and a prerequisite for effectively making use of other procedural rights more generally. In this subchapter, I point to situations in which publication, transparency, and access to documents and information have been explicitly emphasized by the Court as a more independent and autonomous (procedural) element of the right to an effective remedy.

In the practice of the Court, publication, transparency, and access to documents and information have been particularly important in situations in which a speedy procedure is necessary (Section 10.7), for instance, because of irreversible damage. Asylum and extradition procedures that may violate Articles 2 and 3 are illustrative. In such cases, access to information is particularly important to make effective use of remedies.[58] In fact, lack of access to information is often a major obstacle in accessing asylum procedures. Applicants do, therefore, have the right to obtain sufficient information so that they can gain effective access to the relevant procedures and substantiate their complaints.[59] Similarly, in cases concerning conditions of detention, because of the irreversible nature of potential damage, information to the applicant and his/her representatives is particularly important.[60] The information must, *inter alia*, be sufficiently detailed and communicated to the applicant in such a manner that he/she may make use of the relevant remedies.[61]

Gaining access to documents may be particularly difficult if the documents concern questions of national security. This question must be seen in connection with the burden of proof and the obligation to provide evidence in cases in which the relevant information is in the possession of the authorities (Section 10.3.3). In the practice of the Court, restricted access to information in cases concerning national security has mostly been considered from the viewpoint of whether the remedial authority is in a position to deal with the substance of the complaint (Section 10.5), even though the information is (partly) kept secret from the authority, not just the applicant. Where an allegation of threat to national security is made, the remedial authority must, as a minimum, be informed of the reasons grounding the deportation decision, even if such reasons are not made publicly available.[62] Further, the authority must be competent to reject the executive's assertion

---

[58] See, for example, *M.S.S.* v. *Belgium and Greece* (Grand Chamber 2011) paras. 304 and 318.
[59] See, for example, *Hirsi Jamaa a.o.* v. *Italy* (Grand Chamber 2012) para. 204.
[60] See, for example, *Rupa* v. *Romania (no. 2)* (2011) paras. 38–39.
[61] See, for example, ibid.
[62] See, for example, *Al-Nashif* v. *Bulgaria* (2002) para. 137.

that there is a threat to national security, where it finds it to be arbitrary or unreasonable. There must, also, be some form of adversarial proceedings, if need be, through a special representative after a security clearance. Finally, the question of whether the measure would interfere with the individual's right to respect for family life and, if so, whether a fair balance is struck between the public interest involved and the individual's rights must be examined.[63] Thus, the national authority must receive a minimum of information which enables it to scrutinize the reasons for the measure sufficiently, reject the assertion that there is a threat to national security on the grounds that it is arbitrary or unreasonable, examine whether there has been interference, and, if so, examine the proportionality of the issue.[64] In *C.G. a.o.* v. *Bulgaria* (2008), for example, the remedy did not satisfy theses minimum requirements, *inter alia*, because the applicant was initially given no information concerning the facts which had led the executive to make such an assessment and later had no fair and reasonable opportunity to refute the facts. The review performed was, therefore, not sufficiently effective.[65] Indeed, the Court holds, more generally, that, without the proper information as to the reasons for the security classification, the remedial authority cannot be in a position to challenge the administrative decisions. To this end, full disclosure of, for instance, sources may not be necessary, but the minimum requirements must be fulfilled.[66]

The Court often links the requirements of publication and transparency with that of accessibility.[67] The wording "adequate and accessible" is applied more generally under Article 35(1), but also, albeit to a lesser degree, under Article 13.[68] One explanation may be that the remedy considered under Article 13, more often than not, is exhausted, whereas the remedy considered under Article 35(1) normally has not been exhausted. Under Article 35(1), it is, therefore, important to emphasize a general criterion of accessibility to determine whether the applicant should have given the State the opportunity to set things rightly by using the remedy. Under Article 13, on the other

---

[63] Ibid.
[64] See, more generally, Sections 9.4 and 10.5.4.
[65] *C.G. a.o.* v. *Bulgaria* (2008) para. 60.
[66] *Csüllög* v. *Hungary* (2011) para. 48.
[67] See, for example, *Kadikis* v. *Latvia (no. 2)* (2006) para. 60; *Ignatov* v. *Bulgaria* (2009) paras. 48–50.
[68] The wording "adequate and accessible" was, for instance, not used in para. 113 of the landmark judgment *Silver a.o.* v. *the UK* (1983), but see, subsequently, for example, *Doran* v. *Ireland* (2003) para. 56; *Sürmeli* v. *Germany* (Grand Chamber 2006) para. 100, which also adds "sufficient"; *M.S.S.* v. *Belgium and Greece* (Grand Chamber 2011) para. 292.

hand, accessibility, as such, is, in the main, not a problem. It is more common that specific problems with regard, for instance, to transparency and access to documents arise.[69]

10.3.5 *Legal Assistance*

Everyone charged with a criminal offence has, according to Articles 6(3) *litra* c and d, the minimum right to defend himself/herself in person and to have legal assistance of his/her own choosing, and, if he/she does not have sufficient means to pay for legal assistance, to be given it free when the interests of justice so require. The applicant also has the right to have the free assistance of an interpreter if he/she cannot understand or speak the language used in court. Indeed, Article 6 normally requires that the accused be allowed to benefit from the assistance of a lawyer already at the initial stages of the police interrogation, although this right, which is not explicitly set out in the Convention, may be subject to restriction for a good cause.[70] Further, the right to have legal assistance and to make oneself heard, to be given assistance free of charge when the interests of justice require it, and the assistance of an interpreter are all an integral part of the right to a fair trial in Article 6(1). These rights may thus also apply in civil cases, although the required scope of assistance may differ, compared to criminal cases.

Under Article 13, too, legal assistance of various forms may need to be granted. Generally, more is demanded when the applicant is in a vulnerable situation or state of mind. An applicant may, for instance, be mentally ill and not in a position to avail himself personally of remedies against decisions regarding imprisonment and segregation violating Article 3. Review may, therefore, need to be initiated automatically, independently of whether the applicant has legal aid and representation or not.[71] Also in asylum and deportation procedures that may violate Articles 2 and 3, lack of access to legal assistance may prevent the applicants from effectively raising their allegations under the Convention.[72]

Notice that Article 13 does not require children to be able to institute and conduct proceedings on their own. It suffices that a legal representative is able

---

[69] However, lacking publicity may give rise to questions of effectiveness under Article 13, but then usually when the Court, also under Article 13, considers the effectiveness of remedies not exhausted; see, for example, *Kadikis v. Latvia (no. 2)* (2006) para. 60; *Ignatov v. Bulgaria* (2009) paras. 48–50; *Dbouba v. Turkey* (2010) paras. 44 and 31–32.

[70] See, for example, *John Murray v. the UK* (Grand Chamber 1996) para. 63.

[71] *Keenan v. the UK* (2001) paras. 126–127.

[72] See, for example, *Abdolkhani and Karimnia v. Turkey* (2009) paras. 114–115.

to do so on the child's behalf.[73] The legal representative must thereto have sufficient contact and possibility of communicating with the child.[74]

10.3.6 *Exemption from Court Fees*

In order for the remedy to be effective, it may be necessary to grant exemptions from court fees or other costs pertaining to the procedures.

With regard to effective remedies against excessive length of proceedings, even though States, as a starting-point, are free to choose the form of remedial procedures, "special rules concerning legal costs (in particular, registration fees) may be appropriate to avoid excessive costs constituting an unreasonable restriction on the right to file such claims."[75] Also in proceedings concerning conditions of detention, exemptions from court fees have been considered. As a starting-point, as long as requirements to pay court fees or request a waiver do not prevent the applicant from using the proceedings, the remedy is effective.[76] However, if, for instance, indigence prevents the applicant from paying a court fee, an exemption must be available.[77] Similarly, in a case concerning an arguable claim under Article 8, a financial threshold for obtaining a residence permit may make the remedy ineffective. Although the Court is not concerned with administrative charges in the abstract nor with the level at which the administrative charge is set, as such, the Court considers whether a charge prevents the applicant from seeking effective recognition of his/her arguable claim under Article 8.[78]

10.3.7 *Adversarial Proceedings*

Adversarial proceedings are a central element of the right to a fair hearing and an integral part of the principle of equality of arms in Article 6(1), which applies in both criminal and civil cases.[79] It is thus also a constituent element of the right to an effective remedy in Article 13.[80] However, lack of adversarial

---

[73] *Margareta and Roger Andersson* v. *Sweden* (1992) para. 101.

[74] See the majority in *Margareta and Roger Andersson* v. *Sweden* (1992) paras. 101–103 and compare the partly dissenting opinion of Judge De Meyer joined by Judges Pinheiro Farinha, Petitti, and Spielmann.

[75] *Vlad a.o.* v. *Romania* (2013) para. 112.

[76] See, for example, *Generalov* v. *Russia* (2009) para. 118.

[77] See, for example, *Orlov* v. *Russia* (2011) paras. 88 and 71.

[78] See, for example, *G.R.* v. *the Netherlands* (2012) para. 51.

[79] See, for example, *Brandstetter* v. *Austria* (1991) paras. 66–67.

[80] See, for example, *Csüllög* v. *Hungary* (2011) para. 46; *de Tommaso* v. *Italy* (Grand Chamber 2017) para. 182.

proceedings has not been central in the Court's case law under Article 13. The Court has more often referred to the lack of publication, transparency, and access to information, which can, indeed, be seen as an integral element of adversarial proceedings, but without referring to adversarial proceedings explicitly, or equality of arms for that sake, as the general standard under which the question is considered. The reason is probably that this question is often considered to have been sufficiently dealt with under Article 6(1). However, in some cases under Article 13, the Court generally refers to adversarial proceedings as the decisive standard. An example of this can be found in the minimum of adversarial proceedings that has to be offered in cases concerning national security.[81]

10.4 THE POWERS OF THE NATIONAL AUTHORITY

The domestic remedial authority must not only offer procedural guarantees similar to those of Article 6(1) but also possess the power to grant sufficient relief, including a binding decision (Section 11.2). But procedural guarantees and powers are connected.[82] Without the power to provide a legally binding determination on the substance of the complaint, the remedial authority is not capable of providing sufficient relief.[83] Indeed, procedures in which a right cannot be claimed, but in which the applicant only attempts, for instance, to obtain a favor, does not satisfy Article 13. Recourse to a national Ombudsman is, therefore, normally not satisfactory, as ombudsmen cannot usually provide legally binding decisions.[84] The same goes for a Chancellor of Justice,[85] various Governmental commissions and appeal boards,[86] prosecuting authorities,[87] the supervision of conditions of detention by the President

---

[81]	See, for example, *Al-Nashif* v. *Bulgaria* (2002) para. 137; *C.G. a.o.* v. *Bulgaria* (2008) para. 57; *Madah a.o.* v. *Bulgaria* (2012) para. 39.

[82]	However, on a principled level, the Court distinguishes; see, for example, *Klass a.o.* v. *Germany* (Plenary 1978) para. 67, *Silver a.o.* v. *the UK* (1983) para. 113; *Rotaru* v. *Romania* (Grand Chamber 2000) para. 69.

[83]	See, for example, *Lorsé a.o.* v. *the Netherlands* (2003); *Chatzigiannakou* v. *Greece* (2019).

[84]	See, for example, *Silver a.o.* v. *the UK* (1983) para. 115 (Parliamentary Ombudsman); *Leander* v. *Sweden* (1987) para. 82 (Parliamentary ombudsman); *E. a.o.* v. *the UK* (2002) para. 112 (local authorities Ombudsman); *Mandić and Jović* v. *Slovenia* (2011) para. 117 (Human-Rights Ombudsman); *Ananyev a.o.* v. *Russia* (2012) para. 106, *Dirdizov* v. *Russia* (2012) paras. 78–79; and *Sergey Babushkin* v. *Russia* (2013) para. 40 (various regional and federal Ombudsmen).

[85]	See, for example, *Leander* v. *Sweden* (1987) para. 82; *Segerstedt-Wiberg a.o.* v. *Sweden* (2006) para. 118.

[86]	See, for example, *Zazanis a.o.* v. *Greece* (2004) para. 47 (Governmental commission); *Lorsé a.o.* v. *the Netherlands* (2003) para. 94 (Appeal board).

[87]	See, for example, *Reshetnyak* v. *Russia* (2013) para. 63.

of a district court,[88] or other decisions by court officials or judges to the extent that the decisions, recommendations, and instructions, independently of what they are called, do not provide a legally binding determination of the substance of the complaint.[89] This is an absolute requirement. Even though the activities of the authority usefully contribute to the improvement of the applicant's situation, for instance, by improving the conditions of detention, the lack of power to issue a legally binding decision always renders the remedy ineffective.[90]

The required relief may depend upon, *inter alia*, the situation and the violation (Chapters 8 and 11). Accordingly, the powers required of the remedial authority may, also, vary. If the situation requires compensation, the authority or authorities must have the power to award sufficient compensation. The fact that the authority can impose a fine on a perpetrator is then, for example, not sufficient.[91] Similarly, if, for instance, a decision must be quashed, a measure suspended, property returned, proceedings reopened, access to information granted, or a record deleted, the national authority must have the power to do just that. However, having the power is not the same as being required to use the power. If the national authority may, in principle, afford sufficient redress, Article 13 is not necessarily violated if sufficient redress is not granted in the concrete case (Sections 9.4 and 10.6). As a consequence, the applicant may still be a victim and may need to turn to the Court in order to achieve sufficient redress. A string of judgments against Italy concerning excessive length of proceedings, to which domestic courts did not award sufficient compensation, but in which domestic courts had, in principle, the power to grant sufficient compensation, also for nonpecuniary damages, is illustrative of this.[92]

Further, in many cases, a binding decision needs enforcement, for instance, an award of compensation or a decision granting access to documents. The national authority providing the binding decision is not required to enforce the binding decision, as such, nor is it usual that independent courts have such powers. However, Article 13 obliges States to ensure that the redress granted is enforced through competent authorities (Section 11.9). The enforcing authority must not necessarily provide the same procedural safeguards as the authority rendering the binding decision, but, if the remedy is not enforced, the whole remedial procedure is considered ineffective.[93]

[88] See, for example, *Mandić and Jović v. Slovenia* (2011) para. 117.
[89] See, for example, *Karimov v. Ukraine* (2008) para. 74.
[90] See, for example, *Ananyev a.o. v. Russia* (2012) para. 106.
[91] See, for example, *Peck v. the UK* (2003) para. 109 (UK Media Commissions).
[92] See Section 11.5.
[93] See, for example, *Kenedi v. Hungary* (2009) paras. 371 and 47–48.

10.5 THE SCOPE OF DOMESTIC REVIEW

10.5.1 *Introduction*

Article 13 requires the national authority to be able to "deal with the substance of the relevant Convention complaint".[94] This not only presupposes the procedural safeguards and powers accounted for in Sections 10.3 and 10.4 but also requires the remedial authority to be able to deal with facts and apply substantive standards in a manner which secures that the substance of the complaint is dealt with. This is, possibly, the most important practical requirement stemming from Article 13.[95]

The requirement must not be confused with the Article 6(1) requirement that domestic courts and tribunals need have "full jurisdiction" when dealing with administrative decisions concerning civil rights and obligations. This requirement sets out the competences that domestic courts and tribunals must have when they review such decisions, but does not define the substantive content of those same rights and charges. Indeed, Article 6 does not require domestic courts and tribunals to be able to come to specific substantive outcomes. Article 13, on the other hand, requires the domestic remedial authority to apply specific substantive (Convention) standards irrespectively of whether the right or obligation is civil or criminal in nature or of whether the complaint is related to an administrative decision or not, as long as the applicant has an arguable claim that his/her Convention rights are violated.

The requirement must, further, be distinguished from the Court's practice to apply a wider or narrower margin of appreciation under substantive rights depending on the quality of the domestic review. Indeed, this practice only provides States with the opportunity to be granted a wider margin of appreciation under substantive Articles and is, in contrast to Article 13, no requirement concerning the domestic review that has to be performed (Section 13.2).

In the following, I first account for how the domestic review required by Article 13 is negatively delimited in two important aspects: (1) States are not required to incorporate the Convention and (2) Article 13 grants no right to challenge primary legislation, as such. I then account for the positive content of the requirement, seen in the light of these two delimitations.

---

[94] This requirement was first formulated in this manner in *Soering v. the UK* (Plenary 1989) para. 120, but was indirectly applied much earlier, in *Klass a.o. v. Germany* (Plenary 1978) para. 66.

[95] Similarly, Lorenzen, Christoffersen *et al.* (2011) 948.

10.5.2 *No Requirement to Incorporate the Convention*

Since early case law, the Court holds that neither Article 13 nor the Convention in general lays down, for the Contracting States, any given manner for ensuring within their internal law, the effective implementation of any of the provisions of the Convention.[96] As a consequence, Article 13 does not require the Convention to be incorporated into national law.[97] That being said, incorporation is considered to be the best manner to implement the Convention, and, in many cases, the Court recommends it.[98] This is linked to the supervisory role of the Court which:

> should be easier in respect of States that have effectively incorporated the Convention into their legal system and consider the rules to be directly applicable since the highest courts of these States will normally assume responsibility for enforcing the principles determined by the Court.[99]

Indeed, even though there is no formal obligation to incorporate the Convention, it follows from the principle of subsidiarity that:

> the national courts must, where possible, interpret and apply domestic law in accordance with the Convention. While it is primarily for the national authorities to interpret and apply domestic law, the Court is in any event required to verify whether the way in which domestic law is interpreted and applied produces consequences that are consistent with the principles of the Convention.[100]

The fact that there is no formal requirement to incorporate the Convention is of less importance today. The Convention has, in some manner, been incorporated in all Member States.[101] Most notably, the Convention has been incorporated in the United Kingdom and the Scandinavian countries, whose reluctance to incorporate the Convention was a significant underlying reason as to why the Court did not impose a requirement of this sort in early years.[102]

---

[96] *Swedish Engine Drivers' Union* v. *Sweden* (1976) para. 50. However, in the earliest legal literature, many held that the Convention needed to be directly applicable at national level, under which Article 13 was one of the main arguments; see, for example, Golsong (1958) 8; Pelloux (1961) 64–65; Buergenthal (1965) 80 ff.

[97] See, for example, *Swedish Engine Drivers' Union* v. *Sweden* (1976) para. 32; *Silver a.o.* v. *the UK* (1983) para. 113; *Khan* v. *the UK* (2000) para. 44.

[98] See, for example, *Abdulaziz, Cabales and Balkandali* v. *the UK* (Plenary 1985) para. 93.

[99] *Apicella* v. *Italy* (Grand Chamber 2006) para. 80.

[100] *Scordino* v. *Italy (no. 1)* (Decision 2003) (under "The Court's assessment").

[101] See, for example, Polakiewicz (2001); Ando (2013) 703. Against this background, Chryssogonos (2001) 52 and Pfeffer (2009) 150 argue that there is an implicit acceptance of an obligation to incorporate the Convention.

[102] Similarly, Chryssogonos (2001) 52.

However, incorporation does not guarantee that the obligations arising from Article 13 are safeguarded in practice. Indeed, ordinary domestic law and legislation may still, for various reasons, prevail in domestic remedial proceedings.[103] The problem, therefore, is not a matter of formal incorporation, but of effectively integrating the Convention in national adjudication.[104]

10.5.3 *No Right to Challenge Primary Legislation as Such*

10.5.3.1 The Existence of the Principle

The Court first had the possibility to take a stand on the principle that Article 13 grants no rights to challenge primary legislation, as such, in *Young, James and Webster* v. *the UK* (Plenary 1981). In the case, Article 11 was violated because the applicants faced the dilemma of either joining a trade union or being dismissed from their jobs.

A majority of eight to two Commission members had concluded that Article 13 was not violated. Although domestic courts had to apply national legislation, which expressly held that a dismissal on the ground of refusing to join a trade union was legitimate, Article 13 was not violated, since it could not be "deduced from Article 13 that there must be a remedy against legislation as such which is considered not to be in conformity with the Convention." Indeed, this would amount to requiring judicial review of legislation, which could not be demanded without a clear indication in the text of Article 13. On the contrary, the wording "notwithstanding that the violation has been committed by persons acting in an official capacity" indicated that Article 13 was concerned only with individuals acting on behalf of the State, not reviewing legislation. The Commission majority thus concluded that Article 13 "does not relate to legislation and does not guarantee a remedy by which legislation could be controlled as to its conformity with the Convention."[105]

However, the Commission minority, the members Opsahl and Trechsel, could not find "any basis" for restricting the scope of application of Article 13 in this manner. They agreed that Article 13 did not require a "remedy against legislation as such", but only in the sense that national authorities must not have the competence to declare a national law invalid in the abstract. But Article 13 would be deprived of much of its importance if the right to an

---

[103] See, for example, Greer (2006) 83–85, 88–93; Helfer (2008) 137–138; Bates (2010) 158–159, 163 and, more generally, Krisch (2008).

[104] Greer (2006) 321.

[105] *Young, James and Webster* v. *the UK* (Plenary Commission report 1979) paras. 177–178.

effective remedy was excluded whenever an alleged violation was based upon a national law. Article 13, therefore, had to require, in a given case, that the national authority could remedy the violation, irrespectively of whether the violation had been caused by domestic legislation. The authority, therefore, in some manner, had to be competent to apply the Convention rights, or similar principles or rights, as "correctives," and to interpret national legislation so that it was brought into conformity with Convention rights whenever necessary.[106]

The Court, for its part, did not to comment on this question and simply held that, because of the finding of a violation under Article 11, it was not necessary to determine whether Article 13 had also been violated.[107]

In the more immediate subsequent case law, there are some examples in which the Court, at least implicitly, required national authorities to be able to correct or depart from national legislation, in the sense suggested by the Commission members Opsahl and Trechsel.

Silver a.o. v. the UK (1983) concerned stopping of prisoner's correspondence in violation of Article 8, which was regulated in detail in secondary legislation.[108] English courts had supervisory jurisdiction over the exercise of the powers conferred on the Home Secretary and the prison authorities, but the jurisdiction was limited to determining whether the powers were exercised arbitrarily, in bad faith, for an improper motive, or in an *ultra vires* manner. The Convention, at the time, could not be directly invoked before UK courts, and although it was considered relevant for the interpretation of ambiguous legislation, to the extent that the applicable rules (the secondary legislation) were incompatible with the Convention, there could be no effective remedy because domestic courts were not able to depart from that what followed from these rules.[109]

Similarly, in *Abdulaziz, Cabales and Balkandali v. the UK* (Plenary 1985), a majority found a breach of Article 14 taken together with Article 8 because the applicants had been discriminated on the grounds of sex. It was explicitly regulated in secondary legislation that it was easier for a man settled in the United Kingdom than for a woman to obtain permission for his nonnational spouse to enter or remain in the country for settlement.[110]

---

[106] Dissenting opinion of MM. Opsahl and Trechsel in *Young, James and Webster v. the UK* (Plenary Commission report 1979).

[107] *Young, James and Webster v. the UK* (Plenary 1981) para. 67.

[108] *Silver a.o. v. the UK* (1983) paras. 41–50.

[109] Ibid., paras. 117–119. Almost identical, *Campbell and Fell v. the UK* (1984) paras. 124–128. As accounted for in Section 10.5.3.2 below, the Court and the Commission have, in later case law, distinguished between primary and secondary legislation. This distinction, however, had not been introduced at the time of this judgment.

[110] *Abdulaziz, Cabales and Balkandali v. the UK* (Plenary 1985) paras. 74 and 23–25.

The majority found that there could be no effective remedy as required by Article 13 because the courts were not able to depart from the legislation in force.[111] A minority of three judges agreed to the result, but found that the reasoning of the majority would always and automatically lead to a violation of Article 13 if (1) the Convention does not form part of the internal law of a given State and (2) the internal law of the State violates a right guaranteed by the Convention, which could not be accepted. However, the minority submitted to what they perceived to be the established jurisprudence since *Silver a.o. v. the UK* (1983) and argued *de lege ferenda*, that this jurisprudence should be modified since it did not conform to the object and purpose of Article 13.

However, in *James a.o. v. the UK* (Plenary 1986), the Court explicitly excluded legislation from the scope of application of Article 13. The case concerned compulsory transfer of property which, arguably, violated P1 Article 1 and Article 14. The transfer was explicitly foreseen in UK primary legislation (the Leasehold Reform Act 1967). The largest majority fraction simply concluded, without referring to any previous case law, that Article 13 "does not go so far as to guarantee a remedy allowing a Contracting State's laws as such to be challenged before a national authority on the ground of being contrary to the Convention."[112] Four judges agreed with the *ratio*, but regretted that the majority had not justified its reasoning. As a point of departure, they expressed that Article 13 was one of the most ambiguous Articles in the Convention and that the Court's doctrine with regard to its application had not yet been firmly established. Further, the wording of Article 13 contained no limitations with regard to legislation. On the contrary, a literal reading indicated that a remedy had to exist even when the alleged violation resulted from the operation of a statute. They also admitted that this opinion had been expressed in several recent judgments. However, in their view, it seemed improbable that the drafting fathers had intended to extend the scope of Article 13 to this point, because, when the Convention had been ratified, only a few Contracting States made legislative provision for individuals to test the constitutionality of a statute (or its compatibility with the Convention). They added that this was still the position. They further argued that the wording "persons acting in an official capacity" indicated that Article 13 primarily

---

[111] Ibid., para. 93. The Commission had, at this point, distinguished between primary and secondary legislation, holding that only primary legislation was encompassed by the principle; see *Abdulaziz, Cabales and Balkandali v. the UK* (Plenary Commission report 1983) para. 127. The Court, however, did not distinguish explicitly.

[112] *James a.o. v. the UK* (Plenary 1986) para. 85.

covered violations of the Convention committed by entities belonging to the executive or the judiciary. Such reasoning would, in their opinion, have to be elaborated on and considered more thoroughly in future judgments, not only in a concurring opinion.[113] Three judges, on the other hand, saw no reason to make an exception for acts of the legislature and added that this had been the position of the Court in *Silver a.o. v. the UK* (1983), *Campbell and Fell v. the UK* (1984), and *Abdulaziz, Cabales and Balkandali v. the UK* (Plenary 1985).[114]

Lithgow a.o. v. the UK (Plenary 1986) had almost identical facts as in *James a.o. v. the UK* (Plenary 1986), and the same majority and dissenting opinions, but the majority did not present any further justification, nor was there a concurring opinion by Judges Bindschedler-Rober, Gölcüklü, Matscher, and Spielmann. Further, the minority, again consisting of Judges Pinheiro Farinha, Pettiti, and Russo, simply stated, without any further justification, that, under the system and the terms established by the United Kingdom, there was no effective remedy before a national authority to test the compatibility of the act with the rights guaranteed by the Convention and P1 Article 1.

In *Leander v. Sweden* (1987), the principle was then listed as a general principle under Article 13, still without any further justification.[115] In the subsequent case law, the existence of the principle has been firmly established, but still without any further justification.[116]

10.5.3.2 The Scope of the Principle

In early case law, the Court did not distinguish between different forms of legislation. However, in *Abdulaziz, Cabales and Balkandali v. the UK* (Plenary Commission report 1983), the Commission distinguished between primary, secondary, and administrative legislation (guidelines/directives) and held that

---

[113] Concurring opinion of Judges Bindschedler-Rober, Gölcüklü, Matscher and Spielmann in *James a.o. v. the UK* (Plenary 1986).

[114] Concurring opinion of Judge Pinheiro Farinha and concurring opinion of Judges Pettiti and Russo. Notice, however, that the conclusion of the judgment states that the finding of no violation with regard to Article 13 was unanimous.

[115] *Leander v. Sweden* (1987) para. 77. But the principle was of no significance to the result in the case. Moreover, Judges Pettiti and Russo, in their dissenting opinion, did not comment on this question.

[116] See, for example, *Powell and Rayner v. the UK* (1990) para. 36; *Murray v. the UK* (Grand Chamber 1994) para. 102; *Gustafsson v. Sweden* (Grand Chamber 1996) para. 70; *Christine Goodwin v. the UK* (Grand Chamber 2002) para. 113; *Maurice v. France* (Grand Chamber 2005) para. 107; *Debelianovi v. Bulgaria* (2007) para. 63; *A. a.o. v. the UK* (Grand Chamber 2009) para. 135; *Chervenkov v. Bulgaria* (2012) para. 83; *Nada v. Switzerland* (Grand Chamber 2012) para. 208; *Sadak v. Turkey* (2015) para. 96; *Kulinski and Sabev v. Bulgaria* (2016) para. 49.

only primary legislation was encompassed by the principle.[117] Further, during the pleadings in *Boyle and Rice* v. *the UK* (Plenary 1988), there was considerable argument as to whether the principle only extended to primary legislation. The Court, however, considered it unnecessary to go into these issues of interpretation since the applicant's claims were not arguable.[118] Indeed, the Court first explicitly referred to primary legislation in *Willis* v. *the UK* (2002),[119] but no justification as to why it should be distinguished was given.

In subsequent case law, the Court occasionally refers to primary legislation,[120] but mostly only legislation or laws. However, I have not seen later cases where the Court applies the principle on secondary legislation or administrative guidelines, and, in legal theory, the general opinion is that the principle only applies to primary legislation.[121] That being said, the Court has never, in the abstract, justified the distinction. However, the underlying arguments concerning judicial review of legislation mainly show deference toward the primary domestic legislator, *i.e.* Parliaments.[122] Still, the Court has not taken a formal view on the form of the legislative decision. For instance, in *Debelianovi* v. *Bulgaria* (2007), a moratorium in the form of a Parliamentary decision was not considered domestic legislation *"proprement dite"* but was still sufficient to make the principle applicable.[123] Similarly, "a general policy as such", is encompassed by the principle, even though the policy does not formally stem from primary legislation.[124] The Court has, also, excluded constitutional court made precedent with statutory force from the scope of

---

[117] *Abdulaziz, Cabales and Balkandali* v. *the UK* (Plenary Commission report 1983) paras. 126–128. The Court, however, did, at this point, not explicitly recognize this distinction; see *Abdulaziz, Cabales and Balkandali* v. *the UK* (Plenary 1985) para. 93 and the concurring opinion of Judge Bernhardt joined by Judges Pettiti and Gersing.

[118] *Boyle and Rice* v. *the UK* (Plenary 1988) para. 87. The Commission, on the other hand, had distinguished and held that the norms in question (prison rules, standing orders and administrative circulars) did not stem from primary legislation and that legislation, as such, therefore, was not challenged; see *Boyle and Rice* v. *the UK* (Plenary Commission report 1986) paras. 78–79.

[119] *Willis* v. *the UK* (2002) para. 62.

[120] See, for example, *A.* v. *the UK* (2002) para. 112 (with reference to *James a.o.* v. *the UK* (Plenary 1986) para. 85 which, however, only refers to "laws"); *Connors* v. *the UK* (2004) para. 109; *Klyakhin* v. *Russia* (2004) para. 114; *Roche* v. *the UK* (Grand Chamber 2005) para. 137; *Petrov* v. *Bulgaria* (2008) para. 65; *A. a.o.* v. *the UK* (Grand Chamber 2009) para. 135; *Shahanov* v. *Bulgaria* (2012) para. 62.

[121] See, for example, Harris, O'Boyle *et al.* (2018) 746.

[122] Also in other contexts, the Court has shown particular deference toward the implementation freedom of the domestic legislator; see, for example, *Hatton a.o.* v. *the UK* (Grand Chamber 2003) para. 97; *S.A.S.* v. *France* (Grand Chamber 2014) para. 129.

[123] *Debelianovi* v. *Bulgaria* (2007) paras. 63–64.

[124] See, for example, *Hatton a.o.* v. *the UK* (Grand Chamber 2003) para. 138.

application of Article 13.[125] Indeed, in some cases, the Court, more generally, refers to primary legislation or "equivalent domestic norms".[126]

Clearly, the distinction between primary and secondary legislation is of great practical importance. Indeed, "any other finding would have had a devastating effect on the role Article 13 could play."[127] But when, then, is primary legislation, as such, actually challenged? And how consistent is the principle applied by the Court?

Undoubtedly, the abstract challenging of primary legislation, *i.e.*, a claim that legislation must be declared null and void, is excluded from the scope of application of Article 13. Indeed, in the earliest case law, it seemed as though the Court distinguished between the abstract challenging of legislation in this form and any other application of legislation.[128] However, later cases do not only concern the abstract challenging of legislation, but are more or less connected to the concrete application of legislation, for instance, the stopping of prisoner correspondence,[129] the denial of visits in prison,[130] the placement of a restaurant under a blockade because the owner refused to sign a collective agreement with an employment association,[131] and no possibility of deducting maintenance payments for tax purposes.[132]

Further, the Court, and the former Commission, has used and uses wording that could encompass different situations and degrees of causality between the legislation and its application, for instance, referring to the legislation in question as "the source of the grievance complained of",[133] stating that the applicant's complaint was "essentially directed against the fact that the union action was lawful",[134] or "related in essence to one of the principles underlying the applicable legal regime",[135] stating that Article 13 cannot be interpreted as requiring a remedy against "the state of domestic law",[136] or complaints "related to" the immunity and the unavailability of legal aid under primary

---

[125] See, for example, *Paksas v. Lithuania* (Grand Chamber 2011) para. 114.
[126] See, for example, *Peck v. the UK* (2003) para. 101.
[127] Harris, O'Boyle *et al.* (2009) 559 in note 14.
[128] See, for example, *Lithgow a.o. v. the UK* (Plenary 1986) paras. 206–207.
[129] For example, *Petrov v. Bulgaria* (2008) para. 65.
[130] For example, *Shalimov v. Ukraine* (2010) para. 99.
[131] For example, *Gustafsson v. Sweden* (Grand Chamber 1996).
[132] For example, *P.M. v. the UK* (2005).
[133] For example, *Sigurdur A. Sigurjónsson v. Iceland* (Commission report 1992) para. 77.
[134] For example, *Gustafsson v. Sweden* (Grand Chamber 1996) para. 70; *Klyakhin v. Russia* (2004) para. 114.
[135] For example, *Supreme Holy Council of the Muslim Community v. Bulgaria* (2004) paras. 106–107.
[136] For example, *Christine Goodwin v. the UK* (Grand Chamber 2002) para. 113; *Appleby a.o. v. the UK* (2003) para. 56; *I.G. a.o. v. Slovakia* (2012) para. 156; *Voynov v. Russia* (2018) para. 46.

legislation,[137] or because discrimination "derived",[138] or "resulted from",[139] primary legislation, or conditions of detention stemming from "the very nature of the detention scheme",[140] or simply that the "impugned measure was contained in primary legislation".[141] In addition, the principle is usually only applied with a brief summary of the applicant's and the Government's arguments and facts of the case.[142] This makes it difficult to foresee when primary legislation, as such, actually is being challenged. Indeed, if traced back far enough, almost any action has some connection to legislation.[143]

However, the case law indicates that there must be sufficient causality between the primary legislation and the concrete action or nonaction causing the violation (the application). For instance, in *Peck v. the UK* (2003), Article 8 was violated because of the disclosure of sensitive information. Under Article 13, the Court held that since the relevant legislation "did not require disclosure of the material" and the complaint was "about the Council's exercise of its powers to disclose", legislation, as such, was not challenged.[144] On the other hand, in *Petrov v. Bulgaria* (2008), Article 13 was not violated because the monitoring of prison correspondence did not result from an individual decision of the prison administration or another authority, but was "systematic and directly resulting from the application of the express wording" of the relevant legislation.[145] Accordingly, at least when administrative authorities have broad discretion when applying legislation, legislation, as such, is not challenged.[146] But, the Court has not provided an answer as to how broad this discretion must be.

In addition, the implementation of legislation is considered to fall outside the principle.[147]

That being said, although the principle has potential far-reaching consequences, the Court has not used the principle in many cases. And, in a

---

[137] For example, *A. v. the UK* (2002) para. 112.
[138] For example, *P.M. v. the UK* (2005) para. 34.
[139] For example, *Holy Synod of the Bulgarian Orthodox Church (Metropolitan Inokentiy) a.o. v. Bulgaria* (2009) para. 178.
[140] *A. a.o. v. the UK* (Grand Chamber 2009) para. 135.
[141] For example, *Vrountou v. Cyprus* (2015) para. 89.
[142] See, for example, *Willis v. the UK* (2002) para. 62; *Maurice v. France* (Grand Chamber 2005) para. 107; *Roche v. the UK* (Grand Chamber 2005) para. 137.
[143] Compare Christoffersen (2009) 389.
[144] *Peck v. the UK* (2003) para. 101.
[145] *Petrov v. Bulgaria* (2008) para. 65. Similarly, *Konstantin Popov v. Bulgaria* (2009) para. 23; *Tsonyo Tsonev v. Bulgaria* (2009) paras. 47–48; *Iliev a.o. v. Bulgaria* (2011) para. 77; *Iordan Petrov v. Bulgaria* (2012) para. 173; *Oreshkov v. Bulgaria* (2012) para. 66; *Chervenkov v. Bulgaria* (2012) para. 83; *Halil Adem Hasan v. Bulgaria* (2015) para. 83.
[146] See, also, for example, *Fevzi Saygılı v. Turkey* (2008) paras. 31–32.
[147] See, for example, *Greens and M.T. v. the UK* (2010) paras. 77–90.

number of cases, it could be argued that legislation, as such, was challenged, but the principle not applied.[148] As to the reasons why, one may only speculate, but one central reason is that many States do not claim that legislation, as such, is being challenged, although they could have and that the Court does not apply the principle *ex officio*.

10.5.3.3 The Principle Reconsidered in the Light of Present Day Circumstances

In the following, I argue that the Court should depart from its precedent and explicitly require that domestic remedial authorities, in some manner, have the power to remedy violations caused by primary legislation. I do so by first analyzing the formal justification for introducing the principle and then reconsider the principle and its justification in the light of present day circumstances.

As we have seen above, the Court has never explicitly justified the principle, but the Commission did, in particular, the majority in *Young, James and Webster* v. *the UK* (Plenary Commission report 1979). In addition, some indications can be found in the Court's practice. The case law reveals three primary arguments:

First, such a remedy would require judicial review of legislation, which could not be demanded.[149] The underlying reasons for this can be divided in two.

First, judicial review of legislation was only accepted by a few Member States.[150] And, certainly, if the Court and Commission envisaged a judicial review which allows courts to strike down legislation in the abstract and declare legislation null and void, then only a few Member States accepted such

---

[148] See, for example, *Riener* v. *Bulgaria* (2006) (denial of permission to leave the State explicitly foreseen in legislation); *Ivan Vasilev* v. *Bulgaria* (2007) (use of force legitimate according to primary legislation); *Bashir a.o.* v. *Bulgaria* (2007) (expulsion foreseen by domestic primary legislation); *Association for European Integration and Human Rights and Ekimdzhiev* v. *Bulgaria* (2007) (gathering and use of information foreseen by domestic primary legislation); *Marcu* v. *Romania* (2010) (automatic withdrawal of parental right foreseen in primary domestic penal legislation); *Boychev a.o.* v. *Bulgaria* (2011) (prohibition of religious gathering foreseen by primary domestic legislation); *Milen Kostov* v. *Bulgaria* (2013) (prohibition to leave the country, because of a criminal conviction, foreseen in primary legislation); *International Bank for Commerce and Development AD a.o.* v. *Bulgaria* (2016) (bank required by primary domestic legislation to freeze accounts); *S.K.* v. *Russia* (2017) (administrative authorities and courts precluded by primary legislation from examining risks of violations of Articles 2 and 3).

[149] See, in particular, *Young, James and Webster* v. *the UK* (Plenary Commission report 1979) para. 177.

[150] See, for example, *Young, James and Webster* v. *the UK* (Plenary Commission report 1979) para. 177 and the concurring opinions of Judge Pinheiro Farinha and Judges Pettiti and Russo in *James a.o.* v. *the UK* (Plenary 1986).

judicial review. However, as the Commission members Opsahl and Trechsel pointed out in *Young, James and Webster* v. *the UK* (Plenary Commission report 1979), Article 13 could limit itself to require a weak form of review that applies Convention rights, or comparable rights, as "correctives" in concrete cases, but which do not declare legislation to be null and void.[151]

Second, it was improbable that the drafting fathers intended the scope of Article 13 to extend to this point.[152] However, at least the *travaux préparatoires* provide no clear answer as to what the drafting fathers thought about this issue. Indeed, although there was considerable disagreement as to whether the Court should have the power to strike down and declare domestic legislation null and void,[153] this does not imply that domestic remedial authorities should not have, in some manner, in individual cases, the power to "correct" national legislation contravening the Convention. And even though the general opinion was that States should have considerable freedom to implement the Convention in their national legal systems, this was connected to the understanding of the general rules on State responsibility, under which States have the freedom of choice as to how they fulfill their obligations as long as they do not fail to achieve the objective.[154] But the fact that the objective – in this case, achieve a remedy that, in some manner, can deal with the substance of the complaint – potentially, under the legal regime in a given State, only can be achieved through judicial review of legislation is of no relevance to the international obligation (to achieve the objective).[155]

On the other hand, the drafting fathers had numerous discussions concerning the question of enforcement, more generally, although not explicitly linked up to the scope of Article 13. Indeed, many emphasized that it was of the uttermost importance that the rights were actually enforced – without indicating how or whether it should be done at international or national level. In the first session of the Consultative Assembly, Lord Layton, for example, held that:

> Purely paper declarations, however, are rightly discredited. Our statement will have force only if it is converted into action, and the most immediate and practical way of doing this is by the adoption of a Charter of Human Rights, *coupled with a definite method of enforcement*. (My emphasis)[156]

---

[151] See, also, for example, Tuori (2002) 229.
[152] See, for example, the concurring opinion of Judges Bindschedler-Rober, Gölcüklü, Matscher and Spielmann in *James a.o.* v. *the UK* (Plenary 1986).
[153] See, for example, the CETP Volume I 94 and 300–302; Volume II 126–130; Volume V 300–302; Volume VI 14 and compare the CETP Volume VI 32–34, 58 and 64.
[154] See, for example, Christoffersen (2009) 296.
[155] Similarly, Christoffersen (2009) 388.
[156] The CETP Volume I 30. See, also, for example, Mertens (1968) 467–468.

Further, a significant argument of those who opposed the establishment of the Court was that the Court was unnecessary, because once the facts were established by the Commission, this would give rise to immediate restitution by the Member States, who were all anxious to see human rights respected.[157] And many, including M. Edberg (Sweden), explicitly held that the rights had to be regarded as "supreme and binding upon all Governments".[158] Indeed, under the work with the collective guarantee (the Teitgen proposal), it was presupposed that a future Convention should have supremacy over domestic legislation.[159] The drafting fathers were also acutely aware of the linkage between the responsibility to secure rights and remedy violations.[160] The many changes in the wording of Article 1 to ensure that the rights were made "immediately effective" so that they could "be relied on before the [domestic] courts",[161] could, therefore, have bearings for the interpretation and understanding of Article 13. The drafting fathers were, also, acutely aware of the fact that legislation could violate the international guarantees, but did not explicitly exclude legislation from the scope of application of Article 13.[162]

On the other hand, the drafting fathers, more generally, showed great deference toward national Parliaments, and many States, in particular those which opposed the establishment of the Court, were anxious that the Court should overrule decisions by democratically elected Parliaments. Some even asked whether laws passed by democratically elected Parliaments could ever be "arbitrary" in the sense that they violated fundamental rights,[163] and Sir David Maxwell-Fyfe (UK) held that the only way in which the position of a national court could be dealt with in Strasbourg, was:

> when the law was so arbitrary, so contrary to all these rights which we have approved, that the national court was prevented from giving a judgment which would really be the satisfactory judgment of a court. In that case there would be an appeal, and only in that would it include a reflection on the

---

[157] See, for example, M. Rolin (Belgium), in the CETP Volume II 148, 152 and the CETP Volume III 18.

[158] See, for example, M. Edberg (Sweden), in the CETP Volume I 78.

[159] See, for example, the CETP Volume I 158–160.

[160] See Section 4.2.

[161] See Teitgen (1976) 39. See, also, Christoffersen (2009) 394–395 with further references.

[162] See, for example, the CETP Volume I 278. See, also, Christoffersen (2009) 392–394 concerning the significance of the so-called Solemn declaration, which he, in my opinion, reads too much into. Gerards and Fleuren (2014a) 343 hold that the drafting fathers clearly held that the substantive provisions of the Convention were to have direct effect in domestic law.

[163] See, for example, the CETP Volume II 126–128.

fact that the national court had been forced to put into effect arbitrary and undemocratic laws.[164]

Further, M. Rolin (Belgium), who supported the establishment of the Court, including the competences to declare legislation null and void, held that:

> None of the courts of our countries would have the power to judge our laws in this field, and we deplore having to give to external organs a jurisdiction which we do not allow our national organs.[165]

However, this statement specifically concerned the suggested competence of the Court to declare legislation null and void. Indeed, M. Rolin generally held that "[n]o State can shelter behind a national law to evade an international Convention."[166]

In summary, although there are some statements that might be taken to the contrary, if anything, the *travaux préparatoires*, read more globally, provide support for demanding, at the very least, that domestic remedial authorities, in some manner, need to be able to apply Convention rights, or comparable rights, as "correctives" in concrete cases, notwithstanding that the violation has been caused by primary legislation.

The second argument was that judicial review of legislation could only be imposed through a clear indication in the text of Article 13.[167] However, it is difficult to deduce any limitations of this sort in the wording of Article 13,[168] and the request for a "clear indication" finds no support in Article 31(1) of the VCLT.[169] This argument, however, was also connected to the understanding of some specific elements in the wording of Article 13. *First*, since Article 13 only requires a remedy by a "national authority", requiring judicial review would go beyond the scope of Article 13.[170] However, this is turning the wording on its head. Indeed, the fact that Article 13 only requires review by a national authority does not imply that, if judicial review is the only remedy actually made available, the possibility of challenging legislation must be excluded.

---

[164] CETP Volume II 200.

[165] Ibid. 130.

[166] Ibid.

[167] See, in particular, *Young, James and Webster* v. *the UK* (Plenary Commission report 1979) paras. 177–178

[168] Similarly, the dissenting opinion of MM. Opsahl and Trechsel in *Young, James and Webster* v. *the UK* (Plenary Commission report 1979); Matscher (1988) 330; Kilpatrick (2000) 23; Grabenwarter and Pabel (2012) 488.

[169] Similarly, Harris, O'Boyle et al. (2014) 765–766.

[170] See, for example, *Young, James and Webster* v. *the UK* (Plenary Commission report 1979) para. 177.

Second, the wording "notwithstanding that the violation has been committed by persons acting in an official capacity" indicated that Article 13 primarily had violations committed by entities of the executive or the judiciary, and not the legislature, in mind.[171] However, as the majority in *Young, James and Webster v. the UK* (Plenary Commission report 1979) was acutely aware of, this passage was inserted to exclude any doctrine of immunity.[172] Indeed, it is difficult to see how this reference can be used as an argument to restrict the scope of Article 13 to acts of the executive and judiciary.[173]

The third argument was that if domestic judicial review of legislation was to be demanded, the Convention would have to be incorporated into domestic law.[174] But, clearly, the State has a number of ways of complying with the obligation to provide an effective remedy, and the fact that domestic law in some States may be so organized that only incorporation, in practice, may provide effective remedies is primarily a concern for domestic law, not the understanding of the international obligation.

In summary, the arguments for introducing the principle that Article 13 grants no rights to challenge primary legislation were, at best, weak.

If we, then, turn to reconsidering the formal justification in the present context,[175] we first notice that even though constitutional review of legislation still is formally prohibited in a few Member States,[176] all Member States allow for some form of judicial review of legislation. That being said, the form and consequences may vary, most notably the extent to which courts may strike down legislation in the abstract and declare legislation null and void.[177] Further, all Member States have now, in some manner, incorporated the Convention. It is, in this context, particularly noteworthy that the principle

---

[171] Ibid.

[172] Ibid.

[173] Similarly, Matscher (1988) 330; Kilpatrick (2000) 23; Christoffersen (2009) 387; Grabenwarter and Pabel (2012) 488.

[174] See, for example, *James a.o. v. the UK* (Plenary 1986) paras. 84–87; *Lithgow a.o. v. the UK* (Plenary 1986) para. 206 and compare *Lithgow et al. v. the UK* (Plenary Commission report 1984) para. 482 and *Christine Goodwin v. the UK* (Grand Chamber 2002) para. 113.

[175] Compare Holoubek (1992) 148–151; Chryssogonos (2001) 53; Grote and Marauhn (2006) 1094–1096; Christoffersen (2009) 364 ff.

[176] For instance, Article 120 of the Dutch Constitution holds that the constitutionality of Acts of Parliament and treaties shall not be reviewed by courts. But the Dutch judiciary is still able to review primary legislation against rights of a constitutional character contained in European and international law, including the Convention, via Articles 93 and 94 of the Constitution; see, for example, Adams and van der Schyff (2006).

[177] See, for example, Law and Versteeg (2012) 766, 793–796 and, more generally, Gerards and Fleuren (2014). See, also, Tuori (2011) 245–255.

that Article 13 grants no right to challenge primary legislation was developed in a number of cases against the United Kingdom, which, at the time, had not incorporated the Convention and was chiefly critical of the establishment of the Court. The United Kingdom, at the time, did neither allow for judicial review of legislation nor did she accept the jurisdiction of the Court unconditionally, but applied the optional clause so as to reconsider on a yearly basis whether the jurisdiction of the Court should be binding on the United Kingdom. However, with the adoption and entry into force of the UK Human Rights Act, the Convention, with some exceptions, was incorporated in the UK law. The Court has accepted that, as of October 2, 2000, UK applicants, in principle, have an effective remedy available before domestic courts, also in judicial review cases.[178]

On the other hand, the Court has, and rightly so, been reluctant to set out requirements that could change the power balance between domestic democratic institutions.[179] And, certainly, if the Court were to require that domestic remedial authorities need have the power to strike down legislation in the abstract and declare legislation null and void, the power balance between many domestic legislators and courts would change. However, as should have become clear by now, the Court could limit itself to require a procedure that, in concrete cases, verifies whether legislation is in conformity with the Convention, without requiring that legislation be declared null and void, in accordance with that what the Commission members Opsahl and Trechsel proposed in *Young, James and Webster* v. *the UK* (Plenary Commission report 1979). Indeed, this is what the Court, indirectly, requires under substantive Articles, under which the Court does not hesitate declaring violations even though the violation stems from primary legislation.[180] In some newer cases, the Court has even declared violations of procedural aspects of substantive Articles explicitly because domestic remedial authorities could not review the Convention issue, even though the violation stemmed from primary legislation.[181]

---

[178] See, for example, *Christine Goodwin* v. *the UK* (Grand Chamber 2002) para. 113; *Appleby a.o.* v. *the UK* (2003) para. 56. Alas, the English *Sonderweg* with emphasis on parliamentary supremacy and rejection of constitutional review is approaching its end; see Tuori (2011) xix and his Chapter 7.

[179] See, for example, Christoffersen (2009) 388. But, in a number of areas, the Court has nudged judicial reform with significant consequences for the relationship between domestic legal institutions; see, for example, Kosař (2017).

[180] See, as a few examples, *Paulić* v. *Croatia* (2009) para. 42; *Losonci Rose and Rose* v. *Switzerland* (2010) para. 50; *Brežec* v. *Croatia* (2013) paras. 49–50.

[181] See, for example, *Koch* v. *Germany* (2012) paras. 66–68. However, the scope of this practice is uncertain; see, for example, *Nicklinson and Lamb* v. *the UK* (Decision 2015) paras. 83–84.

Further, following the judgments of the Court, States must implement both the individual and general measures necessary, subject to the procedures foreseen in Article 46 of the ECHR, which, again, may require changes in primary legislation.[182] Also the Court, and increasingly so, sets out remedial requirements with consequences for domestic legislation, in particular under substantive Articles and through the Pilot judgment procedure (Section 13.2). It remains a paradox that such remedial requirements may have to be stricter and more specific because the domestic remedial authority could not – and is not required to – provide a remedy against violations caused by primary legislation. It is, also, a paradox that the Court's scrutiny under substantive Articles may need be more rigorous when no domestic remedy is available. In *Kennedy* v. *the UK* (2010), for example, the Court, under Article 8, considered whether the mere existence of surveillance measures entailed a threat of surveillance for all those to whom the legislation (on surveillance) could be applied.[183] And, because there was no possibility of challenging the secret surveillance measures at domestic level, there was, indeed, greater need for scrutiny by the Court.[184]

Clearly, such paradoxes do not chime well with the principle of subsidiarity. Indeed, in the current situation, one of the main obstacles to achieving a subsidiary protection of human rights is that the Convention, in many States, is not given priority over domestic legislation. Many, therefore, hold that national courts have both the right and duty to ensure the supremacy of the Convention, also over domestic legislation.[185] However, under Article 13, the Court does not require this supremacy.[186] This not only makes the protection of human rights less effective because the individual has to turn to Strasbourg, but makes the Court's review more complicated as there is less to review.[187]

The principle, also, creates the additional paradox that only States in which primary legislation still prevails over the Convention, in practical terms,

[182] See, for example, notes 1 and 2 to Rule 2 of the Rules of the Committee of Ministers for the supervision of the execution of judgments and of the terms of friendly settlements.
[183] *Kennedy* v. *the UK* (2010) paras. 99–100. See, also, for example, *Kulinski and Sabev* v. *Bulgaria* (2016) paras. 49–51.
[184] *Kennedy* v. *the UK* (2010) para. 124.
[185] See, for example, Costa (2009) 474; Jagland (2014) 15–16.
[186] Surprisingly, this has not explicitly been an issue in the process of the reform of the Court. Philippe Boillat, for example, has emphasized that the solution must be found in dialogue between the Court and domestic courts; see, for example, Boillat (2009b) 19 and Boillat (2009a) 554, but without commenting on the fact that Article 13 does not require the primacy of the Convention over domestic legislation. See, however, more generally, the introductory part of Section B in the Brussels declaration.
[187] Similarly, Christoffersen (2009) 391.

may invoke it. Indeed, States that have effectively integrated the law of the Convention in their legal systems, *inter alia*, through harmonious interpretation and by taking the case law of the Court into account have few practical possibilities and incentives for invoking the principle. However, States in which the Convention and the case law of the Court still remain separate from domestic law may invoke it. But, it may very well be that these are the States with the greatest need to improve their domestic remedies. Further, the distinction between primary and secondary legislation may have the skewed effect of providing incentives for States to adopt more primary legislation at the expense of secondary legislation. And, in any case, the extent to which States have chosen to adopt laws in the form of primary and/or secondary legislation varies considerably. The distinction may, therefore, cause unjustified differences in the minimum level of protection of human rights.[188]

The development and perseverance of the principle is particularly striking if one compares how the doctrine of primarity and direct effect has developed and persisted within EU law. Indeed, at its inception, the project of European human rights was closely linked to the initiative of integrating Europe in terms of politics and economics,[189] and the EU system and the Convention system have – ever since – been closely connected.[190] However, whereas the ECJ, in its early case law, required the primacy of EC law over domestic law, by introducing the doctrine of direct effect, and by insisting that the domestic judiciary upholds this primacy, the Court in Strasbourg has, at least in its early years, been more focused on establishing limits for the use of Article 13.[191]

10.5.4 *The Substance of the Complaint*

With these limitations in the back of our minds, we can proceed to analyze what is required of the national authority in order to be able to "deal with the substance of the relevant Convention complaint".[192]

---

[188] Similarly, Matscher (1988) 334.
[189] See, for example, Bates (2013) 25.
[190] See, for example, Popelier, Heyning *et al.* (2011) 3.
[191] Compare Flauss (1991) 326.
[192] The principle was so first formulated by the Court in *Soering* v. *the UK* (Plenary 1989) para. 120. Later, the principle has mostly been formulated in the same manner; see, for example, *Chahal* v. *the UK* (Grand Chamber 1996) para. 145; *M.S.S.* v. *Belgium and Greece* (Grand Chamber 2011) para. 291, but, occasionally, the Court uses slightly different wording, for instance, "enforce the substance of the Convention rights"; see, for example, *Keegan* v. *the UK* (2006) para. 41, or that the applicant has the right "having the relevant issues examined with sufficient procedural safeguards and thoroughness by an appropriate domestic forum"; see, for example, *Riener* v. *Bulgaria* (2006) para. 138.

Any assessment of substance relates to questions of both law and facts. As a starting-point, if the national authority cannot deal with the facts that are causing the violation, the remedy is not effective.[193] But the relevant facts may be subject to different degrees of scrutiny and governed by a variety of domestic laws and principles, which may be more or less similar to the Convention rights, and the application of such laws and principles, including the degree of scrutiny, may vary.

As a starting-point and background to the analyses below, the following two overarching points should be taken into account.

First, the domestic remedial authority must not comment upon every argument that the applicant addresses during domestic proceedings. The argument must have some bearing for the substance of the Convention complaint.[194] On the other hand, if relevant arguments and facts are not examined at all,[195] or if the domestic authority is not competent to deal with the Convention issue, be it related to law or facts, Article 13 will be violated.[196] Indeed, immunity from review not only violates Article 13, but is "incompatible with the rule of law in a free and democratic society."[197]

Second, the form of the proceedings is, as such, not decisive, as long as the substance of the complaint can be dealt with. The substance may, therefore, in principle, be dealt with in, for example, admissibility proceedings.[198] However, if the authority only rules on formal issues, such as whether a decree is issued by the competent body,[199] or if the underlying issue on which the national authority may decide is only indirectly related to the issue under the Convention, for instance, the action of the police officer and not the underlying permission permitting the action of the police officer,[200] Article 13 has been violated. The same applies if the remedial authority may, in principle, deal with the substance of the complaint, but it is

[193] See, for example, *Iustin Robertino Micu v. Romania* (2015) para. 107; *Chiragov a.o. v. Armenia* (Grand Chamber 2015) paras. 214 and 118.

[194] See, for example, *Verein der Freunde der Christengemeinschaft a.o. v. Austria* (2009) paras. 60–64.

[195] See, for example, *Hagyó v. Hungary* (2013) para. 97; *Hirtu a.o. v. France* (2020) para. 90.

[196] See, for example, *Friedl v. Austria* (Plenary Commission report 1994) para. 77; *E.B. a.o. v. Austria* (2013) para. 92.

[197] See, for example, *Fevzi Saygılı v. Turkey* (2008) para. 41.

[198] See, for example, *Amann v. Switzerland* (Grand Chamber 2000) para. 89; *Metropolitan Church of Bessarabia a.o. v. Moldova* (2001) para. 139: *Lorsé a.o. v. the Netherlands* (2003) para. 93.

[199] See, for example, *Hasan and Chaush v. Bulgaria* (Grand Chamber 2000) para. 100; *Glas Nadezhda EOOD and Elenkov v. Bulgaria* (2007) paras. 69–70.

[200] See, for example, *Avanesyan v. Russia* (2014) para. 22.

settled case law that only persons who are still affected have *locus standi* to lodge a complaint.[201]

If we then look at the case law of the Court more concretely, we notice that there has been a clear development toward demanding both that (1) the legal starting-points must be more similar to those applied by the Court and (2) the concrete scrutiny of both facts and law must be more rigorous.

Indeed, in early case law, the Court accepted that the substance could be dealt with in proceedings which applied legal criteria and standards quite different from those applied by the Court. The prime example is that UK Courts were considered able to deal with the substance of the complaint under the so-called Wednesbury principles. The first example can be found in *Soering* v. *the UK* (Plenary 1989). Article 3 would have been violated if a prisoner were extradited to the United States. The decision was taken by the Secretary of State and reviewed by UK courts. The review was limited to finding "the exercise of executive discretion unlawful" on the grounds that it was "illegal, irrational or amounted to procedural impropriety".[202] Although this test applies criteria very different from those applied by the Court under Article 3,[203] the review was performed "in the light of the kind of factors relied on by Mr. Soering before the Convention institutions", which was sufficient to satisfy Article 13.[204] That being said, in some cases, the review of UK courts was even more limited, most notably in deportation cases which raised issues of national security, in which UK courts confined themselves to examining whether the evidence showed that the Secretary of State had carried out a balancing of the risk against the perceived threat to national security. These legal starting-points were too different, with the consequence that Article 13 was violated.[205] And although the legal starting-points could be different, the threshold of irrationality could not be set so high that it effectively excluded any consideration of the relevant criteria under the Convention.[206]

Hatton v. *the UK* (Grand Chamber 2003), then, indicates a general change with regard to the review according to the Wednesbury principles. Article 8 was violated because of the failure to protect against increased noise from an airport.

---

[201] See, for example, *Camenzind* v. *Switzerland* (1997) para. 54.
[202] *Soering* v. *the UK* (Plenary 1989) para. 121.
[203] Ibid., paras. 100–104.
[204] Ibid., paras. 121 and 124. The majority of seven to four members of the Commission, on the other hand, had found the review insufficient; see, *Soering* v. *the UK* (Commission report 1989) para. 166.
[205] See, for example, *Chahal* v. *the UK* (Grand Chamber 1996) paras. 143 and 151.
[206] See, for example, *Smith and Grady* v. *the UK* (1999); *Bensaid* v. *the UK* (2001); *Beck, Copp and Bazeley* v. *the UK* (2002); *Peck* v. *the UK* (2003).

Under Article 13, a majority of 16 to 1 found that the scope of judicial review was too limited,[207] because it "was limited to the classic English public-law concepts, such as irrationality, unlawfulness and patent unreasonableness."[208] Nothing was said about the relationship to the Court's earlier case law.

The review in UK tort law cases, also, illustrates how the legal starting-points now have to be more similar to those applied by the Court. In *Murray* v. *the UK* (Grand Chamber 1994), which concerned the searching of the applicant's house arguably violating Article 8, Article 13 was not violated, even though the applicant had very feeble prospects of success because the Army had lawful authority for its search according to domestic law.[209] However, in *Keegan* v. *the UK* (2006), the Court simply held that domestic courts "were unable to examine issues of proportionality or reasonableness" and that "the balance was set in favour of protection of the police." Domestic courts could, therefore, not deal with the substance of the complaint under the Convention.[210] No mention of previous case law was made.

In other areas, too, the Court now requires that the domestic remedial authorities apply legal starting-points that are more similar to those applied by the Court.

In *Riener* v. *Bulgaria* (2006), the applicant had not been allowed to leave Bulgaria for more than nine years because of tax obligations, which violated P4 Article 2. Since domestic courts did not consider and attach weight to several concerns pertinent for the assessment of proportionality under Article 8 and P4 Article 2, they were not able to deal with the substance of the complaint as required by Article 13.[211] In *Pfeifer* v. *Bulgaria* (2011), the Court went one step further and explicitly required that the individual need be able to "put forward all arguments impacting on the proportionality – in the Convention sense of the word – of the measure."[212] And, in *Stamose* v. *Bulgaria* (2012), domestic courts "could not scrutinise the authorities' discretionary assessment of the need for the ban – ... a key part of the balancing exercise required under Article 2 § 3 of Protocol No. 4."[213]

---

[207] The minority, consisting of Sir Brian Kerr, found that in reality the "state of domestic law" was challenged and that Article 13, therefore, did not apply.
[208] *Hatton a.o.* v. *the UK* (Grand Chamber 2003) paras. 138–142.
[209] *Murray* v. *the UK* (Grand Chamber 1994) para. 100 and *Murray* v. *the UK* (Plenary Commission report 1993) para. 91.
[210] *Keegan* v. *the UK* (2006) para. 42. See, also, for example, *Wainwright* v. *the UK* (2006) para. 55 (strip-searches violating Article 8).
[211] *Riener* v. *Bulgaria* (2006), paras. 140–143.
[212] *Pfeifer* v. *Bulgaria* (2011) para. 67.
[213] *Stamose* v. *Bulgaria* (2012) para. 51.

Also in expulsion cases, which, arguably, may violate, in particular, Articles 2, 3, and 8, the Court now requires, directly and explicitly under Article 13, that domestic remedial authorities apply more or less the same starting-points as the Court. For instance, in *Al-Nashif* v. *Bulgaria* (2002), concerning Article 8, the Court held that Article 13 requires that "the question whether the impugned measure would interfere with the individual's right to respect for family life and, if so, whether a fair balance is struck between the public inter-est involved and the individual's rights" is examined.[214] *C.G. a.o.* v. *Bulgaria* (2008) is even more explicit and requires that "the authority has to carry out a balancing exercise and examine whether the interference with the applicants' rights answered a pressing social need and was proportionate to the legitimate aims pursued."[215] *Vasil Sashov Petrov* v. *Bulgaria* (2010) is very explicit concern-ing a substantive and procedural violation of Article 2 because of life threat-ening use of force in circumstances where this was not deemed absolutely necessary. The Court held, more generally, that Article 13 required that alle-gations of breaches of Article 2 must be examined in line with the standards developed in the Court's case law "which demand a careful review of whether life-threatening force used during arrest operations is more than 'absolutely necessary', that is, strictly proportionate in the circumstances."[216]

The Court now, also, requires that the concrete scrutiny of both law and facts need be more rigorous. But the scrutiny may vary, depending on, *inter alia*, the violation and the circumstances (Chapter 8). For instance, in pro-ceedings raising issues of national security, the scrutiny may, more generally, be less rigorous, and when there is danger of irreparable damage, the scrutiny must, more generally, be more rigorous. Both these aspects are illustrated in expulsion cases, which, most notably, may violate Articles 2, 3, and 8.

Chahal v. *the UK* (Grand Chamber 1996) concerned the scope of review by UK courts and authorities in deportation proceedings which could lead to a violation of Article 3 and which had to be balanced against the interests of national security. UK courts could not review the evidence on which the Secretary of State had based his decision that the applicant constituted a dan-ger to national security, or undertake any evaluation of the Article 3 risks, but had to confine themselves to examine whether the evidence showed that the

---

[214] *Al-Nashif* v. *Bulgaria* (2002) para. 137.
[215] *C.G. a.o.* v. *Bulgaria* (2008) paras. 62–63. Similarly, for example, *Raza* v. *Bulgaria* (2010) paras. 62–63; *Kaushal a.o.* v. *Bulgaria* (2010) paras. 39–40; *Asalya* v. *Turkey* (2014) para. 119; *Voynov* v. *Russia* (2018) paras. 42–43; *Gorlov a.o.* v. *Russia* (2019) para. 108; *Kungorov* v. *Russia* (2020) para. 24.
[216] *Vasil Sashov Petrov* v. *Bulgaria* (2010) para. 60.

Secretary of State had carried out the balancing of these interests as required by domestic law.[217] But, in assessing whether there was a real risk of treatment in breach of Article 3, the fact that the person was a danger to national security is not a material consideration, in contrast to assessments under Articles 8 and 10.[218] Therefore,

> given the irreversible nature of the harm that might occur if the risk of ill-treatment materialised and the importance the Court attaches to Article 3, the notion of an effective remedy under Article 13 requires *independent scrutiny* of the claim that there exist substantial grounds for fearing a real risk of treatment contrary to Article 3. This scrutiny must be carried out *without regard to what the person may have done to warrant expulsion or to any perceived threat to the national security of the expelling State.* (My emphasis)[219]

However, where national security considerations are involved, certain limitations on the type of remedies available to the individual may be justified. For instance, in cases concerning secret surveillance and the use of secret information for the screening of job candidates who would have access to sensitive information which, arguably, may violate Article 8, Article 13 only requires a remedy "as effective as it can be" because a restricted scope for recourse is inherent in any system of secret surveillance.[220] That being said, concerns regarding national security do not imply that there can be no scrutiny. In secret surveillance cases, there must, as a minimum, be a possibility of challenging the holding of personal information or of refuting the truth of the information. It is not sufficient that it may be possible to disclose the information about the identity of some of the secret surveillance collaborators and agents.[221] And, in cases of expulsion of aliens on grounds of national security which, arguably, may violate Article 8, the remedial authority must, as a minimum, "be informed of the reasons grounding the deportation decision, even if such reasons are not publicly available." Further, the authority "must be competent to reject the executive's assertion that there is a threat to national security where it finds it arbitrary or unreasonable." There must, also, be "some form of adversarial proceedings, if need be through a special representative after a security clearance." The remedial authority must also examine "the question whether the impugned measure would interfere with

---

[217] *Chahal* v. *the UK* (Grand Chamber 1996) para. 143.
[218] See, for example, *Chahal* v. *the UK* (Grand Chamber 1996) paras. 149–150, and compare, for example, *Klass a.o.* v. *Germany* (Plenary 1978) and *Leander* v. *Sweden* (1987).
[219] *Chahal* v. *the UK* (Grand Chamber 1996) para. 151.
[220] See, for example, *Al-Nashif* v. *Bulgaria* (2002) para. 136.
[221] *Rotaru* v. *Romania* (Grand Chamber 2000) paras. 71–72.

the individual's right to respect for family life and, if so, whether a fair balance is struck between the public interest involved and the individual's rights."[222] Accordingly, the scrutiny must not be as strict as in expulsion cases which, arguably, violate Article 3, but must be stricter than in secret surveillance cases which, arguably, violate Article 8.[223]

In some areas, the Court requires a particularly intensive scrutiny. Again, expulsions that arguably may violate Article 3 are illustrative. In *Jabari v. Turkey* (2002) the Court, for example, held that:

> given the irreversible nature of the harm that might occur if the risk of torture or ill-treatment alleged materialised and the importance which it attaches to Article 3, the notion of an effective remedy under Article 13 requires *independent and rigorous scrutiny of a claim that there exist substantial grounds for fearing a real risk of treatment contrary to Article 3 and the possibility of suspending the implementation of the measure impugned.* (My emphasis)[224]

In contrast, in deportation procedures arguably violating Article 8, Article 13:

> requires that States must make available to the individual concerned the effective possibility of challenging the deportation or refusal-of-residence order and of having the relevant issues *examined with sufficient procedural safeguards and thoroughness by an appropriate domestic forum* offering adequate guarantees of independence and impartiality. (My emphasis)[225]

Further, *M.S.S. v. Belgium and Greece* (Grand Chamber 2011) underlines that the rigorous scrutiny required by Article 13 in conjunction with Article 3 cannot be limited to "verifying whether the persons concerned had produced concrete proof of the irreparable nature of the damage that might result from the alleged potential violation of Article 3." Indeed, the remedial authority has an independent responsibility for shedding light on the arguable violation.[226] It is, for instance, necessary to specify exactly where the applicant will be deported. If not, any meaningful examination of the risks involved in the deportation will be hampered, rendering Article 13 illusory.[227] And even though, as a starting-point, the applicant must cite evidence capable of proving that there are substantial grounds for believing that he/she would be

---

[222] See, for example, *Al-Nashif v. Bulgaria* (2002) para. 137.
[223] Such lack of scrutiny has been a persistent problem in Bulgaria; see, for example, *C.G. a.o. v. Bulgaria* (2008); *Kaushal a.o. v. Bulgaria* (2010); *Baltaji v. Bulgaria* (2011); *M. a.o. v. Bulgaria* (2011); *Auad v. Bulgaria* (2011).
[224] *Jabari v. Turkey* (2000) para. 50.
[225] *Al-Nashif v. Bulgaria* (2002) para. 133.
[226] See, for example, *M.S.S. v. Belgium and Greece* (Grand Chamber 2011) para. 389.
[227] See, for example, *Asalya v. Turkey* (2014) para. 113.

exposed to a real risk of being subjected to treatment prohibited by Article 3, the Government must dispel any doubts about it. In this context, the Court recognizes that asylum-seekers are often in a special situation, which frequently necessitates giving them the benefit of the doubt when assessing the credibility of their statements and the supporting documents that they have submitted. But, when information is lacking, or when there is a strong reason to question the veracity of an asylum-seeker's submissions, the individual must provide a satisfactory explanation for the discrepancies.[228] The best way for an asylum-seeker to prove his/her identity is usually by submitting an original passport. But if this is not possible on account of the circumstances, other documents and circumstances may prove his/her identity, for instance, a birth certificate. That being said, depending on the circumstances, domestic authorities may assume, for example, that a birth certificate is not capable of proving the applicant's origins.[229] Further, for the review to be rigorous, it cannot only confirm a decision by an administrative authority that lacks the necessary scrutiny of the risks concerned.[230] The merits of the arguable claim need be rigorously examined.[231] It does not, for example, suffice to question particular provisions of an Alien Act with the domestic Constitution in general.[232]

Concerning excessive length of proceedings arguably violating Article 6(1), the remedial authority must analyze all the relevant periods and provide "a proper assessment of the overall length of the proceedings."[233] It may, thereto, be necessary to examine in detail the concrete steps of, for example, a criminal investigation, for instance, "why, after more than four years, the investigative authorities still needed to obtain key evidence."[234]

More generally, even though States, as a starting-point, may set out their own rules governing evidence, the remedial authority cannot take a too formalistic approach with regard to the admittance of evidence.[235] In addition, if the applicant provides the remedial authority with reasons to believe that the Government is in a position to deliver evidence of significance, this evidence has to be delivered. If not, the scrutiny incumbent on national authorities may be rendered illusory.[236]

---

[228] See, for example, *A.A.* v. *Switzerland* (2014) para. 60.

[229] Ibid., para. 61.

[230] See, for example, *Diallo* v. *the Czech Republic* (2011) para. 79.

[231] Ibid., para. 81.

[232] Ibid., para. 83. See, also, for example, *Budrevich* v. *the Czech Republic* (2013) para. 111.

[233] See, for example, *Tur* v. *Poland* (2007) para. 64.

[234] *Golovkin* v. *Russia* (2008) para. 34.

[235] See, for example, *Stelian Roşca* v. *Romania* (2013) para. 99.

[236] Ibid., para. 100. See, also, for example, *Csüllög* v. *Hungary* (2011) para. 48.

Further, the manner in which the Court deals with the lack of scrutiny illustrates two points of importance.

First, the relationship between the requirement that the authority need be able to deal with the substance of the complaint and the requirement that remedy must be effective not only in theory but also in practice, is not always easy to draw. In early case law, the Court mostly found that Article 13 had not been violated if the remedial authority, in principle, was able to deal with the substance of the complaint, without considering whether the remedy was effective in practice.[237] In more recent case law, however, a remedy is often found to be ineffective even though the remedial authority had it within its powers to deal with the substance of the complaint (Section 9.4).[238] Indeed, the Court has even held, more recently, that "what matters is the reality of the situation rather than appearances ..." and that the case, therefore, "must have *in fact been examined consistently with the standards flowing from the Court's case-law.*" (My emphasis)[239]

Second, and connected to the foregoing, the Court is more prone to consider that domestic courts have taken the authorities' assertions at face value, rather than subjecting them to a rigorous scrutiny, when domestic courts are silent on the issues in question.[240] Indeed, silence, or lack of justification by the domestic remedial authorities, is particularly alarming and should make it easier to find a violation of Article 13, more generally, in particular, if the applicant is not able to access all the information used against him.[241] In this sense, the considerations under both the requirement that the authority be able to deal with the substance of the complaint and the requirement that the remedy be effective in practice are dependent on the actual justification provided by domestic remedial authorities. But the Court has not, in a principled manner, explained how lacking justification relates to the requirements, in particular to what extent justification may be perceived as a separate and independent requirement. However, in many cases, the lack of justification, as such, at least indirectly, seems to be decisive[242]

---

[237] See, for example, *Vereinigung demokratischer Soldaten Österreichs and Gubi v. Austria* (1994) para. 55.

[238] See, for example, *Debelić v. Croatia* (2005) paras. 45–46; *Vladimir Kharitonov v. Russia* (2020) para. 56; *Kargakis v. Greece* (2021) paras. 82 and 83.

[239] *Neshkov a.o. v. Bulgaria* (2015) para. 187. See, also, for example, *Yengo v. France* (2015) para. 62; *Kiril Ivanov v. Bulgaria* (2018) paras. 59–60.

[240] See, for example, *Asalya v. Turkey* (2014) para. 117 and contrast with, for example, *D v. the UK* (1997) paras. 71–73.

[241] See, for example, *Asalya v. Turkey* (2014) para. 118.

[242] See, for example, *Garayev v. Azerbaijan* (2010) para. 84 and the dissenting opinion of Judges Spielmann and Malinverni in *Maksimov v. Russia* (2010) para. 12. Justification is formally required under Article 6; see, for example, *Taxquet v. Belgium* (Grand Chamber 2010) para. 91.

10.6 PROSPECT OF SUCCESS

Under Article 35(1), the applicant only needs to exhaust the remedies which have "reasonable prospect of success" (Chapter 5). Under Article 13, the Court holds that certainty of success is not decisive, as long as the national authority is able to deal with the substance of the complaint,[243] or that Article 13 does not guarantee a remedy bound to succeed, but simply an accessible remedy before an authority competent to examine the merits of the complaint.[244] On the other hand, if the remedy offers no prospect of success, the remedy is not effective under Article 13. Many cases concerning effective investigations, in which the Court holds that, without effective investigations, no remedy has any prospect of succeeding, are illustrative of this.[245]

Also when an existing remedy is, in general, not enforced, for instance, because of systemic failures in the State concerned, the Court considers that the remedy has no prospect of success, with the consequence that the remedy is ineffective.[246] And, when the remedy is required to have automatic suspensive effect, the remedy needs be successful in the sense that it must be suspensive.[247]

Moreover, in many cases concerning Article 13, the Court often only refers to the assessment under Article 35(1), even when the requirement of "reasonable prospect" of success was decisive and finds a violation of Article 13 on similar grounds.[248] In a few cases, the Court has, also, used the wording "reasonable prospect of success" directly under Article 13.[249] The question then arises as to whether there is a requirement of a prospect of success under Article 13, and, if so, what prospect of success is required (Fig. 10.1)?

Based upon the case law of the Court, it is hard pressed to maintain that there is a general requirement of "reasonable" prospect of success under Article 13, in a similar manner as under Article 35(1). Indeed, under Article 13, the Court mostly refers to *no prospect* of success. If some other standard

---

[243] See, for example, *Swedish Engine Drivers' Union* v. *Sweden* (1976) para. 50; *Amann* v. *Switzerland* (Grand Chamber 2000) para. 88; *Shchebetov* v. *Russia* (2012) para. 90.

[244] See, for example, *Lorsé a.o.* v. *the Netherlands* (2003) para. 96; *Düzgören* v. *Turkey* (2006) para. 36; *I.G. a.o.* v. *Slovakia* (2012) para. 154.

[245] See Section 11.7 and, for example, *Menteş a.o.* v. *Turkey* (Grand Chamber 1997).

[246] See Section 11.9 and, as an example, *A.B.* v. *the Netherlands* (2002) paras. 98 and 72–73.

[247] See Section 11.3.2.

[248] See, for example, *Rodić and 3 Others* v. *Bosnia and Herzegovina* (2008) paras. 85 and 58.

[249] See, for example, *D.M.T. and D.K.I.* v. *Bulgaria* (2012) para. 126; *O'Keeffe* v. *Ireland* (Grand Chamber 2014) para. 177; *Apap Bologna* v. *Malta* (2016) para. 79.

```
|------------------------------------?------------------------------------|
No prospect              Reasonable prospect               Certainty
```

FIGURE 10.1 *Prospect of success*

was sufficient, why not refer to that? *M.S.S.* v. *Belgium and Greece* (Grand Chamber 2011) is illustrative, in which the Court held that "while the effectiveness of a remedy does not depend on the certainty of a favourable outcome for the applicant, *the lack of any prospect of obtaining adequate redress raises an issue under Article 13.*" (My emphasis)[250]

The Court has not explained why the approaches under Articles 13 and 35(1) are different. But different purposes and more practical considerations may justify the different approaches. Such differences should mostly lead to the conclusion that the hurdle of effectiveness is easier to climb under Article 35(1), at least with regard to the required prospect of success (Chapter 5). The Court should, therefore, avoid using the term "reasonable prospect of success" as a general criterion under Article 13. Indeed, a flexible requirement of success may then be applied under the evaluation of whether the remedy is effective not only in theory but also in practice (Section 9.4). This allows for a broader assessment under which the prospect of success, as such, is not decisive, but under which national authorities have to take the positive measures required in the circumstances to ensure that the applicant's complaint is properly dealt with and that the remedy is effective in practice.[251] The required prospect of success could then vary, depending on the type of violation and the specific circumstances.[252]

That being said, when the State, under Article 13, puts forward alternative remedies, which have not been used by the applicant, and which he/she was not required to exhaust under Article 35(1), the State must, as a minimum, present an example showing the application of the alternative remedies in a similar case,[253] or that the remedy exists with a sufficient degree of certainty.[254] For instance, in *Horvat* v. *Croatia* (2001), concerning excessive length of proceedings, a complaint to the Constitutional Court was not effective, *inter alia*, because the Government only produced one case in which the Constitutional Court had ruled under the relevant section of the Constitutional Act to

---

[250] *M.S.S.* v. *Belgium and Greece* (Grand Chamber 2011) para. 394.
[251] See, for example, *Onoufriou* v. *Cyprus* (2010) para. 123.
[252] See Chapter 8 and, for example, *Lorsé a.o.* v. *the Netherlands* (2003) para. 96.
[253] See, for example, *Rotaru* v. *Romania* (Grand Chamber 2000) para. 70; *Bazjaks* v. *Latvia* (2010) paras. 133 and 134; *Voynov* v. *Russia* (2018) paras. 40 and 45; *Ter-Petrosyan* v. *Armenia* (2019) para. 57.
[254] See, for example, *Lukenda* v. *Slovenia* (2005) paras. 87 and 53; *Burdov* v. *Russia* (no. 2) (2009) para. 104; *Khider* v. *France* (2009) paras. 141–145; *O'Keeffe* v. *Ireland* (Grand Chamber 2014) para. 186.

support their argument concerning the effectiveness of the remedy.[255] Most notably, in repetitive cases, the Court may perform a very detailed assessment of the certainty of the existence of the remedy in practice.[256]

In numerous cases, the Court has dealt with claims that changes in practice, in particular from national courts, must lead to a different evaluation with regard to the existence of the remedy, compared to previous cases in which the Court has found a violation of Article 13. In *Peck v. the UK* (2003), for example, the Government argued that the scope of national judicial review in cases concerning arguable violations of the right to privacy now satisfied Article 13 because UK case law had introduced a general principle of proportionality. However, this case law was not sufficiently established, most notably because the references to proportionality were made in an *obiter dictum*, and, in any event, did not demonstrate the full application by domestic courts of the proportionality principle in a judicial review context.[257]

The Court seems to demand more evidence for the existence of the remedy when the State points to a general remedy which is not specifically directed at the problem in hand.[258] A special branch of this question is to what extent the State can point to the fact that the Convention is incorporated into national law and that redress could be obtained by applying the Convention directly before national courts or other national authorities. In such cases, the Court has demanded examples of litigants successfully relying on the Convention in order to obtain redress and clarity as to how it is possible to achieve redress against the specific problem at issue, for example, to what authority the applicant could apply, what procedure would be followed, and what the concrete legal effects of the complaint would be.[259] The Court has applied similar

---

[255] *Horvat v. Croatia* (2001) paras. 65 and 41–45. The Croatian Constitution was later amended and the Court has found this remedy effective for the purposes of both Article 35(1) and Article 13; see, for example, *Slaviček v. Croatia* (decision 2002) with regard to Article 35(1) and *Rados a.o. v. Croatia* (2002) with regard to Article 13.

[256] See, for example, *Sergey Babushkin v. Russia* (2013) para. 43; *Yarashonen v. Turkey* (2014) paras. 63–64.

[257] *Peck v. the UK* (2003) para. 106. See, also, for example, *D.M. v. Poland* (2003) para. 48 and, thereafter, for example, *Cegielski v. Poland* (2003) para. 42; *Zynger v. Poland* (2004) para. 63; *Krasuski v. Poland* (2005) paras. 68–69, which confirm the existence of new effective remedies concerning excessive length of proceedings. See, for a similar development in the Czech Republic, for example, *Slezák a.o. v. the Czech Republic* (2005).

[258] See, for example, *Gavrielidou a.o. v. Cyprus* (2006) para. 50; *Sürmeli v. Germany* (Grand Chamber 2006) paras. 110 and 113; *Saarekallas OÜ v. Estonia* (2007) paras. 65–66.

[259] See, with regard to excessive length of proceedings, for example, *Rachevi v. Bulgaria* (2004) para. 100; *Wasserman v. Russia (no. 2)* (2008) para. 54; *Paroisse gréco-catholique Sfântul Vasile Polonă v. Romania* (2009) paras. 103–104 and, with regard to conditions of detention, for example, *Marcu v. Romania* (2010) para. 77; *Mandić and Jović v. Slovenia* (2011) paras. 112–114.

reasoning in several complaints against Russia, in which the effectiveness of a general judicial complaint of infringements of rights and freedoms was considered.[260]

Concerning the scope of redress, the Court accepts that, if the national authority could, in principle, afford sufficient redress, Article 13 is not necessarily violated even though sufficient redress was not granted in the specific case.[261] However, under the substantive Article, the applicant may then still be a victim according to Article 34 and thus granted additional redress by the Court under Article 41.[262] In fact, in cases concerning compensatory remedies, if the national authority is competent to grant sufficient redress and there is no indication of a systemic error, a lower redress than that awarded by the Court will only render the remedy ineffective under Article 13 if the "amount of compensation awarded by the domestic courts was so derisory as to raise issues of the effectiveness of the redress."[263]

10.7 SPEED

Article 13 requires that the remedial action be performed with a minimum of speed. Requirements of speed are, also, expressly included in Articles 5(3), 5(4), and 6(1). Under Article 13, the Court has not emphasized general criteria to be taken into account, in a similar manner as, for example, under Article 6(1). However, also under Article 13, the complexity of the proceedings, the conduct of the domestic authorities, and the applicant, as well as what is at stake for the applicant, must be relevant factors (Chapter 8).

The required speed may vary, depending on the violation and circumstances of the case. When complaining about conditions of detention which, arguably, violate Article 3, for instance, isolation, the requirement is strict. The Court has, for instance, found a Latvian law that more generally afforded the authorities between 15 and 30 days to deal with such complaints to be ineffective.[264] And even if the applicant is released from prison – and there is no danger of new irreversible damage – the authorities have been required to act with the speed required, both during the investigations and the trial, so as not to render the

---

[260] See, for example, *Dirdizov* v. *Russia* (2012) paras. 85–90; *Reshetnyak* v. *Russia* (2013) paras. 74–79.

[261] See, for example, *Šidlová* v. *Slovakia* (2006).

[262] See Section 6.3.

[263] See, for example, *Wainwright* v. *the UK* (2006) para. 55; *Nicolò Santilli* v. *Italy* (2013) para. 86. However, if a systemic practice of awarding lower compensation is established, the remedy is not effective in practice; see, for example, *Apap Bologna* v. *Malta* (2016) paras. 80–91. See, also, Section 11.5.4.

[264] *Kadiķis* v. *Latvia* (no. 2) (2006) para. 62.

remedial action ineffective.[265] However, a particular prompt response is required when there is risk of irreversible damage, in particular in cases arguably violating Articles 2 and 3.[266] Further, if the adequate nature of the remedy may be undermined by time, the Court pays particular attention to the speediness of the remedial action.[267] In some cases, the remedial action must, for instance, be performed before a planned action is set into motion (Section 11.3.3).

In cases concerning excessive length of proceedings, the Court attaches particular importance to the speed of the remedial action itself. In order for a preventive remedy to be effective, the totality of the procedures must be taken into account. The effectiveness of the preventive remedy may thus depend on "whether it has a significant effect on the length of the proceedings as a whole."[268] If not, compensation may also be necessary to provide sufficient redress. A remedy awarding compensation must then in itself comply with the "reasonable time" requirement in Article 6(1). In addition, the procedural rules applied to the remedy must not be the same as those applied to ordinary applications for damages.[269] This could mean that ordinary civil procedures for claiming damages cannot be used. In *Vlad a.o. v. Romania* (2013), for instance, the compensatory remedy followed ordinary civil procedures for claiming damages, which could last several years through three jurisdictions. Such "a lapse of time would not be reconcilable with the requirement that the remedy for delay be sufficiently swift."[270] In other cases, lack of speed is one of the several factors which, in total, make the remedy ineffective.[271]

Also in relation to violations of Articles 8, 12, and Protocol 1 Article 1, the Court has found the remedial action to be ineffective because of insufficient speed.[272]

---

[265] See, for example, *Hüseyin Esen v. Turkey* (2006) para. 63.

[266] See, for example, *M.S.S. v. Belgium and Greece* (Grand Chamber 2011) para. 293.

[267] See, for example, *Sürmeli v. Germany* (Grand Chamber 2006) para. 100; *M.S.S. v. Belgium and Greece* (Grand Chamber 2011) para. 292; *de Souza Ribeiro v. France* (Grand Chamber 2012) para. 81.

[268] See, for example, *Djangozov v. Bulgaria* (2004) para. 52; *Bartha v. Hungary* (2014) para. 17.

[269] *Vlad a.o. v. Romania* (2013) para. 112.

[270] Ibid., para. 118.

[271] See, for example, *Raudsepp v. Estonia* (2011) paras. 82 and 65.

[272] See, for example, *Ratushna v. Ukraine* (2010) (claim for compensation, arguable violation of right to home, Article 8); *Jaremowicz v. Poland* (2010) para. 71 (belated permission to marry in detention, violation of Article 12); *East/West Alliance Limited v. Ukraine* (2014) (claim for return of property lasted 12 years, violation of P1 Article 1). Concerning P1 Article 1, see, also, the considerations of the Court under Article 46 in, for example, *Driza v. Albania* (2007); *Ramadhi a.o. v. Albania* (2007); *Vrioni a.o. v. Albania and Italy* (2009).

11

Redress

11.1 INTRODUCTION

Article 13 not only requires access to an authority that can deal with the substance of the arguable complaint (Chapter 10), but that appropriate relief for violations be granted and enforced.[1]

Many questions dealt with in this chapter on redress could have been dealt with in the previous chapter on access to justice and *vice versa*. The most notable examples are the requirements of effective investigations (Section 11.7) and requirements which seek to prevent substantive violations (Section 11.3). These requirements are analyzed in this chapter because I seek to underline their function as redress, as such. However, this must not detract from the fact that the requirements promote both access to justice and redress as part of the collective enterprise to achieve one effective remedy.

The Court sometimes indicates that redress only has to be provided "if appropriate".[2] However, as a minimum, the national authority must provide redress in the form of a binding decision on the substance of the arguable complaint (Sections 10.4 and 11.2). The question in this chapter is primarily whether additional redress is required. The answer here depends, *inter alia*, on the context and the violation. Indeed, the implementation freedom, which the Court so often refers to under Article 13 (Chapter 8), is particularly important in this area.[3] This is not surprising considering that there are different

---

[1] See, for example, *Kudla v. Poland* (Grand Chamber 2000) para. 157; *Vilho Eskelinen a.o. v. Finland* (Grand Chamber 2007) para. 80; *de Souza Ribeiro v. France* (Grand Chamber 2012) para. 78; *Abdilla v. Malta* (2018) para. 65; *Mugemangango v. Belgium* (Grand Chamber 2020) para. 130.

[2] See, for example, *Amann v. Switzerland* (Grand Chamber 2000) para. 88; *Z a.o. v. the UK* (Grand Chamber 2001) para. 103.

[3] See, as an example, *Mugemangango v. Belgium* (Grand Chamber 2020) para. 138.

forms of redress that individually or in various combinations may provide redress, as illustrated by, for example, the Committee of Ministers' surveillance of the execution of the Court's judgments. Concrete requirements of redress may, also, have significant consequences for areas which States have normally wished to control and which they had not foreseen being regulated by the Convention. For instance, if the Court should require that compensation for nonpecuniary damages always be provided when the Convention has been violated, many States would have to change their systems of tort law.[4]

On the other hand, no formal legal sources prevent the Court from specifying the redress required by Article 13. And such specifications could contribute to a more effective protection of human rights. Indeed, indeterminacy with regard to the required redress makes it harder to succeed with a claim for redress. If, for example, compensation for nonpecuniary damage is required by Article 13, the domestic remedial authority must, at the very least, be empowered to award compensation for nonpecuniary damages. And, consequently, remedial procedures must be facilitated so that it is possible to achieve this.

Further, the Court could specify the required redress in many ways. The least degree of specification is to demand that redress be provided, but without specifying either the form or the specific measures. However, this could be complemented by, for example, specifying the purposes that redress must promote (Chapter 3) and leave it in the hands of the States to justify how their remedial systems accommodate for these purposes. The Court could then limit itself to procedurally test whether the form and/or specific measures sufficiently accommodate these purposes. At the other end of the scale, the Court could specify both the general purposes, the form of redress, and the specific measures required in different situations.

The below demonstrates that in early years, the Court mostly limited itself to a statement that redress had to be provided, without any further specification. But, increasingly, the Court, at least in some specific contexts, now lays down the form and the specific measures required. This is a parallel to the development of the Court's own remedial practice under Articles 41 and 46.[5] However, the Court has, to a limited extent, specified the more general purposes of redress (Chapter 3), including how different purposes potentially relate to each other.[6] Still, the Court holds that the domestic remedy must be

---

[4] See, for example, Rijnhout and Emaus (2014) on the consequences for Dutch and German private law concerning the right to damages for nonpecuniary losses in cases of wrongful deaths.

[5] See, for example, Leach (2005); Buyse (2008); Fyrnys (2011); Leach (2013); Haider (2013); Leach (2013a); Jahn (2014); Cremer (2014); Çalı (2018); Czepek (2018); Glas (2019).

[6] Compare, for example, Roach (2021).

able either to prevent the alleged violation or its continuation, or to provide adequate redress for any violation that has already occurred.[7] The use of the alternative "or" could indicate that States are free to choose between prevention and redress. And, theoretically, one could imagine different variations of those two elements:

- Prevention is necessary and sufficient. No further redress is required.
- Redress is necessary and sufficient. Prevention is not required.
- Both prevention and redress are necessary. The degree of prevention and redress may vary.

The practice of the Court shows that there is no contradiction between prevention and redress and that Article 13 may require several combinations of these elements, depending on the violation and the situation. The analyses below, further, demonstrate that in most areas, it is not only uncertain what the general purpose(s) of redress are, but the concrete form of redress, required in specific circumstances.[8]

11.2 DECLARATORY RELIEF

The primary relief required by Article 13 is the binding decision on the substance of the complaint.[9] In the practice of the Court, this is usually not expressed as a form of relief, as such, but a competence that the national authority needs to have in order to be able to provide effective access to justice (Section 10.4). However, the binding decision may satisfy other purposes, such as correcting injustice and providing deterrence and legal certainty, finality and procedural justice, thus contributing to upholding the rule of law. The question, therefore, arises, on the one hand, to what extent and how the binding decision must accommodate for such purposes, and, on the other hand, to

---

[7] See, for example, *Kudla v. Poland* (Grand Chamber 2000) para. 159; *Burdov v. Russia (no. 2)* (2009) para. 97; *Piskunov v. Russia* (2016) para. 45; *Mugemangango v. Belgium* (Grand Chamber 2020) para. 133.

[8] See, for example, McGregor (2012) 746. More generally, the decision-making by international courts with regard to remedies is very inconsistent; see, for example, Gray (2014) 873. That being said, the main elements of redress must be considered customary international law, even though it remains uncertain how specific that right is; compare Shelton (2014) 1201.

[9] Similarly, the primary redress offered by the Court is a declaratory judgment; see, for example, Klein (2000) 707–709. Also in the practice of the ICJ, the declaratory judgment is the remedy most commonly awarded; see, for example, Gray (2014) 876. In contrast, under the general rules on State responsibility, the declaratory judgment is a subordinate form of relief – the main forms being restitution and compensation; see, for example, Crawford (2002) 231.

what extent the remedial authority needs to provide additional redress (other than the binding decision on the substance).

The violation of the Convention – or similar rights at national level – must not necessarily be explicitly recognized, for instance, in the operative part of a judgment.[10] It suffices that the remedial authority deals with the substance of the complaint, which, at least in principle, could be performed in different manners. However, the violation must be acknowledged in substance. A favorable outcome that does not, in substance, acknowledge the violation is not sufficient.[11] On the other hand, the Court has not in the abstract explained how, nor required, that the binding decision has a form and content that is able to correct injustice, deter future violations, and promote other potential remedial purposes. If the Court were to specify how and to what extent the binding decision needed to contribute to such purposes, it could reduce the need to apply other forms of redress, for instance, compensation and restitution in kind.

Further, the subchapters below demonstrate that in many areas, additional redress may be necessary, but that, often, there are different opinions and controversy as to when declaratory relief is sufficient. *Goranova Karaeneva* v. *Bulgaria* (2011) is illustrative. Tapping of conversations (of the accused and the applicant), in connection with criminal proceedings, arguably violated Article 8. A majority of five to two judges found that a domestic decision, stating that surveillance had been unlawful, did not, in itself, constitute sufficient redress. Since there were no other avenues in which additional redress could be obtained, Article 13 had been violated. The majority did not specify what other forms of redress would have proved sufficient, but a claim for damages was not considered effective, under the circumstances (no prospect of success).[12] The minority, on the other hand, simply found that a declaration of unlawfulness, within the criminal trial, constituted sufficient redress.[13]

11.3 INDIVIDUAL PREVENTION

11.3.1 *Introduction*

Below, I analyze three interrelated questions – suspensive effect, decision before a planned action, and cessation.

---

[10] See, for example, *I.D.* v. *Norway* (Decision 2017) paras. 68–69.
[11] See, for example, *Kuzin* v. *Russia* (2005) para. 45. See, also, for example, Grabenwarter (2014) 334.
[12] *Goranova-Karaeneva* v. *Bulgaria* (2011) paras. 58–64.
[13] Dissenting opinion of Judges Garlicki and Mijović.

The question of whether Article 13 requires the remedy to have suspensive effect arises when there is danger of irreparable damage: To what extent must the remedy have suspensive effect so that irreparable damage is avoided? Suspensive effect is related to the question of whether the remedy must stop continuous violations (cessation). In both situations, an act or decision is stopped, but, whereas suspensive effect aims at preventing a future violation, cessation aims at redressing (ending) a violation. Suspensive effect is, also, linked to the question of whether the remedy has to provide a final or binding decision before a planned act takes place – for instance, a decision on the legality of a prohibition to demonstrate on a particular date. However, in this case, an action or decision is not suspended, but the legality of the action is finally dealt with, before the action is to take place. That being said, in both cases, the purpose is to avoid future damage.

The Court has provided little abstract and principled reasoning concerning the content of these requirements. One could, for instance, have expected the Court to set out clear starting-points, with (proportional) exceptions because of competing concerns, in a similar manner to the general rules on State responsibility. However, the Court has, for example, not emphasized as a clear starting-point that continuous violations have to be ended.[14] That being said, in all areas, there has been development in the sense that the Court now demands suspensive effect, a decision before a planned action, and cessation, in more specific situations than before.

11.3.2 *Suspensive Effect*

In the Court's case law, the question of suspensive effect has, most notably, arisen when decisions to expel, extradite, or not to permit residence may lead to violations of Articles 2, 3, 8, and P4 Article 4.[15]

In *Soering* v. *the UK* (Plenary 1989), extradition to the United States would violate Article 3, but UK courts were not required to grant interim junctions against the decision taken by the Government because there was no suggestion that the applicant actually would be surrendered before a final decision by UK courts.[16] Accordingly, formal suspensive effect was not required. This

---

[14] Compare, for example, Crawford (2002) 196.

[15] P7 Article 1 provides additional procedural safeguards relating to expulsion of aliens, but no requirement of suspensive effect. The existence of P7 Article 1 was important when the Court found that expulsion proceedings do not amount to civil rights or obligations under Article 6(1); see *Maaouia* v. *France* (Grand Chamber 2000) paras. 36–37. Article 13 is, therefore, particularly important in this field.

[16] *Soering* v. *the UK* (Plenary 1989) para. 123.

was partly reversed in *Čonka* v. *Belgium* (2002), which concerned expulsions violating P4 Article 4 (prohibition of collective expulsion of aliens). A majority of four to three judges found that a complaint to the Belgian *conseil d'état* had not been effective because Article 13 "requires that the remedy *may prevent* the execution of measures that are contrary to the Convention and whose effects are potentially irreversible" (my emphasis).[17] The wording "may prevent" could indicate that the remedy need not have automatic suspensive effect, but simply that the possibility must exist with some prospect of success in practice.[18] Indeed, in Belgium, several possibilities for staying the execution existed, but the majority considered that these possibilities were too uncertain.[19] A minority of three judges, on the other hand, found that these possibilities were sufficiently certain, in practice.[20] However, in *Gebremedhin [Gaberamadhien]* v. *France* (2007), automatic suspensive effect was required in relation to expulsion and risk of ill-treatment violating Article 3:

> In view of the importance which the Court attaches to Article 3 of the Convention and the irreversible nature of the damage which may result if the risk of torture or ill-treatment materialises, this finding [in *Čonka*!] obviously applies also to cases in which a State Party decides to remove an alien to a country where there are substantial grounds for believing that he or she faces a risk of that nature: Article 13 requires that the person concerned *should have access to a remedy with automatic suspensive effect.* (My emphasis)[21]

Automatic suspensive effect is a strict formal requirement. The remedy is not effective, even if it is suspensive in practice, as, for instance, in the *Soering* case.[22] The consequence is that in the time between the application to use the remedy and the decision from the remedial authority, the decision to extradite or expel cannot be executed.

The requirement of automatic suspensive effect has, in relation to expulsion and arguable violations of Article 3, been more or less consistently upheld.[23]

---

[17] *Čonka* v. *Belgium* (2002) para. 79.

[18] Similarly, for example, *Jabari* v. *Turkey* (2000) para. 50: "Article 13 requires independent and rigorous scrutiny of a claim that there exist substantial grounds for fearing a real risk of treatment contrary to Article 3 and *the possibility* of suspending the implementation of the measure impugned." (My emphasis).

[19] *Čonka* v. *Belgium* (2002) para. 83.

[20] Partly concurring and partly dissenting opinion of Judge Velaers and partly dissenting opinion of Judge Jungwiert joined by Judge Küris.

[21] *Gebremedhin [Gaberamadhien]* v. *France* (2007) para. 66. But notice that the reference to *Čonka*, in order to justify a formal requirement of automatic suspensive effect, is flawed.

[22] See, for example, *M.A.* v. *Cyprus* (2013) paras. 136–137.

[23] See, for example, *Abdolkhani and Karimnia* v. *Turkey* (2009) para. 108; *M.S.S.* v. *Belgium and Greece* (Grand Chamber 2011) para. 293; *Mohammed* v. *Austria* (2013) para. 72; B; *M.A. a.o.*

The requirement also applies when expulsion exposes the applicant to a real risk of violation of the right to life (Article 2).[24] However, concerning arguable violations of Article 8, most notably, interferences in family life, because of expulsions, a majority in *de Souza Ribeiro* v. *France* (Grand Chamber 2012), found that Article 13 does not require the remedy to have automatic suspensive effect. That being said, Article 13 requires that the individual has the:

> effective possibility of challenging the deportation or refusal-of-residence order and of having the relevant issues examined with sufficient procedural safeguards and thoroughness by an appropriate domestic forum offering adequate guarantees of independence and impartiality.[25]

And even though formal automatic suspensive effect is not required, the national authority, taking all circumstances into account, must have sufficient time to scrutinize the complaint. In *de Souza Ribeiro*, the majority, for example, found that the remedy was not effective because of the haste with which the removal order was executed, which, in return, rendered all available remedies ineffective in practice.[26] Two minority fractions found that Article 13, also in conjunction with arguable violations of Article 8, in cases of expulsion, required the remedy to have automatic suspensive effect.[27]

Indirectly, in *de Souza Ribeiro* v. *France* (Grand Chamber 2012), the Court held that automatic suspensive effect is required also in cases of arguable violations of P4 Article 4.[28] This was confirmed in *Khlaifia a.o.* v. *Italy* (2015),[29] but reversed in *Khlaifia a.o.* v. *Italy* (Grand Chamber 2016).[30] In the latter judgment, the Grand Chamber seems to hold that in extradition cases, only arguable violations of Articles 2 or 3 may cause "harm of a potentially irreversible nature", which thus requires automatic suspensive effect.[31] Indeed, in a

---

v. *Lithuania* (2018) para. 119; *D a.o.* v. *Romania* (2020) para. 128, but contrast, for example, *Chankayev* v. *Azerbaijan* (2013) para. 89; *M.D.* v. *Belgium* (2013) para. 60. Notice that the requirement of automatic suspensive effect only applies in relation to possible violations of Articles 2 and 3 in the receiving country; see, *Moustahi* v. *France* (2020) para. 154.

[24] See, for example, *de Souza Ribeiro* v. *France* (Grand Chamber 2012) para. 82; *Asalya* v. *Turkey* (2014) para. 11; *Khlaifia a.o.* v. *Italy* (Grand Chamber 2016) para. 276.

[25] *de Souza Ribeiro* v. *France* (Grand Chamber 2012) para. 83.

[26] Ibid., para. 95. Similarly, for example, *Moustahi* v. *France* (2020) para. 163.

[27] See the concurring opinion of Judge Pinto de Albuquerque, joined by Judge Vučinić and the concurring opinion of Judge Kalaydjieva.

[28] *de Souza Ribeiro* v. *France* (Grand Chamber 2012) para. 82.

[29] *Khlaifia a.o.* v. *Italy* (2015) para. 167.

[30] *Khlaifia a.o.* v. *Italy* (Grand Chamber 2016) paras. 276–277. Later confirmed in, for example, *N.D. and N.T.* v. *Spain* (Grand Chamber 2020).

[31] *Khlaifia a.o.* v. *Italy* (Grand Chamber 2016) para. 277. See, however, *M.K. a.o.* v. *Poland* (2020) para. 220.

similar manner as in *de Souza Ribeiro*, concerning Article 8, the Convention, in cases of arguable violations of P4 Article 4, "merely requires that the person concerned should have an effective possibility of challenging the expulsion decision by having a sufficiently thorough examination of his or her complaints carried out by an independent and impartial domestic forum."[32] In addition, if the applicants do not make use of existing and proportional official entry procedures, which allow them to assert rights under the Convention, the lack of individual removal decisions can be attributed to the conduct of the applicants. This may not only deprive them of their protection under P4 Article 4, but the right to an effective remedy under Article 13 altogether.[33]

In other areas, the Court has dealt with the question of suspensive effect only sporadically.

With regard to Article 3 (outside the expulsion/extradition scenario), the question has arisen whether the remedy must be able to suspend a decision of disciplinary isolation (so that the individual is not placed in isolation while awaiting the final decision) and, if so, whether the suspension need be automatic. In these cases, the remedies in question have mostly been found ineffective, but the question of suspensive effect has only been one element in more global assessments,[34] although some of the more general statements seem to require, at the very least, the possibility of suspensive effect, although not automatic.[35]

Concerning Article 8, the question arose in *M.S. v. Sweden* (1997) of whether the applicant should have been able to challenge the communication of medical records containing sensitive and personal information before it was communicated. The Court held that, since the applicant could bring criminal and civil proceedings before ordinary courts against the relevant staff, and claim damages for breach of professional secrecy, she had access to an authority that could deal with the substance of the Article 8 complaint and grant relief. These *ex post facto* remedies satisfied Article 13, given "the limited nature of the disclosure" and "the different safeguards concerning the communication".[36]

---

[32] *Khlaifia a.o. v. Italy* (Grand Chamber 2016) para. 279. Judge Serghides dissented and found that Article 13 required automatic suspensive effect also in extradition proceedings arguably violating P4 Article 4. However, in a similar manner as in *de Souza Ribeiro v. France* (Grand Chamber 2012), the fact that the expulsion actually is executed may deprive the applicant of any meaningful examination of the substance of the complaint, and thus violate Article 13; see, for example, *N.D. and N.T. v. Spain* (2017), but compare *N.D. and N.T. v. Spain* (Grand Chamber 2020).

[33] *N.D. and N.T. v. Spain* (Grand Chamber 2020) para. 231.

[34] See, for example, *Yankov v. Bulgaria* (2003) paras. 156–157; *Payet v. France* (2011) paras. 132–133.

[35] See, for example, *Payet v. France* (2011) para. 129.

[36] *M.S. v. Sweden* (1997) paras. 55–56.

In conjunction with Article 10, the question arose in *Özgür Radyo-Ses Radyo Televizyon Yayın Yapım Ve Tanıtım A.Ş.* v. *Turkey* (2006) of whether the execution of sanctions against a radio channel for broadcasting several programs had to be suspended until the case had been dealt with by the national authority. The Court held that in "certain cases" Article 13 requires the remedy to have suspensive effect.[37] In this case, however, the possibility of obtaining compensation, seen in conjunction with the theoretical possibility of suspending the sanctions, was sufficient to satisfy Article 13, regardless of their effectiveness in practice.[38]

Because of this case-by-case approach, outside the specific scenarios in which the Court has dealt with the question of suspensive effect, it remains uncertain when suspensive effect is required, and, if so, whether it needs be automatic. Jonas Christoffersen claims that the reason why suspensive effect has not been generally recognized by the Court, is the limited scope of review required by Article 13 – in particular, the fact that Article 13 does not grant a right to challenge legislation, as such.[39] However, even though it cannot be excluded that this has been at the back of the Court's mind, in the outspoken reasoning, this argument is not visible. In contrast, the main guiding criterion is whether the damage is irreparable, and, if so, whether this, under the circumstances, requires the remedy to have suspensive effect.[40] Further, the case law reveals that irreparable damage is, in many cases, not a sufficient criterion, and, on the other hand, that even though it could be argued that it should be an absolute criterion, at least in the sense that damages which cannot be restituted should always be considered irreparable,[41] the Court has not made this linkage. In fact, automatic suspensive effect is not required, even in case of many irreversible violations of Articles 2 and 3. For instance, a prisoner could, under the circumstances, be placed in isolation, before the question is considered by domestic remedial authorities, at least for shorter periods because, it could be necessary to protect the lives or fundamental rights of others.[42] However, in such cases, the applicant must have access to a remedy that can deal with the case as soon as possible and with the power to put an end to continuing violations.[43] On the other hand, also in cases in which

[37] *Özgür Radyo-Ses Radyo Televizyon Yayın Yapım Ve Tanıtım A.Ş.* v. *Turkey (no. 1)* (2006) para. 90.
[38] Ibid., paras. 93–94.
[39] Christoffersen (2009) 407.
[40] The reasoning in *Khlaifia a.o.* v. *Italy* (Grand Chamber 2016) paras. 276–279 is illustrative.
[41] See, for example, Keller and Marti (2015) 834.
[42] An indirect expression of this is Article 5(1) *litra c* ECHR.
[43] Compare, for example, Articles 5(2) and 5(3) and *Keenan* v. *the UK* (2001) para. 127. See, also, Section 11.3.4.

the damage is considered to be reparable, one could imagine that suspensive effect is required. Purely monetary damages can, for example, in some cases, amount to violations of, for instance, P1 Article 1. In such cases, even though the damages in principle can be repaired through monetary compensation, the arguments against suspensive effect may not be very weighty. Irreparable damage should thus, not necessarily, be an absolute criterion.[44] However, also in this respect, it is difficult to deduce general criteria and guidance from the Court's case law.

If a remedy needs be suspensive, the case law indicates that, as long as the first proceedings satisfy the requirement of an effective remedy, the remedy need not be suspensive on appeal.[45]

11.3.3 *Decision before a Planned Action*

The question of whether the remedial decision needs to be taken before the time at which an action is planned, has, in the Court's case law, most notably, arisen when demonstrations and manifestations are planned at a specific time, but are forbidden, or not permitted, by an administrative decision. Such prohibitions, or lack of permissions, may, most notably, violate Articles 11 and 10.

In *Ivanov a.o. v. Bulgaria* (2005), an organization informed the authorities that they planned a rally on a specific date, which was prohibited by the Mayor. The prohibition violated Article 11. Further, judicial review could, in principle, provide an effective remedy, but this "implied the possibility to obtain a ruling before the time of the planned events."[46] Indeed, freedom of assembly could well be rendered meaningless if it is prevented from being exercised at a propitious time.[47] The State may usefully provide reasonable time limits in which the authorities have to act,[48] but for these time frames to be effective, they may have to be legally binding on the national authority.[49] The decision from the national authority also needs to be enforceable before the planned date.[50]

With regard to Article 10, a decision concerning access to reports and exclusions from court hearings may have to be rendered before the hearing and/

---

[44] Similarly, irreversible damage to particularly important rights cannot be considered a necessary condition for the binding effect of rule 39 decisions; see Christoffersen (2009) 401–402.
[45] See, for example, *Z.M. v. France* (2013) para. 83; *S.K. v. Russia* (2017) para. 76.
[46] *Ivanov a.o. v. Bulgaria* (2005) para. 74. Similarly, *Bączkowski a.o. v. Poland* (2007) para. 81.
[47] *Bączkowski a.o. v. Poland* (2007) para. 82.
[48] Ibid., para. 83.
[49] See, for example, *Alekseyev v. Russia* (2010) para. 99; *Genderdoc-M v. Moldova* (2012) paras. 35–37; *Lashmankin a.o. v. Russia* (2017) para. 351.
[50] See, for example, *Lashmankin a.o. v. Russia* (2017) para. 352.

or final decision in the main case. In *Mackay & BBC Scotland* v. *the UK* (2010), in the aftermath of an exclusion order, Scottish courts had the competence to give the media the opportunity to make representations for the recall of the order in advance of the proceedings. The Court did not doubt that, in such hearings, Scottish courts would give appropriate consideration to any submissions concerning Article 10. However, Scottish courts were under no obligation to hear representations from the media. And even when such representations were held, there was "no obligation upon it to do so within a reasonable period of time and in any event prior to the proceedings."[51] The fact that domestic courts considered the exclusion order some three months after the main proceedings had ended could not render the remedy effective since the impact of any report was seriously diminished by that time.[52] Reading the Court's analysis of the general requirements stemming from Article 13, one could get the impression that there is always an obligation to deliver a final decision before the relevant act or action takes place. However, in concrete, this element was included in a more general consideration of the safeguards provided by Scottish courts, *inter alia*, the lack of a personal right on the part of the media and the certainty/uncertainty of the courts actually dealing with the question.

Outside the areas in which the Court has explicitly demanded that a decision be taken before the planned action, it remains uncertain to what extent the domestic remedial authority must actually do so or whether *ex-post* redress may be sufficient.

11.3.4 *Stop (Put an End to) Continuous Violations*

A violation may be limited to a single point of time, but also extend to longer periods. The question then arises as to whether the remedy must put an end to the continuing violation.

The question of whether we are faced with a continuous violation may vary in relation to different situations and legal contexts.[53] In the context of Article 13, the question, in principle, only arises if the violation is ongoing at the time when the national authority renders its decision (or should have rendered its decision). However, the Court has applied the continuous

---

[51] *Mackay & BBC Scotland* v. *the UK* (2010) para. 32.
[52] Ibid., para. 33.
[53] See, generally, on the concept of continuous violations in public international law, for example, Pauwelyn (1996); Crawford (2002) 135–140, 96–200; Crawford (2013) 258–264, 461–469, and, in the context of the Convention, for example, Loucaides (2000); Buyse (2006).

nature of the violation with flexibility. For instance, in cases of conditions of detention arguably violating Article 3, the Court considers that regular inter-ruptions in the detention, depending on the circumstances, do not prevent the Court from treating such detention(s) as a "continuing situation", adding that it would be excessively formalistic, in the circumstances, to insist that the applicant lodge a new complaint after the end of each of the multiple periods of detention at the same detention facility.[54]

Before we analyze the case law, more concretely, it may be queried whether a remedy ever could be effective without being able to put an end to the viola-tion? Seen from the point of view of the applicant, this is normally the most important issue, and the obligation to put an end to continuing violations is unquestionable in international law.[55] Some even hold that the obligation is a direct consequence of the primary obligation, and, therefore, simply derives from the operation of the law.[56] Further, the importance of putting an end to continuing violations is explicitly recognized under many substantive Articles in the Convention.[57] Why, then, should not Article 13 require, more generally, that the national authority must put an end to continuing violations?

The Court has never provided an abstract justification, but, in a similar manner, as States have a certain discretion with regard to how past violations must be redressed, the answer must be that States have some discretion with regard to how ongoing violations must be put to an end. Clearly, the State is obliged, in one way or the other, to end the violation, but this must not neces-sarily be done by the national (remedial) authority. In particular, if a violation could be ended in several manners, it could be argued that it must not be the national remedial authority that states how the violation must be ended. On the other hand, seen from the perspective of the applicant, it is usually prefer-able that the national (remedial) authority also ends the violation.

---

54 See, for example, *Grossman v. Russia* (2013) paras. 64 and 48, and compare Article 30 *litra* a of the ILC Draft Articles on Responsibility of States for Internationally Wrongful Acts and Crawford (2002) 196 under para. 3.

55 Compare Article 30 *litra* a of the ILC Draft Articles on Responsibility of States for Internationally Wrongful Acts and, for example, Crawford (2013) 461–469, but notice that the van Boven/Bassiouni principles do not consider cessation a primary consequence of the violation, but a form of satisfaction that "should" include, where applicable, effective mea-sures aimed at the cessation of continuing violations; see Principle 22 *litra* a of the van Boven/Bassiouni principles.

56 See, for example, Gray (2014) 879.

57 See, for example, Article 5(4) that requires domestic courts to order release if a detention is not lawful. Article 5(3) contains no explicit obligation to order release, but the Court has incorporated this in the wording "competent legal authority"; see, for example, *Ireland v. the UK* (Plenary 1978) para. 199. Under Article 6, depending on the circumstances, courts must be able to quash decisions; see, for example, *Veeber v. Estonia (no. 1)* (2002) para. 71.

The case law of the Court reveals that whether Article 13 requires the remedial authority to have the power to put an end to continuing violations may vary, depending, *inter alia*, on the violation and the situation.

Concerning continuing violations of Articles 2 and 3, the remedy must be able to put an end to the violations. An example can be found in *Keenan v. the UK* (2001), which, *inter alia*, concerned conditions of detention, in particular, punishment in the form of segregation, of a prisoner suffering from mental illnesses. Article 13 was violated because no remedy was available that could either quash the punishment before it was executed or had come to an end.[58] Indeed, in many cases concerning conditions of detention, the Court has held that purely compensatory remedies are not sufficient.

> Where the fundamental right to protection against torture and inhuman and degrading treatment is concerned, the preventive and compensatory remedies have to be complementary in order to be considered effective. The existence of a preventive remedy is indispensable for the effective protection of individuals against the kind of treatment prohibited by Article 3 of the Convention. Indeed, the special importance attached by the Convention to that provision requires, in the Court's view, that the States Parties establish, over and above a compensatory remedy, an effective mechanism in order to put an end to any such treatment rapidly. Had it been otherwise, the prospect of future compensation would have legitimised particularly severe suffering in breach of this core provision of the Convention.[59]

Accordingly, remedies of a purely compensatory nature may be effective only in respect of applicants who have been either released or actually placed in conditions of detention which satisfy the requirements of Article 3.[60]

In contrast to continuing violations of Articles 2 and 3, compensation may be a sufficient remedy with regard to continuous violations of Article 6(1), at least in cases concerning excessive length of proceedings and nonenforcement of judgments.

With regard to excessive length of proceedings, the case law of the Court has been consistent.[61] The remedy may be purely compensatory, regardless of whether the excessively lengthy proceedings are terminated or pending.[62]

---

[58] *Keenan v. the UK* (2001) para. 127.

[59] *Dirdizov v. Russia* (2012) para. 73. Similarly, for example, *Ananyev a.o. v. Russia* (2012) paras. 97–98; *W.D. v. Belgium* (2016) para. 153.

[60] See, for example, *Mandić and Jović v. Slovenia* (2011) para. 111; *Harakchiev and Tolumov v. Bulgaria* (2014) paras. 222–225; *G.B. a.o. v. Turkey* (2019) para. 136.

[61] See, however, the concurring opinions of Judge Malinverni, joined by Judges Rozakis and Jebens in *Vitzthum v. Austria* (2007), *Stempfer v. Austria* (2007) and *Schutte v. Austria* (2007).

[62] See, for example, *Slezák a.o. v. the Czech Republic* (2005) para. 33; *Apicella v. Italy* (Grand Chamber 2006) para. 76.

However, the Court emphasizes that the best solution is to combine the two types of remedies.[63] The situation is different if the State has actually introduced acceleratory remedies. The Court then tests whether the acceleratory remedy, in combination with compensatory remedies, in aggregate, satisfies the requirement of an effective remedy.[64] But in contrast to compensation, which may be sufficient on its own, even though prevention is seen as preferable, an acceleratory remedy may, in itself, not sufficiently redress a situation in which proceedings are already excessively long.[65] Further, when the excessive length of proceedings, as such, affects other Convention rights, for example, the applicant's family life, a remedy which is both preventive and compensatory is required.[66]

With regard to nonenforcement of judgments, violating only Article 6(1), not involving continuing violations of other Convention rights, the picture is more unclear. Some of the Court's general statements indicate that the situation is the same as with excessive length of proceedings.[67] However, the case law reveals that it must be distinguished between different situations and aspects of nonenforcement and/or execution.

First, in the cases in which the Court's general statements indicate that compensation is sufficient, the national judgment has (1) either been enforced, and the question under Articles 6(1) and 13, in reality, only concerns the delay (not the total lack) of enforcement,[68] or (2) concerns an award of money against the State,[69] or property which mainly has economical value.[70] In both scenarios, a purely compensatory remedy is sufficient. And, at least in the latter scenario, the general statements seem more directed at indicating that the applicant should not be compelled to initiate separate enforcement proceedings, instead of indicating that compensation is sufficient.[71]

Second, in cases which concern excessive length of proceedings still pending, and in which the State has introduced both acceleratory and compensatory

[63] See, for example, *Apicella v. Italy* (Grand Chamber 2006) para. 75; *Sürmeli v. Germany* (Grand Chamber 2006) para. 100.
[64] See Section 9.3 and, for example, *Stefanova v. Bulgaria* (2007) paras. 66–74.
[65] See, for example, *Apicella v. Italy* (Grand Chamber 2006) para. 74; *Karov v. Bulgaria* (2006) para. 74.
[66] See, for example, *Kuppinger v. Germany* (2015) para. 137.
[67] See, for example, *Burdov v. Russia (no. 2)* (2009) para. 99; *Ananyev a.o. v. Russia* (2012) para. 98; *Stoyanov and Tabakov v. Bulgaria* (2013) para. 92.
[68] See, for example, *Burdov v. Russia (no. 2)* (2009) para. 62.
[69] See, for example, *Simaldone v. Italy* (2009); *Manushaqe Puto a.o. v. Albania* (2012).
[70] See, for example, *Stoyanov and Tabakov v. Bulgaria* (2013) and contrast with *Kanellopoulos v. Greece* (2008).
[71] See, for example, *Delvina v. Albania* (2011) paras. 71–72; *Manushaqe Puto a.o. v. Albania* (2012) para. 71; *Stoyanov and Tabakov v. Bulgaria* (2013) para. 91.

remedies, and in which the Court tests the aggregate of remedies, the nonenforcement of a domestic order to speed up proceedings may be perceived from
different angles: on the one hand, as a prolongation of the excessive length
of proceedings and, on the other hand, a separate violation of Article 6(1)
because of the nonexecution of the order to speed up the proceedings.[72]

Third, in other situations, the primary goal is to enforce judgments (put an
end to the continuing violation – the nonenforcement).[73] This is particularly
important with regard to domestic judgments, which provide redress against
other arguable Convention complaints, and is analyzed in Section 11.9

In other areas, the question of whether the domestic remedy must put an
end to continuing violations has arisen only rarely in the Court's case law. But
in a number of cases, it has been an underlying question.

Sampanis a.o. v. Greece (2008) concerned violations of Article 14 in combination with P1 Article 2 because Roma children were continuously discriminated in educational matters. The Government argued that the applicants
could have lodged administrative complaints of the annulment of the administrative act. The Court concluded that none of the remedies cited by the
Government could have annulled the act, but did not comment on the question of whether annulment was necessary, but added, in a general manner,
that Article 13 had been violated since the Government had not pointed to any
other avenues in which the applicants could be awarded redress.[74]

Listing in registers and storage of information may continuously violate,
inter alia, Article 8. The question then arises as to whether Article 13 requires
that the domestic remedial authority must be able to order that the information be deleted. A confirmative example can be found in *Nada v. Switzerland*
(Grand Chamber 2012). Article 13 was violated because the applicant "did
not have any effective means of obtaining the removal of his name from
the list annexed to the Taliban Ordinance."[75] Similarly, in *Segerstedt-Wiberg
a.o. v. Sweden* (2006), Article 13 was violated in conjunction with Articles 8,
10, and 11 because the applicants "had no direct access to any legal remedy
as regards the erasure of the information in question." These shortcomings
could not be "offset by any possibilities for the applicants to seek compensation."[76] On the other hand, in *Dimitrov-Kazakov v. Bulgaria* (2011), the applicant

[72] See, as an illustration, *Kaić a.o. v. Croatia* (2008).
[73] See, for example, *Kanellopoulos v. Greece* (2008) paras. 33 and 20; *Vasilev and Doycheva v. Bulgaria* (2012) paras. 59, 30, and 69.
[74] *Sampanis a.o. v. Greece* (2008) para. 58.
[75] *Nada v. Switzerland* (Grand Chamber 2012) para. 213.
[76] *Segerstedt-Wiberg a.o. v. Sweden* (2006) paras. 120–121.

was unlawfully listed in a police register and had no possibility of getting the inscription deleted. However, the Court did not conclude that deletion was necessary, but investigated whether a compensatory remedy was effective.[77] *Linkov* v. *the Czech Republic* (2006) concerned the opposite situation – a refusal to register a political party violated Article 11. However, the Court did not consider it necessary to examine whether Article 13 had also been violated,[78] including the question of whether the domestic remedial authority needed to order the registration.

Under Article 8 in conjunction with Article 13, the Court has indirectly held that the continued refusals of family visits in prisons may necessitate a remedy that can quash the refusal.[79] In *Panteleyenko* v. *Ukraine* (2006), on the other hand, the Court held that the remedy against a continuing disclosure of sensitive psychiatric information in a public court room was not effective as it "did not result in the discontinuation of the disclosure of confidential psychiatric data in the court case file *or any award to the applicant of compensation for damages suffered* as the result of the unlawful interference with his private life." (My emphasis)[80]

Further, in a number of cases, the Court has not deemed it necessary to comment on these questions under Article 13 in conjunction with the finding of a violation under Article 8. In *Airey* v. *Ireland* (1979), for example, Article 8 was violated because the applicant was unable to seek effective recognition in law of her *de facto* separation from her husband.[81] However, the Court did not deem it necessary to examine the case under Article 13, including the question of whether the remedy needed to recognize her separation.[82] And in *Mikulić* v. *Croatia* (2002), Article 8 was violated because of uncertainty caused with regard to the applicant's personal identity, *inter alia*, because it was not possible to compel the father to take a DNA-test. However, because of the assessment under Article 8, the Court did not deem it necessary to examine Article 13 separately,[83] including the question of whether the remedy actually needed to compel the father to take the DNA-test. Similarly, in

---

77 *Dimitrov-Kazakov* v. *Bulgaria* (2011) paras. 37–39.

78 *Linkov* v. *the Czech Republic* (2006) para. 50.

79 See, for example, *Schemkamper* v. *France* (2005) para. 44 (refusal of permission) and *Moisejevs* v. *Latvia* (2006) para. 163 (family visits in prison).

80 *Panteleyenko* v. *Ukraine* (2006) para. 83.

81 *Airey* v. *Ireland* (1979) para. 33. For similar reasons, the right to access to court in Article 6(1) was violated; see para. 28.

82 See, in particular, the conclusions point 7 and paras. 34–35.

83 *Mikulić* v. *Croatia* (2002) paras. 72–73. Similarly, in *Paulík* v. *Slovakia* (2006), Article 8 was violated because it was not possible to challenge paternity because of new biological evidence, but it was not necessary to examine Article 13; see para. 50.

Mincheva v. *Bulgaria* (2010), Article 8 was violated because the State did not do what was sufficient to reinstate family life – in concrete, give the applicant access to her daughter. Under Article 13, however, the Court simply concluded that it was not necessary to examine Article 13,[84] without commenting on the question of whether the remedial authority needed to have the competence to order the reinstatement of family life.[85]

With regard to Article 10 in conjunction with Article 13, the question has arisen in some cases. *Association Ekin* v. *France* (2001) concerned a ban on the circulation, distribution, and sale of a book. The applicant association claimed that it did not have access to an urgent procedure to review the ban, and, if necessary, to lift it promptly. However, the Court did not deem it necessary to consider the question under Article 13 as it had, *inter alia*, considered the question of the form and extent of judicial review under Article 10, as a component of the assessment of whether the ban was necessary in a democratic society.[86] The question of whether it was necessary for the remedy to be able to quash the ban was thus not dealt with. In contrast, in *Halis Doğan a.o.* v. *Turkey* (2005), which concerned the continuous prohibition of distributing a newspaper, the Court found a violation also of Article 13, just by pointing to its considerations under Article 10, in which the central consideration was that there was no legal control against abuse.[87] However, the Court did not comment explicitly on the question of whether the remedy needed to quash the decision, even though this was alleged by the applicant.[88]

Grosaru v. *Romania* (2010) deserves particular mention because it illustrates development and disagreement as to how far the development should go. The case concerned a refusal to allocate the applicant a seat in the Romanian Parliament to represent the Italian Minority. The Court found that the very essence of the applicant's rights under P1 Article 3 had been violated because of the lack of clarity of an electoral law concerning national minorities, the lack of impartiality of the bodies responsible for examining the applicant's challenges, and because no court had ruled on the interpretation of the law or the dispute.[89] The Court, further, concluded unanimously that Article 13

---

[84] *Mincheva* v. *Bulgaria* (2010) para. 112.

[85] Compare, for example, *Görgülü* v. *Germany* (2004) para. 64.

[86] *Association Ekin* v. *France* (2001) para. 76. It might be that the rationale was connected to the fact that legislation appeared to "be in direct conflict" with Article 10, see para. 62, and that the Court did not want to state that Article 13 did not require an effective remedy in this situation; see Section 10.5.3.

[87] *Halis Doğan a.o.* v. *Turkey* (2006) paras. 35 and 27. And this even if the ban derived directly from legislation.

[88] *Halis Doğan a.o.* v. *Turkey* (2006) para. 33.

[89] *Grosaru* v. *Romani* (2010) para. 57.

had also been violated, contrary to, for example, *Podkolzina v. Latvia* (2002), which concerned similar issues, and in which the Court did not deem it necessary to examine whether Article 13 had been violated.[90] A majority declared a violation of Article 13 simply by pointing to its considerations under Article 3 of Protocol 1.[91] By looking at the references from the majority, the impression remains that the decisive factor, under Article 13, was the limited review performed by domestic courts. This approach, however, was criticized by Judge Ziemele, because in doing so, the Court had missed the opportunity to clarify the scope of the obligations arising from Article 13 in this context.[92] She particularly pointed to the fact that the applicant under Article 13 had alleged that there was no remedy "capable of restoring his seat in Parliament" and that the answer of the majority was not sufficient in this regard.[93] The answer might have come in *Paunović and Milivojević v. Serbia* (2016), in which the remedy, in concrete, was not effective because the parliamentary mandate could not be restored, although the Court is not very explicit.[94]

More recently, in *Bartolo Parnis a.o. v. Malta* (2021), Article 13 was violated in conjunction with P1 Article 1 because domestic courts did not award the applicants a higher rent or evicted tenants and, thereby, stopped the continuous violation, even though domestic courts had awarded compensation for damages already incurred.[95]

However, if anything, the above reveals an unclear picture. Indeed, outside the areas in which the Court has explicitly stated that the remedy must, or must not, put an end to continuous violations, it remains uncertain whether the remedy must do this. This uncertainty is primarily caused by the Court's case-by-case approach, seen in conjunction with the fact that the Court has provided few general and abstract guiding criteria. In the case of suspensive effect (Section 11.3.2), the criterion "irreparable damage" provides some guidance, but, in the case of putting an end to continuous violations, no similar general criterion is visible. The closest starting-point might be the Court's justification for dealing differently with cases under Article 3 and cases concerning excessive length of proceedings:

> In contrast to the cases concerning the length of judicial proceedings or non-enforcement of judgments, where the Court accepted in principle that

[90] *Podkolzina v. Latvia* (2002) para. 45.
[91] *Grosaru v. Romani* (2010) para. 62.
[92] Paras. 1 and 2 in the dissenting opinion.
[93] Ibid., para. 5.
[94] *Paunović and Milivojević v. Serbia* (2016) paras. 72 and 48.
[95] *Bartolo Parnis a.o. v. Malta* (2021) paras. 60–70.

a compensatory remedy alone might suffice ... the existence of a preventive remedy is indispensable for the effective protection of individuals against the kind of treatment prohibited by Article 3. Indeed, the special importance attached by the Convention to that provision requires, in the Court's view, that the States parties establish, over and above a compensatory remedy, an effective mechanism in order to put an end to any such treatment rapidly. Had it been otherwise, the prospect of future compensation would have legitimized particularly severe suffering in breach of this core provision of the Convention and unacceptably weakened the legal obligation on the State to bring its standards of detention into line with the Convention requirements.[96]

One could, of course, argue that, faced with any continuous violation, to which it is not required that the remedy puts an end to the violation, the prospect of future compensation could legitimize the continuous violation and weaken the primary obligation to avoid human-rights violations. On the other hand, in some cases, continuous violations could be ended in different ways, and with contributions from several authorities, depending on the domestic legal situation. Take the example of excessive length of proceedings, which could be ended, for instance, by orders from superior courts, transfer of jurisdiction, and providing additional resources. That being said, if the national legislator, in a given situation, is not content with how a remedial authority puts an end to the violation, the legislator would, normally, be empowered to change the manner in which the violation is to be ended, at least with regard to future violations. In any case, the remedial authority must not necessarily determine specifically how the violation must end, only be required to identify continuous violations and state that the violation needs to end, without stating specifically how. However, at least if the violation may only be ended in one manner, the domestic remedial authority should be able to state also how, for instance, order the release of a prisoner, access to a child, conditions of detentions improved, or quash an administrative decision. But, the Court has not required this, in general and abstract terms, under Article 13.[97]

---

[96] *Ananyev a.o.* v. *Russia* (2012) para. 98. Similarly, for example, *Dirdizov* v. *Russia* (2012) para. 73; *Reshetnyak* v. *Russia* (2013) para. 60.

[97] However, in relation to the Court's own remedial powers, the Court has specified how a violation must be ended, at least when there is only one alternative; see, for example, *Assanidze* v. *Georgia* (Grand Chamber 2004) (release prisoner); *Ilić* v. *Serbia* (2007) (enforce domestic judgment); *Sławomir Musiał* v. *Poland* (2009) (transfer patient to an establishment capable of providing necessary psychiatric treatment); *Oleksandr Volkov* v. *Ukraine* (2013) (reinstate Supreme Court judge). Further, in some cases, the Court has offered advice on what it considers an appropriate individual measure, or even the most appropriate measure, although it

11.4   RESTITUTION

Restitution or reparation in kind seeks to reestablish the situation which existed before the wrongful act was committed (*restitutio in integrum*).

Under the general rules of State responsibility, restitution is the preferred form of redress. Compensation and satisfaction are secondary forms.[98] Indeed, restitution may only be left out if it is "materially impossible" or involves "a burden out of all proportion to the benefit deriving from restitution instead of compensation."[99] This strict starting-point, under which competing concerns play a limited role, is confirmed by the official commentaries which hold that proportionality only applies "where there is a grave disproportionality between the burden which restitution would impose on the responsible State and the benefit which would be gained."[100] That being said, this proportionality requirement has not been applied consistently by international courts and claims tribunals.[101]

Also under Articles 41 and 46 ECHR, the Court expresses a preference for restitution in kind.[102] And, at least in one case, the Court has ordered restitution without reservations.[103] However, because the Court mostly awards compensation in the form of money under Article 41, compensation is, at least in practice, the general rule.[104] Indeed, even though the Committee of Ministers insists on achieving *restitutio in integrum*, it mostly does so in cases in which the Court has not awarded just satisfaction.[105] Consequently, at the international level, the practical preference for compensation, to the detriment of

---

still leaves the choice of the measures in the hands of the State, under the surveillance of the Committee of Ministers. In this respect, the remedial requirements under Article 13 should not be less strict than those pertaining to the Court.

[98] See the ILC Draft Articles on Responsibility of States for Internationally Wrongful Acts Articles 35–37.

[99] See Article 35 of the ILC Draft Articles on Responsibility of States for Internationally Wrongful Acts.

[100] Crawford (2002) 217.

[101] See, for example, Shelton (2005) 53.

[102] See, more generally, Somers (2018) 240 and, for example, *Papamichalopoulos a.o. v. Greece* (Article 50) (1995) paras. 34–40 and paras. 2 and 3 of the operative part; *Brumarescu v. Romania* (*Article 41*) (Grand Chamber 2001) paras. 20–24 and paras. 1 and 2 of the operative part.

[103] *Borzhonov v. Russia* (2009) para. 69 and para. 7 *litra* a of the operative part (return bus expropriated in violation of P1 Article 1).

[104] That being said, in some cases, the Court may choose not to award just satisfaction and leave the choice between restitution and/or compensation to the State under the surveillance of the Committee of Ministers; see, as an example, *Lindheim a.o. v. Norway* (2012).

[105] See, for example, Ichim (2014) 33. See, also, Rule 6 para. 2 *litra* b(i) of the Rules of the Committee of Ministers for the supervision of the execution of judgments and of the terms of friendly settlements.

restitution in kind, is highly influenced by the division of powers between the Court and the Committee of Ministers. Further, it is not given that an international court or the Committee of Ministers are well placed to consider the adequacy of restitution in concrete cases. The justification for the practical rule of compensation, to the detriment of restitution, does, therefore, not necessarily apply at domestic level.[106]

However, under Article 13, the Court has not emphasized restitution as a general starting-point, even though the deepest desire for any victim of human-rights violations is to turn back the clock.[107] True, the Court often accepts restitution as a sufficient form of redress, often in combination with monetary compensation for both pecuniary and nonpecuniary damages.[108] And, in cases concerning the lack of execution of domestic judgments, in which restitution has been ordered at domestic level, for instance, the return of property, the judgment must be enforced. Indeed, compensation cannot substitute the binding decision on the return of the property.[109] Moreover, some of the cases in which the Court requires the domestic authority to put an end to continuous violations may be seen under the heading of restitution.[110]

On the other hand, under Article 13, the Court explicitly, and increasingly, requires compensation for both pecuniary and nonpecuniary damages (Section 11.5). Consequently, also under Article 13, at least in practice, domestic remedial authorities stand free to choose compensation to the detriment of restitution, without any justification and assessment of proportionality. The Court, therefore, at least indirectly, promotes a preference for compensation, not only at international level but also at domestic level. As for the underlying reasons, one can only speculate. The Court might have felt more familiar demanding compensation, as compensation already had some explicit grounds in the Convention, most notably in Article 5(5), P7 Article 3, and Article 41.[111] Demanding compensation could, also, be perceived as less intrusive toward

---

[106] See Section 11.5 and Christoffersen (2009) 422. See, also, for example, *Association of Real Property Owners in Łódź a.o. v. Poland* (Decision 2011) para. 86.

[107] Buyse (2008) 129.

[108] See, for example, *Klass a.o. v. Germany* (Plenary 1978) para. 71 (return of documents confiscated in violation of Article 8).

[109] See Sections 11.3.4 and 11.9 and, as an example, *Guseva v. Bulgaria* (2015) paras. 69 and 46.

[110] Restitution may be difficult to distinguish from cessation. In the earlier approaches under the general rules of State responsibility, cessation and nonrepetition were, for example, considered as "satisfaction"; see, for example, Shelton (2005) 87. See, also, Crawford (2002) 213 under para. 1 where he holds that releasing a prisoner wrongly detained may be considered restitution, which in the practice of the Court is perceived as cessation; see, for example, *Assanidze v. Georgia* (Grand Chamber 2004).

[111] Similarly, Christoffersen (2009) 439.

States. Indeed, whereas the effects of compensation, at least intuitively, seem clear-cut and with a limited number of possible skewed effects, in particular on third parties, it is more difficult to foresee the skewed effects that restitution may have. However, the Court could require restitution as a principled starting-point, with the possibility of providing compensation when restitution is not possible, or not proportional, for instance, because of skewed effects, or because the victim prefers compensation instead of restitution.[112] Further, in this assessment, a wide margin of appreciation could be left in the hands of the State. But, at least to date, the Court has not engaged in such principled reasoning (Section 13.3).

11.5 COMPENSATION

11.5.1 *Introduction*

With the exceptions of Article 5(5) and P7 Article 3, the Convention does not explicitly recognize a right to compensation at national level.[113] Below, I analyze to what extent, and how, the Court requires compensation under Article 13.[114]

Compensation is a substitute – something is compensated for. In principle, the substitute can take different forms, but, in practice, compensation usually means monetary awards, which is the most common remedy both at international and domestic levels.[115] Indeed, I have not seen the Court require compensation in other forms than money. However, the Court has accepted other forms of compensation as sufficient. Excessive length of proceedings in penal cases may, for example, be compensated for by reducing the penalty.[116]

Compensation may only compensate for harms that have already occurred. It cannot put an end to continuing violations. Still, the Court accepts that compensation may be sufficient redress against some continuous violations, most notably, excessive length of proceedings (Section 11.3.4).

Because compensation is a substitute and because it is usually awarded in the form of money, it becomes particularly important to identify the purposes

---

[112] Similarly, Buyse (2008) 132–133.
[113] Some human-rights treaties contain general provisions on compensation at national level, for example, Article 14 CAT.
[114] Notice that under Article 5(5) compensation is required, unlike under Article 13, even if the violation stems from primary domestic legislation; see, for example, *S.B.C. v. the UK* (2001) paras. 22–24; *Stoichkov v. Bulgaria* (2005) paras. 73–75 and compare Section 10.5.3.
[115] See, for example, Crawford (2002) 218 under para. 2.
[116] See, for example, *Apicella v. Italy* (Grand Chamber 2006) para. 75.

of the right to an effective remedy (Chapter 3), not least because the purposes clarify the object that is to be substituted, which, *inter alia*, is important for the level of generic compensation (money).[117]

11.5.2 *Compensation Necessary?*

The Court increasingly demands that the domestic remedial authority be able to provide compensation.[118] Some even argue that the Court is moving toward a general right of compensation.[119] However, this reads too much into the case law. In a number of areas, a declaratory judgment may be sufficient, especially in cases revealing only nonpecuniary damages. And even though the Court does not emphasize a preference for restitution under Article 13, the Court accepts that restitution may be sufficient, with the consequence that additional compensation is not necessary.[120] Indeed, many criticize the Court for not requiring compensation, more generally. Such criticism is often based upon the assumption that human-rights violations always entail some form of moral damage which needs to be compensated.[121]

Under Article 13, the Court initially held that compensation, in some specific situations, had to be provided "where appropriate", for instance, for arguable claims of torture,[122] or the destruction of homes and possessions by agents of the State.[123] Subsequently, the Court has held, more generally, that "in appropriate cases" compensation for both pecuniary and nonpecuniary damage flowing from the breach "in principle" should be available as part of the range of redress.[124] The reference to "appropriate cases" is, as such, not very informative, but, at the very least, emphasizes that compensation for both pecuniary and nonpecuniary damages may be necessary.

---

[117] Under EC law, compensation must, at least under specific directives, both correct injustice and deter future violations; see, for example, Shelton (2015) 220–224.

[118] However, that does not mean that compensation is sufficient. Indeed, as demonstrated in the subchapters above and below, the remedial authorities may, depending on the violation and the circumstances, need to perform a number of other tasks; see, as a general expression, for example, *Apap Bologna v. Malta* (2016) para. 77.

[119] See, for example, Christoffersen (2009) 439–443. Also under substantive Articles, the Court increasingly demands compensation. The most notable example is violations of P1 Article 1; see, for example, Fischborn (2010).

[120] This is also admitted by Christoffersen (2009) 442.

[121] See, for example, Shelton (2015) 286.

[122] See, for example, *Aydin v. Turkey* (Grand Chamber 1997) para. 103.

[123] See, for example, *Menteş a.o. v. Turkey* (Grand Chamber 1997) para. 89.

[124] See, for example, *Anguelova v. Bulgaria* (2002) para. 161; *Karácsony a.o. v. Hungary* (2014) para. 96.

In some areas, the Court has provided further guidance. In *Keenan v. the UK* (2001), the Court held that, in cases of a breach of Articles 2 and 3, compensation for nonpecuniary damage flowing from the breach should, "in principle," be available as part of the range of possible remedies.[125] This must include the possibility for a mother to apply for compensation, both for her nonpecuniary damage and for that of her son, which he suffered before his death.[126] Indeed, for a bereaved parent, the possibility of claiming compensation for the failure to protect life "is an essential element of a remedy under Article 13."[127] This includes the possibility of obtaining compensation for nonpecuniary damages because of violations of the procedural aspects of Articles 2 and 3, most notably ineffective investigations.[128]

Consequently, in cases concerning Articles 2 and 3, the applicant must have the possibility of seeking and obtaining compensation for any damages of both pecuniary and nonpecuniary character.[129] But, if the possibility exists, Article 13 is not necessarily violated if the national authority does not award compensation, or awards compensation that does not fully redress the violation, as long as the authority had the possibility of awarding sufficient compensation.[130] That being said, there is a "strong presumption" that violations of Article 3, at the very least, occasions nonpecuniary damages.[131]

Also with regard to arguable violations of Article 8, the Court has explicitly stated that there must be a possibility of obtaining compensation for any damage suffered, including any nonpecuniary damages.[132]

Moreover, in cases concerning excessive length of proceedings, "there is a strong but rebuttable presumption that excessively long proceedings will occasion non-pecuniary damage." In some cases, the length of the proceedings may result in only minimal nonpecuniary damage, or no nonpecuniary damage at all, but domestic courts "will then have to justify their decision by giving sufficient reasons."[133] The applicant is not obliged to prove any specific amount

[125] *Keenan v. the UK* (2001) para. 130. Similarly, for example, *Z a.o. v. the UK* (Grand Chamber 2001) para. 109; *Zavoloka v. Latvia* (2009) para. 35 *litra* c; *Stanev v. Bulgaria* (Grand Chamber 2012) para. 218; *Mirzoyan v. Armenia* (2019) para. 78.
[126] *Keenan v. the UK* (2001) para. 131.
[127] See, for example, *Paul and Audrey Edwards v. the UK* (2002) para. 101.
[128] See, for example, *Bubbins v. the UK* (2005) paras. 171–172.
[129] See, for example, *Mosendz v. Ukraine* (2013) para. 121; *Kirins v. Latvia* (2017) paras. 86–87; *Teymurazyan v. Armenia* (2018) para. 71.
[130] See Sections 9.4 and 10.6.
[131] See, for example, *Neshkov a.o. v. Bulgaria* (2015) para. 190; *Roth v. Germany* (2020) para. 93.
[132] See, for example, *R.K. and A.K. v. the UK* (2008) para. 45; *X a.o. v. Russia* (2020) paras. 73–78.
[133] See, for example, *Scordino v. Italy (no. 1)* (Grand Chamber 2006) para. 204 concerning the victim requirement in Article 34 ECHR, which must apply similarly in cases concerning Article 13, compare, for example, *Hartman v. the Czech Republic* (2003) paras. 83 and 68.

of nonpecuniary damage,[134] but only specific circumstances ("*circumstances particuliere*") may justify not according to compensation for nonpecuniary damages. In penal cases, the reduction of the penalty may provide "sufficient reasons".[135]

This doctrine of "sufficient reasons" could be taken to express a more general principle: If States do not allow for the possibility of obtaining compensation (no matter what the violation), even for nonpecuniary damages, they have to justify why. Indeed, the Court does not generally set out the circumstances in which compensation has to be provided, but mostly only considers whether the State has provided sufficient reasons as to why compensation, most notably for nonpecuniary damages, was not awarded. The question then arises, what reasons may justify not awarding compensation?

Lack of fault on the part of authorities may not, at least in cases of direct infringements violating Articles 2 and 3, justify not providing compensation.[136] Also in cases concerning excessive length of proceedings and nonenforcement of judgments, lack of fault on the part of, for example, the judges who are to expedite the proceedings, is not a sufficient justification.[137] Neither may a doctrine of "absence of good faith" justify not providing compensation for a direct violation of Article 8.[138]

On the other hand, when the State is responsible under the positive obligation for the lack of protection against actions from third persons, or natural hazards, lack of compensation for nonpecuniary damages may be justified with reference to broader competing concerns. An example is *Zavoloka v. Latvia* (2009), which concerned an alleged violation of Article 2 because of the failure to protect the life of a child who died in a car accident (caused by a third person). The applicant claimed that the failure to award compensation for nonpecuniary damages, for the death of her child, violated Article 13 in combination with Article 2. A majority of six to one judge found no violation of Article 13 because the applicant did not have an arguable claim against the State (the death of the child was exclusively due to the negligence of a particular car driver who was prosecuted and penalized).[139] However, in an *obiter dictum*, the majority held, more generally, that, because of the grand diversity

---

[134] See, for example, *Hartman v. the Czech Republic* (2003) paras. 83 and 68; *Zwoźniak v. Poland* (2007) para. 50.
[135] See, for example, *Apicella v. Italy* (Grand Chamber 2006) para. 75.
[136] See, for example, *Kochetkov v. Estonia* (2009) paras. 58–59; *Dirdizov v. Russia* (2012) para. 80; *Reshetnyak v. Russia* (2013) paras. 65–68; *Roth v. Germany* (2020) paras. 93 and 96.
[137] See, for example, *Rutkowski a.o. v. Poland* (2015) para. 184.
[138] *S.W. v. the UK* (2021) para. 72.
[139] *Zavoloka v. Latvia* (2009) para. 39.

between States with regard to compensation in cases of such deaths, the Court could not deduce an absolute and general obligation to award damages for nonpecuniary losses in cases such as the present one.[140] By contrast, in her dissenting opinion, Judge Ziemele held that Article 13 was violated because the applicant had no possibility of obtaining an integral compensation which took into account both material and moral loss.

Some claim that *Zavoloka v. Latvia* (2009) must be so understood that compensation for nonpecuniary losses must only be part of redress mechanisms when the right to life is directly infringed by the State and not in any private law relationships.[141] But even though the obligations under the Convention primarily pertain to States, both the positive obligation and the right to an effective remedy may oblige States to take actions which affect third parties, including placing both obligations and responsibility on those individuals, even in private law relationships (so-called indirect horizontal effect or *Drittwirkung*).[142] Further, in the *obiter dictum*, the majority only held that, with regard to one specific breach of the positive obligation (these types of car accidents), compensation for nonpecuniary damages was not necessary. That being said, also, for example, *Budayeva a.o. v. Russia* (2008) illustrates that, in emergency situations, in particular if caused by natural hazards, it may be justified not to provide compensation for both pecuniary and nonpecuniary damages.[143]

Because the Court does not positively set out the circumstances in which compensation has to be provided, but mostly only considers whether the State has provided "sufficient reasons" as to why compensation was not awarded, it is difficult to say to what extent compensation has to be provided, outside the scenarios explicitly dealt with by the Court. However, the trend, in a similar manner as under Article 41,[144] goes in the direction of demanding, in more and more scenarios, that compensation for both pecuniary and nonpecuniary damages has to be provided, and the Court scrutinizes, in a stricter manner, whether States have provided "sufficient reasons" for not providing compensation.

[140] Ibid., para. 40.
[141] See, for example, Rijnhout and Emaus (2014) 97.
[142] See, more generally, Somers (2018).
[143] Presuming that compensation for nonpecuniary damages for such breaches has to be made available, the question arises in what procedures the applicant may claim compensation? To what extent may the State remedy the breach of the positive obligation by making a third-person liable to pay compensation, and to what extent must the State make the private individual responsible, even for nonpecuniary damages? Schultz (2011) holds that Article 13, at the very least, should have some effect in relationships between private individuals. See, also, more generally, Somers (2018) 52–57.
[144] See, for example, Ichim (2014).

11.5.3 *Level of Compensation*

In the Court's case law, there is little guidance concerning the level of compensation. This is only natural because the level of compensation may vary considerably between States.[145] In the framework of excessive length of proceedings, this is justified in the following manner:

> Where a State has made a significant move by introducing a compensatory remedy, the Court must leave a wider margin of appreciation to the State to allow it to organise the remedy in a manner consistent with its own legal system and traditions and consonant with the standard of living in the country concerned. It will, in particular, be easier for the domestic courts to refer to the amounts awarded at domestic level for other types of damage – personal injury, damage relating to a relative's death or damage in defamation cases for example – and rely on their innermost conviction, even if that results in awards of amounts that are lower than those fixed by the Court in similar cases.[146]

Further, the level of compensation may depend on the characteristics and effectiveness of the remedy, as such, which may vary from country to country.[147] Accordingly, the compensation required in one State does not necessarily provide guidance for the level of compensation in another. However, the Court has (1) emphasized some general elements of significance directly under Article 13 and (2) considered whether the level of compensation under Article 41, in cases against the same State, need be the same under Article 13.

Directly under Article 13, the Court has, as starting-points, held that the amounts need to be "reasonable",[148] "adequate",[149] or "capable of resulting in an award of fair and reasonable damages proportionate to the loss suffered".[150] Further, this must be assessed "in the light of all the circumstances of the case", such as the type and severity of the violation, and "the value of the award judged in the light of the standard of living in the State concerned".[151] The Court has, also, in a similar manner as under Article 41, held that pecuniary

---

[145] See, for example, Ichim (2014) 159 and 277 ff.

[146] *Apicella v. Italy* (Grand Chamber 2006) para. 78. See, also, for example, *Bara and Kola v. Albania* (2021) para. 110.

[147] Ibid., para. 94.

[148] See, for example, *Bako v. Slovakia* (Decision 2005).

[149] See, for example, *Apicella v. Italy* (Grand Chamber 2006) para. 84.

[150] See, for example, the partly dissenting opinion of Judges Spielmann and Malinverni in *Maksimov v. Russia* (2010).

[151] *Bako v. Slovakia* (Decision 2005). See, also, for example, *Rutkowski a.o. v. Poland* (2015) para. 174.

damages must put the applicant, as far as possible, in the position he would have enjoyed had the breach not occurred (*restitutio in integrum*).[152]

Indirectly, the Court has recognized that the main function of compensation is to correct individual injustice. For instance, in *Keenan v. the UK* (2001), when considering whether compensation for nonpecuniary damages was necessary to redress violations of Articles 2 and 3, the Court referred to the need to take into account the applicant's "pain, stress, anxiety and frustration".[153] Further, in *Maksimov v. Russia* (2010), effective investigations could not alone "redress the physical and psychological damage flowing from the direct and deliberate invasion of the applicant's bodily integrity."[154] In this regard, the type and degree of violation has to be taken into account,[155] and with regard to excessive length of proceedings, the Court has emphasized that the national authority must be able to take all periods and instances of delay into account,[156] including the length of execution before the compensation is paid.[157]

Under Article 41, the Court has, in addition to the correction of injustice, explicitly attached weight to general deterrence by awarding higher levels of compensation in cases that reveal systemic and repetitive problems, the most notable example being cases concerning excessive length of proceedings.[158]

Under Article 13, the Court mostly only indirectly indicates that, for instance, it must be possible to obtain pecuniary damages at national level, presumably with the purpose of deterring. However, domestic courts are then "clearly in a better position to determine the existence and quantum".[159] But, the cases of *Shilbergs v. Russia* (2009) and *Ananyev v. Russia* (2010) illustrate that, at least in cases which concern violations of Article 3, it may be necessary to take into account the need both to correct and deter. The cases concerned inhuman and degrading conditions of detention in extremely cold and humid cells, without adequate lighting, food, or a personal sleeping place for prolonged periods.[160] The motives and conduct of the defendant, and the circumstances in which the wrong was committed, were also relevant to take into account. On the

---

[152] *Portanier v. Malta* (2019) para. 55.
[153] *Keenan v. the UK* (2001) para. 130. See, also, for example, *Poghosyan and Baghdasaryan v. Armenia* (2012) paras. 46–47.
[154] *Maksimov v. Russia* (2010) para. 63.
[155] See Chapter 8.
[156] See, for example, *Barry v. Ireland* (2005) para. 55; *Dobál v. Slovakia* (2006) para. 57; *Donner v. Austria* (2007) para. 44.
[157] See, for example, *Apicella v. Italy* (Grand Chamber 2006) para. 98.
[158] See, for example, ibid., para. 65.
[159] See, for example, ibid., para. 192. See, also, for example, *Kirins v. Latvia* (2017) para. 91.
[160] *Shilbergs v. Russia* (2009) paras. 70–79, under Article 35(1), but *Ananyev a.o. v. Russia* (2012) paras. 113–118 includes the same reasoning under Article 13.

other hand, financial and logistical difficulties, as well as the lack of a positive intention to humiliate or debase the applicant, were irrelevant. Further, the Court underlined that the award had to mark:

> disapproval of the State's wrongful conduct to the extent of awarding an adequate and sufficient quantum of damages to the applicant, taking into account the fundamental importance of the right of which they had found a breach, even if they considered that breach to have been an inadvertent rather than an intended consequence of the State's conduct. As a corollary this would have conveyed the message that the State could not set individual rights and freedoms at nought or circumvent them with impunity.[161]

Moreover, the Court has accepted, more generally, that lower levels of compensation may be provided at domestic level than at international level.[162] Most notably, in cases concerning excessive length of proceedings, the Court grants States a wide margin of appreciation with regard to the level of compensation required by Article 13. Indeed, even though nonpecuniary damages, as a starting-point, must be provided, the length of proceedings may result in only minimal nonpecuniary damage or no nonpecuniary damage at all, as long as the domestic courts justify their decision by giving "sufficient reasons".[163] However, the domestic awards cannot be "unreasonable", compared to the amounts awarded by the Court, and the relevant decisions must be "consonant with the legal tradition and the standard of living in the country concerned, ... speedy, reasoned and executed very quickly."[164]

In a number of cases, the Court has found domestic awards "unreasonable" compared to what the Court would have awarded. For instance, in *Shilbergs* v. *Russia* (2009), the applicant was awarded RUB 1,500 (less than 50 euros) for nonpecuniary damages, whereas the Court awarded the applicant 10,500 euros.[165] That being said, for example, *Maksimov* v. *Russia* (2010) illustrates that the difference may be fairly large. The case concerned serious ill-treatment in violation of Article 3 by a police officer, under which domestic courts had awarded the applicant compensation for nonpecuniary damages to the amount of RUB 10,000 (approximately EUR 340), whereas the Court awarded EUR 9,000.[166]

---

[161] *Ananyev a.o.* v. *Russia* (2012) para. 117.
[162] See, for example, Christoffersen (2009) 449–454 with further references.
[163] *Apicella* v. *Italy* (Grand Chamber 2006) paras. 92–93.
[164] See, for example, *Apicella* v. *Italy* (Grand Chamber 2006) para. 95; *Liseytseva and Maslov* v. *Russia* (2014) para. 158; *Roth* v. *Germany* (2020) para. 93.
[165] *Shilbergs* v. *Russia* (2009) para. 129.
[166] A minority of two judges, Judges Spielmann and Malinverni, found the amount disproportionately low compared to what the Court had awarded in similar Russian cases. Since

The Court has provided no abstract explanation as to why the levels of compensation may be different, but several factors speak for allowing different levels.[167]

First, Article 13 does not guarantee a remedy that is bound to succeed (Section 10.6). As a consequence, and at least as a starting-point, as long as the domestic authority in principle can afford sufficient compensation, and as long as insufficient compensation does not stem from a systemic or structural problem, Article 13 is mostly not found to be violated by the Court, even though the domestic authority did not award sufficient compensation. Lower compensation has been accepted, for example, in a number of cases concerning excessive lengths of proceedings against, *inter alia*, Malta,[168] Slovakia,[169] Italy,[170] and Croatia.[171]

Second, assessing and calculating damages in human-rights cases is difficult. This difficulty has been recognized by the Court when considering whether the applicant is a victim under Article 34. In *Scordino* v. *Italy (no. 1)* (Decision 2003), which concerned excessive length of proceedings, the Court, for example, held that:

> [i]t cannot be disputed that the assessment of the length of proceedings and the effects thereof, particularly as regards non-pecuniary damage, does not lend itself to precise quantification and must by its very nature be carried out on an equitable basis. The Court consequently accepts that judicial or other authorities may calculate compensation in a length-of-proceedings case in a manner not entailing strict and formalistic application of the criteria adopted by the Court.[172]

Third, compensation at domestic level is, under normal circumstances, awarded and enforced more promptly.[173] Indeed, if the applicant has to resort

---

domestic courts made no reasonable attempt to justify the amount of the award, Article 13 had been violated. Compare, also, *Ananyev a.o.* v. *Russia* (2012) para. 230: "The right not to be subjected to inhuman or degrading treatment is so fundamental and central to the system of the protection of human rights that the domestic authority or court dealing with the matter will have to provide *exceptionally compelling and serious reasons to justify their decision to award lower or no compensation in respect of non-pecuniary damage*" (my emphasis). However, this statement was only made under Article 46, as an element of the Pilot judgment procedure, and not repeated directly under Article 13.

[167] See, also, Christoffersen (2009) 454.
[168] For example, *Zarb* v. *Malta* (2006) para. 51.
[169] For example, *Rišková* v. *Slovakia* (2006) paras. 100–101.
[170] For example, *Di Pietro* v. *Italy* (2006) para. 49; *Simaldone* v. *Italy* (2009) paras. 71–72.
[171] For example, *Kaić a.o.* v. *Croatia* (2008) para. 39.
[172] See, for example, *Scordino* v. *Italy (no. 1)* (Decision 2003).
[173] See, for example, *Bako* v. *Slovakia* (Decision 2005).

to the Court, he/she must exhaust domestic remedies and use additional time and resources to obtain redress. It is, therefore, conceivable that the Court will "acknowledge its own delay and that accordingly, and in order not to penalize the applicant later, it will award a particularly high amount of compensation in order to make good the further delay."[174]

Fourth, the subsidiary review of the Court influences how the Court scrutinizes domestic decisions, including the appropriateness of both awarding compensation and the concrete level awarded. Indeed, domestic compensation procedures may be influenced by several factors, *inter alia*, other available forms of redress, national legal cultures, and socioeconomic conditions.[175] Because of this, States are granted a wide margin of appreciation concerning the concrete level of compensation. Seen from the point of view of the Court, the question is, therefore, rather whether domestic authorities have awarded compensation in accordance "with the spirit of the Convention".[176] This implies a procedural (in contrast to substantive) review of the justification from the domestic authority.

But what, then, is to be justified? As we have seen earlier, the Court considers that both the deviation from the level of compensation under Article 41 and the extent to which domestic compensation satisfies the purposes of Article 13 are relevant. However, additional guidance and clarification from the Court is necessary. At the very least, the Court should explicitly recognize and clarify the following:

First, if restitution is not granted, the starting-point must be that the full economic loss caused by the violation is compensated,[177] in accordance with the overall goal of achieving *restitutio in integrum* for the individual victim.[178] There may be difficulties in calculating the economic loss, establishing causality between the loss and the violation, considering proportionality between the violation and the loss, *etc.*[179] However, if the substantive Article has been violated, and if compensation is required, no additional grounds for accountability, for instance, *culpa*, can be required.[180]

---

[174] *Apicella* v. *Italy* (Grand Chamber 2006) para. 96.
[175] Compare Cameron (2006) 124–125.
[176] Compare *Scordino* v. *Italy (no. 1)* (Decision 2003) concerning the assessment under Article 34 ECHR.
[177] Compare the ILC Draft Articles on Responsibility of States for Internationally Wrongful Acts Article 36.
[178] See, for example, Shelton (2013) 678. See, also, Proceedings under Article 46 § 4 of the Convention in the case of *Ilgar Mammadov* v. *Azerbaijan* (Grand Chamber 2019) paras. 150–152.
[179] As is amply illustrated under Article 41 ECHR; see, for example, Ichim (2014).
[180] Similarly, under Article 41 ECHR, Bydlinski (2011) 96 holds that the only possible ground for reduction of pecuniary damages is the contributory responsibility of the victim.

Second, whereas economic loss may be established with reference to economic principles, the calculation of nonpecuniary damages must be made with reference to underlying purposes (Chapter 3). Without taking a stand here on the normative question as to what extent various purposes should be of significance, the Court, at the very least, needs to take a stand on the following:

(1) To what extent is compensation above an economic loss necessary to correct individual injustice? Both past and future (noneconomic) suffering may be alleviated through compensation. Compensating moral damage may, also, affirm public respect to the victim and recognize fault. On the other hand, even valuating moral damage in money may be considered degrading.[181] And, even if one normatively accepts money as a substitute for moral damage, the appropriateness may, in practice, vary considerably between States. For instance, many States have extensive systems of social security and health insurance, which may alleviate and correct injustice and, therefore, diminish the need for monetary compensation.[182] To the extent that nonpecuniary damages are necessary to correct individual injustice, domestic authorities should, therefore, have considerable discretion with regard to the concrete level of nonpecuniary damages. But the Court may require that the domestic authorities justify the level.

(2) To what extent is compensation necessary to compensate wrongs against society more generally, and, if so, should the individual victim be able to collect this compensation? To date, there is little evidence in the practice of the Court that this is a relevant concern when setting out the required compensation.

(3) To what extent should compensation aim at promoting other purposes, most notably, deterrence? Some may find it easier to justify, in particular, nonpecuniary damages in deterrence, in contrast to correcting injustice. And, domestically, compensation for human-rights violations is, usually, awarded both to correct and to deter.[183] Further, if deterrence is recognized as a purpose of Article 13, it must be clarified against whom deterrence should be aimed. Even though there is some evidence that the Court requires domestic authorities to attach weight to deterrence, in particular in cases concerning Articles 2 and 3 revealing systemic and

---

[181] See, for example, Sandel (2009) 98.
[182] Iain Cameron holds that, in Sweden, rights have, by many, not been regarded as necessary in a generous welfare State; see Cameron (2006) 98.
[183] Shelton (2005) 38.

structural problems, the extent to which domestic authorities must do so remains unclears (Chapter 3).

(4) Independently of the stand taken on the purposes that redress is to serve, every legal system must strive for some certainty and coherence when calculating damages.[184] But the assessment of damages is complicated, not least in human-rights cases. In national law, many countries, therefore, use charts, grids, and tables based upon preset factors or a comparison of similar cases. However, seen from the point of view of the Court, setting out such charts is extremely difficult and controversial due to, *inter alia*, the differences between States.[185] That being said, the Court could emphasize the need to achieve certainty and equality when calculating damages.

It should be underlined that an alternative could be to perceive compensation purely as a method for vindicating rights. The main purpose of requiring compensation under Article 13 would then be to assure that there actually is a procedure in which private parties may vindicate their rights.[186] However, this accepts that the only purpose of redress is to correct individual injustice and, also, implies that a declaratory judgment (without a finding of compensation) could be sufficient in most cases, which, clearly, does not correspond with the Court's case law. Further, as we have seen earlier, the case law demonstrates, at least indirectly, that deterrence, both at an individual and systemic level, may be necessary. Moreover, if this approach is accepted, a very wide margin of appreciation on the part of States with regard to compensation (and redress, more generally) would have to be granted, which again allows for considerable differences between the redress required in different States. However, at least to the extent that redress is to be perceived as a right for the individual, a minimum level of equal application would have to be demanded.[187] And, as long as the Court has started to sketch out the redress required by Article 13, and, at least indirectly, some of the purposes that the redress must promote, the Court is moving toward recognizing specific forms of redress as rights for the individual. Accepting that compensation is only a method for vindicating rights, is a step backward.

---

[184] See, for example, Shelton (2015) 31.

[185] It could be argued that the Court should make public the tables and charts which it uses when setting out compensation in the framework of Article 41; see, for example, Ichim (2014) 161, and that these could serve as guidance also for the national level – in particular States which have a large number of similar cases at the Court. However, the level of compensation awarded under Articles 41 and 13 may, as accounted for above, vary considerably.

[186] This seems to be the main point of, for example, Rijnhout and Emaus (2014) 104–106.

[187] See, as an expression, Article 14 ECHR.

11.5.4 *Compensation from Whom?*

The Court has not demanded that a claim of compensation must be directed against specific authorities of the State,[188] but the internal legal framework of the State may require so.[189] This seems unproblematical, as long as the required redress is provided. More problematical is the question as to whether the State may fulfill its obligation to provide redress by allowing the applicant to claim compensation from private persons or entities? Surely, the State cannot be released from its obligation to provide redress by obliging third persons, with no connection to the violation, to pay compensation. But the question arises as to whether the obligation may be fulfilled by allowing, for example, personal claims against agents of the State?

Maximov v. Russia (2010) indicates, more generally, that it may be sufficient that the agent or entity directly responsible for the violation be held liable.[190] Article 3 was violated because of ill-treatment by a police officer. The applicant attempted to obtain redress in two tort actions. Domestic courts awarded the victim compensation from the police officer in the criminal proceedings against the latter. However, this action was never enforced because the officer did not have sufficient funds. But the applicant, also, initiated proceedings against a number of State agencies, in which he alleged that the amount awarded was not sufficient, and, in any case, never enforced. He argued that the State, as such, had to be held responsible so as to deter future violations. Domestic courts did not allow this action. A majority of the Court (five to two judges) found that the award against the police officer was sufficient. The minority, on the other hand, held that Article 13 required the remedy to be capable of actually resulting in an award of fair and reasonable damages proportionate to the loss suffered. Since it was not possible to get this award enforced, and since the domestic system offered no other alternative for obtaining compensation, Article 13 had been violated.[191]

11.5.5 *Time of Payment*

The Court accepts that domestic authorities need time to make payment, but the period cannot be too long. It is, simply, an admission that there are some

---

[188] At domestic level, the answer to the question of whether the State, or specific agents of the State, should be held liable for human-rights violations, vary greatly. However, most States accept some form of joint responsibility; see, for example, Shelton (2005) 33–34.

[189] See, for example, *Liseytseva and Maslov v. Russia* (2014).

[190] See, more generally, also, Somers (2018) 45–57.

[191] Joint partly dissenting opinion of Judges Spielmann and Malinverni. Critical is, also, for example, McGregor (2012) 747.

practical barriers, which may hinder immediate payment, for example, the transfer of funds and the obtaining of the necessary permission(s) within the State. Indeed, in cases of excessive length of proceedings, and this could probably be seen as a more general guideline,[192] the Court has held that the period should generally not exceed six months from the date on which the decision awarding compensation becomes enforceable.[193]

11.6 INDIVIDUAL GUARANTEES AND ASSURANCES AGAINST NONREPETITION

Under the general rules on State responsibility, individual guarantees and assurances against nonrepetition are, together with cessation and reparation, the primary consequences of the international wrongful act. In the ILC Draft Articles on Responsibility of States for Internationally Wrongful Acts, such guarantees and assurances are dealt with in Article 30, together with cessation. But whereas cessation looks to the past and present by seeking to end a continuing wrongful conduct, guarantees and assurances against nonrepetition serve a preventive function. Indeed, whereas cessation is considered the negative aspect of future performance, guarantee against nonrepetition is seen as a positive reinforcement of future performance.[194] These positive reinforcements are directed at the relationship between the parties. They do not aim at preventing similar violations between other parties.[195]

The case law of the Court does not demand guarantees and assurances against nonrepetition to be issued in the relationship between the parties, nor have such guarantees and assurances been demanded by the Committee of Ministers. True, in its surveillance activity, the Committee of Ministers require States to implement measures not only to redress the individual violation but also general measures to prevent future violations. Thus, occasionally, the Committee of Ministers has, for instance, considered it necessary to make changes in domestic legislation. This necessity has also, albeit indirectly, been recognized by the Court in individual cases and not just Pilot judgments.[196] However, such measures and indications seem to have a more

---

[192] See, for example, *Liseytseva and Maslov v. Russia* (2014) para. 158.

[193] See, for example, *Apicella v. Italy* (Grand Chamber 2006) para. 87.

[194] See, for example, Crawford (2002) 196 under para. 1.

[195] By contrast, Principle 23 of the van Boven/Bassiouni Principles includes measures directed at preventing similar violations between other parties in the concept of guarantees against nonrepetition. See, also, Tomuschat (2007) 590.

[196] See, as an example, *Norris v. Ireland* (Plenary 1988) para. 50.

general preventive function. They are not required as "guarantees" or "assurances" of nonrepetition to be provided to the individual.[197] They are thus not "a positive reinforcement of future performance",[198] and not primarily concerned with restoring "confidence in a continuing relationship" between the parties,[199] but aim at repairing the general situation, so as to avoid any type of similar violation, even between different parties.

The Court has not given any justification as to why it does not demand guarantees and assurances against nonrepetition. One reason may be that they are not perceived as being inherent to the remedial task, as such – it is not a form of redress directed against past and present violations, but a guarantee against future violations.[200] On the other hand, when requiring specific forms of redress, in particular, compensation, the Court has, on several occasions, attached weight to general deterrence, although not as a guarantee between the parties. Nor has the ICJ or the IACtHR demanded specific guarantees against nonrepetition, but refer, more generally, to commitments with regard to future behavior.[201]

11.7 EFFECTIVE INVESTIGATIONS

11.7.1 *Introduction*

Since the early 1990s, the Court has required effective investigations under substantive Articles, most notably, Articles 2 and 3.[202] The Court, also, includes a requirement of effective investigations under Article 13, in combination with, most notably, Articles 2, 3, 5, 8, and P1 Article 1. The requirement was developed in a string of cases against Turkey concerning deaths, disappearances, inhuman treatment, and destruction of homes and property inflicted by State

---

[197] See, in a similar manner, Ichim (2014) 254.

[198] Compare Crawford (2002) 196 under para. 1 and 199 under para. 11.

[199] Crawford (2002) 198 under para. 9.

[200] See, in this regard, the ILC Draft Articles on Responsibility of States for Internationally Wrongful Acts Articles 30 and 31, which distinguish between cessation, nonrepetition, and reparation. This, however, has not prevented the Court from requiring cessation, both under Articles 13, 41, and 46. Further, in the practice of the ICJ, guarantees against nonrepetition are often analyzed under the heading of reparation; see, for example, Gray (2014) 880. However, in the *La Grand Case*, the ICJ assumed that, as a general rule, there is no reason to suppose that a State whose act has been declared wrongful would repeat that act in the future. Thus, good faith must be presumed. The ICJ will, therefore, only order guarantees against nonrepetition when there are special circumstances; see, for example, Gray (2014) 880–881.

[201] Gray (2014) 880.

[202] See, for example, *McCann a.o.* v. *the UK* (Grand Chamber 1995).

agents and unknown perpetrators in southeast Turkey, which suffered from disturbances between Turkish security forces and the PKK (Worker's party of Kurdistan). In later years, the requirement has been important in a number of cases against Russia, most notably in cases arising out of the conflict in Chechnya, but also in many cases against, for example, the United Kingdom, Bulgaria, and Ukraine.[203]

Aksoy v. *Turkey* (1996) was the first case, which considered whether Article 13 had been violated because of ineffective investigations. Article 3 was violated because of torture by State agents. The Court did not include a procedural requirement of effective investigations under Article 3, but considered the issue solely under Article 13,[204] and held that:

> The nature of the right safeguarded under Article 3 of the Convention has implications for Article 13. Given the fundamental importance of the prohibition of torture … and the especially vulnerable position of torture victims, Article 13 imposes, without prejudice to any other remedy available under the domestic system, an obligation on States to carry out a thorough and effective investigation of incidents of torture. Accordingly, as regards Article 13 where an individual has an arguable claim that he has been tortured by agents of the State, the notion of an "effective remedy" entails, in addition to the payment of compensation where appropriate, a thorough and effective investigation capable of leading to the identification and punishment of those responsible and including effective access for the complainant to the investigatory procedure.[205]

Since no investigation of the alleged torture had taken place, Article 13 was violated.[206] In *Aydin* v. *Turkey* (Grand Chamber 1997), the Court added that the investigation must be "capable of establishing the truth" and of "leading to the identification and punishment of those responsible".[207]

The Court may review the investigations intensely and in detail, both under substantive Articles and Article 13, for instance, on a case-by-case basis setting out what is necessary with regard to, for example, the amount of forensic evidence, for instance, an autopsy which provides a complete and accurate record of possible signs of ill-treatment and injury and an objective analysis of

---

[203] See Section 4.3.
[204] The applicant also claimed that Article 6(1) had been violated because of lacking investigations, but the Court only considered the case under Article 13, see *Aksoy* v. *Turkey* (1996) para. 94, and, later, for example, *Aydin* v. *Turkey* (Grand Chamber 1997) paras. 88 and 101–102; *Kaya* v. *Turkey* (1998) para. 105. See, also, Section 4.5.2.
[205] *Aksoy* v. *Turkey* (1996) para. 98.
[206] Ibid., para. 100.
[207] *Aydin* v. *Turkey* (Grand Chamber 1997) para. 105.

clinical findings, including the cause of death,[208] the collection of evidence, for example, the questioning of witnesses and the collection of other factual evidence,[209] the independence of the investigating authority,[210] the scope and duration of the investigation,[211] the length of time before the investigation starts,[212] unexplained omissions,[213] and the speed of the investigation (prompt, adequate, and effective).[214] The extent to which such factors are necessary depends on the particular circumstances of the case and may be influenced by the passage of time.[215]

From a structural and analytical point of view, it is problematical that effective investigations may be considered necessary on several legal grounds. But this, also, makes it difficult to deduce the more concrete content of the obligation in practice. Under Article 2 and Article 13 seen in conjunction with arguable violations of Article 2, effective investigations may, for example, be required on four different grounds:

- the general positive obligation to protect life, seen in conjunction with Article 1;
- the specific positive obligation to protect life "by law" in Article 2(1) first sentence;
- the procedural obligation inherent in Article 2;
- the right to an effective remedy in Article 13 seen in conjunction with Article 2.

The question then arises as to whether these requirements are the same? Similar questions arise in relation to other substantive Articles.

Section 11.7.2 demonstrates that the relationship between the requirements under Article 13 and substantive Articles is highly unclear.[216] Although some differences are certain, Section 11.7.3 argues that the Court should clarify the relationship by making abstract distinctions with reference to purposes. This recommendation must be read in conjunction with the following Sections 11.7.4 and 11.7.5, which analyze what extent Article 13 sets out an autonomous right to know the truth and requires identification, punishment,

---

[208] See, for example, *Salman* v. *Turkey* (Grand Chamber 2000) para. 105.
[209] See, for example, Tanrikulu v. Turkey (Grand Chamber 1999) para. 107.
[210] See, for example, *Mahmut Kaya* v. *Turkey* (2000) para. 95.
[211] See, for example, *Kilic* v. *Turkey* (2000) para. 83.
[212] See, for example, *Timurtaş* v. *Turkey* (2000) para. 89.
[213] See, for example, *Velikova* v. *Bulgaria* (2000) para. 79.
[214] See, for example, *Taş* v. *Turkey* (2000) para. 52.
[215] See, for example, *Brecknell* v. *the UK* (2007) para. 72.
[216] Similarly, for example, Klinkner and Davis (2020) 139–140.

and establishment of liability. Section 11.7.6 accounts for the relationship between effective investigations and some other requirements and principles arising under Article 13.

11.7.2 *Relationship with Substantive Articles*

After the first cases finding violations of Article 13 in conjunction with only Article 3, the Court, in a number of cases, found violations of both Articles 3, 8, and P1 Article 1 for the destruction of homes and eviction from villages.[217] In a similar manner as in *Aksoy* and *Aydin*, this assessment was made solely under Article 13.[218]

However, in a number of successive cases, the Court found an inherent procedural requirement of effective investigations under Article 3 to have been violated, as well as Article 13 in conjunction with Article 3. The first case was *Assenov a.o.* v. *Bulgaria* (1998). No substantive violation of alleged beatings by police officers was found because it was impossible to establish the alleged facts. However, there was "reasonable suspicion" that the injuries were caused by the police. In these circumstances, similarly as in previous cases under Article 2, which I account for below, the Court held that:

> where an individual raises an arguable claim that he has been seriously ill-treated by the police or other such agents of the State unlawfully and in breach of Article 3, that provision, read in conjunction with the State's general duty under Article 1 of the Convention to secure to everyone within their jurisdiction the rights and freedoms defined in … [the] Convention, requires by implication that there should be an effective official investigation. This investigation, as with that under Article 2, should be capable of leading to the identification and punishment of those responsible … If this were not the case, the general legal prohibition of torture and inhuman and degrading treatment and punishment, despite its fundamental importance … would be ineffective in practice and it would be possible in some cases for agents of the State to abuse the rights of those within their control with virtual impunity.[219]

Under Article 13, the Court, then, reiterated the statements in *Aksoy* and *Aydin*, concerning the necessity of effective investigations under Article 13, which are almost identical to those made under Article 3. The Court, thereafter, only referred to its finding under Article 3 and found a violation also of Article 13.[220] The subsequent case law is not consistent.

---

[217] See, for example, *Selçuk and Asker* v. *Turkey* (1998).
[218] See, for example, *Tekin* v. *Turkey* (1998) para. 66.
[219] *Assenov a.o.* v. *Bulgaria* (1998) para. 102.
[220] Ibid., paras. 117–118.

In some cases, the Court includes a right to effective investigations in a more global assessment under Article 3, thus seemingly included in the substantive obligation of Article 3 (and not part of the positive obligation or an independent procedural obligation) and at the same time finds a violation of Article 13 in conjunction with Article 3, but with no explanation of the relationship between the requirements.[221] In other cases, the Court finds that it is not necessary to examine the investigations under Article 3, but finds a violation of Article 13 in conjunction with Article 3,[222] or the question is simply not commented upon under Article 3, but a violation is found under Article 13.[223]

However, in a few cases, the Court has attempted to explain why it is not necessary to examine the investigations under Article 3, in addition to Article 13. The primary example is *İlhan v. Turkey* (Grand Chamber 2000) in which Article 2 was arguably violated and Article 3 violated because of threats to life and mistreatment by security forces. In addition, Article 13 was violated in conjunction with both Articles 2 and 3, but the Court considered it unnecessary to examine whether the inadequate investigations violated both Articles 2 and 3, as such. The Court held, more generally:

> Procedural obligations have been implied in varying contexts under the Convention, where this has been perceived as necessary to ensure that the rights guaranteed under the Convention are not theoretical or illusory but practical and effective. The obligation to provide an effective investigation into the death caused by, inter ali[a], the security forces of the State was for this reason implied under Article 2 which guarantees the right to life … This provision does, however, include the requirement that the right to life be 'protected by law'. It may also concern situations where the initiative must rest on the State for the practical reason that the victim is deceased and the circumstances of the death may be largely confined within the knowledge of State officials.[224]

The Court then distinguished more explicitly between Articles 2 and 3:

> Article 3, however, is phrased in substantive terms. Furthermore, although the victim of an alleged breach of this provision may be in a vulnerable position, the practical exigencies of the situation will often differ from cases

---

[221] See, for example, *Karayiğit v. Turkey* (2005).

[222] See, for example, *Mahmut Kaya v. Turkey* (2000) para. 120; *Salman v. Turkey* (Grand Chamber 2000) para. 117; *Akdeniz a.o. v. Turkey* (2001) paras. 112–114.

[223] See, for example, *Egmez v. Cyprus* (2000); *Dizman v. Turkey* (2005); *Ortsuyeva a.o. v. Russia* (2016).

[224] *İlhan v. Turkey* (Grand Chamber 2000) para. 91.

of use of lethal force or suspicious deaths. The Court considers that the requirement under Article 13 of the Convention that a person with an argu-able claim of a violation of Article 3 be provided with an effective remedy will generally provide both redress to the applicant and the necessary procedural safeguards against abuses by State officials. The Court's case law establishes that the notion of effective remedy in this context includes the duty to carry out a thorough and effective investigation capable of leading to the identifi-cation and punishment of those responsible for any ill-treatment and permit-ting effective access for the complainant to the investigatory procedure ... Whether it is appropriate or necessary to find a procedural breach of Article 3 will therefore depend on the circumstances of the particular case.[225]

The Court, thereafter, concluded that the lack of any effective investigation into the cause of the alleged torture was to be dealt with solely by Article 13 in conjunction with Article 3.[226]

The Court thus established a preference for using Article 13 in conjunc-tion with Article 3. Indeed, declaring a procedural violation under Article 3, should only be necessary to ensure that the prohibition in Article 3 was ren-dered practical and effective. But the Court did not explain when this would be necessary, in addition to Article 13, only stating that this will "depend on the circumstances of the particular case."

In a number of later cases, the Court has only considered the effectiveness of the investigations under Article 13, not also Article 3. In many of these cases, the Court has done so with a simple reference to *Ilhan*, but without any further explanation,[227] in others without reference to *Ilhan*, but still without any further explanation.[228] But in a few cases, the Court has attempted to provide additional justifications. The Court has, for instance, held that the procedural aspect of Article 3 (including the requirement of effective investi-gations) is only to be invoked when it is not possible to find a violation of the substantive aspect of Article 3,[229] or, "in particular," when the Court is unable to reach any conclusion on the substantive aspect.[230] However, in many cases, the Court finds violations of both the substantive and procedural aspects of Article 3, as well as Article 13, without any further explanation as to why it is

---

[225] Ibid., para. 92.
[226] Ibid., para. 93.
[227] See, for example, *Büyükdağ v. Turkey* (2000) paras. 59–60; *Gennadi Naoumenko v. Ukraine* (2004) para. 130; *Veli Tosun v. Turkey* (2007) para. 50.
[228] See, for example, *Mehmet Emin Yüksel v. Turkey* (2004); *Khashiyev and Akayeva v. Russia* (2005); *Nazif Yavuz v. Turkey* (2006); *Mikadze v. Russia* (2007).
[229] See, for example, *Rashid v. Bulgaria* (2007) para. 58; *Bitiyeva and X v. Russia* (2007) para. 109.
[230] See, for example, *Petropoulou-Tsakiris v. Greece* (2007) para. 46.

necessary.[231] And, in some cases, the Court finds no substantive violation of Article 3, but only considers the investigations under Article 13.[232] The Court has, also, found violations of both the substantive and procedural aspect of Article 3, but not considered it necessary to consider Article 13,[233] or not mentioned the investigations under Article 13.[234] There are also cases, in which only the procedural aspect under Article 3 is violated (not the substantive), and in which the Court does not consider it necessary to consider the complaint under Article 13.[235]

Further, in many cases of deaths (or threats against life) and disappearances, the Court finds substantive violations of both Articles 2 and 3 (in many cases also Article 5). In most of these cases, the investigations are assessed under the procedural aspect of Article 2. Under Article 3, the question is, then, mostly not touched upon. But, in other cases, the Court, explicitly, states that it is not necessary to consider the procedural aspect under Article 3 due to the finding of a procedural violation of Article 2. In many of these cases, the Court, also, finds violations of Article 13. In most of these cases, the assessment under Article 13 is only seen in conjunction with Article 2 (not Article 3 as well).[236] However, in other cases, the assessment under Article 13 is also linked up to Article 3.[237] In other cases, it remains unclear whether Article 3 is included in the assessment under Article 13.[238] The Court may, also, find no

---

[231] See, for example, *Menesheva v. Russia* (2006) paras. 63, 71, and 77; *Rupa v. Romania (no. 1)* (2008) paras. 121, 128, 176, 179, and 188–193; *Davydov a.o. v. Ukraine* (2010) paras. 272, 291, 301, and 312; *Mesut Deniz v. Turkey* (2013) paras. 49, 56, and 62; *Abu Zubaydah v. Lithuania* (2018) paras. 622, 644, and 677.

[232] See, for example, *Aksakal v. Turkey* (2007).

[233] See, for example, *M.C. v. Bulgaria* (2003) para. 187; *Bekos and Koutropoulos v. Greece* (2005) para. 57; *Kucheruk v. Ukraine* (2007) para. 166; *Kasymakhunov v. Russia* (2013) para. 157; *Shestopalov v. Russia* (2017) para. 71; *Abdulkhanov v. Russia* (2021) para. 122.

[234] See, for example, *Akkoç v. Turkey* (2000) paras. 118–119 and 100–105, in which Article 13 was violated, but seemingly only in relation to Article 2. See, also, for example, *Taş v. Turkey* (2000) paras. 79–80; *Idalov v. Russia (no. 2)* (2016) paras. 90 and 94–95.

[235] See, for example, *Gömi a.o. v. Turkey* (2006) para. 83; *Zelilof v. Greece* (2007) para. 64; *Iordan Petrov v. Bulgaria* (2012) para. 162; *Aleksandr Nikonenko v. Ukraine* (2013) para. 51; *Adzhigitova a.o. v. Russia* (2021) para. 225.

[236] See, for example, *Abdurrahman Orak v. Turkey* (2002) paras. 95–99; *Süheyla Aydın v. Turkey* (2005) paras. 2014–210; *Musayev a.o. v. Russia* (2007) paras. 171–175; *Dangayeva and Taramova v. Russia* (2009) para. 117. Most of the cases against Russia concern disappearances, in which the sufferance of relatives constitutes a separate substantive element under Article 3.

[237] See, for example, *İkincisoy v. Turkey* (2004) para. 125; *Akdeniz v. Turkey* (2005) para. 140; *Imakayeva v. Russia* (2006) paras. 194–196; *Syltogov a.o. v. Russia* (2014) para. 470; *Alikhanovy v. Russia* (2018) para. 105.

[238] See, for example, *Anguelova v. Bulgaria* (2002) paras. 150 and 161; *Tanış a.o. v. Turkey* (2005) paras. 222–227; *Ognyanova and Choban v. Bulgaria* (2006) paras. 124 and 136–138; *Carabulea v. Romania* (2010) paras. 165–167.

substantive violation of Articles 2 and 3, a violation of the procedural aspect under Article 2, and a violation of Article 13 which only refers to the assessment under Article 2.[239]

In contrast to Article 3, where the obligation was first required in conjunction with Article 13, effective investigations under Article 2 were first required under Article 2 in combination with Article 1.[240] *Kaya* v. *Turkey* (1998), then, included a right to effective investigations under Article 13 in conjunction with Article 2. In a similar manner as the first judgments concerning effective investigations under Article 13, seen in conjunction with Article 3,

> the nature of the right which the authorities are alleged to have violated in the instant case, one of the most fundamental in the scheme of the Convention, must have implications for the nature of the remedies which must be guaranteed for the benefit of the relatives of the victim. In particular, where those relatives have an arguable claim that the victim has been unlawfully killed by agents of the State, the notion of an effective remedy for the purposes of Article 13 entails, in addition to the payment of compensation where appropriate, a thorough and effective investigation capable of leading to the identification and punishment of those responsible and including effective access for the relatives to the investigatory procedure.[241]

The Court added that, seen in these terms, "the requirements of Article 13 are broader than a Contracting State's procedural obligation under Article 2 to conduct an effective investigation."[242] The Court, then, simply referred to its findings under Article 2 and concluded that Article 13 had also been violated.[243] These starting-points have been repeated in a number of judgments against Turkey, and, later, other States, most notably Russia, in which the Court has found violations of both Article 2 and Article 13 seen in conjunction with Article 2. In most cases, the Court holds that the requirements of effective investigations under Article 13 "are broader" than those under Article 2,[244]

---

[239] See, for example, *Tepe* v. *Turkey* (2003) paras. 194–197; *Tekdag* v. *Turkey* (2004) paras. 96–99.

[240] *McCann a.o.* v. *the UK* (Grand Chamber 1995) para. 161.

[241] *Kaya* v. *Turkey* (1998) para. 107.

[242] Ibid. This phrase has, also, but much later, been included under Article 13 in conjunction with Article 3. Indeed, the first case was *Cobzaru* v. *Romania* (2007) para. 83. In later cases, this phrase is occasionally, and not as consistently as in conjunction with Article 2, included under Article 13 in conjunction with Article 3; see, for example, *Denis Vasilyev* v. *Russia* (2009) paras. 134–135; *El-Masri* v. *FYROM* (Grand Chamber 2012) para. 256; *Husayn (Abu Zubaydah)* v. *Poland* (2014) para. 542.

[243] *Kaya* v. *Turkey* (1998) para. 108.

[244] See, for a few examples, *Tanrikulu* v. *Turkey* (Grand Chamber 1999) para. 119; *Mordeniz* v. *Turkey* (2006) para. 109; *Khalidova a.o.* v. *Russia* (2008) para. 122; *Predică* v. *Romania* (2011) para. 80; *Shchiborshch and Kuzmina* v. *Russia* (2014) para. 277.

but, in other cases, the Court holds that the requirements "may be broader",[245] or makes no reference to broader requirements under Article 13.[246] The Court may, also, hold that it is not necessary to examine the investigations under the positive and procedural obligations of Article 2, but finds a violation of Article 13,[247] but may conclude that only the procedural limb of Article 2 has been violated and that there has been no violation of Article 13,[248] or that it is not necessary to examine the complaint under Article 13.[249]

In a few cases, the Court has attempted to distinguish between the assessments under Article 2 and Article 13 seen in conjunction with Article 2.

In *İlhan v. Turkey* (Grand Chamber 2000), the investigations were only considered under Article 13 seen in conjunction with Article 2. The Court seemed to attach decisive weight to the fact that the killers were known (in contrast to previous Turkish cases in which the perpetrators were unknown).[250] However, the reasoning under Article 13 was mainly linked to the finding of a violation of Article 3 – not Article 2.[251]

In four cases against the United Kingdom in 2001, the Court, then, considered the requirement outside the situation in southeast Turkey.[252] The Court took stock of its previous case law and emphasized that the applicants in these cases were in a vulnerable position due to the ongoing conflict between the security forces and the PKK. Further, the most accessible means of redress for these applicants was to complain to the public prosecutor, who was under a duty to investigate alleged crimes. In the Turkish system, however, the complainant could join criminal proceedings, as an intervener, and apply for damages at the conclusion of successful prosecution. The public prosecutor's fact-finding function was, therefore, essential in any attempt to take civil

---

[245] See, for example, *Salman v. Turkey* (Grand Chamber 2000) paras. 121–123; *Ceyhan Demir a.o. v. Turkey* (2005) para. 117; *Bozkır a.o. v. Turkey* (2013) para. 80.

[246] See, for example, *Velikova v. Bulgaria* (2000); *İpek v. Turkey* (2004); *Kontrová v. Slovakia* (2007); *Akhmadova a.o. v. Russia* (2008); *Er a.o. v. Turkey* (2012).

[247] The first case was *İlhan v. Turkey* (Grand Chamber 2000).

[248] See, for example, *Slimani v. France* (2004) paras. 42 and 49; *Nachova a.o. v. Bulgaria* (Grand Chamber 2005) para. 123.

[249] See, for example, *Makaratzis v. Greece* (Grand Chamber 2004) para. 86; *Ramsahai a.o. v. the Netherlands* (Grand Chamber 2007) para. 363; *Ekrem v. Turkey* (2007) para. 73; *Brecknell v. the UK* (2007) para. 84; *Budayeva a.o. v. Russia* (2008) para. 195; *Dzidzava v. Russia* (2016) para. 75; *Adzhigitova a.o. v. Russia* (2021) para. 195.

[250] *İlhan v. Turkey* (Grand Chamber 2000) paras. 73 and 103. Notice that the majority found no violation of the substantive obligation under Article 2, and, compare, the approach under Article 3, under which the Court holds that it is particularly important, under such circumstances, to declare a procedural violation.

[251] *İlhan v. Turkey* (Grand Chamber 2000) paras. 94 and 103.

[252] *Hugh Jordan v. the UK* (2001); *Shanaghan v. the UK* (2001); *McKerr v. the UK* (2001); *Kelly a.o. v. the UK* (2001).

proceedings. There was, accordingly, a close procedural and practical relationship between the criminal investigation and the remedies available in the
legal system as a whole. The legal system in Northern Ireland, however, was
different. Applicants who claimed that the use of force by soldiers or police
officers was unlawful had to initiate civil proceedings, by which courts would
examine the facts, determine liability, and, if appropriate, award compensation. These proceedings were independent of any criminal investigation, and
their efficacy was not shown to rely on the proper conduct of criminal investigations or prosecutions and could provide redress (compensation), in respect
of the excessive use of force. The Court, then, simply pointed to the assessment under the procedural aspect of Article 2 and found that "no separate
issue" arose under Article 13.[253]

A similar approach was applied in *Öneryildiz v. Turkey* (Grand Chamber
2004). Thirty-nine people had died, and the life of several others had been
threatened, in a methane explosion at a municipal waste-collection site. The
substantive aspect of Article 2 was violated because the State had not put in
place a legislative and administrative framework that effectively provided deterrence against threats to life, and the procedural aspect of Article 2 because of
the ineffective judicial response in the aftermath of the accident, including
ineffective investigations. The Court emphasized that neither Article 2 nor
Article 13 entails a right for an applicant to have third parties prosecuted or
sentenced for a criminal offence, or an absolute obligation for all prosecutions to result in conviction, or a particular sentence.[254] However, national
courts cannot allow life-endangering offences go unpunished. Indeed, this is
"essential for maintaining public confidence and ensuring adherence to the
rule of law and for preventing any appearance of tolerance of or collusion in
unlawful acts."[255] The Turkish criminal justice system was not able to secure
the full accountability of the State officials or the authorities for their role in
the tragedy and the effective implementation of provisions of domestic law
guaranteeing respect for the right to life, in particular, the deterrent function
of criminal law. On the other hand, it was not necessarily true that Article 13
had been violated, even though the procedural obligation under Article 2 had.
What was important under Article 13 was:

> the impact the State's failure to comply with its procedural obligation under
> Article 2 had on the deceased's family's access to other available and effective

---

[253] See, for example, *Hugh Jordan v. the UK* (2001) paras. 161–165 and *McShane v. the UK* (2002)
paras. 140–146.
[254] *Öneryildiz v. Turkey* (Grand Chamber 2004) paras. 96 and 147.
[255] Ibid., para. 96.

remedies for establishing liability on the part of State officials or bodies for acts or omissions entailing the breach of their rights under Article 2 and, as appropriate, obtaining compensation.[256]

Indeed, without an effective investigation initiated by the State, the individual may not be in a position to use any remedy available to him/her for obtaining relief, given that the knowledge necessary to elucidate facts is often in the sole hands of State officials or authorities. The Court's task under Article 13, at least in the case in question, was, therefore, "to determine whether the applicant's exercise of an effective remedy was frustrated on account of the manner in which the authorities discharged their procedural obligation under Article 2."[257]

Accordingly, in contrast to the approach under Article 13 seen in conjunction with Article 3, where the Court has expressed a preference for applying Article 13 in conjunction with Article 3 in the abstract (although the practice is not clear), under Article 13 seen in conjunction with Article 2, the Court has, in the abstract, expressed a preference for applying Article 2. However, this stands in opposition to the general statements that the requirements of effective investigations under Article 13 are broader than those under Article 2 and, also, that the notion of an effective remedy entails, in addition to the payment of compensation where appropriate, a thorough and effective investigation capable of leading to the identification and punishment of those responsible and including effective access to the investigatory procedure for the relatives of the victims.[258] However, in a string of later cases, most notably against Russia and Ukraine, the Court only seems to attach weight to how the failure of criminal investigations undermines the effectiveness of other remedies, although when referring to the general requirements of Article 13, the aspects of truth, identification, and punishment are pointed to, in a similar manner as, for example, *Kaya* v. *Turkey* (1998). But, when considering whether Article 13 has been violated in the concrete, the Court only points to the effect that lack of investigations has on other remedies.[259] Only in a very few other cases has the Court concluded on both aspects.[260] But, at the very least, an award of a

---

[256] Ibid., para. 148.
[257] Ibid., para. 149. See, also, for example, *Ihsan Bilgin* v. *Turkey* (2006) para. 80; *Budayeva a.o.* v. *Russia* (2008) paras. 163 and 195; *Kolyadenko a.o.* v. *Russia* (2012) paras. 227–228.
[258] See, for example, *Kaya* v. *Turkey* (1998) para. 107.
[259] See, for example, *Tanrikulu* v. *Turkey* (Grand Chamber 1999) para. 119; *Menteşe a.o.* v. *Turkey* (2005) para. 85; *Bazorkina* v. *Russia* (2006) para. 161; *Makhauri* v. *Russia* (2007) para. 131; *Predică* v. *Romania* (2011) para. 80; *Shchiborshch and Kuzmina* v. *Russia* (2014) para. 277; *Alikhanovy* v. *Russia* (2018) paras. 104–105.
[260] See, for example, *Gongadze* v. *Ukraine* (2005) paras. 191–193.

lump sum of money, without any meaningful findings as to the perpetrators, and the establishment of the responsibility is not sufficient under Article 13, even though the procedural obligation under Article 2 has been violated.[261]

Effective investigations have, also, been required under Article 13 in conjunction with Article 8. The first case was *Menteş a.o. v. Turkey* (Grand Chamber 1997) in which homes and possessions were destroyed by State agents. In a similar manner as in conjunction with Article 3, "the nature and gravity of the interference" had implications for Article 13 and the State had an obligation to carry out a thorough and effective investigation of allegations "of deliberate destruction by its agents of the homes and possessions of individuals."[262] The Court, further, underlined that ineffective investigations undermined the exercise of any other remedies that the applicants had at their disposal, including the pursuit of compensation.[263] In later cases against Turkey, the Court also found violations of Article 3 and P1 Article 1, in addition to Article 8, for the destruction of homes and eviction from villages,[264] in which the requirement under Article 13 was seen in conjunction with both Articles 3, 8 and P1 Article 1, and in which it was not deemed necessary to consider the investigation under the substantive Articles.[265] However, in some cases, concerning substantive violations of both Articles 3 and 8, the Court has only considered the investigations under Article 3, thus excluding the question under both Articles 8 and 13.[266] In other cases, the Court has considered the investigations under Article 3 and also included both Article 3 and P1 Article 1 under Article 13.[267] Moreover, in cases involving both Article 2 and P1 Article 1 (death and violations of property), it remains unclear to what extent P1 Article 1 may play a role under Article 13 (in addition to Article 2).[268] However, in other cases, the Court seems to consider the question under Article 13 mainly in conjunction with P1 Article 1, not Article 2,[269] whereas in other cases, the Court considers that Article 13 has been violated both in conjunction with Article 2 and P1 Article 2.[270]

[261] See, for example, *Esmukhambetov a.o. v. Russia* (2011) para. 161.
[262] *Menteş a.o. v. Turkey* (Grand Chamber 1997) para. 89.
[263] Ibid., para. 92.
[264] In *Menteş a.o. v. Turkey* (Grand Chamber 1997) para. 77 the Court did not deem it necessary to examine the matter under Article 3.
[265] See, for example, *Selçuk and Asker v. Turkey* (1998) paras. 83–87; *Bilgin v. Turkey* (2000); *Aksakal v. Turkey* (2007); *Karimov a.o. v. Russia* (2009); *Husayn (Abu Zubaydah) v. Poland* (2014).
[266] See, for example, *Sečić v. Croatia* (2007) para. 61; *Al Nashiri v. Poland* (2014) paras. 541–551.
[267] See, for example, *Sadykov v. Russia* (2010) paras. 275–278.
[268] See, for example, *Isayeva, Yusupova and Bazayeva v. Russia* (2005) para. 138.
[269] See, for example, *Abdurashidova v. Russia* (2010) para. 108.
[270] See, for example, *Abdulkhadzhiyeva and Abdulkhadzhiyev v. Russia* (2016) paras. 98–100.

Similarly, the Court's case law concerning effective investigations in conjunction with arguable violations of Article 5 reveals an unclear picture. The first case, *Kurt* v. *Turkey* (1998), concerned a disappearance, which gave rise to violations of Articles 2, 3, and 5. The substantive complaint concerning the applicant's son and his disappearance was dealt with exclusively from the angle of Article 5. However, the mother was also a victim, under Article 3, because of the disappearance (inhuman and degrading suffering).[271] Article 5 had been violated, in part, because no meaningful investigation had been conducted into the applicant's insistence that her son was in detention.[272] But, Article 13, in conjunction with Article 5, had also been violated because the authorities had failed to conduct an effective investigation into the disappearance. Indeed,

> where the relatives of a person have an arguable claim that the latter has disappeared at the hands of the authorities, the notion of an effective remedy for the purposes of Article 13 entails, in addition to the payment of compensation where appropriate, a thorough and effective investigation capable of leading to the identification and punishment of those responsible and including effective access for the relatives to the investigatory procedure ... Seen in these terms, the requirements of Article 13 are broader than a Contracting State's obligation under Article 5 to conduct an effective investigation into the disappearance of a person who has been shown to be under their control and for whose welfare they are accordingly responsible.[273]

The Court, thereafter, simply referred to the finding under Article 5 and added that this was "tantamount to undermining the effectiveness of any other remedies that may have existed."[274]

In *Çakıcı* v. *Turkey* (Grand Chamber 1999), the substantive aspects of Articles 2 and 3, as well as Article 5 in relation to the disappearance of the applicant's brother, had been violated.[275] Articles 2 and 5 had also been violated because of the lack of "effective procedural safeguards," in concrete, inadequate investigations. Further, under Article 5, as such, the Court held:

> Given the responsibility of the authorities to account for individuals under their control, Article 5 requires them to take effective measures to safeguard

---

[271] *Kurt* v. *Turkey* (1998) para. 117.
[272] Ibid., para. 128.
[273] Ibid., para. 140.
[274] Ibid., para. 141.
[275] This was the first of a string of cases against Turkey in which the Court found substantive violations of Article 2, even though it was not established that the missing person was dead, because the person had to be "presumed dead following an unacknowledged detention by the security forces"; see para. 87.

against the risk of disappearance and to conduct a prompt and effective investigation into an arguable claim that a person has been taken into custody and has not been seen since.[276]

Under Article 2, the Court only referred to the assessment under Article 5, and under Article 3, the Court did not deem it necessary to make a separate finding in respect of the deficiencies in the investigation because this aspect was to be examined under Article 13.[277] Under Article 13, the Court, then, held that:

> Given the fundamental importance of the rights in issue, the right to protection of life and freedom from torture and ill-treatment, Article 13 imposes, without prejudice to any other remedy available under the domestic system, an obligation on States to carry out a thorough and effective investigation apt to lead to those responsible being identified and punished and in which the complainant has effective access to the investigation proceedings.[278]

The Court, thereafter, simply pointed to the assessment under Article 5 and added that this undermined the effectiveness of any other remedies which might have existed.[279]

In later cases, the Court has found procedural violations under Articles 2 and 5, as well as Article 13, but in which the assessment under Article 13 is primarily linked to Article 2, without any specific mention of Article 5.[280] In some other cases, the assessment is more explicitly linked to also Article 5.[281] Further, the Court may find it more appropriate to examine the question only under Article 13, in particular, if it finds that Article 5 has not been violated.[282] However, in most cases, Article 5 is explicitly excluded from the assessment under Article 13, even if the Court finds that Article 13 has been violated in conjunction with Articles 2 and 3, but in which it is hard to see why Article 5 should be excluded. In some cases, the Court refers to the fact that Article 5 contains a number of procedural guarantees, seemingly in contrast

---

[276] *Çakıcı v. Turkey* (Grand Chamber 1999) para. 104.
[277] Ibid., paras. 87 and 93.
[278] Ibid., para. 113.
[279] Ibid., para. 114.
[280] See, for example, *Taş v. Turkey* (2000) para. 93; *Yasin Ateş v. Turkey* (2005) para. 154; *Akdeniz a.o. v. Turkey* (2001) paras. 112–114.
[281] See, for example, *Orhan v. Turkey* (2002) paras. 373–374, but see, however, the general conclusion in para. 396. See, also, for example, *Husayn (Abu Zubaydah) v. Poland* (2014) paras. 544–545.
[282] See, for example, *Şarlı v. Turkey* (2001) paras. 69–70.

to Articles 2 and 3.[283] In other cases, Article 5 is excluded under Article 13, but without any explicit justification.[284] In most cases, however, the Court holds that:

> according to its established case law the more specific guarantees of Article 5 §§ 4 and 5, being a lex specialis in relation to Article 13, absorb its requirements … It also notes that it has found a violation of Article 5 of the Convention as a whole on account of the applicant's unacknowledged detention. Accordingly, it considers that no separate issue arises in respect of Article 13 read in conjunction with Article 5 of the Convention in the circumstances of the present case.[285]

Most of these cases concern disappearances in Russia,[286] in particular during the second Chechen conflict, which, mostly, reveal violations of Articles 2, 3, and 5, including lack of effective investigations.[287] In these cases, the applicants were mainly relatives of the disappeared persons. Under Article 13, the Court mostly held that the requirements of effective investigation under Article 13 seen in conjunction with Article 2 are broader than the procedural obligations of Article 2 and explicitly excluded both Articles 3 and 5 seen in conjunction with Article 13 – Article 5 linked to Articles 5(4) and 5(5), but Article 3 without any specific justification.[288] In other cases, the exclusion of Article 5 is not specifically linked to Articles 5(4) and 5(5), but a general reference to stricter requirements under Article 5.[289] In other cases, no mention of Article 5 is made under Article 13, even though this was alleged by the applicant.[290]

As of 2013, however, the Court mostly includes Article 3, in addition to Article 2, in the assessment under Article 13, but not Article 5.[291] In other cases, the Court also excludes Article 3, at least with regard to the mental suffering

---

[283] See, for example, *Bazorkina v. Russia* (2006) para. 165; *Baysayeva v. Russia* (2007) para. 159; *Aziyevy v. Russia* (2008) para. 118; *Zaurbekova and Zaurbekova v. Russia* (2009) para. 120.

[284] See, for example, *Imakayeva v. Russia* (2006) paras. 195–197.

[285] See, for example, *Gisayev v. Russia* (2011) para. 161.

[286] See, generally, on the right to effective investigations in case of enforced disappearances, for example, Jötten (2010). See, also, for example, Sarkin (2014).

[287] See, generally, on the practice of the Court in relation to the Chechen conflict, for example, Leach (2008).

[288] See, for example, *Meshayeva a.o. v. Russia* (2009); *Guluyeva a.o. v. Russia* (2010); *Mutsolgova a.o. v. Russia* (2010); *Dzhabrailovy v. Russia* (2010).

[289] See, for example, *Bitiyeva a.o. v. Russia* (2009); *Sasita Israilova a.o. v. Russia* (2010).

[290] See, for example, *Khaydayeva a.o. v. Russia* (2009); *Dzhabirailova and Dzhabrailova v. Russia* (2010); *Turluyeva v. Russia* (2013); *Abu Zubaydah v. Lithuania* (2018).

[291] See, for example, *Aslakhanova v. Russia* (2012) para. 157; *Malika Yusupova a.o. v. Russia* (2015) para. 213; *Khachukayevy v. Russia* (2016) para. 77. See, however, *Al Nashiri v. Romania* (2018) para. 710, which, also, includes Article 5, but without any justification.

of the applicants.[292] However, in some cases concerning direct torture, which has been proved, also in applications from relatives, and in which both the substantive and procedural aspects of Articles 2 and 3 had been violated, the Court includes both Articles 2 and 3 under Article 13.[293] Accordingly, it could be that the Court has attempted to distinguish between cases, which primarily concern direct torture and cases which primarily concern the mental suffering of relatives.[294]

I have not seen the question of effective investigations explicitly emphasized under Article 13 in conjunction with other Articles.[295] However, if necessary to establish responsibility, the truth about the violation, and any other remedy is dependent upon effective investigations performed by the State, the requirement of effective investigations must apply under Article 13, at least as the clear starting-point, also in conjunction with other Articles.[296]

11.7.3   Concrete and Abstract Differences

Although the case law, as accounted for above, reveals an uneven picture, some differences are clear. In the following, I first summarize some concrete differences that can be deduced from the case law before I illustrate how the Court could distinguish, on a more abstract level, with reference to purposes.

Even though the Court holds that the requirements of effective investigations under Article 13 are or may be broader, most notably in conjunction with Article 2, the case law reveals that the requirements may, under some circumstances, be broader, whereas, in other circumstances, the requirements under substantive Articles may be broader.

First, for Article 13 to apply, it suffices that the substantive (procedural) violation be arguable. Therefore, even though a requirement of effective investigations is found not to be violated under substantive Articles, the claim may be arguable under Article 13.[297] The applicant may, therefore, need a

---

[292] See, for example, *Arapkhanovy v. Russia* (2013) para. 178; *Khava Aziyeva a.o. v. Russia* (2015) para. 112; *Abdurakhmanova and Abdulgamidova v. Russia* (2015) para. 100.

[293] See, for example, *Isayev a.o. v. Russia* (2011) paras. 186–190.

[294] See, for example, *Aslakhanova v. Russia* (2012) paras. 151–157.

[295] The IACtHR holds, more generally, that States are obligated to investigate every situation involving a violation of the rights protected by the ACHR; see, for example, Antkowiak (2001–2002) 985–986.

[296] Compare Wildhaber (2002) 161, who argues, more generally, that "practically all the Convention guarantees contain an implied positive obligation to set up and render effective procedures making it possible to vindicate the right concerned at the national level."

[297] See Chapter 7 and, as one example, *D.P. & J.C. v. the UK* (2002) paras. 135–138. Seemingly to the contrary, Jötten (2010) 123.

remedy against (arguable) procedural violations of substantive Articles.[298] If, for instance, a public prosecutor does not institute criminal proceedings, and no other possibility of obtaining effective investigations exists, the applicant needs to have a remedy against the decision not to institute criminal proceedings, for instance, the possibility to appeal against the decision.[299]

Second, ineffective investigations may undermine the effectiveness of any other remedy, in particular, (other) required forms of redress, most notably, compensation.[300]

Third, under substantive Articles, criminal liability and criminal investigations may be required,[301] not only to prosecute and punish direct acts committed by State agents or third persons but, in cases of negligence, also to protect life against dangerous activities or natural disasters.[302] Under Article 13, however, a requirement of criminal investigations does not chime well with the starting-point that Article 13 does not require any particular form of remedy.[303] That being said, Article 13 requires, at least in conjunction with Articles 2 and 3, "a thorough and effective investigation capable of leading to the identification and punishment of those responsible."[304] And, in many domestic remedial systems, this is only possible to achieve through criminal proceedings. But, in principle, civil investigations may be sufficient,[305] although some statements could indicate that criminal investigations may be required under Article 13 too.[306]

Fourth, under the procedural limbs of Articles 2 and 3, at least in cases involving direct infringements of State agents or bodies, the authorities must act on their own initiative and cannot leave it to the initiative of, for example, the next of kin, either to lodge a formal complaint or to take responsibility for

---

[298] See, for example, *Güngör v. Turkey* (2005) paras. 98 and 101.

[299] See, for example, *Stoica v. Romania* (2008) paras. 94–110.

[300] See, for example, *Kaya v. Turkey* (1998) para. 105.

[301] See, for example, *X and Y v. the Netherlands* (1985) para. 27; *M.C. v. Bulgaria* (2003) para. 153. However, this is not uncontroversial; see, for example, *X and Y v. the Netherlands* (1985) para. 24 and the concurring opinion of Judge Tulkens in *M.C. v. Bulgaria* (2003).

[302] See, for example, *Öneryıldız v. Turkey* (Grand Chamber 2004) para. 92–43; *Tarariyeva v. Russia* (2006) para. 75; *Zavoloka v. Latvia* (2009) para. 34 litra d. The fact that criminal liability is not consistently demanded under Article 2 was criticized by, for example, Harris, O'Boyle *et al.* (2009) 40–41, but the critique has been removed in later editions.

[303] See Chapter 8 and, for example, *Budayeva a.o. v. Russia* (2008) para. 190. See, also, Stephens (2002) 5.

[304] See, for example, *Aydin v. Turkey* (Grand Chamber 1997) para. 105.

[305] See, for example, *Z a.o. v. the UK* (Grand Chamber 2001); *Paul and Audrey Edwards v. the UK* (2002); *Peev v. Bulgaria* (2007); *Betayev and Betayeva v. Russia* (2008); *I.P. v. the Republic of Moldova* (2015).

[306] See, for example, *Carabulea v. Romania* (2010) para. 166; *Pankov v. Bulgaria* (2010) para. 70.

the conduct of any investigatory procedures.[307] Under Article 13, however, the authorities must not necessarily undertake the responsibility for investigating the allegations.[308] But, there must be a mechanism available, in which any liability of State officials or bodies can be established for acts or omissions which are in breach of Convention rights.[309]

However, such differences do not explain the uneven practice of, as accounted for above, in some cases applying only substantive Articles, in other cases only Article 13, and, in other cases both Articles.[310] Indeed, the Court has not, in the abstract, explained how and why the requirements may differ,[311] and what the purposes of the various requirements under substantive Articles and Article 13 are. Indeed, independently of whether the assessment of the investigations is performed under substantive Articles or Article 13, the Court mostly only indicates why investigations, in the concrete, are or are not effective.[312] And, when the Court finds parallel violations of substantive Articles

---

[307] See, for example, *Musayeva a.o.* v. *Russia* (2007) para. 85. That being said, in some cases the applicant may be understood to have chosen a civil remedy, and taken responsibility for the procedures, including forfeiting the right to investigations under substantive Articles. The Court may, then, accept that no specific investigatory procedures have been instituted by the authorities; see, for example, *V.C.* v. *Slovakia* (2011) paras. 126–129.

[308] See, for example, *Slimani* v. *France* (2004) paras. 48 and 42.

[309] See, for example, *Z a.o.* v. *the UK* (Grand Chamber 2001) para. 109; *Paul and Audrey Edwards* v. *the UK* (2002) para. 97, *D.P. & J.C.* v. *the UK* (2002) para. 135; *E. a.o.* v. *the UK* (2002) para. 110; *Centre for Legal Resources on behalf of Valentin Câmpeanu* v. *Romania* (Grand Chamber 2014) para. 149; *Tagayeva a.o.* v. *Russia* (2017) paras. 619–620.

[310] See, also, for example, Mowbray (2004) 64. Concerning the relationship between Articles 2 and 13, some claim that the Court, more or less consistently, has found concurring violations; see, for example, Dijk, Hoof *et al.* (2018) 1050, who, however, in note 74, give examples of "a few" cases, in which the Court has found that the obligation to perform effective investigations under Article 13 was absorbed by Article 2. Others claim that the Court's general approach seems to be that it will not examine Article 13 separately, once it has examined the procedural aspects under Article 2; see, for example, Harris, O'Boyle *et al.* (2018) 761. As far as I can see, the cases, in which the Court has not declared a violation of Article 13 in conjunction with Article 2, are in a minority, but the practice is not consistent; see Section 11.7.2. Similarly, Jötten (2010) 116.

[311] Compare, for example, Harris, O'Boyle *et al.* (2018) 761. Some claim, more generally, that the investigations required by Article 13 cannot be less elaborate than those under substantive Articles, while others claim that the investigations under Article 13 may be less elaborate; see, for example, Jötten (2010) 121–122 with further references. In my opinion, the answer here must depend on the purposes investigations are to serve under substantive Articles and Article 13, respectively.

[312] Some dissenting opinions, which criticize the majority for finding "list of shortcomings", are illustrative, for example, the partly concurring and partly dissenting opinion of Judge Gölcüklü in *Şemsi Önen* v. *Turkey* (2002) and the dissenting opinion of Judges Costa, Bratza, Lorenzen, and Thomassen in *Ramsahai a.o.* v. *the Netherlands* (Grand Chamber 2007).

and Article 13, it usually only refers to the assessment performed under the one or the other Article, without any additional justification. But, clearly, effective investigations may serve different purposes.

Investigations may, in the first place, be a prerequisite for obtaining effective access to justice. Information and evidence may, for example, be in the hands of the State, or cannot, for other reasons, be expected to be obtained by the applicant. The claim that Convention rights have been violated can, then, neither be effectively determined. Further, effective access to justice is a central element in the rule of law, as such, but ineffective investigations may also undermine other elements of the rule of law, *inter alia*, legality and legal certainty, the prohibition of arbitrariness, and nondiscrimination and equality.[313] Further, ineffective investigations may undermine any possibility for obtaining other forms of redress, most notably, compensation. But, investigations may, also, serve as a form of redress, as such, and contribute to correct injustice, facilitate prosecution, punishment, and other forms of liability, and promote deterrence, both on an individual and a general level. Investigations and their results, for instance, convictions, civil consequences (e.g., compensation), and disciplinary reactions, may also serve as retribution and a foundation for achieving restorative justice. Further, investigations contribute to establishing the truth about the violation, which may be seen as an intrinsic purpose of redress and a wider purpose of remedial justice.[314]

There are some signs in the case law that effective investigations under substantive Articles primarily seek to make substantives rights effective by deterring future violations and upholding the rule of law. This, for example, seems to be the reason why criminal liability and investigations may be required under substantive Articles, most notably under Article 2.[315] More generally, at least under the substantive and positive obligations of Article 2, the essential purpose of the investigation is:

> to secure the effective implementation of the domestic laws which protect the right to life and, in those cases involving state agents or bodies, to ensure

---

[313] This may lie underneath the attempt to distinguish in *Tagayeva a.o.* v. *Russia* (2017) para. 627.

[314] See, more generally, Chapter 3.

[315] See, for example, the majority in *X and Y* v. *the Netherlands* (1985) para. 27. However, the assumption that criminal law is the best way to achieve deterrence and that deterrence actually works preventively is controversial; see, for example, Ashworth and Horder (2013) 16; Jareborg (2002) in his Chapter 6. This controversy is also present within the Court; see, for example, the concurring opinion of Judge Tulkens in *M.C.* v. *Bulgaria* (2003).

their accountability for deaths occurring under their responsibility. What form of investigation will achieve those purposes may vary in different circumstances.[316]

And, in particular the reference to "the effective implementation of laws" indicates a purpose of general deterrence, not necessarily linked up to the specific situation of the individual.

On the other hand, under Article 13, the Court often emphasizes the effect that ineffective investigations have on any other remedies, in particular, compensation. This could indicate that the Court does not perceive investigations as a form of redress, as such. However, several judgments which find violations of both Articles 2 and 13 indicate that effective investigations are an inherent requirement in Article 13, as such, independently of how it influences the possibility of access to any other remedies.[317] And, in other cases, the Court emphasizes, under Article 13, the need for the investigations to be capable of establishing the truth of the complaint,[318] and that there must be a meaningful finding as to liability and responsibility.[319] That being said, there seems to be considerable reluctance, on the part of the Court, to declare a violation of Article 13 solely because of such issues if the question of effective investigations has been dealt with under substantive Articles. As a consequence, since the requirement of effective investigations under substantive Articles primarily seems to aim at promoting deterrence, other purposes that effective investigations may have, in particular those which could be necessary in order to correct injustice, remain undercommunicated.

This is not only an analytical and abstract problem. Indeed, the uneven and case-specific case law makes it difficult to predict the specific elements necessary to satisfy the requirement. To what extent is, for example, an autopsy necessary to correct injustice, punish the perpetrator, set a correct amount of compensation, and/or establish the truth? In addition, if the Court were to clarify the purposes that the effective investigations are to serve under different legal grounds, it would facilitate a more subsidiary protection of human rights by placing legal interpreters, and, most importantly in this context, domestic courts, in a position where they in an independent manner can set

[316] *Avşar v. Turkey* (2001) para. 393. Under Article 13, the Court only referred to the assessment under Article 2, see para. 431.
[317] See, for example, *Kaya v. Turkey* (1998) para. 107; *Arzu Akhmadova a.o. v. Russia* (2009) para. 219; *Carabulea v. Romania* (2010) para. 165.
[318] See, for example, *Aydin v. Turkey* (Grand Chamber 1997) para. 105; *Selçuk and Asker v. Turkey* (1998) para. 97.
[319] See, for example, *Esmukhambetov a.o. v. Russia* (2011) para. 161.

out the necessary (concrete) remedial requirements concerning investigations (Section 13.3).

11.7.4 *An Autonomous Right to Know the Truth?*

Over the last 20 years, a right to the truth has developed in international law.[320] Within international humanitarian law, international human-rights law, and international criminal law, several legal instruments now explicitly recognize an autonomous right to the truth for victims of violations of their international rights.[321] Some even hold that the right to know the truth is approaching a customary right (albeit with differing contours).[322] However, none of the more general human-rights instruments explicitly recognize an autonomous right to the truth. But the Inter-American Commission and the IACtHR have accepted an autonomous right to know the truth, which is perceived both as a form of redress for the individual and as a collective right for society.[323] Also the Human Rights Committee has accepted an autonomous right to the truth.[324]

The Court has not recognized the right to truth as an autonomous right, but recognizes that it is an important factor when considering whether specific rights have been violated. For instance, under Article 3, uncertainty with regard to the whereabouts and conditions of a relative taken into custody may amount to a continuous violation of Article 3 because of the inhuman suffering caused by not knowing.[325] Most importantly in this context, however, is that the establishment of the truth is a factor when considering whether domestic authorities have performed effective investigations, although it remains uncertain how central this purpose (factor) is under substantive Articles and Article 13, respectively.

---

[320] See, for example, Groome (2011) 175; Shelton (2015) 115–116. On the right to truth, more generally, see for example, Antkowiak (2001–2002); Naqvi (2006); David (2014); Klinkner and Smith (2015); Klinkner and Davis (2020).

[321] See, for example, Article 32 of the First Additional Protocol to the Geneva Conventions of August 12, 1949, relating to the Protection of Victims of International Armed Conflicts; Principles 11, 22(b), and 24 of the van Boven/Bassiouni principles; Human Rights Resolution 2005/66, Right to the truth, adopted by the UN Commission on Human Rights April 20, 2005; Parliamentary Assembly of the Council of Europe (PACE) Resolution 1463 (2005) on Enforced Disappearances para. 10.2; Resolution 12/12 adopted by the UN Human Rights Council, Right to the truth, on October 1, 2009.

[322] See, for example, Naqvi (2006) 267.

[323] See, for example, Naqvi (2006) 257; David (2014) 277–279, and, compare, Antkowiak (2001–2002) 990–996.

[324] See, for example, David (2014).

[325] See, for example, *Cyprus* v. *Turkey* (Grand Chamber 2001) para. 157.

Moreover, *El-Masri* v. *FYROM* (Grand Chamber 2012) indicates that there may be a movement within the Court toward accepting the right to know the truth as an autonomous right.[326] The substantive aspects of Articles 3, 5, and 8 were violated because of ill-treatment and unlawful custody,[327] and the procedural aspects of Articles 3 and 5, and Article 13 more generally, were violated because of ineffective investigations.[328] But the Court expressed diverging opinions concerning the justification. The majority performed the primary assessment under the procedural limb of Article 3, and, more explicitly, and in greater length than in previous cases,[329] considered how the establishment of the truth was relevant for the requirement of effective investigations under Article 3:

> the Court also wishes to address another aspect of the inadequate character of the investigation in the present case, namely its impact on *the right to the truth* regarding the relevant circumstances of the case. In this connection it underlines the great importance of the present case not only for the applicant and his family, but also for other victims of similar crimes and the general public, who had the right to know what had happened.[330] (My emphasis)

The prosecuting authority should, therefore, have undertaken an adequate investigation to "prevent any appearance of impunity in respect of certain acts." Further,

> investigating allegations of serious human rights violations, as in the present case, may generally be regarded as essential in maintaining public confidence in their adherence to the rule of law and in preventing any appearance of collusion in or tolerance of unlawful acts. For the same reasons, there must be a sufficient element of public scrutiny of the investigation or its results to secure accountability in practice as well as in theory … "impunity must be fought as a matter of justice for the victims, as a deterrent to prevent new violations, and to uphold the rule of law and public trust in the justice system". The inadequate investigation in the present case deprived the applicant of being informed of what had happened, including of getting an accurate account of the suffering he had allegedly endured and the role of those responsible for his alleged ordeal.[331]

---

[326] See, for example, Fabbrini (2014).
[327] *El-Masri* v. *FYROM* (Grand Chamber 2012) paras. 204, 211, 221, 240, and 249.
[328] Ibid., paras. 194, 243, and 262.
[329] Compare, for example, *Aydin* v. *Turkey* (Grand Chamber 1997) para. 105.
[330] *El-Masri* v. *FYROM* (Grand Chamber 2012) para. 191.
[331] Ibid., para. 192.

The majority concluded that the investigations could not be considered "effective ... capable of leading to the identification and punishment of those responsible for the alleged events *and of establishing the truth.*" (My emphasis)[332]

The fact that the majority starts out by making reference to "the right to truth" may indicate that the establishment of the truth is considered a separate and autonomous issue (a right) inherent in the procedural limb of Article 3.[333] However, the following concrete assessment indicates that the truth is one of many underlying, and potentially conflicting, purposes of effective investigations, for example, the fight against impunity, the promotion of the rule of law, the deterrent of future violations, and the establishing of responsibility (identification and punishment). Further, the majority did not only consider the establishment of the truth important for the victim, but for others in similar situations and the public more generally.[334] Under Article 13, on the other hand, the majority made no reference to a right to the truth,[335] but concluded that Article 13 had been violated because "no effective criminal investigation can be considered to have been carried out in accordance with Article 13 with regard to the applicant's complaints under Articles 3 and 5 of the Convention",[336] and because "the ineffectiveness of the criminal investigation undermined the effectiveness of any other remedy, including a civil action for damages."[337] Two minority fractions had diverging justifications.

Judges Casadevall and López Guerra held that the majority under the procedural limb of Article 3 should have performed no "separate analysis" with respect to the existence of a "right to the truth" as something different from, or additional to, the requisites already established by the previous case law of the Court. The right to a serious investigation was, in their view, "equivalent to the right to the truth" and applied equally in cases, which attracted wide public coverage and in other cases. It was, therefore, only the victim, not the general public, who was entitled to the right resulting from Article 3.[338]

Judges Tulkens, Spielmann, Sicilianos, and Keller, on the other hand, perceived the right to the truth as "an accurate account of the suffering endured

---

[332] Ibid., para. 193.
[333] Compare the joint concurring opinion of Judges Casadevall and López Guerra.
[334] Compare para. 3 of the joint concurring opinion of Judges Tulkens, Spielmann, Sicilianos, and Keller.
[335] *El-Masri* v. FYROM (Grand Chamber 2012) para. 255.
[336] Ibid., para. 259.
[337] Ibid., para. 261.
[338] See the joint concurring opinion of Judges Casadevall and López Guerra.

and the role of those responsible for that ordeal." But this "right" should, primarily, have been considered under Article 13. The scale and seriousness of the human-rights violations at issue, together with the widespread impunity observed in multiple jurisdictions, gave real substance to the right to an effective remedy, which included a right of access to the relevant information about alleged violations, both for the persons concerned and for the general public. Indeed, the right to the truth was not a novel concept in the case law of the Court, nor a new right. It was broadly implicit in other provisions of the Convention, in particular, the procedural aspects of Articles 2 and 3. But "the search for the truth" was more than that – it was:

> … the objective purpose of the obligation to carry out an investigation and the raison d'être of the related quality requirements (transparency, diligence, independence, access, disclosure of results and scrutiny). For society in general, the desire to ascertain the truth plays a part in strengthening confidence in public institutions and hence the rule of law. For those concerned – the victims' families and close friends – establishing the true facts and securing an acknowledgment of serious breaches of human rights and humanitarian law constitute forms of redress that are just as important as compensation, and sometimes even more so. Ultimately, the wall of silence and the cloak of secrecy prevent these people from making any sense of what they have experienced and are the greatest obstacles to their recovery.

The Court, therefore, should have acknowledged the right to the truth, in the context of Article 13, in order to "cast renewed light on a well-established reality". Indeed, the "timid allusion" to the right to the truth in the context of Article 3 and the lack of an explicit acknowledgment in relation to Article 13 gave "the impression of a certain over-cautiousness".[339]

The justifications reveal differences both in starting-point and emphasis. Should the starting-point be the establishment of the truth, or effective investigations? One minority fraction emphasized Article 13 and the truth as the starting-point – although as "the objective purpose" of requiring effective investigations. Accordingly, the truth is the purpose, the effective investigations (one of) the means to achieve that purpose. The other minority fraction, however, emphasized that no "separate analysis" with respect to the existence of a "right to the truth" should be performed. Accordingly, the starting-point is a right to an investigation, which promotes, among other purposes, the establishment of the truth. The majority landed somewhere in between – on a principled level emphasizing a right to the truth under Article 3, but in the

---

[339] Joint concurring opinion of Judges Tulkens, Spielmann, Sicilianos, and Keller.

concrete assessment the truth was only one of several factors when consider-ing whether the investigations were effective.

However, the question of starting-point and emphasis could be traced fur-ther back. Is the establishment of the truth important as a means to secure the effectiveness of human rights more globally, as a prerequisite for achieving access to justice, or as a form of redress, as such? Those who consider the establishment of the truth as being (more) important in order to secure the effectiveness of human rights more globally, or as a means to obtain access to justice, would seem to lean toward considering the truth as one element under the procedural limb of substantive Articles, whereas those who consider the truth as an autonomous form of redress, toward including it under Article 13.

The fact remains that the establishment of the truth may be considered important, for different reasons. Indeed, the truth is important both as a means to secure the effectiveness of human rights more globally, as a prerequisite for obtaining access to justice, and as a form of redress, as such. However, it is not necessarily equally important for all these aspects.

In my opinion, the Court should and could (still) choose a fourth path. In a similar manner as the minority opinion of Judges Tulkens, Spielmann, Sicilianos, and Keller, the establishment of the truth should be emphasized as a factor under Article 13, however, not as an autonomous right, but as one factor when considering the effectiveness of investigations. This is best in accordance with the previous case law of the Court.[340] Further, the establish-ment of the truth through effective investigations should be perceived as a form of redress, as such, necessary not only to correct injustice against the individual victim, but toward society more generally. In this sense, the fourth path is more similar to the opinion of Judges Casadevall and López Guerra, but with the difference that the assessment is performed under Article 13 (so as to emphasize the necessity of effective investigations also in order to achieve redress). In any case, for reasons of clarity and foreseeability, and put-ting domestic authorities in a position to apply the Convention correctly, the Court must strive to clarify how, and to what extent, the truth is important, both under substantive Articles and Article 13.

11.7.5 *Identification, Punishment, and Establishment of Liability*

Both under substantive Articles and Article 13, identification, punishment, and establishment of other forms of liability are emphasized as goals of the

---

[340] See Section 11.7.2.

investigation.[341] Although Article 13 does not require criminal investigations and liability,[342] there must be some form of proceedings that can establish liability. Indeed, establishment of liability is an essential element of the right to an effective remedy.[343] However, it is not an autonomous right.[344]

Further, in a similar manner as the establishment of the truth, identification, punishment, and liability may serve different purposes. To date, the Court has consistently rejected revenge as a purpose (Section 3.4.4). However, identification, prosecution, punishment, and establishing liability may correct injustice, both for individual victims and for society more generally. In particular, from the point of view of the victims and their families, punishment and/or other forms of establishing liability is an important form of redress.[345] Identification, prosecution, punishment, and liability may also serve as tools to obtain access to justice and enhance the effectiveness of human rights more generally, most notably, by promoting deterrence. However, the Court has provided little guidance as to how such purposes are important, both under the substantive Articles and under Article 13, and/or if there are differences.

11.7.6 Relationship with Other Requirements

On some occasions, investigations are considered as part of other principles and requirements under Article 13 – not a separate and distinct requirement. The Court may, for instance, apply a more global approach that considers the process and procedural guarantees at various stages, for example, the trial before courts, the reason being, that under both substantive Articles and Article 13, the procedural requirements go beyond the stage of preliminary investigations.[346] In some cases, the Court seems to attach more weight to how the process before courts has been conducted, for example, the fact that a central witness could not appear as well as the refusal to the hear reasons as to why this was important.[347] In other cases, the Court attaches more weight to the

---

[341] See, for example, *Aksoy* v. *Turkey* (1996) para. 98; *Arzu Akhmadova a.o.* v. *Russia* (2009) para. 219; *El-Masri* v. *FYROM* (Grand Chamber 2012) para. 193. See, also, Principle 3 *litra* b of the van Boven/Bassiouni principles.
[342] See Section 11.7.3 and, for example, *Avanesyan* v. *Russia* (2014) para. 34.
[343] See, for example, *Keenan* v. *the UK* (2001) para. 132.
[344] See, for example, *Öneryıldız* v. *Turkey* (Grand Chamber 2004) para. 147; *Trykhlib* v. *Ukraine* (2005) para. 33; *Budayeva a.o.* v. *Russia* (2008) para. 191.
[345] See, for example, Shelton (2005) 119.
[346] See, explicitly, with regard to Articles 2 and 3, for example, *Feyzi Yıldırım* v. *Turkey* (2007) para. 77. See, also, for example, *Zavoloka* v. *Latvia* (2009) para. 34 *litra* b.
[347] For example, *Uslu* v. *Turkey* (2007) paras. 49–54.

lack of investigations, but still considers the process more globally.[348] In some cases, the global approach is performed under the substantive Articles and the Court finds it unnecessary to examine whether Article 13 has been violated.[349] In other cases, the Court concludes, more generally, under Article 13, that:

> ... the system in question was incapable of effectively preventing the commission of unlawful acts by agents of the State or of offering appropriate redress for an infringement of the principles enshrined in Article 2 of the Convention.[350]

The Court may, also, include the question of investigations in a more global assessment and, in addition, conclude separately on the question of whether the investigations, as such, were effective.[351]

The effectiveness of investigations may, also, be one of several elements when the Court considers whether the domestic remedial authority is able to deal with the substance of the complaint.[352] Accordingly, mistakes and flaws in the investigatory process may make the review of the remedial authority flawed. Indeed, even if the investigatory process is not flawed, the considerations of the remedial authority with regard to facts stemming from the investigations may be flawed, with the consequence that the substance of the complaint has not been dealt with.[353]

11.8 OTHER NONMONETARY REMEDIES

To the extent that something more than declaratory relief is required, the practical rule, under Article 13, has been compensation (Section 11.5). Below, I point to nonmonetary remedies not previously accounted for and which the Court has accepted as redress (although not required).

Under Articles 41 and 46, the Court has accepted that a public apology may serve as redress,[354] but it has not required that the State provide it.[355] In some cases, the applicant has asked the Court to issue an order for the State

---

[348] See, for example, *Fahriye Çalışkan v. Turkey* (2007) paras. 48–51.
[349] See, for example, *97 members of the Gldani Congregation of Jehovah's Witnesses and 4 Others v. Georgia* (2007) paras. 124–125 and 137; *Kolyadenko a.o. v. Russia* (2012) paras. 202 and 228.
[350] *Feyzi Yıldırım v. Turkey* (2007) paras. 96–96.
[351] See, for example, *Mahmut Kaya v. Turkey* (2000) paras. 96, 108, and 126.
[352] See Section 10.5.4 and, as an example, *Vasil Sashov Petrov v. Bulgaria* (2010) paras. 60–61.
[353] See, for example, *Ivan Vasilev v. Bulgaria* (2007) paras. 77–79.
[354] See, for example, *Darnell v. the UK* (1993) para. 24.
[355] The IACtHR, on the other hand, has demanded an official apology, for example, in cases of torture; see, for example, Sandoval and Duttweiler (2011) 131. For a *Plädoyer* for court-ordered apologies in the United States as civil rights remedies; see White (2005–2006).

to provide a public apology. However, the Court has not been willing to discuss the value of such an apology as a form of redress. In some cases, the Court has simply not commented upon the question, even though a violation has been found and compensation for nonpecuniary damages in the form of money was awarded.[356] In other cases, the Court may refer to the statement that the judgments of the Court are essentially declaratory in nature and that the means for executing the judgments are left in the hands of State under the surveillance of the Committee of Ministers.[357]

Under Article 13, the Court has, as far as I can see, never touched upon the question of whether the remedial authority should issue an apology, or issue an order that the State or specific authorities provide an apology.[358] However, a prime goal of victims is often to receive some form of recognition of responsibility.[359] Further, apologies may relieve injuries that cannot be healed by money alone and may also induce changed behavior.[360] From the point of view of States, an official apology may, also, be considered less intrusive than many other forms of remedies, at least as long as apologies are accepted as a sufficient form of redress, which, then, may limit the need for other forms of redress, for example, compensation in the form of money. Actually, in many domestic penal systems, apologies play an important role, in particular, when setting out the punishment.[361]

The Court has not required the reopening of proceedings, neither under Articles 41 and 46, nor Article 13.[362] However, to the extent that such reopening, in practice, is the only way to put an end to continuing violations, it must be considered required, under both Articles 46 and 13.[363]

Further, under Article 13, the Court frequently refers to the importance of obtaining access to documents and information. But such access mostly seems to be perceived as an element of access to justice – not as a form of redress, as such (Section 10.3.4). Similarly, effective investigations must include effective

---

[356] See, for example, *Biskupska* v. *Poland* (2003) para. 51.

[357] See, for example, *Bersunkayeva* v. *Russia* (2008) paras. 155–159.

[358] But it has been demanded by the applicant; see, for example, *Vassiliou a.o.* v. *Cyprus* (2021) para. 106.

[359] See, for example, White (2005–2006) 1271–1272; Antkowiak (2011) 284.

[360] See, for example, White (2005–2006) 1273.

[361] For an overview, see, for example, White (2005–2006) 1268–1270.

[362] See, for example, Reiertsen (2007) 230–231; Christoffersen (2009) 448–449. However, in some dissenting opinions, reopening has been required; see, for example, the joint partly concurring and joint partly dissenting opinion of Judges Lazarova Trajkovska and Pinto de Albuquerque in *Bljakaj a.o.* v. *Croatia* (2014) para. 16.

[363] Compare *Assanidze* v. *Georgia* (Grand Chamber 2004) paras. 202 and 203.

access for the complainant to the investigatory procedure,[364] but is, as such, not considered an independent form of redress. However, under the surveillance of the execution of judgments by the Committee of Ministers, publication and dissemination of judgments are regularly required in order to avoid future violations.[365]

Indeed, the surveillance of the execution of judgments by the Committee of Ministers reveals that both the Committee of Ministers and the Member States hold that a string of individual measures (in addition to the just satisfaction awarded by the Court under Article 41) and, also, general measures may be necessary to execute the judgments of the Court. Such individual and general measures have taken a variety of different forms and levels of concreteness, for example, the striking out of an unjustified criminal conviction from criminal records, the granting of a residence permit and the reopening of domestic proceedings, legislative or regulatory amendments, and changes of case law or administrative practice.[366] Increasingly, also the Court indicates and requires both the individual and general measures to be implemented in order to resolve repetitive (and systemic) problems, most notably in the framework of the Pilot judgment procedure, but normally without specifying exactly how.[367] The general measures in the surveillance by the Committee of Ministers and the Pilot judgment procedure seem to be directed at preventing future violations of a similar kind, independently of whether they improve the situation of the applicant or not.[368] It is, for example, illustrative that the individual is not part of the surveillance proceedings.

There are some indications that the Court requires domestic remedial authorities to attach weight to general deterrence when setting out the individual redress, most notably compensation (Section 11.5). But the Court has

[364] See, for example, *Aksoy v. Turkey* (1996) para. 98; *D.P. & J.C. v. the UK* (2002) para. 135; *El-Masri v. FYROM* (Grand Chamber 2012) para. 259.

[365] The IACtHR demands the publication and dissemination of judgments; see, for example, Sandoval and Duttweiler (2011) 130–131. See, also, Principle 22 *litra* h of the van Boven/ Bassiouni principles.

[366] See, for example, notes 1 and 2 to Rule 2 of the Rules of the Committee of Ministers for the supervision of the execution of judgments and of the terms of friendly settlements. Also the IACtHR has awarded and recognized the importance of a variety of nonmonetary remedies for different purposes; see, for example, Sandoval and Duttweiler (2011) 132. Similarly, the van Boven/Bassiouni principles refer to a wide range of nonmonetary measures that may be required; see Principle 22 of the van Boven/Bassiouni principles.

[367] See, for example, Leach (2013a) 416. On the various elements and different types of Pilot judgments; see, for example, Leach, Hardman *et al.* (2010).

[368] Compare, for example, Ichim (2014) 252–256 and Rule 6 *litra* b(ii) of the Rules of the Committee of Ministers for the supervision of the execution of judgments and of the terms of friendly settlements.

not, in the framework of Article 13, required domestic remedial authorities to be able to set out general measures in order to prevent future violation of the Convention, more generally.

11.9 ENFORCEMENT

Article 13 does not, by its wording, require remedies to be enforced.[369] However, the Court holds that Article 13 encompasses:

> a duty to ensure that the competent authorities enforce remedies when granted … it would be inconceivable that Article 13 provided the right to have a remedy, and for it to be effective, without protecting the implementation of remedies afforded. To hold the contrary would lead to situations incompatible with the principle of the rule of law which the Contracting States undertook to respect when they ratified the Convention … .[370]

The lack of enforcement and execution of judgments and decisions from courts, in cases concerning the determination of civil rights and obligations and a criminal charge, may amount to violations of Article 6(1). To the extent that they are not enforced, such violations may constitute continuing violations of Article 6(1), which must be ended (Section 11.3.4). As a clear starting-point, Article 13 requires judgments and decisions directed at the State to be enforced – the State cannot choose to offer other forms of compensation, for example, money.[371] However, in cases concerning the execution of a final court decision against private actors, the State is, as a general rule, not directly liable for the debts of private actors. In such cases, State obligations under Article 6 and P1 Article 1 are limited to "providing the necessary assistance to the creditor in the enforcement of the respective court awards, for example, through enforcement proceedings or bankruptcy procedures."[372]

In cases in which domestic remedial authorities provide redress against the violation of other substantive Convention rights, apart from violations of Article 6, the unconditional rule is that the redress provided must be enforced.[373] That being said, the domestic judgment will often leave discretion on part of the authorities with regard to the enforcement and execution.

---

[369] Compare Article 2(3) *litra* c ICCPR.

[370] See, for example, *Kaić a.o.* v. *Croatia* (2008) para. 40; *Kenedi* v. *Hungary* (2009) para. 45; *Elvira Dmitriyeva* v. *Russia* (2019) para. 63.

[371] See, for example, *Kanellopoulos* v. *Greece* (2008) paras. 33 and 20; *Vasilev and Doycheva* v. *Bulgaria* (2012) paras. 59, 30, and 69; *Sharxhi a.o.* v. *Albania* (2018) para. 84.

[372] See, for example, *Marinković* v. *Serbia* (2013) para. 38; *Ciocodeică* v. *Romania* (2018) para. 85.

[373] See, for example, *Biserica Adevărat Ortodoxă din Moldova a.o.* v. *Moldova* (2007) para. 53.

In such cases, the domestic authorities have to execute the judgment loyally within the discretion. A loyal execution that does not fully redress the situation will not necessarily render the remedy, as such, ineffective.[374] However, under no circumstance, the execution can be left in the sole discretion of the administration.[375] Further, new court procedures, instigated to enforce the remedies granted, cannot consist of a declaratory judgment simply repeating the original judgment,[376] nor is a simple increase of compensation sufficient. The applicant must, normally, also be compensated for the nonpecuniary damage.[377] In this respect, the presumption for nonpecuniary damages is particularly strong.[378]

---

[374] See, as an example, *Nicolò Santilli v. Italy* (2013) para. 86.
[375] See, for example, *Kanellopoulos v. Greece* (2008) paras. 33 and 21.
[376] See, for example, *Vakulenko v. Ukraine* (2008) para. 17 and 10; *Gjyli v. Albania* (2009) para. 58; *Burdov v. Russia (no. 2)* (2009) para. 103; *VR-Bank Stuttgart eG v. Austria* (2010) para. 31.
[377] See, for example, *Moroko v. Russia* (2008) paras. 48 and 27–28; *Vakulenko v. Ukraine* (2008) paras. 17 and 10.
[378] See, for example, *Burdov v. Russia (no. 2)* (2009) para. 100.

12

A Normative and Contextual Reading

12.1 INTRODUCTION

The previous chapters have demonstrated that, in particular, as from year 2000, there has been a certain development in the Court's case law concerning Article 13. Most notably the Court, now, actually considers whether Article 13 has been violated in addition to substantive Articles (Section 4.3). The Court, also, performs a stricter assessment of many requirements, for example, how an aggregate of remedies may be effective (Section 9.3) and how the domestic remedial authority must deal with the substance of the complaint (Section 10.5.4). Further, the Court increasingly specifies the relief required in concrete situations, most notably, compensation for nonpecuniary damages in more scenarios (Section 11.5.2). However, there is still considerable uncertainty regarding both the content and scope of specific obligations and the role which Article 13 has in the system of protection of human rights under the Convention.

This chapter provides normative and contextual depth that may contribute to our understanding of Article 13 and how it could be construed, applied, and further developed by the Court. The goal is not to provide specific answers as to how every requirement could be construed and applied, but to illustrate, more generally, the role that Article 13 could have in the system of protection of human rights under the Convention. By that I mean the role Article 13 could have in regulating the relationship between international and national protection of human rights.

The selection of materials, which I use below in order to provide this normative and contextual depth, builds on the consideration that Article 13 (still) has the potential to be construed in different ways by the Court (Section 2.4) and that when courts exercise discretion, a range of factors, perceptions, materials, and argumentative techniques may influence how the discretion is exercised.[1] Indeed, it is just as misleading to claim that law admits any and all types of arguments as it is to hold that adjudication is exclusively concerned with shoehorning arguments into formal sources.[2] Sections 12.2 and 12.3, therefore, illustrate how different perceptions and understandings of fundamental normative concepts, values, and structures underlying Convention law and four more general contextual factors may influence how judges construe, apply, and understand the role of Article 13.

12.2 FUNDAMENTAL NORMATIVE CONCEPTS, VALUES, AND STRUCTURES

12.2.1 *Introduction*

The concepts, values, and structures accounted for below are parts of the fundament of Convention law.[3] Indeed, the Convention is, explicitly, based upon democracy (Section 12.2.4), the rule of law (Section 12.2.7), the principle of subsidiarity (Section 12.2.5), and the margin of appreciation (Section 12.2.6). And no lawyer applying the law of the Convention may hide from their understandings of law and human rights (Section 12.2.3), the concept of a right (Section 12.2.2), and the functions of the Court (Section 12.2.8).

Disagreement concerning the best interpretation of a particular statute, and, in this context, Article 13, is often a symptom of submerged and unrecognized disagreements concerning such fundamental conceptions, values, and structures.[4] Further, even though some claim that a distinct legal culture has developed within the Court, most notably a distinct legal method, and that the judges may be more influenced by this legal culture, than that of their home States,[5] it is likely that they have different understandings of the fundamental

---

[1] See, for example, Voeten (2014); Alter, Helfer *et al.* (2016).
[2] Compare, for example, Drobak and North (2008) 131–132; Jacob (2011) 1011; Langford (2015) 57.
[3] Compare Tuori (2002) who distinguishes between three levels of law: the surface level, the cultural level, and the deep structure.
[4] Dworkin (2011) 133, 136, 143. See, also, for example, Sand (2008) 50, 72 and Habermas (1998) 4, 19, 22. Indeed, one of the least contested insights of legal realism is "the manner in which our normative sensibilities and sensitivities condition the very way we experience both facts and the law"; see, Weiler (2014) 641. This realization is, also, a central element of postmodernist thought in which it is criticized how classical legal theory fails to take into account the subjective experience of what we encounter; see, for example, Drobak and North (2008) 140–147; Wacks (2015) 331.
[5] See, for example, Arold (2010). See, also, Voeten (2013), who holds that home-State biases are not very influential in the Court and, more generally, Brandom (1999) 181, who holds that the judge is held accountable to the traditions he/she inherits by the judges yet to come.

concepts, values, and structures that I account for below. Indeed, with such diverse backgrounds from different legal cultures, normative convictions, policy preferences, and cognitive frames could only be expected to be more diverse.[6] Or, to put it another way, "it is differing belief systems that make for judges with differing judicial philosophies and for judges to be labeled either liberal or conservative or either activist or restrained", because "the indeterminacy of the judicial process [legal method] leaves an opening for belief systems to affect outcomes."[7]

The understandings and perceptions that judges may have with regard to such fundamental concepts, values, and structures could be reconstructed from discursive traces in, for example, case law.[8] But because the case law of the Court is very fact specific, I primarily use literature from legal theory, philosophy, sociology, and political sciences, to illustrate and shed light on different understandings and perceptions that judges in the Court may have, and which, therefore, may influence how they construe and apply Article 13.[9] In so doing, I primarily account for contrasting views.

A discourse emphasizing such contrasting views may enlighten us with regard to how different prioritizations of values and goals may lead to different results, which is my primary goal below. A central element in the analyses is, for example, how the aptitude to attach more or less weight to procedure and substance within these concepts, values, and structures may influence how the Court construes and applies Article 13. However, the exercise is dangerous because it may create false dichotomies and give the impression that it is not possible to reconcile values, concerns, and understandings that all are legitimate, within a given system. At the outset, I therefore provide the following warning and clarification: I proceed from the assumption that the system for the protection of human rights set up under the Convention must seek reflective equilibrium, an ideal which has been applied since Socrates, and later, for example, by John Rawls,[10] Martha Nussbaum,[11] Ronald Dworkin,[12] and Jürgen Habermas.[13] Although the concept is debated, the basic idea, and the ideal that I pursue, is that one reflects on and attempts to achieve equilibrium between

---

[6]   See, for example, Venzke (2012) 9.
[7]   Drobak and North (2008) 138.
[8]   Compare Tuori (2002) 186.
[9]   Accordingly, I do not attempt to empirically prove the different perceptions and understandings that the judges in the Court actually have.
[10]   See, for example, Rawls (1971).
[11]   See, for example, Nussbaum (2011) 77.
[12]   See, for example, Dworkin (2011).
[13]   See, for example, Habermas (1998).

several judgments, principles, ideas, and alternative conceptions.[14] The goal is to achieve an "overall satisfactory reflective equilibrium".[15] However, and this is the warning, my take on how this equilibrium should be struck is not accounted for below, but in the concluding Chapter 13. Further, this equilibrium is not only based upon my understanding of these fundamental values, concepts, and structures, but the context accounted for in the next subchapter as well as the previous analyses of case law. Thus, the below primarily illustrate how the interpretation, application, and understanding of Article 13 may be affected to the extent that one is leaning more or less toward one or the other side of the (contrasting) normative positions presented. Many explicit mediating middle positions are, therefore, left out.[16]

Some might question why I do not attempt to transpose these understandings into more formal legal sources and argumentation by explicitly applying the Court's legal method, for example, by making reference to the object and purpose of the Convention, the wording, the context, and the will of the parties.[17] However, because they have not received clear expressions in the Court's case law,[18] any attempt to force such contested understandings into formal sources through legal method could create an impression of certainty where none exists. In the disguise of legal method, we would then claim to verify the validity of a normative theory which has not been established or accepted by the Court. It is, therefore, more honest to remove the disguise and openly admit that the understanding of these factors may influence how Article 13 is construed, applied, and understood by the Court, but, that the understandings, at least to date, are not clearly specified in the case law.

12.2.2 *The Concept of a Right*

Convention rights, including Article 13, are legal rights. Legal rights are distinguished from rights with no legal basis and consequences, most notably, purely moral rights.[19] In the following, I use the terminology developed by the

---

[14] See, for example, Eng (2014) 143.
[15] Eng (2014a) 444.
[16] The approach is, in this sense, similar to that of Janneke Gerard's exposition of "push and pull factors" in the work of the Court; see, Gerards (2014) 19–20. See, also, Tuori (2011) 29.
[17] See, as an example, Emberland (2006) 24, who analyzes to what extent the fundamental values and structures of the Convention, perceived as part of the Court's teleological method of interpretation, protect companies.
[18] Compare Tuori (2002) 154, 196.
[19] That being said, the relationship between moral and legal human rights is controversial; see, for example, Dworkin (1978) 93.

American legal philosopher Wesley Newcomb Hohfeld to illustrate how different descriptive and normative understandings of the concept of legal rights may influence how judges construe, apply, and understand Article 13.[20]

Hohfeld distinguished between claim-rights, liberty-rights (or privileges), power-rights, and immunity-rights. A central element in the typology is correlatives.[21] Since only claim-rights have a duty as a correlative, only duties can be claimed. This strict correlative raises several problems.

First, it must be possible to identify a duty bearer.[22] The Convention contains rights that explicitly place a duty upon States to perform or not perform specific actions, but also liberty- or freedom rights. However, all liberty rights are coupled with a prohibition, a duty on the part of States not to interfere with these freedoms. The Convention also contains a more general obligation on the part of States to protect and safeguard all rights (positive obligations).[23] At the outset, the question of identifying a duty-bearer, therefore, does not pose a problem – the State, as such, is the duty-bearer. However, if one, in addition, demands that the right has a character that makes it possible to identify specific duty-bearers below the level of the State, it becomes more problematical. Indeed, such considerations have led many to argue, for example, that welfare rights are nonjusticiable because it is virtually impossible to identify any duty-bearer below the level of the State.[24]

Second, if the content of the right is too abstract, it becomes difficult to claim what the duty-bearer should do. This problem can be overcome by specification through judicial activity. But in the context of the Convention, legislative initiatives to specify the right to an effective remedy have been rejected,[25] and it remains controversial whether, and if so how, further specification should be done by courts. The Court has gone a long way in specifying the content of substantive rights. Some rights are specified in a detailed manner, setting out specific forms of required actions and nonactions, most notably, under Articles 2, 3, and 5. Other rights appear as balancing or goal-realization norms, most notably, Articles 8–11.[26] Within rights theory, it is often held that purely goals, values, guidelines, and aspirations cannot be claimed or demanded, but merely

---

[20] See, for example, Hohfeld and Cook (1919). Notice, however, that Hohfeld's analysis is purely descriptive. He makes no normative claim as to what a right is.
[21] See, for an overview, for example, Wacks (2015) 273–275.
[22] Compare, in that regard, the capabilities approach in Nussbaum (2011) 167–168.
[23] The most general expression is Article 1 ECHR.
[24] See, for example, O'Neill (2005) and, for a critique, Etinson (2013).
[25] See Section 12.3.3.
[26] On norms seeking to realize goals and not regulating specific actions; see, for example, Nickel (2007) 24–26.

sought or requested.[27] And, it may be particularly problematical for courts to specify required positive actions because they may be fulfilled in different manners. Courts, therefore, tend to specify positive obligations in an abstract manner, leaving the concrete alternatives to the State. Article 13 is one of the few rights in the Convention explicitly formulated as a positive obligation.

Such uncertainties probably contributed to the early view that Article 13 was not a right in itself, but merely a mode by which to secure substantive rights, and to the fact that many monist countries held that Article 13 was not self-executing. Accordingly, they did not conceive Article 13 as a claim-right. However, in time, the case law of the Court contributed to establish the self-executing character and claimability of Article 13 in all monist Member States.[28] Today, after further years of specification, Article 13 is a right including many rights. In some areas, specific requirements to perform actions and nonactions may be deduced, for instance, obligations to perform effective investigations (Section 11.7) and provide compensation (Section 11.5). In other areas, the case law only sets out vague goals, under which it is uncertain what the more specific purposes are, and which, accordingly, provide States with a wide margin of appreciation with regard to how the positive duty should be implemented. In such cases, it could still be questioned to what extent Article 13 is actually perceived as a claim-right.

Connected to perceptions of the claimability of rights, is what aspect of the correlative duty/right one is susceptible to attach weight to. Breaches of duties are mostly sanctioned, whereas breaches of the right are to be remedied (redressed) (Fig. 12.1).

Given the relationships between the right and the duty, between rights and remedies, and between duties and sanctions, one may ask whether all the squares in Fig. 12.1 should be horizontally and diagonally connected – is there a required relationship between rights, remedies, and sanctions?

The judges at the Court may have different understandings of how such relationships should be. Although the Court has never explicitly accepted punitive purposes,[29] sanctions and remedies may have similar effects. Indeed, underlying many remedial decisions, one may sense a punitive purpose, and underlying sanctions, one may sense a restorative (remedial) purpose. For example, in many remedial decisions, the Court attaches weight to deterrence, which is related to punitive purposes and sanctions. It could be that, the more the judge is drawn toward the duty, in contrast to the right, the more the judge attaches weight to deterrence, and maybe also punitive purposes, in contrast to restorative purposes.

---

[27] See, for example, Beitz (2009) 30; Campbell (2013) 1.
[28] See, for example, Mertens (1968) 463–464; Mertens (1973) 95; Flauss (1991) 328.
[29] See, for example, Fikfak (2019) 1095.

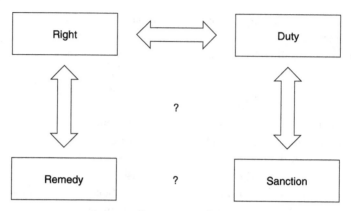

FIGURE 12.1 *Relationship rights, duties, remedies, and sanctions*

This leads me to the two major normative theories as to what the deepest functions of rights are – what do rights do for right holders? Will or choice theories hold that the protected issue is the will or choice of the right-holder.[30] Such theories often emphasize freedom or liberty as the fundament of rights. Intuitively, one could think that such conceptions primarily underscore restorative purposes and, accordingly, are less attached to, for example, systemic concerns, the interests of third parties, and the wider interest of the public. Interest theories, on the other hand, hold that the primary function of rights is to protect certain interests of the right-holders, or even the public, more generally.[31] At the outset, such theories and understandings are more open to integrate, for example, systemic concerns and wider purposes in the right to an effective remedy, in contrast to purely restorative purposes.[32] Clearly, the Court seeks to draw a line between a wide range of considerations.[33] Accordingly, rights in the Convention are not only based upon the will or choice of the individual right-holder, but broader interests, not merely connected to the individual. However, judges, like other legal interpreters, tend, more or less consciously, to favor a perception of rights which lean more against will/choice theories, or more against interest theories, which could influence the interpretation, application, and understanding of Article 13.

Further, the legal system, of which Article 13 is a part, is dynamic. Changes in one part may lead to changes in other parts and *vice versa*. Judges may have different opinions about how to achieve common goals within a system.

---

[30] See, for example, Hart (1973).
[31] See, for example, MacCormick (1977).
[32] Compare, for example, Sathanapally (2012) 1.
[33] See, for example, Christoffersen (2009) 1.

Accordingly, how one structurally perceives the right to an effective remedy, in relation to other rights and principles in the Convention, may influence how Article 13 is construed and applied. For instance, some may hold that remedies are inherent in the concept of any right, as such,[34] others may refute that enforceability and claimability are existence condition for human rights,[35] some may hold that there is no effective rule of law without law enforcement, and, accordingly, that every right must be enforced,[36] and others that remedial and preventive measures are alternative concepts which the State is more or less free to choose between.[37] Under the Convention, domestic remedial action may, conceptually, be required by various Articles and principles, for instance, as an element included in substantive Articles, the Pilot judgment procedure, as part of the rule of law, and, more independently, under Article 13. Which of these tools the individual judges apply in order to promote remedial action may, then, depend upon how one fundamentally perceives that remedies relate to the concept of a right and how that right forms part of the legal system.

12.2.3 *Perceptions of Law and Human Rights*

An interpreter's perceptions of law and human-rights law may influence how Article 13 is construed, applied, and understood.[38]

However, during the negotiations of human-rights treaties, discussions on the foundation of human rights have been explicitly avoided.[39] Indeed, international human rights are the result of complex political bargains reached upon the basis of different normative assumptions and perceptions of human rights.[40] Yet, it is with the why that the dispute begins.[41]

---

[34] See, for example, Buchanan (1984); O'Neill (1996); Dworkin (2011) 331; David (2014) 261.

[35] See, for example, Tasioulas (2007) 81.

[36] See, for example, O'Neill (2005).

[37] See, for example, Beitz (2009) 13, 31, 106.

[38] Compare, more generally, for example, Koskenniemi (2005) 2; Kumm (2009) 267–270; Benhabib (2011) 60; Dworkin (2013) 3; Wacks (2015) 6 and 49–62. With regard to different perceptions and foundations of human rights, more generally; see, for example, Mahoney (2007) 1–70; Pollmann and Lohmann (2012) 1–128; Kim (2012); Scott Sheeran and Rodley (2013) 7–182. That being said, few have been able to integrate descriptive and normative commitments into analytical studies about the content of the law; see Koskenniemi (2005) 1. In Convention law, one notable exception is Letsas (2006) and Letsas (2007).

[39] See, for example, Glendon (2001) 40–41.

[40] Compare, for example, Maduro (2009) 366. In fact, it is frequently impossible to find a uniform intention of the drafters of any multilateral treaty; see, for example, Venzke (2012) 3 and the opinion of the UNESCO philosophers during the drafting of the UDHR, as referred to in, for example, Glendon (2001) 77.

[41] See, for example, Douzinas and Gearty (2014) 2.

Indeed, Ronald Dworkin holds that the question of linkage (or no linkage) between law and morals is the hottest chestnut that has burnt lawyers' fingers for centuries.[42] Historically, there have been two main opposing positions. On the one hand, those who hold that certain moral virtues exist independently of our minds and our conventions, for instance, natural lawyers, Kantians, and modern contemporary lawyers such as Ronald Dworkin. On the other hand, those who deny the existence of deontological mind-independent moral values, for instance, utilitarians, legal positivists, and noncognitivists. Within human-rights law, such contrasting positions are often phrased in practice-based accounts of human rights,[43] and moral-based accounts of human rights.[44]

Further, it seems as though those who consider law and human rights to have independent moral value are more willing to let human rights prevail over democratic concerns, compared to those who hold that law and human rights are the result of a normative understanding developed by people and institutions.[45] Consequently, judges drawn toward natural law and moral theory seem to be more drawn toward promoting aspects of substantive justice (and substantive human rights), whereas judges drawn toward legal positivism and practice-based accounts – emphasizing law as a social construction – toward promoting procedural fairness and practical concerns, independently of substantive outcomes.[46]

However, these initial assumptions are modified by at least two other fundamental perceptions of law and human rights.

First, modern theories and understandings of law and human rights tend to take more integrated and holistic approaches which include both naturalistic (moral) and positivist elements. Nevertheless, also such theories and understandings tend to be leaning more or less toward natural (moral) justice or positivist (procedural) justice.[47] And although those leaning more toward positivism and practice-based accounts has a primary reference to formal rather than moral criteria, at least soft-positivists accept that the rule of recognition may incorporate moral criteria when determining what law is.[48] It is thus a question of degree, rather than a dichotomy. That being said, judges drawn

---

[42] Dworkin (2011) 400.
[43] For example, Beitz (2009).
[44] For example, Griffin (2010).
[45] Compare Neumann (2011) 7–8.
[46] Compare, for example, Brugger (1994) 403.
[47] See, for example, Habermas (1998) 56 ff. and 9, 43, 80, 449, 453, who analyzes the political theories of John Rawls and Ronald Dworkin under the heading of the "return of modern natural law", whereas he places his own discourse theoretic concept of law between the "twin pitfalls" of legal positivism and natural law.
[48] See, for example, Koskenniemi (1997); Venzke (2012) 204.

toward legal positivism and practice-based accounts of human rights tend to find it easier to develop procedural aspects, for example, those of Article 13, at the cost of (absolute) substantive rights.[49]

Second, such conceptions cannot be read in isolation from how domestic law relates to international law – in this context, how domestic law relates to the law of the Convention.[50] Indeed, independently of the fundamental conception which one is drawn toward, one may still disagree as to whether fundamental rights are primarily to be promoted, developed, and enforced at domestic or international level. Consequently, what may be lacking more than anything else is a common understanding of the moral (or not moral) justification of the international system of human rights.[51] However, at least seen from the international level, the primary question seems to be whether the ultimate moral concern is human beings or political communities?[52] Whereas cosmopolitans tend to advocate human beings, social liberals advocate political communities. In this respect, a cosmopolitan liberal stance is more drawn toward developing substantive rights as expressions of international limits on sovereignty,[53] whereas a social liberal stance is more drawn toward developing international and/or domestic procedural aspects, for example, through Article 13.

In addition, some perceptions are fundamentally skeptical about human rights altogether. Communitarians, for example, claim that individual human rights neglect the interests of the community, civic virtues, and social solidarity. Relativists tend to reject the universality of any rights – even human rights must be relative to local culture, history, and social and political conditions. Legal realists also wage war on absolute values. They tend to be empirical, pragmatic, and reject concepts, which have no foundation in reality. And utilitarianism, at least in most versions, seeks to maximize general welfare even at the cost of individual fundamental interests. To the extent that one, more or less, has sympathies toward such perceptions, it could have at least two consequences for how the right to an effective remedy is construed and applied. On the one hand, the wider effects and purposes of remedies could be taken into account when considering whether a remedy is effective. On the other hand, the concept of an effective domestic remedy, in particular its procedural elements, could be promoted at the cost of substantive rights.

---

[49] It is illustrative that some claim, more generally, that Germans view their Constitution as a substantive charter of justice, in contrast to Americans who pay more attention to checks and balances and the fairness of the political process; see, for example, Brugger (1994) 595.
[50] Compare Letsas (2007) 83.
[51] See, for example, Buchanan (2013) vii.
[52] See, for example, Valentini (2011) 399.
[53] See, for example, Benhabib (2011) 62.

12.2.4 *Democracy and Judicial Review*

How to achieve a proper balance between democratic concerns and the effective protection of human rights has been debated ever since the inception of the Convention. A dividing line goes between those arguing for strong international protection of human rights and those defending national sovereignty, of which the most central element is democratic sovereignty.[54]

Clearly, democracy is a fundamental feature of the European public order promoted by the Court.[55] Indeed, democracy has a "primordial place" in the Convention system,[56] and remains the gold standard against which the legitimacy of public authority needs to be assessed, including the authority that the Court exercises by law-making.[57]

However, there are different opinions on how important democracy should be when considering the relationship between the Court and national authorities.[58] And, although everyone agrees that human-rights law is intrinsically linked to democracy,[59] democracy, like human rights, is a contested concept. In fact, democracy is used in a staggering number of different ways,[60] and the Court has never identified the constituent elements of the concept of democracy that the Convention adheres to.[61] Different understandings of democracy and judicial review, and how these concepts should be integrated and applied in an international setting, may, therefore, affect how, *inter alia*, Article 13 is construed, applied, and understood.[62]

By its wording and original meaning, in particular as developed in Greece, democracy means government by the people.[63] But, in time, at least western democracies have developed intricate legal systems in which a central element of democracy is a proper balance of power, in particular between the

---

[54] See, for example, Bogdandy (2004). Mattias Kumm considers that the language of subsidiarity has, largely, replaced that of sovereignty; see, Kumm (2009) 292–293. But underneath subsidiarity lies, in any case, democratic concerns; see Section 12.2.5 and, for example, Besson (2016).

[55] See, for example, *United Communist Party of Turkey a.o. v. Turkey* (Grand Chamber 1998) para. 45; *Ždanoka v. Latvia* (Grand Chamber 2006) para. 98. See, also, more generally, for example, Habermas (1998) in his Chapter 7; Tuori (2002) 234.

[56] Wildhaber (2002) 162. Some consider the promotion of democracy as the main function of international jurisprudence, more generally; see, for example, Martinez (2003).

[57] Bogdandy and Venzke (2014) 520. See, also, for example, Besson (2009) 384; Staden (2012) 1024.

[58] See, for example, Kumm (2004); Langford (2015).

[59] See, for example, Besson (2011).

[60] Dahl (2000) 38.

[61] Wildhaber (2007) 529. See, also, for example, Besson (2011a) 99.

[62] Compare Tuori (2011) 259 with regard to how different conceptions of democracy may lead to divergent appraisals of constitutional review.

[63] *Demos* (the people) and *kratos* (to rule). See, also, for example, Dahl (2000) 11.

legislative, executive, and judicial branches.[64] But how must authorities be responsible to other authorities? How must their powers be limited and controlled? To what extent does the concept of democracy include the protection of fundamental rights? And what is the role of courts in upholding and promoting this protection, not least international courts?

For answering such questions, the distinction between those who primarily define democracy procedurally and those who also tie democracy to substantive constraints, most importantly fundamental rights, is particularly important.[65] That being said, for most it is not a question of either/or, but of degree.[66]

Further, substantive constraints must not necessarily be protected by judicial review.[67] Indeed, judicial review seems less necessary where stable (political) majorities have a strong record of protecting individual rights.[68] The questions of how democracy relates to human-rights law is, thus, intrinsically linked to how the relationship between courts and other authorities should be, in particular, the legislator. Whereas some generally condemn judicial review as offensive to democracy, others claim that it is justified with reference to other values (interference in democracy justified) or that it is democracy enhancing.[69]

Moreover, judicial review of fundamental rights may be performed in different ways. A fundamental distinction, similarly as for the concept of democracy, as such, goes between substantive and procedural forms of judicial review. Whereas substantive forms primarily aim at finding "correct" substantive results (both concerning substantive and procedural rights), procedural forms are more concerned about the process in which other authorities have considered the substantive content of rights. Consequently, those drawn toward procedural concepts of democracy as such would, at least intuitively, find their conceptions of democracy better protected through procedural forms of judicial review, whereas those drawn toward concepts of democracy containing more or less absolute substantive constraints would find their conceptions better promoted through substantive forms of judicial review.[70] Indeed, a prime

---

[64] See, for example, Schermers (2000) 1272 and Habermas (1998) in his Sections 3.3 and 6.3.
[65] For a substantive conception, see, for example, Nussbaum (2011), and, for a more procedural conception, for example, Habermas (1998).
[66] See, for example, Dworkin (2011) 349–350, 384–38.
[67] See, for example, Dahl (2000) 119–129; Dworkin (2011) 385.
[68] Dworkin (2011) 398. See, also, Dahl (2000) 139. Other arguments than those stemming from democracy may, of course, speak for or against judicial review; see, for example, Langford (2015).
[69] See, for example, Dworkin (2011) 348.
[70] See, for example, Bogdandy and Venzke (2012) 32. See, also, more generally, for example, Ely (1980).

underlying assumption of theories of weak and procedural review is that there is room for reasonable disagreement concerning the content of rights and that this disagreement is better solved by (democratic) legislative deliberations, in contrast to what is perceived as unaccountable judicial deliberations.[71] On the other hand, those drawn toward substantive conceptions of democracy tend to hold that no such reasonable disagreement is possible (absolute constraints) and that judicial review is necessary to protect against the tyranny of the majority.[72]

In addition, those who are skeptical against judicial review at domestic level tend to be even more skeptical toward judicial review at international level,[73] because judicial review by international courts is outside domestic democratic control and accountability altogether.[74] On the other hand, those who argue for substantive constraints on democracy tend to hold that the substantive values are better promoted by an international court because States, including domestic courts, should not be judges in their own cause.[75]

An additional problem for the Court is that it develops precedents, which are expected to be followed by many different States. The perceived (domestic) democratic cost may then increase because a coherent jurisprudence to be applied on the many and different is more likely to override local particularities.[76] But also the case against judicial review is faced with an additional problem of diversity in the international setting. Consider, for example, Jeremy Waldron's core case against judicial review, which is based upon four assumptions: reasonably working democratic institutions, reasonably working judicial institutions, commitment of society to basic rights, and persisting disagreement about rights.[77] Within the members of the Council of Europe, these assumptions are satisfied in many, but not all, Member States. Accordingly, the judicial review by the Court seems to be necessary to a different degree, depending on the State concerned.[78]

---

[71] See, for example, Waldron (2006) 1353; Tushnet (2009) 20–21; Gerards (2011) 86. Notice that although the counter-majoritarian argument has been the main focus in the debate for and against judicial review, some contributions have, also, focused on other aspects; see, for example, Langford (2015).

[72] See, for example, Dahl (2000) 48; Besson (2011a) 124.

[73] See, for example, Dahl (2000) 115, 183; Martinez (2003) 461.

[74] See, more generally, for example, Luhmann (1993) 582; Bogdandy and Venzke (2011) 993, and, more concretely concerning the Court, for example, Bellamy (2014) 1020–1021.

[75] See, for example, Cali (2008) 302, with particular reference to the protection of minority groups. See, also, the overview in Bellamy (2014a) 256–261.

[76] See, for example, Moravcsik (2000) 227.

[77] Waldron (2006).

[78] Compare Dworkin (2011) 398. See, also, Dahl (2000) 139. Similarly, States have different incentives to ratify human-rights instruments; see, for example, Moravcsik (2000) 228–229.

Indeed, if, at the outset, a conception of democracy based upon more or less absolute substantive constraints favors a judicial review aimed at achieving "correct" substantive results (substantive judicial review), differences between States may speak for a procedural review by the Court, if not by domestic courts. A reconciliatory middle ground between different domestic conceptions of democracy may, therefore, at least to a certain extent, be to limit international review to verify whether domestic courts have proceeded and considered substantive questions in a proper manner, based upon the general substantive principles developed by the Court. In the context of the Convention, this could be achieved by developing the element of access to justice under Article 13 and, at the same time, decrease substantive review under substantive Articles (Section 13.2). Although such an approach intuitively seems most pleasing to procedural concepts of democracy, even for substantive conceptions, the main concern is that democracy must make fundamental rights effectively available to its citizens.[79]

Concerning the element of redress in Article 13, finding a balance between such different perceptions intuitively seems more difficult. For substantive conceptions of democracy, the development of, for example, detailed injunctions with regard to, for instance, compensation and restitution, could be perceived as democracy enhancing, whereas, for procedural accounts, they could be seen as a violation of the separation of powers, in particular, because such injunctions tend to be polycentric and complex.[80] However, seen from the point of view of the Court, even with regard to the redress required at domestic level, a procedural review is easiest to reconcile with both conceptions of democracy. Indeed, as recommended in the concluding Chapter 13, the Court could develop more general and abstract principles with regard to the redress required, and, then, procedurally test whether these principles have been taken into account by domestic remedial authorities (Section 13.3).

12.2.5 *The Principle of Subsidiarity*

The principle of subsidiarity is a fundamental principle underlying the law of the Convention.[81] It was not explicitly referred to in the drafting, but the main underlying concerns, in particular, achieving a proper balance between

---

[79] Compare Dahl (2000) 49. See, also, David (2014) 260 with further references.
[80] See, for example, Hirsch (2007) 55.
[81] Of the many contributions dealing with the principle of subsidiarity under the Convention; see, for example, Petzold (1993); Mahoney (1997); Ridruejo (2005); Siess-Scherz (2005); Okresek (2006); Shelton (2006); Villiger (2007); Christoffersen (2009); Note by the

sovereignty and the effective protection of human rights, were prevalent.[82] The principle has only, more recently, appeared as an independent argument when construing both substantive Articles and Article 13.[83] The first judgment which, explicitly, refers to subsidiarity as a principle is *United Communist Party of Turkey a.o.* v. *Turkey* (1998),[84] but it was not before *Kudla* v. *Poland* (Grand Chamber 2000) that it received a decisive role in the reasoning of the Court.[85] Thereafter, the Court has made more active and independent use of the principle.[86] The principle has, also, gained importance in the reform process,[87] and has, with the entry into force of Protocol 15, been included in the Preamble, together with a reference to the margin of appreciation. Currently, we might thus be in a phase in which the principle is establishing itself as an explicit part of the Court's legal method.[88]

In 1996, the then presiding president of the Court, Rolv Ryssdal, held that the principle was probably the most important underlying the Convention. It implied a distribution of powers between the international supervisory machinery and the national authorities which played itself out in three more concrete manners.[89] *First*, States can provide a higher level of protection of

Jurisconsult on the Interlaken Follow-Up and the Principle of Subsidiarity (2010); Spano (2014); Mowbray (2015); Huijbers (2017); Popelier and Van De Heyning (2017); Spano (2018); Brems (2019); Cumper and Lewis (2019); Kleinlein (2019). On the principle of subsidiarity, more generally; see, for example; Carozza (2003); Müller (2003); Gosepath (2005); Slaughter and Burke-White (2007); Carter (2009); Føllesdal (2013); Føllesdal (2016); Besson (2016).

[82] See, for example, Bates (2010) 114–132.

[83] But in numerous previous judgments, the Court had referred to the fact that the Convention machinery of protection is "subsidiary" to the national systems safeguarding human rights, but then, mostly, as an introductory phrase (with no added justification or reasoning), most notably when justifying the rule on exhaustion of domestic remedies, for example, *Akdivar a.o.* v. *Turkey* (Grand Chamber 1996) para. 65, or as an element when justifying why a certain margin of appreciation was to be granted, for example in *Handyside* v. *the UK* (Plenary 1976) para. 48.

[84] Previously, the principle had been referred to by the parties, see, for example, *Beldjoudi* v. *France* (1992), and, in some dissenting opinions, see, for example, the dissenting opinion of Judge Gölcüklü in *Akdivar a.o.* v. *Turkey* (Grand Chamber 1996).

[85] *Kudla* v. *Poland* (Grand Chamber 2000) paras. 152–156.

[86] For instance, to limit the Court's fact finding role; see, for example, *Austin a.o.* v. *the UK* (Grand Chamber 2012); to justify a new approach to Article 13, most notably, in *Kudla* v. *Poland* (Grand Chamber 2000); to support the adoption of the Pilot judgment procedure, for example, in *Broniowski* v. *Poland (Merits)* (Grand Chamber 2004) para. 193; to limit the arguments of States before the Court to those put forward before domestic courts, for example, in *A. a.o.* v. *the UK* (Grand Chamber 2009) para. 154.

[87] See Section 12.3.3.

[88] Similarly, Besson (2016). In any case, the development has created an important incentive for the Court to develop a more robust and coherent concept of subsidiarity; see, for example, Spielmann (2013); Spano (2014) 491.

[89] Ryssdal (1996) 24–25.

human rights at national level. *Second*, the Convention does not impose uniform rules, but standards of conduct, which leaves the choice of the means of implementation to the States. *Third*, national authorities are, generally, in a better position to strike the balance between the sometimes conflicting interests of the community and the protection of fundamental rights. This third element was meant as a reference to the margin of appreciation.[90] But subsidiarity is, as Ryssdal's starting-point and reference to the "distribution of powers" imply, also a broader approach to governance, which includes assessments of, in particular, democracy, the scope of human rights, federalism, liberty, and separations of powers.[91] This broader understanding is particularly debated and has led to a complex principle that is understood differently by different actors and institutions.[92]

However, as a starting-point, and as a tool to define the relationship between international and domestic human-rights protection, its primary goal is to regulate the allocation of authority between the international and domestic levels.[93] Further, in all versions, the principle holds that the burden of argument lies with attempts to centralize authority, unless centralization ensures higher comparative effectiveness in achieving specified objectives.[94] Thus, it is in the legitimate objectives that may speak for centralization that controversy begins.

Although many different models of the principle may be perceived,[95] a main dividing line goes between State-centric and individualistic versions.[96] Do we adhere to the principle because it promotes the interests of the individual, or the State? Further, the case law of the Court reveals a third dividing line in the sense that the Court often refers to the principle purely as a means to reduce the Court's case load.[97] In this regard, the principle is an expression of judicial economy.[98]

Considering such differences, maybe the most we can take from the principle, as such, is a procedural presumption that problems are best solved at

---

[90] Indeed, some refer to the principle as more or less synonymous with the margin of appreciation; see, for example, Petzold (1993) 41; Shelton (2003) 129; Ridruejo (2005) 1078–1081; Nollkaemper (2014) 543.

[91] See, for example, Shelton (2006) 4; Okresek (2006) 576. See, also, Greer (2006) 193–230.

[92] Similarly, Besson (2016) 72; Eborah (2014) 240–241.

[93] Compare Follesdal (2011) 37.

[94] Follesdal (2011) 38. Or, put in another manner, unless centralization is justified by "good reasons"; see Kumm (2009) 294.

[95] Føllesdal (2013).

[96] Compare, for example, Neuman (2013) 362.

[97] For instance, *Kudla* v. *Poland* (Grand Chamber 2000).

[98] See, in this direction, also, the Interlaken Declaration para. 9.

national level?[99] The presumption could, then, be countered on the grounds of substance, in particular person-centered arguments, whereas State-centered arguments and judicial economy could speak against rebutting the presumption.[100] Seen from this point of view, the question is rather which human-rights questions are so important that they need a uniform decision at international level and which can be left to a proper political and legal process at domestic level.[101]

Moreover, independently of the conception of subsidiarity to which one adheres, subsidiarity may be achieved in different manners. Indeed, when the Court refers to the principle, it holds, on the one hand, that the task of ensuring respect for the rights in the Convention lies, first and foremost, with States, and, on the other hand, that the Court could and should intervene only when the domestic authorities have failed in that task.[102] Seen from the point of view of the Court, the principle, therefore, has a negative and a positive side: A prohibition for the international authority to intervene when action is not necessary, and an obligation to intervene when the protection at domestic level is not sufficient.[103] In the case law of the Court, both elements are part of the principle of subsidiarity and reflect a shared responsibility, in which the primary responsibility of States must go hand in hand with the subsidiary review of the Court.

That being said, those who are more drawn toward person-centered conceptions of subsidiarity tend to be more drawn toward a uniform decision at the international level, and thus a less subsidiary review of the Court, whereas those more drawn toward State-centered arguments and those emphasizing arguments of judicial economy prefer leaving larger areas in the hands of proper political and legal processes at the domestic level. However, all versions of subsidiarity presuppose that there has actually been a proper political and legal process at domestic level. Accordingly, independently of the conception of subsidiarity to which one adheres, it remains important to bolster how human-rights questions are dealt with in domestic political and legal processes. All versions of subsidiarity, therefore, support that the Court performs a more active, principled, and

---

99 Compare, for example, Shelton (2006) 4.

100 See, for example, Kumm (2004) 922; Kumm (2009) 295. Such a pragmatic approach underlies the Note by the Jurisconsult on the Interlaken Follow-Up and the Principle of Subsidiarity (2010) para. 16: "the principle of subsidiarity itself is neither static nor unilateral. Under the influence of a whole host of factors … it oscillates between judicial self-restraint and judicial activism."

101 Compare, for example, Carozza (2003) 38. See, also, for example, Mahoney (1997); Wildhaber (2002) 162; Shelton (2003) 95.

102 See, for example, the Note by the Jurisconsult on the Interlaken Follow-Up and the Principle of Subsidiarity (2010) 2 and *Scordino v. Italy (no. 1)* (Grand Chamber 2006) para. 140.

103 See, for example, Neuman (2013) 363.

less subsidiary review of the access to justice required by Article 13. This could promote both the primary responsibility of States and make further assistance from the Court concerning substantive Articles less necessary (Chapter 13).[104]

12.2.6 *The Margin of Appreciation*

The margin of appreciation is part of the Court's legal method and culture.[105] As an analytical tool, it guides the Court in the examination of complaints under many, but not all, provisions of the Convention.[106] The basic idea is that States are granted a margin of appreciation when the Court considers whether the Convention has been violated. The margin may vary, depending on a number of factors, most notably, the character of the violation and its gravity.[107]

Both the general concept and its concrete application have received considerable criticism.[108] Some of the criticism could be explained by the fact that the doctrine is not a given or constant in every case because it is contextual and because there is a complex interplay between the doctrine and other legal principles.[109] However, this does not detract from the fact that the Court's case law is abundant, varied, and that, accordingly, it is difficult to know when and what margin the Court is to grant in specific cases.[110]

That being said, some starting-points are clear. Most generally, under some rights, less margin is granted (more absolute rights) while, under others, a wider margin is granted. Most notably, at least under the substantive aspects of Articles 2, 3, and 5, no margin, or very nearly no margin is granted. As a consequence, the Court always performs a fully fledged (or close to fully fledged – in contrast to subsidiary) review, with the exception that the Court is reluctant to review the facts established at domestic level. In other areas, most notably under Articles 8 to 11, the Court will, depending on the circumstances, grant

---

[104] Compare, also, Carozza (2003) 66.
[105] Of the many works concerning the margin of appreciation; see, for example, MacDonald (1993); Lavender (1997); Clashfern (2000); Greer (2004); Brauch (2004–2005); Shany (2006); Letsas (2006); Letsas (2007); Gerards (2011); Heyning (2011); Legg (2012); Spielmann (2013); Hoof (2014); Spielmann (2014a); Bratza (2014); Arnardóttir (2016); Bates (2016); Smet (2017); Vila (2017); Gerards (2018); Evans and Petkoff (2019); Bates (2021); Tripkovic (2021).
[106] See, for example, Spielmann (2014a) 49.
[107] Other elements are, for example, the expertise of the Court in the area (evaluation of facts are, for instance, often left to domestic authorities, whereas the Court may have an advantage in mapping European consensus), respect for domestic democracy and diversity, the need for uniform standards, responsiveness at national level, and European consensus with regard to the question in issue. See, also, Section 2.4 and Chapter 8.
[108] See, for example, Spielmann (2014a) 54–55.
[109] Spielmann (2014a) 58.
[110] See, for example, Ridruejo (2005) 1079; Gerards (2018) 505.

a narrower or wider margin. As a consequence, in many, but not all, areas, the Court accepts pluralism over uniformity.[111] In this book, this is of more concrete importance in two contexts:

First, the margin under substantive Articles (including procedural Articles other than Article 13) is indicative for when applying Article 13 may be an alternative to applying substantive Articles (Sections 4.4 and 13.2). Indeed, if the violation has a character that is considered to require uniformity, there is no room for subsidiarity, and, as a consequence, the substantive Article must be applied exclusively or in addition to Article 13.

Second, to what extent should States have a margin of appreciation under Article 13, as such? The previous chapters have demonstrated that although there has been a certain development in the Court's case law, the Court still grants States considerable leeway when implementing the obligations arising from Article 13. The concluding recommendations in Chapter 13 argue that there is room for reinforcing Article 13, most notably, by performing a stricter procedural review under Article 13, partly at the cost of substantive Articles (Section 13.2), and by providing more principled and abstract reasoning concerning Article 13 (Section 13.3).

12.2.7 *The Rule of Law*

The rule of law is given different meanings in different legal systems and by different legal authors.[112] Even though many hold that the concept is an "exceedingly elusive notion",[113] and doubt its usefulness as a practical legal concept,[114] it is, in various ways, an integral part of national legal systems and a fundamental underlying principle of international human-rights law. In the Convention, the principle is underlined in the Preamble and is one of the three pillars, together with the notions of democracy and human rights, upon which the Council of Europe is based.[115] Further, the Court holds that the rule of law is inherent in all provisions of the Convention, as one of the fundamental principles of a democratic society,[116] including the right to an effective

---

[111] Spielmann (2014a) 49.

[112] General overviews of the rule of law are, for example, Tamanaha (2004); Bingham (2011); Tomuschat (2013). Specifically, in the context of the Convention; see, for example, Lautenbach (2013); Koch (2013); Spano (2021).

[113] Tamanaha (2004) 1, 3. See, also, for example, Tuori (2011) 210.

[114] See, for example, Loughlin (2009). Such skepticism is, usually, related to democratic concerns, in particular, the "danger" of a rule by judges with anti-democratic implications; see, for example, Tamanaha (2004) 4–5.

[115] See the Preamble of the ECHR and Article 3 of the Statute of the Council of Europe.

[116] See, for example, Koch (2013) 331–334, 336–343; Spano (2021). See, also, for example, the Report of the Evaluation Group to the Committee of Ministers on the ECHR, EG Court (2001) 1.

remedy.[117] That being said, the Court has not provided a general definition or description of the constituting elements.

Albeit the scope of the concept remains uncertain, there is relative consensus as to its core meaning.[118] Indeed, to some extent, the notions of legality, legal certainty, prohibition of arbitrariness, access to justice before independent and impartial courts, respect for human rights and nondiscrimination and equality before the law are included.[119] Clearly, remedies may contribute to ensure and promote these elements.[120]

That being said, there is disagreement with regard to the scope and extent to which these elements are included in the concept. A main distinction goes between those who hold that the rule of law, primarily, concerns formal issues related to procedure and institutions (legality, legal certainty, and access to justice),[121] and those who hold that the rule of law, to a larger extent, also concerns the substantive content of the rules, most notably, respect for human rights, equality, and nondiscrimination.[122] The central aspect in this context is that those who are more drawn toward the formal aspects, and less attached to the substantive, intuitively seem to be more drawn toward developing procedural rights and forms of review, in contrast to substantive rights and substantive forms of review, and, most importantly in this context, the right to access to justice, as required by Article 13 (Section 13.2).

12.2.8 *The Functions of the Court*

The roles, purposes, and functions of the Court are not explicitly set out in the Convention.[123] But the Court primarily deals with individual applications, which indicates that the primary function is to settle disputes between

---

[117] See, for example, *Fevzi Saygılı v. Turkey* (2008) para. 41; *A.M. v. the Netherlands* (2016) para. 63.

[118] Report on the Rule of Law, adopted by the Venice Commission at its 86th plenary session, Venice, March 25–26, 2011, CDL-AD(2011)003rev 9.

[119] Ibid. 10. See, also, the Report S/2004/616 of the UN Secretary-General, The rule of law and transitional justice in conflict and postconflict societies, para. 6.

[120] Some even claim that the rule of law is the main idea underlying Article 13; see, for example, Holoubek (1992) 146–148, or that the right to an effective remedy is essential to the rule of law; see, for example, Christoffersen (2009) 263.

[121] For instance, Raz (1979) 211.

[122] See, for example, Bingham (2011) 66–68. See, more generally, on this rough distinction, for example, Tuori (2011) 212, 216. Spano (2021) 6–7 argues that the rule of law under the Convention is not a purely formal concept.

[123] I do not here distinguish strictly between roles, purposes and functions. The central aim is to illustrate how different understandings of the Court's *raison d'être* may influence how Article 13 is construed, applied and understood.

States and individuals.[124] However, the jurisdiction of the Court extends to "all matters concerning the interpretation and application of the Convention",[125] which indicates that the Court, also, has a standard-setting role. Although the Court may be perceived to have other functions,[126] the two major functions are dispute settlement and inducing compliance (by setting standards with regard to the content of the Convention). However, there is controversy concerning how these two functions should be prioritized and balanced against each other.[127]

The drafting fathers assumed that the Court primarily would receive inter-State cases with wider European public interest and did not intend to introduce a system for altering and unifying the practices of the legal systems of the Member States.[128] Consequently, they were chiefly concerned about the systemic elements and tasks of the Court, not providing individual relief.[129] However, in practice, the individual complaint procedure became the main focus and is, today, considered the cornerstone of the Convention system.[130] But the fact that the Court primarily deals with disputes between individuals and States does not necessarily imply that the primary function is dispute settlement between such parties. Indeed, any judgment of the Court has the potential to have effect beyond the individual dispute. When dealing

---

[124] Article 34 ECHR. The Court may deal with inter-State cases (Article 33 ECHR), but this rarely happens in practice. States are, also, only formally obliged to abide by the final judgment of the Court in the cases to which they are parties; see Article 46(1) ECHR.

[125] Article 32 ECHR.

[126] The Court has, albeit not as explicitly as, for example, the ECJ, relied on a doctrine of implied powers; see, for example, Matscher (1993) 80–81, which it has used, for instance, when developing the Pilot judgment procedure; see, for example, Tsereteli (2015) 29–37. Consequently, the Court may have other functions than those explicitly foreseen by the Convention, for example, enforcement and providing concrete legal advice; see, for example, Shelton (2009) 539, 557–571. That being said, under the Convention, enforcement is primarily the task of States and the Committee of Ministers, but the introduction of Articles 46(2)–(5) and the establishment of the Pilot judgment procedure have increasingly involved the Court in enforcement issues. Nor does the Court offer formal legal nonbinding advice, but it may do so indirectly (in its judgments), and has with the entry into force of the advisory opinion procedure (Protocol 16) received the possibility. Other functions that international courts may be perceived to have are, for example, control of States and organs of the State; see, for example, Teubner (2004); assist States in implementing the Convention at domestic level; see, for example, Follesdal (2016) 199; promote peace, stability and democracy; see, for example, Keller and Sweet (2008) 5; support and legitimate the regime that the court forms a part of; see, for example, Shany (2012) 244–247.

[127] See, for example, Greer and Wildhaber (2012) 663; Spano (2014) 490.

[128] See, for example, Madsen (2007) 140; Keller and Sweet (2008) 5.

[129] See, for example, Bates (2013) 31.

[130] See, for example, Spielmann (2014) 27.

with individual cases, the Court may, therefore, attach more or less weight to inducing compliance by developing precedent.[131]

An element of precedent for the system is a core function of law in most fundamental legal theories.[132] It is the consequence of the incompleteness of any system of rules.[133] In *Karner v. Austria* (2003), the Court admitted that its judgments not only serve to decide individual cases but also to elucidate, safeguard, and develop the rules instituted by the Convention, thereby contributing to the observance, on part of the States, of the engagements undertaken by them. Although the primary purpose of the Convention system is to provide individual relief, its mission is also to determine issues on

> public-policy grounds in the common interest, thereby raising the general standards of protection of human rights and extending human rights jurisprudence throughout the community of Convention States.[134]

The question is thus not whether the Court aims at inducing compliance through precedent, but how and to what extent the Court should do it. The more the Court takes upon itself to build precedent for the system, the more it engages in judicial law-making and takes upon itself what could be called a constitutional or quasi-constitutional function.[135]

Even though the primary function of the Court (still) is individual dispute settlement,[136] the constitutional law-making function is growing.[137] But whereas some hold that the primary task of the Court must still be to settle disputes and remedy individual violations, others hold that the systematic

---

[131] See, for example, Bogdandy and Venzke (2011) 979. See, also, Ginsburg (2004) 635–636.

[132] Similarly, Venzke (2012) 146.

[133] See, for example, Ginsburg (2004) 635.

[134] *Karner v. Austria* (2003) para. 26. Similarly, for example, *Konstantin Markin v. Russia* (Grand Chamber 2012) para. 89. See, also, for example, Gerards (2014) 16–17.

[135] See, for example, Ryssdal (1993); Ryssdal (1996); Schermers (2000); Wildhaber (2002); Keller and Sweet (2008) 13; Voβkuhle (2010) 181. Using the constitutional label in an international context is controversial; see, for example, Cali (2008) 305–306. But, at least the issues that the Court deal with are constitutional (fundamental rights), and they are dealt with in a manner that takes into account the (constitutional) task of dividing work between key actors in the system; see, for example, Wildhaber (2002) 161. Increasingly, the constitutional label has found its way into the practice of the Court; see, for example, *Loizidou v. Turkey* (Preliminary objections) (Grand Chamber 1995) para. 75; *Bosphorus Hava Yolları Turizm ve Ticaret Anonim Şirketi v. Ireland* (Grand Chamber 2005) para. 156; *Al-Skeini a.o. v. the UK* (Grand Chamber 2011) para. 141.

[136] Compare, more generally, for example, Barak (2016) 27.

[137] See, for example, Koskenniemi (2005) 42–44; Wildhaber (2007) 525; Sweet and Brunell (2013) 61; Spano (2014); Mowbray (2015); Madsen (2015); Arnardóttir (2018); Spano (2018). The development is illustrated, for example, by procedural changes concerning how the Court deals with cases; see, for example, Glas (2014).

delivery of individual justice was never a credible goal for the Court, and even less so today, because of the Court's case load.[138] Further, in both camps, there are at least two subdirections:

First, those who primarily promote individual justice may hold that the Court should direct its efforts at the past and present, and not be anticipatory in nature.[139] In short, the Court should avoid engaging in law-making by developing Convention rights. Others are primarily concerned that the constitutional mission should not come at the cost of individual relief and are not, as such, opposed to developing Convention rights and Convention law.[140]

Second, those who primarily promote constitutional justice may hold that the Court must concentrate on developing common and principled substantive standards or, alternatively, ensure relevant structures and procedures for vindicating rights at domestic level.[141] Whereas the first group tends to promote universal substantive rights, the second group is more concerned about effectiveness than uniformity.[142]

However, to pit constitutional justice against individual justice leads us astray. The question is, rather, how these two functions are to be balanced.[143] In doing so, the primary goal must be to help as many as possible realize their fundamental human rights, not least their most important fundamental rights. How this is achieved – through individual or constitutional justice – may, at least from a pragmatic point of view, be of lesser importance. But, in the current situation, most commentators seem to hold that the Court needs to attach more emphasis on achieving constitutional justice. This does not mean that the Court should abandon the goal of individual relief, or that individual relief is not important, only that more focus on the Court's constitutional systemic mission would help more people to secure their fundamental rights.[144]

---

[138] See, for example, Keller and Sweet (2008) 13; Barkhuysen and Emmerik (2008) 441; Greer and Wildhaber (2012) 664.

[139] See, for example, Golsong (1988) 244.

[140] See, for example, Hioureas (2006) 720, 731–733.

[141] See, for example, Wildhaber (2002) 162; Wildhaber (2004) 83; Harmsen (2013) 129–130, and, more generally, Greer (2006).

[142] See, for example, Spielmann (2014) 27.

[143] Similarly, Harmsen (2013) 131. See, also, Helfer (2008). Thus, in the reform process, it has repeatedly been underlined that "both functions are legitimate functions for a European Court of Human Rights"; see, for example, CDDH(2003)006 Addendum final para. 11 and the Report of the Group of Wise Persons to the Committee of Ministers, CM(2006)203 para. 24. However, in the said CDDH-report, and, also, later in the reform process, there are primarily views which promote constitutional justice; see Section 12.3.3 and, for example, Greer (2006) 166.

[144] See, for example, Wildhaber (2004) 92; Helfer (2008) 133; Christoffersen (2013) 182; Spano (2018).

To date, the Court has developed Article 13 upon a case-by-case basis with little principled reasoning. This corresponds best with the strict version of individual justice with no, or at least a very limited, goal of being anticipatory in nature. By contrast, substantive rights have been considerably developed. This corresponds best with the substantive form of constitutional justice. Accordingly, the Court has been torn between a function that promotes strict individual justice and a function that promotes substantive constitutional justice. But ever since the entry into force of Protocol 11, competing visions of the Court's functions have been underlying the reform process,[145] although the official debate has not openly discussed what the primary functions should be.[146] However, at least the Brighton Declaration admits that it may be necessary to evaluate the fundamental role of the Court and that, even though the right to individual application remains a cornerstone of the Convention system, any future reforms must enhance the ability of the Convention system to address serious violations promptly and effectively. To this end, the Convention system must support States in fulfilling their primary responsibility to implement the Convention at national level, which, again, should put the Court in a position to focus its efforts on serious or widespread violations, systemic and structural problems, and important questions of interpretation and application of the Convention and, hence, would need to remedy fewer violations itself, and consequently deliver fewer judgments.[147] Although these statements are open to several interpretations, they immediately correspond best to the procedural vision of developing constitutional justice and precedent,[148] a vision to which a further development of Article 13 may contribute (Chapter 13).

12.3 *DER ZEITGEIST* OF CONVENTION LAW

12.3.1 *Introduction*

Judges must have regard for the context in which they live, and the aims which they are serving.[149] A contextual reading of law also requires an historical understanding of law. In order to understand the current meaning of a law, one must first know the original one, and historical knowledge can be gained only by seeing the past in continuity with the present.[150] Sections 12.3.2 to 12.3.5 below

---

[145] See, for example, Christoffersen and Madsen (2013b) 230; Milner (2014).
[146] Greer and Wildhaber (2012) 659.
[147] Brighton Declaration paras. 31–33.
[148] Even more explicitly, for example, Madsen (2018) 206.
[149] Wildhaber (2007) 526.
[150] Gadamer (1975) 335–336.

provide a more general historical and contextual reading of Convention law and some phenomena closely connected to it. The goal is to illustrate how this context may affect how the Court construes, applies, and understands Article 13.

12.3.2 *The Court from Past to Present*

The life and development of the Court in an historical, legal, political, and sociological context has, in recent years, received considerable attention.[151]

In an initial phase (approximately 1959–1975), the Court received few cases and developed its institutional autonomy and jurisprudence in a careful manner. This was necessary to establish the Court's political legitimacy. Indeed, the jurisdiction of the Court was only reluctantly accepted by States, and the authority of the Court was weak, most notably, in the two major political powers, France and the United Kingdom. In fact, France did not accept individual complaints before 1981, and the United Kingdom annually reviewed the procedure,[152] and nominated judges with "sound" diplomatic viewpoints.[153] Consequently, the Court took care not to upset national authorities.[154] In particular, the case law of the Court and Commission was not very progressive in its first 10–15 years.[155] Of particular interest in this context is that the Court found few violations of Article 13, construed its content narrowly, and, more generally, left a wide margin of appreciation in the hands of States (Chapter 4). Two important examples are that Article 13 does not grant a right to challenge legislation as such (Section 10.5.3) and that an aggregate of remedies may satisfy the requirements of Article 13 (Section 9.3). Notice, in this context, that these limitations were set out in cases against the UK, who had expressed herself particularly strongly against the establishment of the Court.[156]

The second phase (approximately 1975–1990s) saw a slight increase in cases, but was, in the main, a reaction to the timid development in the first phase. Indeed, the initial mixture of law and diplomacy, and the deferential interpretation of the Convention, had built the Court's authority and legitimacy.[157] New judges and commissioners made their entrance,[158] and used the increased

[151] See, for example, Madsen (2007); Krisch (2008); Bates (2010); Christoffersen and Madsen (2013); Bates (2013); Alter, Helfer *et al.* (2016); Madsen (2021a).
[152] The UK accepted the optional clause in 1966 and annually reviewed the acceptance in the 1970s, 1980s, and early 1990s. At every occasion, there was a considerable parliamentary debate.
[153] Madsen (2007) 146.
[154] Krisch (2008) 206.
[155] Madsen (2007) 150.
[156] See Section 4.2.
[157] Madsen (2007) 151.
[158] Madsen (2007) 152.

authority and legal autonomy to develop a more progressive jurisprudence in which, for example, the main doctrinal concepts, such as the living instrument, the margin of appreciation, and effective and practical rights, were developed and which were again used to develop the content of substantive Convention rights. This new and progressive approach took many Member States by surprise.[159] However, Article 13, in contrast to most substantive Articles, remained underdeveloped.[160]

The third phase was initiated by the reception of a host of new Member States in the early 1990s, and the following years were characterized by a massive rise in the Court's case load. Further, the Court was presented with new types of cases, most notably, numerous repetitive cases caused by systemic problems on a wide range of issues, such as, excessive length of proceedings, nonenforcement of domestic judgments, lack of effective investigations, and conditions of detention.[161]

The fourth phase started in the early 2000s. It focused on consolidation and effectiveness, and is, above all, characterized by the attempts to deal with the Court's case load and to accommodate calls for a more subsidiary protection of human rights. It has seen several changes in the manner in which the Court deals with cases, for instance, the introduction of Single judge procedures, Pilot judgments, and new admissibility criteria. Further, the Court's substantive case law has taken a procedural turn, most notably in the sense that the Court may award a wider margin of appreciation under substantive Articles when the substance of the complaint has been dealt with in an appropriate manner domestically (Section 13.2).

In this phase, the Court, also, made more active use of Article 13, most notably, and in contrast to earlier years, by finding it necessary to consider whether Article 13 actually had been violated in addition to substantive Articles (Section 4.3). There was, also, some development in the Court's interpretation and application of Article 13, for instance, a stricter and more principled interpretation and application of the requirement that the domestic remedial authority be able to deal with the substance of the complaint (Section 10.5.4) and a stricter assessment of how an aggregate of remedies may satisfy the requirements of Article 13 (Section 9.3). The Court has also provided some specifications concerning the relief required in concrete situations, for instance, automatic suspensive effect in cases of expulsions that may violate Articles 2 and 3 (Section 11.3.2), and compensation for nonpecuniary damages in more cases, for example, excessive length of proceedings (Section 11.5.2). But there is room for further

---

[159] Madsen (2007) 153.
[160] See Chapter 4.
[161] See Sections 4.3 and 4.5.

development. Some of the limitations developed in the first and second phases, for example, seem less appropriate in the present context, for instance, the fact that Article 13 grants no right to challenge legislation, as such (Section 10.5.3) and the linkage between arguability and manifestly ill-founded (Section 7.3). Further, several areas, most notably with regard to redress (Chapter 11), would benefit from clarification, for example, the form of redress required (Section 11.1), when it is necessary to put an end to continuing violations (Section 11.3.4), and, the scope and purposes of, for example, compensation (Section 11.5) and effective investigations (Section 11.7).

   In addition, it seems as though the combined effect of, most notably, the Single judge procedure, the Pilot judgment procedure, and new and stricter application of admissibility criteria has placed the Court in a position to deal with the (incoming) case load (Section 1.3). However, even though the Court has grown more efficient, many Member States have considerable problems protecting human rights. Further, since 2012, in particular, a number of Member States have voiced severe criticism against the Court, not only in individual cases but also on a more systemic level.[162] The fact that the Court now is able to deal with the case load, coupled with a renewed debate with regard to the Court's legitimacy,[163] may have initiated a *fifth phase*, in which the focus could be truly directed at the improvement of the domestic protection and enforcement of human rights, to which the counterpart might be a decreased substantive review of the Court.[164] If so, the obvious tool is Article 13 (Chapter 13).

12.3.3 *The Current Reform Process*

In 1983, the Commission had already expressed its concerns about the "serious backlog" of cases, which risked developing.[165] However, the work with Protocol 11 was not primarily concerned with the backlog of cases,[166] and the attention directed toward the domestic level is a relatively new phenomenon. But, since 2004, the focus has been more explicitly directed toward domestic remedies,[167] and everyone seems to agree that the key to Convention compliance and saving the system lies at domestic level.[168]

---

[162] See, for example, Krisch (2008); Popelier, Lambrecht *et al.* (2016); Madsen (2021); Breuer (2021).
[163] The judges of Court are sensitive to this criticism; see, for example, Björgvinsson (2016) 329; Demir-Gürsel (2021) 126–129.
[164] Similarly, Spano (2018); Madsen (2021a).
[165] See, for example, Harmsen (2013) 121.
[166] Indeed, some hold that, from the point of view of effectiveness, it was an historical mistake to remove the Commission; see, for example, Lester (2013). See, also, Parish (2011) 200.
[167] See, for example, Akçay (2009) 477.
[168] See, for example, Harmsen (2013) 135.

Indeed, the calls to improve domestic remedies have grown steady and unequivocal. Already at the Ministerial conference in Rome on November 3–4, 2000, the former secretary-general of the Council of Europe, Walter Schwimmer, held that:

> Human rights protection begins at home; it requires much more than a stable democratic system. It presupposes the availability and accessibility of effective legal procedures before independent courts capable of providing redress within a reasonable time.[169]

Similarly, Gil Carlos Rodríguez Iglesias, the former Chair of the Group of Wise Persons, has held that:

> … national remedies, which are the first line of defense for the rule of law and human rights, must be effective … National courts bear prime responsibility for protecting human rights within their own legal systems and ensuring respect for the rights guaranteed by the Convention.[170]

And Phillippe Boillat, when summing up the Colloquy organized under the Swedish chairmanship of the Committee of Ministers of the Council of Europe, entitled "Towards Stronger Implementation of the European Convention on Human Rights at National Level", Stockholm, June 9–10, 2008, held that:

> If I had to sum up the substance of our work in a single word, I would have to hold on to 'subsidiarity'. All our reflections have centered on this fundamental notion – a fundamental notion that underpins the whole system of the Convention, and finds its formal expression, above all, in Articles 1, 13 and 35 of the Convention.[171]

Similar expressions have been repeated at the Interlaken, Izmir, Brighton, Brussel, and Copenhagen conferences,[172] and are found in a host of other adopted texts, reports, and declarations.[173] More recently, Guido Raimondi held that:

---

[169] Schwimmer (2009) 21. At the same Conference, Luzius Wildhaber held that the right to an effective remedy is a key element of the Convention system; see Wildhaber (2009a) 34. Wildhaber later held that the Convention "is all about remedies"; see, Wildhaber (2009) 83.

[170] Iglesias (2009) 234.

[171] Boillat (2009a) 553. See, at the same seminar, also, for example, Costa (2009b) 473–474 and Malinverni (2009) 486–487.

[172] See, for example, Widmer-Schlumpf (2014) 73.

[173] For example, Recommendation no. R(2000)2 of the Committee of Ministers to Member States on the re-examination of certain cases at domestic level following judgments of the European Court of Human Rights; Report of the Evaluation Group to the Committee of Ministers on the ECHR, EG Court (2001); Final Activity Report of the CDDH "Guaranteeing the long-term effectiveness of the European Court of Human Rights", CDDH(2003)026

more than ever, the subsidiary nature of the machinery of the European Convention on Human Rights remains the key to the system's success. The very large number of cases contributing to the Court's excessive caseload, whether relating to detention conditions and prison overcrowding or to non-enforcement of judicial decisions, shows that it is primarily at domestic level that an effective remedy is required for human rights violations.[174]

Notice, in particular, how the calls to improve domestic remedies go hand in hand with expressions emphasizing the importance of achieving a more subsidiary protection of human rights. And, at least in the process of the reform of the Court, subsidiarity implies that States have an obligation to implement the Convention at domestic level "on the basis of the clear and consistent guidelines set by the Court's case law" which should "enable the Court to scale down its supervisory function, secure in the knowledge that the domestic courts will have taken due account of the Convention's standards in their assessment."[175] However, under Article 13, clear and consistent guidelines from the Court are, in many areas, lacking.

Theoretically, such guidance could come from the treaty legislator through new and more detailed provisions on domestic remedies. Indeed, this was proposed by the Group of Wise Persons,[176] to which the then presiding President of the Court responded that the idea was "extremely interesting".[177] However, the proposal was set aside by the CDDH, which, instead, expressed interest in the adoption of a soft-law instrument.[178] This resulted in the Guide to good practice in respect of domestic remedies.[179] But this guide only refers to the practice of the Court in very vague terms and points to some well-functioning domestic remedial solutions.

Addendum I Final; Recommendation Rec(2004)6 of the Committee of Ministers to Member States on the improvement of domestic remedies; the Explanatory Report to Protocol 14; CM(2006)203, Report of the Group of Wise Persons to the Committee of Ministers; CM/Rec(2010)3 of the Committee of Ministers to member states on effective remedies for excessive length of proceedings; the Guide to good practice in respect of domestic remedies (adopted by the Committee of Ministers on September 18, 2013); the Explanatory Report to Protocol 15.

[174] Annual Report 2017 of the European Court of Human Rights 7.

[175] Widmer-Schlumpf (2014) 13. See, in a similar manner, for example, Jagland (2014) 15–16; Bratza (2014a) 82; the Interlaken Declaration paras. 4 *litra* d and 7 *litra* a(i), 11; the Brighton Declaration paras. 3, 7, 9 *litra* c(iii) and 10; the Explanatory Report to Protocol 15 paras. 7 and 8.

[176] See the Report of the Group of Wise Persons to the Committee of Ministers, CM(2006)203 paras. 93 and 136 and, for example, Iglesias (2009) 236.

[177] Costa (2009) 243.

[178] See, for example, Boillat (2009a) 555.

[179] Guide to good practice in respect of domestic remedies (adopted by the Committee of Ministers on September 18, 2013).

The justification for not adopting new and more detailed legally binding provisions is not easy to discern in the documents from the Council of Europe and would, in any case, vary between Member States. But a central reason seems to have been that the necessary legal instruments were already in place. Indeed, since Article 13 was of direct application, no real-added value could come from a new, binding legal instrument. What was missing, instead, was the real political will to give full implementation to Article 13.[180] And, indeed, the tool is there. But, the question is rather what to do when the political will is absent, at least in many States. One answer is for the Court to develop Article 13 further, with the goal of providing domestic remedial authorities incentives and help in establishing effective domestic remedies. However, in doing so, the Court would need to take into account that some States have well-functioning remedial systems (the will is there), whereas others do not. The Court, therefore, needs to develop remedial criteria and requirements that provide incentives and guidelines for States with less well-functioning remedial systems, but which, at the same time, does not unduly distort well-functioning domestic remedial systems (Chapter 13).[181]

12.3.4 *Constitutional Pluralism*

The cognitive framework or the lens through which one perceives the relationship between Convention law and domestic law may influence how Article 13 is construed, applied, and understood.[182]

Roughly speaking, international law and domestic law may be perceived as completely separate systems, with their own hierarchical structures, which are not influenced by one another.[183] Seen from the domestic system, domestic apex courts would, then, usually decide on constitutional questions in the last instance, taking international law into account only to the extent that international law has been legally integrated into domestic law, under doctrines of, most notably, monism or dualism. And, even if international law is integrated into domestic law, the latter may not recognize the final authority of international organizations, most notably, international courts. Similarly, seen from the point of international law, an international court could be perceived to decide on the content of international law purely from

[180] Boillat (2009a) 555.
[181] In a similar vein, for example, Spano (2018).
[182] Compare, more generally, for example, Keller and Sweet (2008) 7; Kumm (2009) 266.
[183] See, for example, Tuori (2014) 12, 26.

an international perspective, without regard to how the issue is understood in the domestic context. One might call such perspectives purely domestic constitutional perspectives and purely international constitutional perspectives.[184] That being said, such pure perspectives are growing rare. What seems to dominate in the current context is some version of what might be called constitutional pluralism. Alexander Somek, for example, paints a historical picture in three periods, which leads us to the current phase of constitutional pluralism.[185]

Constitutionalism 1.0 was authored by the free people of independent States. The origin of their constitutions was liberty, collectively exercised, the source, human action. The original constitutions primarily established powers and the core legal question was whether government stayed within its powers. Judicial review was based upon whether government and legislator followed legitimate aims. It did not consider reasonableness of action.[186]

Constitutionalism 2.0 alters the picture, but does not place constitutionalism 1.0 completely in the background. It was primarily developed in Germany and international human-rights instruments in the aftermath of the Second World War. It did not originate from the free choice of people, but the inherent dignity and human rights of people, *i.e.*, universal values such as freedom, equality, and solidarity. As a consequence, the judiciary, through judicial review, became the guardian of values, not just the division of power, in particular, through proportionality review.[187]

Constitutionalism 3.0, or constitutional pluralism, is the current phase. It is a symbiosis of the first two periods and rests on the realization that human rights depend on public authority for their articulation and realization.[188] The main characteristic is that, in order to ascertain that public authorities live up to the standards developed in 1.0 and 2.0, it is necessary to look at how peer members have behaved. This is a practical implication of the abdication of

[184] The appropriateness of applying the constitutional label in international law is disputed; see Section 12.2.8 and, for example, Sweet and Brunell (2013) 62. My goal here is not to single out a correct understanding of constitutionalism, be it at domestic or international level. I simply use the constitutional label to illustrate how international and domestic legal systems (constitutionally) relate to each other and what (constitutional) principles govern this relationship.
[185] Somek (2014).
[186] Somek (2014) 8.
[187] Somek (2014) 16. Notice, however, that Somek underplays the role that Parliaments may play in interpreting and protecting constitutional values, for instance, through weak forms of review.
[188] See, for example, Somek (2014) 282. This has been noted by many others, with different twists, for example, Bogdandy and Venzke (2012).

sovereign authority in the field of human-rights law.[189] Human rights are, therefore, secured through several informal and formal systems of peer review and are characterized by the efforts to reconcile conflicting peer authorities within informal or formal processes of review.

There are different opinions on how peer authorities should relate to each other and how important the discursive relationships should be compared to other factors that may influence how authorities decide cases. However, the central aspect, at least in this context, is that legitimacy is earned, and practice developed, by comparing oneself with others, albeit to a greater or lesser extent. As a consequence, peer authorities yield to other authorities, but only so long as, for some reason (which may vary between different institutions) their understanding of the law warrants defiance. Legitimate authority, therefore, is a derivative of the absence of conscientious objection.[190] In practice, different techniques are used to reconcile diverging opinions, seen from the perspective of the Court, for example, the margin of appreciation, and from the perspective of domestic courts, for example, the *"so lange"* doctrine of the German Constitutional Court. Accordingly, effective constraints do not only emerge from law, as such, but more or less subtle equilibria of power.[191]

Now, responsiveness could manifest itself in different ways. At the extremes, one could distinguish between pure constitutionalists and pure pluralists.[192] Whereas a pure constitutionalist adheres to a strict hierarchy, in which legal results are decided only through reference to hierarchical norms, pluralism leaves the question of the ultimate hierarchy and authority more or less open. However, it is increasingly accepted that no single institution can claim to have the only say on the interpretation and application of supranational law.[193] Indeed, most accept that the interpretation of law by other legitimate authorities could and should influence the interpretation and application of law. Pluralism is an inevitable fact.[194] That being said, it varies how and to what extent the

---

[189] Or, put another way: the content is protected in international instruments and domestic instruments (including international instruments integrated in or transformed to domestic law). It is, therefore, both at domestic and international levels, increasingly difficult to draw a line between national and international constitutional law, which, again, affects the question of authority; see, for example, Besson (2009) 388.

[190] Somek (2014) 20.

[191] Somek (2014) 21.

[192] Krisch (2010) 235; Tuori (2014) 34.

[193] Gerards (2013) 76. See, also, for example, Krisch (2008) 185; Bogdandy (2008) 399–401; Kumm (2009) 272; Maduro (2009) 356; Somek (2014) 19.

[194] Some even hold that the very idea of human rights, in a similar manner as the principle of subsidiarity, entails an affirmation of pluralism and diversity in society; see, for example, Carozza (2003) 47.

discourse from other authorities is considered relevant and legitimate.[195] As a consequence, there is not only pluralism but also constitutionalism: Pluralism is constitutionalized, or governed by more or less formal principles,[196] which may have a domestic, international, or even a cosmopolitan center of gravity.[197]

Different versions of constitutional pluralism do not necessarily provide normative answers as to what judges ought to do in specific cases.[198] However, and this is the important aspect in this context, all models foresee a certain degree of accommodation and responsiveness toward other authorities. Accordingly, constitutional pluralism, at the very least, has an underlying normative claim: The question of final authority is left open,[199] albeit to an extent which varies. The framework, independently of the version, thus suggests a particular responsiveness to issues of diversity,[200] and, at the very least, a preference for solutions found through dialogue and coordination.

Although the Court has developed several doctrines that take national sensitivities, choices, and procedures into account,[201] there is considerable potential in using Article 13 as a tool to foster further responsiveness and diversity in Convention law (Chapter 13).[202]

12.3.5 *Development of Law and Society*

The more general understanding of how law develops in interaction with societal developments may influence how Article 13 is construed, applied, and understood.

---

[195] To what extent one is leaning more toward pluralism or constitutionalism (within constitutional pluralism) depends on what one perceives as advantages and disadvantages with (pure) constitutionalism and (pure) pluralism and the weight one attaches to them, respectively. There are, at least, three main normative arguments for pluralism: capacity for adaptation, space for contestation, and capacity for building checks and balances; see, for example, Krisch (2010) 78–89. The main arguments against pluralism are instability, vulnerability to power, democracy, and the rule of law; see, for example, Krisch (2010), explicitly at 225 and, more generally, his Chapters 7 to 9.

[196] Compare, for example, Ulfstein (2014) 576.

[197] Bogdandy (2008), for example, presents a domestic constitutional pluralist model, whereas, Kumm (2004), for example, presents a more cosmopolitan model, but which encompasses both international and domestic perspectives.

[198] Besson (2011a) 101; Maduro (2009) 372.

[199] Similarly, for example, Fabbrini (2014) 21.

[200] Krisch (2010) 71. Indeed, when pluralism is accepted, deference and diversity must, in some manner, be accepted in order to mitigate conflicts; compare, for example, Gerards (2011) concerning the relationship between EU law and domestic law.

[201] See, for example, Scheek (2005); Krisch (2008); Bratza (2011); Gerards (2013).

[202] Indeed, such responsiveness may be particularly important in the field of remedies; see, for example, Roach (2021).

A central theory in the works of, for example, Gunther Teubner, is that there is a systematic connection between the development of society and law. Teubner builds on Philip Selznik and Philippe Nonet's theory of responsive law,[203] which describes a development from repressive to autonomous and, finally, responsive law. Teubner, in a similar manner, describes a development from formal to material (substantive) and, finally, reflexive law.[204] Formal law's internal rationality is characterized by strict rule-orientation and precise definitions and consequences. Material law is goal oriented with vague standards and open argumentation. Reflexive law is procedurally oriented focusing on organizational and procedural norms and norms of competences in a logical and self-regulating system. Accordingly, reflexive law is characterized by dominating procedural norms, in contrast to substantive norms.[205]

The evolution from a materially centered to a more procedurally oriented law is also central in the theories of, for example, Jürgen Habermas and Max Weber.[206] Although there are important differences between the theories of, for example, Habermas and Teubner,[207] both theories consider reflexive, responsive, and communicative aspects central to our understanding of how law develops in interaction with societal needs.[208] Further, the evolutionary character of law is central – one cannot arrive at responsive or reflexive law, without first having developed substantive norms. And, a prerequisite for arriving at responsive law is well-functioning democratic procedures. Indeed, responsive law functions, and can only function, in societies that are sufficiently developed democratically.[209]

That being said, responsive or reflexive law does not replace substantive law. It is rather a question of degree and development.[210] In complex modern societies, there are layers and different forms of law which, to a varying degree, contain substantive and procedural elements.[211] However, the complexity of modern society indicates a preference for a certain degree of responsiveness and reflexivity between different actors, and, thus, a preference for procedural law.[212]

---

[203] In particular, Nonet and Selznick (1978).

[204] Teubner (1982) 28.

[205] Teubner (1982) 23.

[206] See, for example, Teubner (1982) 23; Habermas (1998) 264, 296, 448, 450; Meuwissen (2000) 906. Sand (2008) 59–64 identifies the same preference in the legal theories of Niklas Luhmann.

[207] Habermas has, for example, criticized the (almost) closed (autopoesis) character of Teubner's legal system; see, for example, Habermas (1998) 52–56.

[208] See, for example, Sand (2008) 47, 48.

[209] Teubner (1982) 48.

[210] Teubner (1982) 23.

[211] See, for example, Sand (2012).

[212] See, for example, Sand (2008) 59; Sand (2012) 202.

Notice, also, that even Ronald Dworkin, the most well-known proponent of "one right answer" theory, does not hold that the "correct" answer is context independent. Indeed, the most fundamental requirement of States toward its citizens is the right to an attitude, which he connects to the concept of dignity as the fundamental value of society. Consequently, human-rights provisions must not be understood as attempts to define human rights in any detail, but as a continuous search for the unacceptable attitude. Hence, only the abstract standard is universal, and the concrete level of protection may vary, according to a variety of different circumstances.[213] On the other hand, in Dworkin's interpretative theory, it is central that the interpreter goes as deep as possible. Accordingly, as a minimum, if one holds that there is no right answer, the philosophers of indeterminacy are required to explain why.[214] The question is, therefore, rather how different legal institutions providing "final" answers should relate, respond, and be reflexive toward each other.

When we compare such general theories of how law develops with how the law of the Convention actually has developed, we notice that the Court has developed substantive norms to a considerable degree. The *first* prerequisite for developing a more reflexive Convention law is, thus, fulfilled. Indeed, we may now experience a procedural turn of Convention law – or a turn to a more responsive and reflexive law. The question then arises: What degree of responsiveness has Convention law actually arrived at, what degree should it have, and, most importantly, in this context, how could and should Article 13 contribute? In this regard, the *second* prerequisite for a more responsive law poses a problem: The quality and level of democratic procedures in the Member States vary greatly. Consequently, a more reflexive and responsive approach to Convention law might be ripe for some States, but not others. Any movement toward a more reflexive and responsive approach, including any use of Article 13 for that purpose, therefore, needs to take such differences into account. In the following and concluding chapter, it is explained how Article 13 could be an important tool to implement a more reflexive and responsive Convention law.

---

[213] Dworkin (2011) 337–338.
[214] Dworkin (2011) 94.

13

Conclusions and Recommendations

13.1 INTRODUCTION

In the world of real politics, including the law-making performed by courts, it is not useful only to call for due consideration of a large variety of factors that everyone concedes relevant without also offering some overall scheme to suggest how these factors should be weighed in a practical decision about a controversial issue.[1]

In this concluding Chapter, I offer two recommendations to the Court in Strasbourg: (1) The Court should engage in more and stricter procedural review by controlling and setting out requirements with regard to how domestic remedial authorities must consider whether the Convention has been violated. To this end, the Court should make more use of Article 13. The counterpart of the increased procedural review should be less substantive review. In short, more procedural review, less substantive review. (2) The Court should engage in more principled and abstract reasoning concerning Article 13, in particular the required form of redress. More principled and abstract reasoning stands in contrast to concreteness. It provides guidance, but allows for flexible implementation in different domestic legal systems.

A more radical shift in the use of Article 13 could be deemed to require a new Protocol.[2] But there is nothing radical in these recommendations. They require a certain development in the case law, but nothing that the Court could not do within its legal method with reference to a dynamic interpretation of the Convention seen in the light of present day circumstances and the need for establishing practical and effective rights (Section 2.4). The recommendations provide what I consider to be the best balance between different

---

[1] Dworkin (2011) 477.
[2] Helfer (2008) 135.

views on the normative and contextual factors presented in Chapter 12, seen in the light of the foregoing analyses of case law.

13.2 MORE PROCEDURAL REVIEW, LESS SUBSTANTIVE REVIEW

Procedural review is characterized by being more concerned about process, relations, and communication, than underlying substantive values, as such. Of course, procedural justice can be perceived a substantive value,[3] which is reflected in, for example, Article 6(1). The central point here, however, is not the promotion of (substantive) values underlying procedural guarantees, but the proposition that the review of the Court should focus more on how domestic remedial authorities have dealt with substantive issues, instead of the outcome of substantive issues, as such,[4] and, more concretely, illustrate how Article 13, in this regard, could play a more central role. That being said, any form of procedural review must be complemented with underlying substantive values. Indeed, it is the procedural testing of these substantive values that is in question.[5] Thus, a procedural review by the Court requires a rational domestic decision-making process, which provides evidence that the substantive criteria in the case law of the Court has been duly considered and guaranteed.[6] In this sense, the more procedural review here recommended is not a fully fledged procedural review, but a semiprocedural or mixed procedural/substantive review.[7]

The recommendation of more procedural review, less substantive review, intuitively finds most support in accounts of law and human rights which are more or less moral independent, such as different versions of legal positivism and practice-based accounts of human rights, in contrast to natural law and moral-based accounts of human rights (Section 12.2.3). Indeed, at least from the outset, legal positivism and practice-based accounts are more concerned about procedure than substance, whereas moral-based accounts promote more or less absolute substantive rights. That being said, most practice-based accounts are not blind to moral and substantive concerns, and moral-based accounts are not blind to procedure. It is, at least for most, a question of

---

[3] See, for example, Ely (1980) 75.

[4] Compare, for example, Gerards and Brems (2017) 1–2. That being said, the distinction between procedure and substance, and, accordingly, procedural and substantive review, is not always easy to draw; see, as an example, the dissenting opinion of Judge Zupancic in *Roche v. the UK* (Grand Chamber 2005).

[5] Compare Tribe (1980) 1064.

[6] Compare Popelier and Van De Heyning (2013); Spano (2018); Popelier (2019).

[7] Compare, for example, Brems (2017).

finding the right balance between procedure and substance. However, ever since the inception of the Convention, the Court has developed detailed abstract and principled reasoning concerning substantive Convention rights. What is needed in the current context is to get domestic remedial authorities truly to apply these substantive rights, instead of leaving it in the hands of the Court (Section 12.3).

The recommendation intuitively also finds more support in procedural – in contrast to substantive – conceptions of democracy, as well as procedural – in contrast to substantive – forms of judicial review (Section 12.2.4). In addition, the perceived advantages and disadvantages of domestic understandings of democracy and judicial review tend to be amplified by judicial review at international level. Indeed, even though, for most, it is not a question of either/ or, those who are more drawn toward substantive concepts of democracy and judicial review tend to find their values better protected by an independent court at international level, whereas those who argue for procedural concepts of democracy and judicial review consider the democratic deficits (within their understanding of democracy) to be amplified at international level. But as long as significant substantive principles actually have been developed, a reconciliatory middle ground may, at least to a larger extent, be to limit international review to verify procedurally whether a substantive review of a certain level has been performed domestically.

Further, at the outset, the recommendation finds most support in State-centered conceptions of subsidiarity, supported by notions of judicial economy (reduce the case load of the Court) (Section 12.2.5). However, person-centered conceptions of subsidiarity are not against improving domestic remedies. Indeed, the different versions of subsidiarity primarily differ when it comes to how the presumption that cases are best solved at national level could be rebutted and to what extent the counterpart should be a less substantive review by the Court. The recommendation here argues that decreased procedural subsidiarity (increased procedural review) must be accompanied by more substantive subsidiarity (decreased substantive review), and that this, overall, strikes the best balance in the system for the protection of human rights under the Convention.[8] Indeed, good procedures not only contribute to good results in concrete cases (process efficacy),[9] but when the Court performs a stricter procedural review, it increases the *res interpretata* effect of its substantive judgments by holding domestic remedial authorities accountable.

---

[8]   Compare, for example; Gerards (2014) 19; Bratza (2014); Spano (2014); Spano (2018).
[9]   See, for example, Christoffersen (2009) 462; Brems (2017) 19–22. That being said, Nussberger (2017) rightly points to the fact that this is not always so.

In doing so, these authorities are provided with incentives to increase substantive Convention protection at domestic level (in accordance with the case law of the Court).[10] In short, increased international procedural review should lead to increased domestic substantive protection.[11]

Notice, in this context, that the domestic substantive review must not necessarily be performed by courts and other remedial authorities.[12] Domestic remedial authorities may perform a procedural review of (substantive) decisions by the legislative and executive branch. The important aspect is that the domestic remedial authority is held accountable (by the Court) for checking and assuring that a substantive review of a satisfactory level actually has been performed.[13] More procedural review by the Court, therefore, allows for flexibility by accommodating different domestic versions of procedural and substantive democracy, as well as procedural and substantive versions of judicial review.

More procedural review finds additional support in the notion of the rule of law, in particular, the principles of legality, legal certainty, access to justice, and avoiding arbitrariness (Section 12.2.7). However, the extent to which the counterpart should be decreased substantive review is controversial and depends on the extent to which one integrates more or less absolute substantive values in the concept of the rule of law.

The recommendation is further supported by an understanding of the functions of the Court which promotes constitutional procedural justice (Section 12.2.8), which again is (primarily) supported by procedural conceptions of democracy (Section 12.2.7), State-centered conceptions of subsidiarity (Section 12.2.5), and an understanding of the relationship between international and domestic law based upon constitutional pluralism (Section 12.3.4). The recommendation is not blind to the importance of granting individual relief, but holds that individual relief must first and foremost, be provided at domestic level, and that the primary task of the Court should be to assist domestic remedial authorities in their task of providing relief.

More procedural review, less substantive review finds considerable and more unequivocal support in the current context (*Zeitgeist*) in which Convention law finds itself (Section 12.3). Indeed, whereas the fundamental normative concepts, values, and structures underlying Convention law (Section 12.2)

---

[10] See Section 2.5 and, already, Strasser (1988) 603–604, and, more recently, for example, Spielmann (2014); Bates (2016); Kartner and Meuwese (2017); Arnardóttir (2018); Spano (2018).

[11] Similarly, Spano (2018) 492.

[12] Compare, for example, Wildhaber (2002) 162; Christoffersen (2009) 529.

[13] This should alleviate the concern that the Court utilizes the procedural turn to grant domestic Parliaments illegitimate substantive discretion; see, for example, Popelier (2019).

may be conceived to point in different directions, this context stakes out a clearer path. Over the years, the Court has developed the content of substantive Articles through considerable principled and abstract reasoning and has, more recently, placed itself in a position in which it can deal with its (at least incoming) case load. Consequently, the focus may be truly directed at the improvement of the domestic protection and enforcement of human rights, to which the counterpart should be a decreased international substantive review. Indeed, in the current reform process, the improvement of domestic remedies, coupled with a more subsidiary protection of human rights, has been consistently called for. This call is supported by an understanding of the relationship between international and domestic law framed in a notion of constitutional pluralism (Section 12.3.4) and theories of how law and society develop and interact (Section 12.3.5), most notably because it promotes responsiveness between authorities which *per se* have no ultimate authority.

But how should the Court implement the recommendation? And, what role could and should Article 13 have? These questions cannot be answered without first considering other tools that the Court has at its disposal, and which could contribute to strike the balance that the recommendation claims to offer.

If the goal was solely to improve the working conditions of the Court, formal amendments to admissibility criteria and/or a stricter application of the current admissibility criteria would be sufficient. But additional formal amendments in admissibility criteria is unlikely.[14] And even though the Court could apply the current admissibility criteria in a stricter and more consistent manner, it does not solve the root cause of the problem: *First,* that violations occur in large numbers, and, *second,* that they are not remedied at national level. That being said, the Court could use the admissibility criteria (and its prioritization policy) to prioritize cases concerning domestic remedies, which could enhance the recommendations offered here.

Remedial requirements may also be promoted through the Pilot judgment procedure. But the Court often adopts remedial orders in Pilot judgments even though it does not consider whether Article 13 was violated. And, independently of whether Article 13 was an issue in the Pilot judgment, the question arises as to whether the specific (remedial) orders are relevant for the general interpretation of Article 13? The answer must depend on an interpretation of the Pilot judgment. But, as long as the remedial question is not explicitly dealt with under Article 13, it may always be claimed that the

---

[14] See, for example, Milner (2014).

remedial order in the Pilot judgment only concerns the State in question. Consequently, if the Court wants to provide precedential guidance to all States, it should do so under Article 13. On the other hand, if the Court wants to provide remedial guidance limited to the concrete State, it should use the Pilot judgment procedure (in repetitive cases) or Article 46 (in nonrepetitive cases). Under Article 13, the Court could, then, issue more general and abstract statements (guidance) with regard to domestic remedies, which could be implemented in different domestic contexts. If these are not followed up, the Court could be more concrete when applying the Pilot judgment procedure and/or Article 46.[15]

Further, and most importantly, remedial requirements may be promoted under substantive Articles. Indeed, a more general procedural turn in the (substantive) law of the Convention has, in recent years, been identified and analyzed by many.[16] This development has taken different forms.[17] *First*, the Court has applied explicit procedural requirements in a stricter manner, most notably the requirements arising under Article 6,[18] but also some of the requirements arising under Article 13, as exposed in the previous Chapters. *Second*, the Court has increasingly developed independent procedural obligations under substantive Articles, most notably in conjunction with positive obligations.[19] The most prominent example is the requirement to perform effective investigations, which has experienced a parallel development under Article 13 (Section 11.7). *Third*, the Court may award States a wider margin of appreciation under substantive Articles when States have fulfilled certain procedural guarantees and have dealt with the Convention issues in a convincing manner (performed a convincing review). Conversely, lack of procedural

---

[15] Some criticize Pilot judgments for their concreteness, *inter alia*, on the grounds that the Court is not able to take into account all the considerations necessary to adopt adequate general measures; see, for example, Christoffersen (2009) 433. But it is more problematic if the Court should issue concrete orders and remedial requirements in the framework of Article 13 because they have the potential, as precedent, to interfere with well-functioning remedial systems in other States; compare, for example, Helfer (2008) 154; Backer (2011) 193.

[16] See, for example, Helfer (2008); Christoffersen (2009) 455–522; Popelier (2012); Rui (2013); Brems and Lavrysen (2013); Popelier and Van De Heyning (2013); Brems (2014); Kavanagh (2014); Spano (2014); Saul (2015); Arnardóttir and Buyse (2016); Bates (2016); Çalı (2016); Arnardóttir (2017); Gerards and Brems (2017); Brems (2017); Gerards (2017); Huijbers (2017); Nussberger (2017); Popelier and Van De Heyning (2017); Arnardóttir (2018); Çalı (2018a); Madsen (2018); Spano (2018); Brems (2019); Cumper and Lewis (2019); Huijbers (2019); Kleinlein (2019); Popelier (2019); Madsen (2021a).

[17] For an overview and typology; see, for example, Gerards (2017).

[18] See, for example, Brems and Lavrysen (2013); Gerards (2017) 136–140.

[19] See, for example, Brems and Lavrysen (2013); Brems (2014); Lavrysen (2016); Gerards (2017); Stoyanova (2018).

guarantees and an unconvincing domestic review may intensify the Court's (substantive) review (narrower margin of appreciation).[20]

These elements are interconnected. Stricter explicit procedural guarantees and requirements may, for example, improve the quality of the domestic decision-making process, which again may grant a wider margin of appreciation.[21] But the Court may, also, more independently of explicit procedural guarantees, grant a wider margin of appreciation when domestic remedial authorities have performed a convincing review of the substantive content of Convention obligations. This is not a new phenomenon.[22] Already in 1996, the then presiding President of the Court, Rolv Ryssdal, held that, to the extent that national authorities had direct regard for the (substantive) principles applied by the Court, it would be easier for the Court to exercise restraint.[23] That being said, in later years, a more intense procedural review by the Court, often, but not always, accompanied by a more lenient substantive review has intensified and increasingly gained attention, not least because of the developing notion of subsidiarity and the current context in which Convention law finds itself (Sections 12.2.5 and 12.3).[24] A parallel development has taken place under Article 13, in the sense that the Court applies the requirement that domestic remedial authorities need be able to deal with the substance of the Convention complaint in a stricter manner (Section 10.5.4).

Few commentators question the Court's development of explicit procedural requirements.[25] But the merits of if, how, and to what extent a more intense procedural review (by the Court) should be accompanied with a wider margin of appreciation under substantive Articles is contested. Indeed, many hold that the Court primarily must strive to strike a correct substantive balance and find it problematical that a more intensive procedural review should weaken

---

[20] See, for example, Spielmann (2014a); Brems (2017); Gerards (2017) 138–140, 146–149 and 150–154; Spano (2018).

[21] See, for example, Gerards (2017) 129.

[22] Seemingly different, Brems (2017) 22; Arnardóttir (2018) 228; Çalı (2018a) 257, although Çalı limits the "new approach" to cases in which the Court previously granted a narrow margin of apreciation.

[23] Ryssdal (1996) 26–27. In a similar manner, for example, Petzold (1993); Wildhaber (2002); Spielmann (2014a); Spano (2014); Spano (2018), all providing several examples from earlier case law.

[24] Similarly, for example, Spano (2014) 492; Spano (2018) 480; Cumper and Lewis (2019) 622.

[25] But see, for example, Kosař (2017) and Nussberger (2017). In addition to arguments such as those presented above, it is, in this regard, also pointed to insight from psychological research, which shows us that people not only care about outcome, but the way in which their case is handled; see, for example, Barkhuysen and Emmerik (2008) 437; Brems and Lavrysen (2013) 177–178, and, more generally, for example, Luhmann (1983). Thus, process has intrinsic value; see, for example, Tribe (1980) 1070–1071.

the Court's substantive review.[26] Support for this view could be found in, for example, substantive versions of democracy and judicial review (Section 12.2.4), substantive versions of the rule of law (Section 12.2.7), person-centered conceptions of subsidiarity (Section 12.2.5), substantive versions of constitutional pluralism (Section 12.3.4), and, more generally, a vision of the functions of the Court which seeks to provide individual substantive justice and relief (Section 12.2.8).[27]

Others argue along similar lines which I have done above.[28] Yet, neither those who argue along such lines nor those who fear the substantive costs emphasize the role which Article 13 could and should play (or not).[29] But, clearly, Article 13 has the potential to play a more prominent role, and in some cases be the primary focus of attention, in a procedural turn which is unquestionably taking place. In the following, I illustrate how Article 13 may do this. The goal is not to map out in every detail how the approach should work, but to demonstrate how Article 13 may be an additional tool in the Court's toolbox and why this tool has advantages compared to the approaches under substantive Articles.

First, when the Court awards States a wider margin of appreciation under substantive Articles because States have fulfilled certain procedural guarantees and/or have dealt with (substantive) Convention issues in a convincing manner, it only provides States with an opportunity to receive a more subsidiary review. It is, in contrast to explicit procedural guarantees under Article 13 (see, in particular, Sections 10.3 and 11.7) and the requirement that the domestic remedial authority must be able to deal with the substance of the

---

[26] See, for example, Popelier and Van De Heyning (2013); Gerards and Brems (2017) 6 and 21; Popelier (2019).

[27] See, for example, Brems (2017) 28 (advocating a substantive version of democracy).

[28] For example, Spano (2014); Spano (2018); Kleinlein (2019). It may, also, be argued that more procedural review, less substantive review accommodates concerns regarding what has been called a human-rights inflation; see, for example, Klein (2013); that when determining the legitimacy of an institution, procedural justice is more important than substantive justice; see, for example, Tribe (1980); or, more generally, that more procedural review, less substantive review does better justice to the doctrine of separation of powers; see, for example, Gerards (2012) 197.

[29] A notable exception is Wolfgang Strasser, who, already in 1988, argued for a more principled shift toward increased use of Article 13, instead of substantive Articles; see Strasser (1988). Strasser argued that this would enhance the system of protection of human rights under the Convention because it would improve the possibility of reaching the desired result domestically and facilitate the work of the Convention organs. See, also, Greer (2006) 87, who, after going through several means which could improve domestic compliance, concludes that there are grounds to believe that judicial remedies which permit Convention standards to be effectively litigated domestically provide the best means. However, he does not explain how Article 13 could contribute.

Convention complaint (Section 10.5), not an obligation. Further, procedural remedial issues under substantive Articles, whether they concern the review performed by domestic remedial authorities or specific procedural aspects, tend to be only one of several elements which may influence the margin of appreciation.[30] This makes it hard to deduce an even indirect (precedential) obligation with regard to remedial action. A more explicit approach under Article 13 could, therefore, enhance the primary implementation obligations of States.

Second, specific procedural obligations and remedial requirements under substantive Articles, for example, the requirement to perform effective investigations, could have other underlying purposes than similar requirements under Article 13. They also tend to be part of broader assessments, for example, as part of the positive obligation, which may undercommunicate remedial goals. They are, further, mostly of a purely procedural nature – they do not include the obligation to provide redress. Consequently, if the Court truly wants to enhance the domestic remedial mission, it is important to clarify and emphasize the specific purpose(s) of Article 13 (Chapter 3), and, at the very least, apply the procedural obligations arising under Article 13 on the basis of such purposes, in addition to substantive Articles (Section 4.4).

Third, and in connection with the foregoing, Article 13 provides the Court with the possibility to perform a truly subsidiary review in the sense that, in some cases, but certainly not all, it may limit itself to consider whether the applicant was provided with an effective remedy. At the very least, if the Court in more cases applied Article 13 in the first hand and, most notably, thoroughly considered whether the domestic remedial authority was able to deal with the substance of the Convention complaint (Section 10.5), the Article 13 review could serve both as an obligation with regard to remedial action and as a firmer basis for the narrower and/or wider margin of appreciation to be granted under the substantive Article.

Although the Court now more often considers whether Article 13 has been violated, in addition to substantive Articles (Section 4.3), the Court only rarely places the primary focus on Article 13, even though the Convention is to be protected "first and foremost" at domestic level.[31] By making Article 13 a primary focus of attention, and not just an "additional guarantee", the Court

---

[30] Compare, for example, Arnardóttir (2017) 11; Gerards (2017) 145, 149, 153–154, and 159.

[31] See, for example, *Kudla* v. *Poland* (Grand Chamber 2000) para. 152; *Al-Nashif* v. *Bulgaria* (2002) para. 132; *Kuppinger* v. *Germany* (2015) para. 136; *de Tommaso* v. *Italy* (Grand Chamber 2017) para. 183. But see, for example, *Toplak and Mrak* v. *Slovenia* (2021) para. 76.

could truly turn its attention to the implementation obligations of States, instead of the discretion that the Court may award under substantive Articles.[32]

Theoretically, and on the extreme, one could foresee that the Court only tested whether Article 13 had been violated and deemed it unnecessary to consider substantive Articles, in addition to Article 13. But, this is neither possible nor acceptable.

The extent to which the approach could be deemed possible would, in the first hand, depend on the margin of appreciation granted under substantive Articles and the perceived need for (substantive) uniform solutions. Indeed, the prerequisite must be that the Court accepts some degree of pluralism with regard to substantive outcomes – that the Court actually grants a margin of appreciation under the substantive rights.[33] To the extent that no margin is granted, the Court must consider whether the substantive Article was violated.[34] In this regard, a rough distinction goes between Articles 2, 3, and 5, under which the Court, for substantive issues, grants no or close to no margin, and Articles 8 to 11, and, for example, P1 Article 1, where a wider margin may be awarded (Section 12.2.6).[35] Accordingly, the approach proposed here is primarily applicable in conjunction with such Articles. That being said, stricter procedural guarantees and/or a more intense procedural review under Article 13 may make the need for finding violations of procedural requirements under substantive Articles, including those arising under Articles 2, 3, and 5, less necessary, in particular if the recommendation of more principled and abstract reasoning concerning Article 13 is followed up (Section 13.3).[36]

The extent to which the approach is possible must further depend on how domestic remedial authorities respond to and apply the substantive requirements set out in the Court's case law. Indeed, a central assumption underlying the recommendation of more procedural review, less substantive review is that it fosters responsiveness and that this, overall, provides a better protection of human rights within the system (Sections 12.3.4 and 12.3.5). Consequently,

---

[32] Compare Christoffersen (2009) 360, who points out that "no one seems to have attempted to develop a general principle addressing the implementation obligation of the States." Christoffersen attempts to do this on a theoretical level (his principle of primarity), but without making Article 13 the primary practical tool of attention, which is my main objective here.

[33] Compare, for example, Gerards (2011) 88; Popelier (2019) 284.

[34] On the margin which may (or may not) be awarded under substantive Articles; see Section 12.2.6 and, for example, more concretely in this context, Popelier and Van De Heyning (2013) 240–244 and Spano (2018) 491–494. On newer case law from the Court emphasizing the systemic elements of the margin of appreciation; see Arnardóttir (2017).

[35] Similarly, Spano (2014) 494; Spano (2018) 483.

[36] Similarly, Spano (2018) 484.

in a similar manner as weak forms of judicial review,[37] the approach tries to get the other party to answer – to respond. To the extent that the other party responds, the Court could, in many cases, but certainly not all, limit itself to applying Article 13. But when the other party does not respond or responds in bad faith,[38] the need to apply also the substantive Article is greater.[39] The Court, therefore, needs to designate instances of bad faith implementation and application of the Convention, which must be tested concretely, also in cases concerning States who normally are on the receiving end of good faith implementations.[40] Two examples may illustrate how the approach could work in practice.

On the one hand, take the case of *E.S. v. Austria* (2018). Domestic courts found the applicant guilty of publicly disparaging Muhammad, the Prophet of Islam, in several seminars at a right-wing education institute. The applicant was imposed a fine of Euro 480. The Court examined whether the fine violated Article 10 by first repeating its previous case law concerning Article 10. Thereafter, the Court considered how the domestic remedial authorities had considered this and concluded that "the domestic courts comprehensively assessed the wider context of the applicant's statements, and carefully balanced her right to freedom of expression with the rights of others to have their religious feelings protected and to have religious peace preserved in Austrian society."[41] The domestic courts did, therefore, not overstep their wide margin of appreciation when imposing the fine. Accordingly, Article 10 had not been violated. But the Court could have performed a similar exercise under Article 13 by considering whether the domestic remedial authority dealt with the substance of the Convention complaint (Section 10.5.4) and concluded that Article 13 had not been violated and that it, therefore, in this case, was not necessary to examine whether also Article 10 had been violated. Alternatively, the Court could have concluded that neither Article 13 nor Article 10 had been violated, but with a primary reference to the considerations under Article 13 and the consequences this had for the margin of appreciation under Article 10.

Conversely, take the case of *OOO Ivpress a.o. v. Russia* (2013). Domestic courts found, in defamation procedures, that several newspaper articles

---

[37] See, for example, Tushnet (2009) in his Chapter 3 and Sathanapally (2012).

[38] See, for example, Çalı (2021); Harutyunyan (2021).

[39] Similarly, Spano (2018).

[40] Similarly, Ulfstein (2020). Such a distinction is present in the substantive case law of the Court in the sense that the Court may award "good faith" interpretations and applications a wider margin of appreciation, whereas "bad faith" interpretations and applications a narrower margin; see Çalı (2018a). See, also, Demir-Gürsel (2021) 129.

[41] *E.S. v. Austria* (2018) para. 57.

violated the honor and reputation of several companies and persons. The applicants had to pay damages and complained to the Court that the newspaper articles were within their freedom of expression. The Court examined whether Article 10 had been violated by first pointing to that there was "no evidence in the domestic judgments that the courts performed a balancing exercise between the need to protect the plaintiffs' reputation and journalists' right to divulge information on issues of general interest."[42] The Court, thereafter, referred to that it on numerous occasions "had pinpointed the structural deficiency of the Russian law on defamation which made no distinction between value judgments and statements of fact." Although some progress had been made on a legislative level, the domestic courts had not taken this distinction sufficiently into account.[43] Article 10 was, therefore, violated. The Court did not explicitly refer to any margin of appreciation, but, clearly, the lack of and false premises in the scrutiny of domestic courts affected the Court's substantive review. Indeed, the review leaves no trace of any margin of appreciation. But, the Court could have started by examining whether the domestic courts were able to deal with the substance of the Convention complaint (Section 10.5.4) and concluded that Article 13 had been violated. In doing so, the Court would have held the domestic courts directly and explicitly responsible for the insufficient review. However, in contrast to *E.S.* v. *Austria* (2018), the Court would need to find a violation of also Article 10. The substantive violation was clear and the State in question, including the remedial authorities, had shown little willingness to adapt to and respond to the Court's previous substantive case law.

Such an approach would have similarities with the Court's Bosphorus-doctrine,[44] which regulates the relationship between the protection of human rights within the Convention system and the EU, and under which the Court presumes that the EU, in principle, provides "equivalent" protection of human rights to that under the Convention.[45] Any measure adopted by an EU Member State, in fulfillment of its obligations under EU law, under the supervision of the ECJ, is, therefore, compatible with the Convention unless a "manifest deficiency" is apparent.[46] In a similar manner, the approach proposed here, at the outset, presumes that domestic remedial authorities have

---

[42] *OOO Ivpress a.o.* v. *Russia* (2013) para. 71.

[43] Ibid. paras. 73–78.

[44] Primarily developed in *Bosphorus Hava Yolları Turizm ve Ticaret Anonim Şirketi* v. *Ireland* (Grand Chamber 2005). Compare, in this sense, Arnardóttir (2017) 34.

[45] *Bosphorus Hava Yolları Turizm ve Ticaret Anonim Şirketi* v. *Ireland* (Grand Chamber 2005) para. 155.

[46] Ibid., para. 156.

provided "equivalent" protection, to the extent that they have provided effective remedies (according to the requirements of Article 13). Accordingly, the crux of the issue then turns to both ascertain and improve the quality of the presumption (the domestic remedies) and clarify when and how the presumption may be rebutted (even though effective domestic remedies have been provided).[47]

If we, then, in the light of the previous analyses of case law, consider how the presumption could be secured and improved, the most important aspect is that the Court must take a more principled stand with regard to the review required by the domestic remedial authority under Article 13 (Section 10.5).[48] Indeed, the Court must *first* require that the applicant, in some manner, be able to challenge primary legislation that violates the Convention before domestic remedial authorities (Section 10.5.3) and *second* actually test whether the remedial authority, in good faith, dealt with the substance of the arguable Convention complaint (Section 10.5.4).[49] In doing so, the Court must distinguish and test separately whether the domestic remedial authority (1) dealt with the relevant facts in a satisfactory manner, (2) tested all the relevant (substantive) Convention criteria and principles in a satisfactory manner, most notably the assessment of proportionality, and (3) did so with sufficient intensity (scrutiny).[50] However, the presumption and, accordingly, the more procedural review proposed, need to be further ascertained:[51]

First, the Court must, in many cases, make use of Article 13 *ex-officio.*[52]

Second, the Court must remove the linkage between the international admissibility criterion "manifestly ill-founded" and the requirement of arguability (Chapter 7).

Third, the Court must clarify the purposes of the required remedy (Chapter 3) and the concrete elements that may influence the relevant standard of effectiveness (Chapter 8).

Fourth, the Court must make a more principled change with regard to how an aggregate of remedies may satisfy Article 13, in accordance with the development already visible in the case law (Section 9.3). In particular, the

---

47 Compare Arnardóttir (2017); Popelier (2019).
48 Compare Keller and Sweet (2008a) 700–701.
49 Compare, for example, Brems (2017) 34. In this sense, the approach may alleviate concerns that only formal issues are tested; see, for example, Brems (2019) 222–223.
50 On these grounds, the domestic review in, for example, the much criticized *Animal Defenders International* v. *the UK* (Grand Chamber (2013), and, accordingly, the Court's lacking review of the domestic review, may be criticized; compare, for example, Popelier (2019).
51 See, for a similar argument, more generally, not linked to Article 13, Brems (2019).
52 Similarly, Strasser (1988) 602.

applicant should not need to initiate several procedures in order to receive access to justice.

Fifth, the Court needs to clarify its use of the requirement that the remedy needs be effective in practice and law, in particular how it relates to the required prospect of success (Sections 9.4 and 10.6). Indeed, even though there has been some development in the case law, the Court still accepts, at least in many cases, that if the remedy is effective in theory, and there is no systemic or structural malfunctioning, the right to an effective remedy has not been violated. The approach proposed here requires that the Court condemns also single procedural mistakes under Article 13, most notably that it actually tests whether the remedial authority dealt with the substance of the arguable Convention complaint (Section 10.5.4), but does not necessarily require a successful outcome (that redress is actually granted).

Sixth, the Court must clarify what competences the national authority needs to have, including the procedural safeguards that it must offer (Sections 10.2 and 10.3). To this end, Article 13 needs to be developed independently of Article 6.

If we, then, turn to the task of clarifying how the reinforced presumption may be rebutted, we may be assisted by the critique from the authors who argue against providing a wider margin of appreciation under substantive Articles on the basis of the quality of the domestic review.

Most notably, the Court (still) needs to be sensitive to unfair outcomes.[53] But remember that the very existence of a margin of appreciation, even when it is to be narrow, presupposes a certain degree of pluralism, which accepts different solutions to similar questions.[54] In this sense, the warning against unjustified double standards is misplaced.[55] Indeed, at least if Article 13 is taken as starting-point, in the manner proposed, it is rather a question of examining whether clear (and more stringent) procedural obligations, on the basis of objective factors, are violated.[56] That being said, any human right protects a minimum (substantive) standard. If the Court suspects that the minimum standard has been violated, it must take a stand on the substantive issue.[57] But the approach allows for additional flexibility in the sense that if the Court judges the substantive outcome unreasonable,[58] even if the Court finds no

---

[53] See, for example, Brems (2017).
[54] Similarly, for example, Spano (2014) 491.
[55] For example, Huijbers (2017) 198–199; Popelier (2019).
[56] Compare Spano (2014) 499.
[57] Compare, for example, *Selami a.o.* v. *FYROM* (2018) para. 101.
[58] Compare, for example, Gerards (2012) 198; Huijbers (2017) 196–197; Spano (2018) 488. See, also, Gyorfi (2019).

violation of Article 13 after a more stringent review, the Court could still examine whether the substantive Article was violated. That being said, if the Court, after having applied the more intensive review here proposed, were to intervene on every occasion in which it felt that national remedial authorities had not found the right (substantive) balance, we would be back to the start. Indeed, subsidiarity is not a one-way street.[59]

The approach can neither be applied at the cost of necessary standard setting under substantive Articles.[60] But remember that most of the Court's cases concern the application of substantive principles that are well established. It could even be argued that fewer substantive judgments could contribute to making the substantive case law more consistent and better reasoned. In any case, what primarily needs to be developed in the current context is the obligation to implement and apply the Convention correctly at domestic level, and, in the case that violations occur, redress these violations at home.

Certainly, if the Court were to include Article 13 in its toolbox and apply it in the manner here proposed, further work on how to improve the quality of the presumption (how to develop Article 13) and how to rebut it would need to be undertaken.[61] The main goal here has been to introduce the basic idea and provide the Court with an additional tool that can contribute to strike the balance that the recommendation of more procedural review, less substantive review claims to offer.

13.3 MORE PRINCIPLED AND ABSTRACT REASONING

Usually, courts provide binding judgments and decisions containing reasons. Indeed, providing reasons is an essential aspect of legal culture.[62] It is a necessary condition for rationality, and a prerequisite for understanding legal decisions.[63] How judges provide reasons could be affected by a number of factors, not least how the functions of the court in question are perceived.[64]

When courts, and any other institution or individual for this sake, provide reasons, they generalize. Reasons are propositions that contain greater

---

[59] Kumm (2004) 922.
[60] See, for example, Brems (2017).
[61] Compare Arnardóttir (2017) 35.
[62] See, for example, Schauer (1995) and, more specifically with regard to the Convention, Letsas (2006) 709.
[63] See, for example, Opinion no. 11 (2008) of the Consultative Council of European Judges (CCJE) to the attention of the Committee of Ministers of the Council of Europe on the quality of judicial decisions para. 32.
[64] See, for example, Pedersen (2016) 20.

generality than the conclusions for which they are reasons. On the other end of the scale is particularity, or the concrete facts of the case. Therefore, when reasons are given, the very particularity of the case is transcended.[65]

In a democratic system, generality pertains to the field of the legislator, whereas the executive and the courts handle individual cases. Unclear and vague rules are often criticized for being undemocratic because they leave too much to be decided by others.[66] Notwithstanding this, faced with open-ended provisions, courts must make law. But court made law may be more or less based upon principled reasoning, or more or less connected to the specific facts of the case (Fig. 13.1).

The main advantage with principled reasoning is that it establishes general rules, which may create predictability for the future.[67] It may also be easier to accept equality on the interpretation of a principled rule, than by accepting that the case distinguishes itself on one out of ten factual circumstances.[68] Principled reasoning may also reduce the likelihood of arbitrary or discriminatory decisions by judges.[69] The major argument against principled reasoning is that it may unduly bind up future authority, not only that of courts sticking to precedent, but that of legislators, especially if it is difficult to amend open-ended provisions, which is the case with international human-rights provisions. The danger for unwanted results arises, in particular, because principled reasoning may build on an imperfect scope of materials (the case in hand) and because it is difficult to predict the future.[70] The trick is, therefore, to carry general principles only as far as they can go.[71] Engaging in principled reasoning may also be time-consuming.

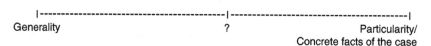

Generality   ?   Particularity/
                                                               Concrete facts of the case

FIGURE 13.1 *Level of principled reasoning*

---

[65] Schauer (1995) 638, 641.
[66] See, for example, Scalia (1989) 1176; Maduro (2009) 362.
[67] See, for example, Scalia (1989) 1179; Strauss (2008) 997. That being said, Scalia and Strauss disagree with regard to how courts should be principled.
[68] Scalia (1989) 1178. See, also, *Taxquet* v. *Belgium* (Grand Chamber 2010) para. 91.
[69] Strauss (2008) 998.
[70] See, for example, Schauer (2006) 897; Strauss (2008) 1003. Some claim that judges are mesmerized by the case before them and, therefore, do not attach sufficient weight to other competing concerns (availability heuristics); see, for example, Schauer (2006) 894–896. Principled reasoning may, therefore, unduly affect fields of law that function well; see, for example, Schauer (2006) 906–908. Bluntly put, it fixes that what does not need to be repaired.
[71] Scalia (1989) 1183.

The arguments for and against case-by-case–based reasoning, limiting one-self to the facts of the case, are the same as the arguments for and against principled reasoning, but with reversed signs. Thus, case-by-case–based precedent offers less predictability, at least outside the facts of the case in hand, and may produce additional cases, but offers flexibility as it does not bind up future authority to the same extent.[72] Further, the case-by-case approach does not promote unity, since differences may develop between States, in particular, because variances between States are a ground for distinguishing cases.[73]

That being said, principled reasoning may be performed in different manners. A rough distinction goes between clearly defined rules, in contrast to broad and less determinate principles,[74] or, put in another manner, strict rules or categorical approaches versus principled standards.[75] The debate on where to draw the line between such approaches has been central in both European and US legal systems.[76] Strict rules tend to provide the greatest predictability, whereas principled standards leave more discretion in the hands of judges,[77] albeit a discretion, which needs to be grounded in the application of background principles or policies.[78]

In short, the Court may develop precedent in at least three different manners: (1) Concrete but not principled, *i.e.*, strictly case-by-case–based reasoning limited to the facts of the case; (2) Principled and abstract, *i.e.*, the standard approach, not clearly defined rules; and (3) Principled and concrete, *i.e.*, clearly defined rules.

The Court primarily adheres to strict case-by-case–based reasoning. For instance, in *Young, James and Webster* v. *the UK* (Plenary 1981) the Court held, more generally:

in proceedings originating in an individual application, it has, without losing sight of the general context, to confine its attention as far as possible to the issues raised by the concrete case before it.[79]

Indeed, some claim that the case-by-case–based reasoning is one of the most distinctive characters of the Court's case law.[80] However, at least in

---

[72] See, for example, Scalia (1989) 1177; Gerards (2008) 420.
[73] See, for example, Scalia (1989) 1179, with explicit reference to the federal US system.
[74] Schauer (2006) 888.
[75] See, for example, Greene (2010) 1289.
[76] In the United States, for example, Scalia (1989) and Strauss (2008), and in Europe, for example, Jürgen Habermas and Robert Alexy, for instance, as accounted for and transcribed to the context of the Convention, in Greer (2004).
[77] See, for example, Strauss (2008) 1006.
[78] See, for example, Greene (2010) 1289.
[79] Para. 53.
[80] Gerards (2008) 419.

newer case law concerning substantive Articles, the Court has developed more principled reasoning based upon coherence and predictability.[81] This development builds on the realization that it is difficult for domestic judges and authorities to decide fundamental rights cases based upon the case-by-case precedent, in particular, when the numbers are growing.[82] That being said, the case load seems to have reduced the amount of reasoning provided in the Court's judgments.[83] And many question the quality of the Court's reasoning, more generally.[84]

Further, even though the case law of the Court primarily has been case-by-case based, it has been incremental, in particular, through the use of analogy. This has significantly expanded the scope of Convention rights and is one reason for the Court's case load problem.[85] With regard to substantive Articles, the case law of the Court has, therefore, provided considerable content. However, this has mostly happened without presenting clear and principled (abstract) meaning of the fundamental rights at stake.[86] This incremental step-by-step approach, which lacks a clear aim and direction, has been criticized, in particular, because it may unconsciously lead the judge to a place where he did not want to be, or to outcomes that the judge would not have reached if he had been able to foresee the consequences.[87] Further, the original justification for the case-by-case approach was deference toward States: The Court should not engage in broad questions of policy with uncertain consequences.[88] However, with the enormous case load, it may be questioned to what extent this justification sticks. Consequently, many have argued that the Court needs to move away from "patchwork case law" when it finds itself confronted with questions of principle.[89]

More concretely, although there has been a certain development, the case law concerning Article 13 has been very case specific. This makes it difficult to deduce general criteria and, for all practical purposes, provides a low threshold for satisfying the different requirements of Article 13 (Section 2.3).[90]

---

[81] See, for a general statement, for example, *Karner v. Austria* (2003) para. 26.
[82] Gerards (2008) 427.
[83] Brems and Lavrysen (2013) 186.
[84] See, for example, Gerards (2008); Barkhuysen and Emmerik (2008) 443.
[85] Gerards (2012) 178–182.
[86] This is a general problem in interpretations of fundamental rights which rely on analogical reasoning by using precedent; see, for example, Sunstein (1996) in his Chapter 3.
[87] Gerards (2012) 183.
[88] See, for example, Mahoney (1990) 77.
[89] See, for example, the dissenting opinion of Judge Bonello in *Al-Skeini a.o. v. the UK* (Grand Chamber 2011) and the dissenting opinion of Judge Pinto de Albuquerque in *Centre for Legal Resources on behalf of Valentin Câmpeanu v. Romania* (Grand Chamber 2014).
[90] Compare, for example, Kilpatrick (2000) 24.

Further, the development of Article 13 has primarily gone in the direction of what I call principled concreteness, for instance, in more and more (concrete) scenarios, demanding effective investigations and compensation for nonpecuniary damages. The recommendation of more principled and abstract reasoning, in particular concerning redress, recommends that the Court departs from both the case-by-case approach and the emerging trend of principled concreteness concerning Article 13.

More principled and abstract reasoning, in particular concerning redress, builds on a conception of rights which holds that rights, including Article 13, need a certain degree of specification in order to be effectively claimed, and, accordingly, a clear duty identified (Section 12.2.2). Indeed, a claim of a right is incomplete until it is spelled out what it means for a certain right to be fulfilled and enjoyed.[91] In many aspects, Article 13, as currently construed and applied by the Court, lacks such clarity, in particular with regard to the required redress.

More principled and abstract reasoning is supported by a vision of the Court which develops precedent not only to solve individual cases but to safeguard and develop the system of protection of human rights setup under the Convention (Sections 12.2.8 and 2.5). Indeed, in order to be effectively complied with, and to have the potential to function as precedent, judicial opinions need sufficient clarity.[92] Domestic authorities commonly consider the Convention inapplicable, or give national concerns primacy, if the rights in the Convention (as understood in the practice of the Court) are not sufficiently specific and determinate.[93] However, it is not necessarily the lack of concreteness that is the problem, but the lack of principled and abstract reasoning, which provides domestic institutions little to build (concreteness) on. What is needed is, therefore, to build precedent which provides guidance to a variety of different States on how to achieve effective domestic remedies. In fact, the reason why the Convention's position in many domestic systems remains weak is, at least partly, the Court's narrow interpretation of Article 13.[94]

More principled and abstract reasoning, seen in conjunction with the recommendation of more procedural and less substantive review, aim to square substantive versions of democracy and judicial review with procedural versions (Section 12.2.4). In fact, the prerequisite for the more procedural review

---

91 Etinson (2013) 464.
92 Compare Huneeus (2014) 448; Letwin (2021) 129–132.
93 Christoffersen (2009) 544.
94 Some also claim that this has contributed to the Court's case load; see, for example, Christoffersen (2009) 362.

recommended is not only sufficiently developed substantive rights but sufficiently developed principled and abstract reasoning concerning Article 13.
Only in this manner may the Court truly check whether the requirements
of Article 13 have been fulfilled. Indeed, it is justification and reasoning that
allows us to control and legitimize judicial power,[95] and it is justification that
allows the Court to extend the effects of its judgments and decisions to the
Member States. It is, thus, the justification that allows the Court's judgments
to be one of several elements that contribute to finding the proper balance
between legitimate powers, which is essential in a democracy. Hence, if the
Court wants to influence and strengthen domestic democratic processes, it
must justify, and it must do so in a manner that is understandable and can be
responded to.

This leads us to the current context of Convention law (Section 12.3), which
lends considerable support not only to the recommendation of more procedural review but to that of more principled and abstract reasoning. Indeed,
whereas the Court had few incentives to develop Article 13 in early years,
what is needed, and what is called for, in the current situation, is the improvement of the domestic implementation and enforcement of the Convention,
in particular, domestic remedial systems. In addition, subsidiarity, at least as
understood in the process of the reform of the Court and the Convention
system, aims to relieve the international order of some of its legitimatory burden by transferring the burden to the domestic level.[96] The Court, therefore,
needs to enable, encourage, and oblige national courts and tribunals to take
the relevant principles of the Convention into account.[97] The Convention
system, including the Court, must, indeed, support States in fulfilling their
primary responsibility to implement the Convention at national level.[98] The
recommendation here holds that the Court should do this by providing clarity
through principled and abstract reasoning concerning Article 13.

Further, the recommendation of more principled and abstract reasoning
finds considerable support in constitutional pluralism and modern theories of
how law and society interact, most notably by holding that modern law must
be responsive and reflexive (Sections 12.3.4 and 12.3.5).[99] But in order to achieve
this, not only is real political will (at domestic level) required to put Article 13
into real use,[100] but guidance from the Court. This guidance is best provided

[95] Bogdandy and Venzke (2011) 986. See, also, more generally, for example, Habermas (1998).
[96] Compare Venzke (2012a) 245.
[97] Compare the Brighton Declaration para. 9 *litra* c(iv).
[98] See Article 1 ECHR and, for example, the Brighton Declaration para. 32.
[99] This is, also, central in the dialogical approach in Roach (2021).
[100] Compare Boillat (2009b) 22.

by being principled and abstract. Such purposeful reasoning through general and abstract principles promotes dialectical interactions (rather than purely hierarchical interactions),[101] and is adaptable to a variety of different domestic settings. This stands in contrast to principled concreteness, which provides one answer for all.

Certainly, the more principled and abstract reasoning here proposed could be controversial, in particular, because it requires development in the Court's case law. Such development, independently of whether it relates to substantive or procedural norms, is almost *per se* criticized by many and under different headings.[102] The Court is, also, reluctant to interfere with the constitutional arrangements of States.[103] However, even if both more procedural review and more principled and abstract reasoning require development in the case law, and hold that the gauntlet must be picked up at domestic level, it does not say by whom, or how. Indeed, the Court should refrain from imposing such arrangements *per se* because the Court is not formally embedded in a responsive political system.[104] Accordingly, what the Court should do, in particular concerning the redress required by Article 13, is to develop more general and abstract principles, and procedurally test how these principles are implemented domestically.[105] Thus, more principled and abstract reasoning is a prerequisite for the more procedural review recommended.[106] If so followed up, the Court's judgments concerning Article 13 may "generate democratic potential" by advancing public discourse on judicial decisions, and inform and guide future practice at domestic level.[107] In this sense, the greatest benefit is not necessarily that more principled and abstract reasoning accommodates for a more procedural review by the Court, but that it is an incentive for domestic authorities, including domestic remedial authorities, to perform their functions.[108] The Court may thus "directly engage national justice systems, cultivating them into compliant partners."[109] To this end, more principled and abstract reasoning, as the procedural turn, must allow for differences between States in the application and procedural testing of these principles.

---

[101] Compare Martinez (2003) 493; Bogdandy and Venzke (2011a); O'Boyle (2014) 102–103 and, more generally, Luhmann (1993) 159.

[102] See, for example, Mahoney (1990); Popovic (2008).

[103] See, for example, Ioannidis (2011) 662.

[104] Bogdandy and Venzke (2011) 993.

[105] Similarly, Hampson (2010) 157, 161–163. See, also, for example, Buyse (2008) 143.

[106] Compare, more generally, Gerards (2012) 197–199.

[107] Bogdandy and Venzke (2011a) 1349.

[108] See, for example, Fletcher (1982) 696.

[109] Huneeus (2011) 494, 495.

More principled and abstract reasoning could, also, be a tool for building an orderly relationship with the rule on the exhaustion of domestic remedies (Chapter 5). Indeed, because the exhaustion rule does not require every remedy to be exhausted, the Court is reluctant to examine nonexhausted remedies, under Article 13. To put it somewhat imprecisely, the substantive problem may be exhausted, but not the remedial. For instance, in torture cases, litigants are mostly able to fulfill the requirement of the exhaustion of domestic remedies, without having exhausted the possibility of obtaining substantive redress in the form of, for example, compensation. Thus, the victim may obtain a remedy at international level, but the Court is inhibited in its capacity to inquire into the broader deficiencies in remedies for torture at national level.[110] As a consequence, at least in such cases, if the Court wants to send a signal to the domestic level concerning domestic remedies, it needs to do so in a principled and abstract manner, in contrast to case-specific and concrete-principled approaches.

Intuitively, the case load and, implicitly, the work load of the Court seem to be counter arguments against more principled and abstract reasoning. However, once the principled and abstract reasoning is performed, it must not, and should not, be performed anew in every case. The Court, most notably the Grand Chamber, need only set out the abstract principles and, in subsequent cases, (procedurally) test to what extent these principles have been implemented.[111]

In concrete, and taking the previous analyses of case law into consideration, the more principled and abstract reasoning should, at the very least, provide the following.

First, the Court must take a more principled stand on the purposes Article 13 is to promote (Chapter 3). The case law indicates that the primary purpose of domestic redress is to correct injustice, but that individual and/or general deterrence may be of relevance. It is, however, unclear what the correction of justice must aim at, and consist of, and when, and if so, to what extent, individual and/or general deterrence must be of relevance. The Court's case law concerning compensation (Section 11.5) is particularly illustrative. It is, further, unclear if, and to what extent, domestic remedies must accommodate other purposes, such as, for example, establish accountability and truth (Sections 11.7.4 and 11.7.5). In short, the Court must clarify the "very essence" of Article 13. In doing so, the Court must, also, clarify the relationship between Article 13 and similar

---

[110] McGregor (2012) 744–745.
[111] Compare, in this regard, the German *"Effizienzprinzip"* as part of the *"Rechtsstaatsprinzip"*; see, for example, Brink (1999) 72.

remedial and procedural requirements arising under substantive Articles, for example, the requirement of effective investigations (Section 11.7). By taking a more principled and abstract stand on the purposes which Article 13 is to serve, seen in conjunction with the recommended procedural turn, the domestic authorities, including domestic remedial authorities, are obliged to justify how their domestic remedies accommodate these purposes. The Court could, then, limit itself to reviewing to what extent the domestic solution sufficiently accommodates the purposes, but without necessarily specifying the alternative. The domestic authorities would, then, be provided more deference than the specific path (clearly defined rules) that the Court has embarked on, most notably by requiring compensation for nonpecuniary damages in more and more situations (Section 11.5).

Second, the Court must take a more principled stand on to what extent major forms of redress are required, but without specifying how these forms must be implemented. The Court should, thereto, distinguish more explicitly between what is required to prevent violations, end ongoing violations, and redress past violations (Section 11.3).[112] Seen from the perspective of the applicant, and against the backdrop of, *inter alia*, the general rules on State responsibility, it is more important to end ongoing violations, than to redress past violations. However, the Court has never, under Article 13, set out the principled starting-point that ongoing violations must be ended (Section 11.3.4). Further, with regard to past violations, the Court has never, under Article 13, emphasized a preference for restitution, in contrast to compensation, such as, for example, the general rules on State responsibility (Sections 11.4 and 11.5). The practice of the Court rather goes in the opposite direction, emphasizing the need to award and make available compensation in more and more situations. Moreover, at international level, the declaratory judgment is the main form of redress. However, under Article 13, the Court has never promoted declaratory relief as a primary form of redress (Section 11.2). But also the specific forms of redress, that the Court has required, need more principled and abstract justification, in order to enable domestic remedial authorities truly to implement such requirements, most notably the requirements of effective investigations (Section 11.7) and compensation (Section 11.5).

---

[112] This is, also, central in Roach (2021).

Bibliography

Adams and van der Schyff (2006)	Adams, Maurice and Gerhard van der Schyff, 'Constitutional Review by the Judiciary in the Netherlands', *Zeitschrift für ausländisches öffentliches Recht*, Vol. 66 (2006), 399–413.
Akçay (2009)	Akçay, Deniz, 'A Reminder of the Main Elements of the Reforms Agreed by the Committee of Ministers, Speech at the Colloquy Organized under the Swedish Chairmanship of the Committee of Ministers of the Council of Europe, "Towards Stronger Implementation of the European Convention on Human Rights at National Level", Stockholm, 9–10 June 2008', in: *Reforming the European Convention on Human Rights. A Work in Progress*, Council of Europe (ed.), Council of Europe Publishing, 2009, 477–481.
Alter, Helfer *et al.* (2016)	Alter, Karen J., Laurence R. Helfer and Mikael Rask Madsen, 'How Context Shapes Authority of International Courts', *Law and Contemporary Problems*, Vol. 79 (2016), 1–36.
Amerasinghe (2004)	Amerasinghe, Chittharanjan Felix, *Local Remedies in International Law*, Cambridge University Press, 2004.
Ando (2013)	Ando, Nisuke, 'National Implementation and Interpretation', in: *The Oxford Handbook of International Human Rights Law*, Dinah Shelton (ed.), Oxford University Press, 2013, 698–718.
Andresen, Boasson *et al.* (2012)	Andresen, Steinar, Elin Lerum Boasson and Geir Hønneland, 'An International Environmental Policy Takes Shape', in: *International Environmental Agreements: An Introduction*, Steinar Andresen, Elin Lerum and Geir Hønneland (eds.), Routledge, 2012, 3–19.
Antkowiak (2001–2002)	Antkowiak, Thomas M., 'Truth as Right and Remedy in International Human Rights Experience', *Michigan Journal of International Law*, Vol. 23 (2001–2002), 977–1006.
Antkowiak (2008)	Antkowiak, Thomas M., 'Remedial Approaches to Human Rights Violations: The Inter-American Court of Human Rights and Beyond', *Columbia Journal of Transnational Law*, Vol. 46 (2008), 351–419.

Antkowiak (2011)	Antkowiak, Thomas M., 'An Emerging Mandate for International Courts: Victim Centered Remedies and Restorative Justice', *Stanford Journal of International Law*, Vol. 47 (2011), 279–332.
Arnardóttir (2016)	Arnardóttir, Oddný Mjöll, 'Rethinking the Two Margins of Appreciation', *European Constitutional Law Review*, Vol. 12 (2016), 27–53.
Arnardóttir (2017)	Arnardóttir, Oddný Mjöll, 'The "Procedural Turn" under the European Convention on Human Rights and Presumptions of Convention Compliance', *International Journal of Constitutional Law*, Vol. 15 (2017), 9–35.
Arnardóttir (2018)	Arnardóttir, Oddný Mjöll, 'The Brighton Aftermath and the Changing Role of the European Court of Human Rights', *Journal of International Dispute Settlement*, Vol. 9 (2018), 223–239.
Arnardóttir and Buyse (2016)	Arnardóttir, Odný Mjöll and Antoine Buyse (eds.), *Shifting Centers of Gravity in Human Rights Protection. Rethinking Relations between the ECHR, EU and National Legal Orders*, Routledge, 2016.
Arold (2010)	Arold, Nina-Louisa, 'The Melting Pot or the Salad Bowl Revisited – Rendezvous of Legal Cultures at the European Court of Human Rights', in: *Rendezvous of European Legal Cultures*, Jørn Øyrehagen Sunde and Knut Einar Skodvin (eds.), Fagbokforlaget, 2010, 61–76.
Ashworth (2013)	Ashworth, Andrew and Jeremy Horder, *Principles of Criminal Law*, Seventh Edition, Oxford University Press, 2013.
Backer (2011)	Backer, Inge Lorange, 'Definition und Entwicklung der Menschenrechte im internationalen Kontext und Volkssouveränität', in: *Menschenrechte und Volkssouveränität in Europa: Gerichte als Vormund der Demokratie?*, Gret Haller, Klaus Günther and Ulfrid Neumann (eds.), Campus, 2011, 187–196.
Barak (2016)	Barak, Aharon, 'On Judging', in: *Judges as Guardians of Constitutionalism and Human Rights*, Martin Scheinin, Helle Krunke and Marina Aksenova (eds.), Edward Elgar Publishing, 2016, 27–49.
Bårdsen (1999)	Bårdsen, Arnfinn, *Krenkelser og klager: vilkårene for realitetsbehandling av private klager ved Den europeiske menneskerettighetsdomstolen*, Universitetsforlaget, 1999.
Barkhuysen (1998)	Barkhuysen, Tom, *Artikel 13 EVRM: Effectieve nationale rechtsbescherming bij schending van mensenrechten* (thesis Leiden University), Koninklijke Vermande, 1998.

Barkhuysen and Emmerik (2008)   Barkhuysen, Tom and Michiel van Emmerik, 'Legitimacy of European Court of Human Rights Judgments: Procedural Aspects', in: *The Legitimacy of the Highest Courts' Rulings: Judicial Deliberations and Beyond*, Nick Huls, Maurice Adams and Jacco Bomhoff (eds.), Springer, 2008, 437–450.

Bates (2010)   Bates, Ed, *The Evolution of the European Convention on Human Rights: From Its Inception to the Creation of a Permanent Court of Human Rights*, Oxford University Press, 2010.

Bates (2013)   Bates, Ed, 'The Birth of the European Convention on Human Rights – and the European Court of Human Rights', in: *The European Court of Human Rights between Law and Politics*, Paperback Edition, Jonas Christoffersen and Mikael Rask Madsen (eds.), Oxford University Press, 2013, 17–42.

Bates (2016)   Bates, Ed, 'Activism and Self-Restraint: The Margin of Appreciation's Strasbourg Career ... Its "Coming of Age"?', *Human Rights Law Review*, Vol. 36 (2016), 261–276.

Bates (2021)   Bates, Ed, 'Strasbourg's Integrationist Role, or the Need for Self-restraint?', *European Convention on Human Rights Law Review*, Vol. 1 (2021), 14–21.

Beitz (2009)   Beitz, Charles R., *The Idea of Human Rights*, Oxford University Press, 2009.

Békés (1998)   Békés, Imre, 'L'Article 13', in: *The Birth of European Human Rights Law: Liber Amicorum Carl Aage Nørgaard*, Michelle de Salvia and Mark E. Villiger (eds.), Nomos, 1998, 25–29.

Bellamy (2014)   Bellamy, Richard, 'The Democratic Legitimacy of International Human Rights Conventions: Political Constitutionalism and the European Convention on Human Rights', *European Journal of International Law*, Vol. 25 (2014), 1019–1042.

Bellamy (2014a)   Bellamy, Richard, 'The Democratic Legitimacy of International Human Rights Conventions: Political Constitutionalism and the Hirst Case', in: *The Legitimacy of International Human Rights Regimes: Legal, Political and Philosophical Perspectives*, Andreas Føllesdal, Johan Schaffer Karlsson and Geir Ulfstein (eds.), Cambridge University Press, 2014, 243–271.

Benhabib (2011)   Benhabib, Seyla, *Dignity in Adversity: Human Rights in Troubled Times*, Polity Press, 2011.

Bernt (2002)   Bernt, Jan Fridthjof, 'Hvorfor skal vi bry oss om prejudikater?', in: *Rettsteori og rettsliv: Festskrift til Carsten Smith til 70-årsdagen 13. juli 2002*, Peter Lødrup, Steinar Tjomsland, Magnus Aarbakke and Gunnar Aasland (eds.), Universitetsforlaget, 2002, 81–96.

Besson (2009) Besson, Samantha, 'Whose Constitution(s)? International Law, Constitutionalism, and Democracy', in: *Ruling the World? Constitutionalism, International Law, and Global Governance*, Jeffrey L. Dunoff and Joel P. Trachtman (eds.), Cambridge University Press, 2009, 381–408.

Besson (2011) Besson, Samantha, 'Das Menschenrecht auf Demokratie – Eine moralische Verteidigung mit einer rechtlichen Nuance', in: *Menschenrechte und Volkssouveränität in Europa, Gerichte als Vormund der Demokratie?*, Gret Haller, Klaus Günther and Ulfried Neumann (eds.), Campus, 2011, 61–101.

Besson (2011a) Besson, Samantha, 'European human rights, supranational judicial review and democracy. Thinking outside the jud[i]cial box', in: *Human rights protection in the European legal order: The interaction between the European and the national courts*, Patricia Popelier, Catherine Van De Heyning and Piet Van Nuffel (eds.), Intersentia, 2011, 97–146.

Besson (2016) Besson, Samantha, 'Subsidiarity in International Human Rights Law – What is Subsidiary about Human Rights?', *The American Journal of Jurisprudence*, Vol. 61 (2016), 69–107.

Bingham (2011) Bingham, Tom, *The Rule of Law*, Penguin, 2011.

Bjorge (2015) Bjorge, Eirik, *Domestic Application of the ECHR, Courts as Faithful Trustees*, Oxford University Press, 2015.

Björgvinsson (2016) Björgvinsson, David Thór, 'The Role of Judges of the European Court of Human Rights as Guardians of Fundamental Rights of the Individual', in: *Judges as Guardians of Constitutionalism and Human Rights*, Martin Scheinin, Helle Krunke and Marina Aksenova (eds.), Edward Elgar Publishing, 2016.

Bogdandy (2004) von Bogdandy, Armin, 'Globalization and Europe: How to Square Democracy, Globalization, and International Law', *European Journal of International Law*, Vol. 15 (2004), 885–906.

Bogdandy (2008) von Bogdandy, Armin, 'Pluralism, Direct Effect, and the Ultimate Say: On the Relationship Between International and Domestic Constitutional law', *International Journal of Constitutional Law*, Vol. 6 (2008), 397–413.

Bogdandy and Venzke (2011) von Bogdandy, Armin and Ingo Venzke, 'Beyond Dispute: International Judicial Institutions as Lawmakers', *German Law Journal*, Vol. 12 (2011), 979–1003.

Bogdandy and Venzke (2011a) von Bogdandy, Armin and Ingo Venzke, 'On the Democratic Legitimation of International Judicial Lawmaking', *German Law Journal*, Vol. 12 (2011), 1341–1370.

Bogdandy and Venzke (2012) — von Bogdandy, Armin and Ingo Venzke, 'In Whose Name? An Investigation of International Courts' Public Authority and its Democratic Justification', *European Journal of International Law*, Vol. 23 (2012), 7–41.

Bogdandy and Venzke (2014) — von Bogdandy, Armin and Ingo Venzke, 'The Spell of Precedents: Lawmaking by International Courts and Tribunals', in: *The Oxford Handbook of International Adjudication*, Cesare P. R. Romano, Karen J. Alter and Yuval Shany (eds.), Oxford University Press, 2014, 503–522.

Boillat (2009) — Boillat, Philippe, 'Final Observations at the Regional Conference Organized by the Directorate General of Human Rights and Legal Affairs and the Supreme Court of Serbia in the Framework of Serbia's Chairmanship of the Committee of Ministers of the Council of Europe, "The Role of Supreme Courts in the Domestic Implementation of the European Convention on Human Rights", Belgrade, 20–21 September 2007', in: *Reforming the European Convention on Human Rights. A Work in Progress*, Council of Europe (ed.), Council of Europe Publishing, 2009, 376–378.

Boillat (2009a) — Boillat, Philippe, 'Summary Conclusions of the Colloquy Organized under the Swedish Chairmanship of the Committee of Ministers of the Council of Europe, "Towards Stronger Implementation of the European Convention on Human Rights at National Level", Stockholm, 9–10 June 2008', in: *Reforming the European Convention on Human Rights. A Work in Progress*, Council of Europe (ed.), Council of Europe Publishing, 2009, 553–557.

Boillat (2009b) — Boillat, Philippe, 'Vers une mise en oeuvre renforcée de la Convention européenne des droits de l'homme au niveau national', *Revue trimestrielle des droits de l'homme*, Vol. 20 (2009), 17–26.

Bossuyt (1987) — Bossuyt, Marc J., *Guide to the "travaux préparatoires" of the International Covenant on Civil and Political Rights*, M. Nijhoff Publishers, 1987.

Boyle (2007) — Boyle, Alan and Christine Chinkin, *The Making of International Law*, Oxford University Press, 2007.

Brandom (1999) — Brandom, Robert B., 'Some Pragmatist Themes in Hegel's Idealism: Negotiation and Administration in Hegel's Account of the Structure and Content of Conceptual Norms', *European Journal of Philosophy*, Vol. 7 (1999), 164–189.

Bratza (2011) — Bratza, Nicolas, 'The Relationship between the UK Courts and Strasbourg', *European Human Rights Law Review* (2011), 505–512.

Bratza (2014)   Bratza, Nicolas, 'Living Instrument or Dead Letter – the
                       Future of the European Convention on Human Rights',
                       European Human Rights Law Review (2014), 116–128.
Bratza (2014a)   Bratza, Nicolas, 'Opening Address at the High Level
                       Conference on the Future of the European Court of
                       Human Rights, Brighton, 19–20 April 2012', in: *Reforming
                       the European Convention on Human Rights. Interlaken,
                       Izmir, Brighton and Beyond*, Council of Europe (ed.),
                       Council of Europe Publishing, 2014, 80–83.
Brauch (2004–2005)   Brauch, Jeffrey A., 'Margin of Appreciation and the
                       Jurisprudence of the European Court of Human
                       Rights: Threat to the Rule of Law', *Columbia Journal of
                       European Law*, Vol. 11 (2004–2005), 113–150.
Brems (2014)   Brems, Eva, 'Procedural Protection: An Examination
                       of Procedural Safeguards Read into Substantive
                       Convention Rights', in: *Shaping Rights in the ECHR:
                       The Role of the European Court of Human Rights in
                       Determining the Scope of Human Rights*, Eva Brems
                       and Janneke Gerards (eds.), Cambridge University Press,
                       2014, 137–161.
Brems (2017)   Brems, Eva, 'The 'Logics' of Procedural-Type Review by
                       the European Court of Human Rights', in: *Procedural
                       Review in European Fundamental Rights Cases*, Janneke
                       Gerards and Eva Brems (eds.), Cambridge University
                       Press, 2017, 17–39.
Brems (2019)   Brems, Eva, 'Positive Subsidiarity and Its Implications
                       for the Margin of Appreciation Doctrine', *Netherlands
                       Quarterly of Human Rights*, Vol. 37 (2019), 210–227.
Brems and Lavrysen   Brems, Eva and Laurens Lavrysen, 'Procedural Justice in
(2013)   Human Rights Adjudication: The European Court of
                       Human Rights', *Human Rights Quarterly*, Vol. 35 (2013),
                       176–200.
Breuer (2021)   Breuer, Martin, 'Principled Resistance to the European
                       Court of Human Rights and Its Case Law: A Comparative
                       Assessment', in: *The European Court of Human Rights.
                       Current Challenges in Historical Perspective*, Helmut
                       Philipp Aust and Esra Demir-Gürsel (eds.), Edward
                       Elgar Publishing, 2021, 43–70.
Brink (1999)   Brink, Stefan, *Über die richterliche Entscheidungs-
                       begründung: Funktion-Position-Methodik*, Peter Lang
                       GmbH, 1999.
Brooks (2014)   Brooks, Thom (ed.), *Deterrence*, Taylor & Francis Ltd, 2014.
Brugger (1994)   Brugger, Winfried, 'Legal Interpretation, Schools of
                       Jurisprudence, and Anthropology: Some Remarks
                       From a German Point of View', *American Journal of
                       Comparative Law*, Vol. 42 (1994), 395–421.

Bruyn (2000)   de Bruyn, Donatienne, 'Le droit à un recours effectif', in: *Les droits de l'homme au seuil du troisième millénaire: Mélanges en hommage à Pierre Lambert*, Bruylant (ed.), Bruylant, 2000, 185–205.

Buchanan (1984)   Buchanan, Allen, 'What's So Special about Rights?', *Social Philosophy & Policy*, Vol. 2 (1984), 61–83.

Buchanan (2013)   Buchanan, Allen, *The Heart of Human Rights*, Oxford University Press, 2013.

Buergenthal (1965)   Buergenthal, Thomas, 'The Effect of the European Convention on Human Rights on the Internal Law of Member States', *International & Comparative Law Quarterly*, Supplementary Publication, Vol. 11 (1965), 79–106.

Buyse (2006)   Buyse, Antoine, 'A Lifeline in Time – Non-retroactivity and Continuing Violations under the ECHR', *Nordic Journal of International Law*, Vol. 75 (2006), 63–88.

Buyse (2008)   Buyse, Antoine, 'Lost and Regained? Restitution as a Remedy for Human Rights Violations in the Context of International Law', *Zeitschrift für ausländisches öffentliches Recht und Völkerrecht*, Vol. 68 (2008), 129–153.

Buyse (2014)   Buyse, Antoine, 'Significantly Insignificant? Studies in the Margins of the Admissibility Criterion in Article 35(3)(b) European Convention on Human Rights', in: *The Realisation of Human Rights, Studies in Honor of Leo Zwaak*, Yves Haeck, Brianne McConigle Leyh, Clara Burbano-Herrera and Diana Contreras-Garduño (eds.), Intersentia, 2014, 107–123.

Bydlinski (2011)   Bydlinski, Franz, 'Methodological Approaches to the Tort Law of the ECHR', in: *Tort Law in the Jurisprudence of the European Court of Human Rights*, Attila Fenyves, Ernst Karner, Kelmut Koziol and Elisabeth Steiner (eds.), De Gruyter, 2011, 29–128.

Cali (2008)   Cali, Basak, 'The Purposes of the European Human Rights System: One or Many?', *European Human Rights Law Review* (2008), 299–306.

Çalı (2016)   Çalı, Başak, 'From Flexible to Variable Standards of Judicial Review: The Responsible Domestic Courts Doctrine at the European Court of Human Rights', in: *Shifting Centers of Gravity in Human Rights Protection. Rethinking relations between the ECHR, EU and national legal orders*, Odný Mjöll Arnardóttir and Antoine Buyse (eds.), Routledge, 2016, 144–160.

Çalı (2018)   Çalı, Başak, 'Explaining Variation in the Intrusiveness of Regional Human Rights Remedies in Domestic Orders', *International Journal of Constitutional Law*, Vol. 16 (2018), 214–234.

Çalı (2018a)   Çalı, Başak, 'Coping with Crisis: Whither the Variable Geometry in the Jurisprudence of the European Court of Human Rights', *Wisconsin International Law Journal*, Vol. 35 (2018), 237–276.

Çalı (2021)   Çalı, Başak, 'Autocratic Strategies and the European Court of Human Rights', *European Convention on Human Rights Law Review*, Vol. 2 (2021), 11–19.

Callewaert (2000)   Callewaert, Johan, 'La Convention européenne des droits de l'homme entre effectivité et prévisibilité', in: *Les droits de l'homme au seuil du troisième millénaire: Mélanges en hommage à Pierre Lambert*, Bruylant (ed.), Bruylant, 2000, 93–108.

Cameron (2006)   Cameron, Iain, 'Damages for Violations of ECHR: The Swedish Example', *Swedish Studies in European Law*, Vol. 1 (2006), 97–128.

Campbell (2013)   Campbell, Tom, 'Human Rights: Moral or Legal?', in: *Human Rights: Old Problems, New Possibilities*, David Kinley, Wojciech Sadurski and Kevin Walton (eds.), Edward Elgar Publishing, 2013, 1–26.

Carozza (2003)   Carozza, Paolo G., 'Subsidiarity as a Structural Principle of International Human Rights Law', *The American Journal of International Law*, Vol. 97 (2003), 38–79.

Carter (2009)   Carter, William M., 'Rethinking Subsidiarity in International Human Rights Adjudication', *Hamline Journal of Public Law and Policy*, Vol. 30 (2009), 319–334.

Chavez (2017)   Chavez, Leiry Cornejo, 'New Remedial Responses in the Practice of Regional Human Rights Courts: Purposes beyond Compensation', *International Journal of Constitutional Law*, Vol. 15 (2017), 372–392.

Christoffersen (2009) Christoffersen, Jonas, *Fair balance: proportionality, subsidiarity and primarity in the European Convention on Human Rights*, Brill, 2009.

Christoffersen (2013) Christoffersen, Jonas, 'Individual and Constitutional Justice: Can the Power Balance of Adjudication be Reversed', in: *The European Court of Human Rights between Law and Politics*, Paperback Edition, Jonas Christoffersen and Mikael Rask Madsen (eds.), Oxford University Press, 2013, 181–203.

Christoffersen and   Christoffersen, Jonas and Mikael Rask Madsen (eds.), *The*
Madsen (2013)   *European Convention on Human Rights between Law and Politics*, Paperback Edition, Oxford University Press, 2013.

Christoffersen and   Christoffersen, Jonas and Mikael Rask Madsen,
Madsen (2013a)   'Introduction: The European Court of Human Rights between Law and Politics', in: *The European Court of Human Rights between Law and Politics*, Paperback Edition, Jonas Christoffersen and Mikael Rask Madsen (eds.), Oxford University Press, 2013, 1–13.

Christoffersen and Madsen (2013b)	Christoffersen, Jonas and Mikael Rask Madsen, 'Postscript: Understanding the Past, Present and Future of the European Court of Human Rights', in: *The European Court of Human Rights between Law and Politics*, Paperback Edition, Jonas Christoffersen and Mikael Rask Madsen (eds.), Oxford University Press, 2013, 230–250.
Chryssogonos (2001)	Chryssogonos, Kostas, 'Zur Inkorporation der Europäischen Menschenrechtskonvention in den nationalen Rechtsordnungen der Mitgliedstaaten', *Europarecht*, Vol. 36 (2001), 49–61.
Clapham (1993)	Clapham, Andrew, *Human Rights in the Private Sphere*, Oxford University Press, 1993.
Collected edition of the "Travaux préparatoires" (1975–1985), CETP	Collected edition of the "Travaux préparatoires" of the European Convention on Human Rights / Council of Europe, Martinus Nijhoff, 1975–1985, 8 vols.
Clashfern (2000)	Lord Mackay of Clashfern, 'The Margin of Appreciation and the Need for Balance', in: *Protecting Human Rights: The European Perspective – Studies in Memory of Rolv Ryssdal*, Paul Mahoney, Franz Matscher, Herbert Petzold and Luzius Wildhaber (eds.), Carl Heymanns Verlag, 2000, 837–844.
Costa (2009)	Costa, Jean-Paul, 'Comments on the Wise Persons' Report from the Perspective of the European Court of Human Rights, Speech at the Colloquy Organized by the San Marino Chairmanship of the Committee of Ministers of the Council of Europe, "Future Developments of the European Court of Human Rights in the Light of the Wise Persons' Report", San Marino, 22–23 March 2007', in: *Reforming the European Convention on Human Rights. A work in Progress*, Council of Europe (ed.), Council of Europe Publishing, 2009, 238–244.
Costa (2009a)	Costa, Jean-Paul, 'Les aspects nationaux de la réforme du système de protection des droits de l'homme: les attents de la Court européenne des droits de l'homme', *Revue trimestrielle des droits de l'homme*, Vol. 20 (2009), 7–16.
Costa (2009b)	Costa, Jean-Paul, 'National Aspects of the Reform of the Human Rights Protection System: The Expectations of the ECHR, Speech at the Colloquy Organized under the Swedish Chairmanship of the Committee of Ministers of the Council of Europe, "Towards Stronger Implementation of the European Convention on Human Rights at National Level", Stockholm, 9–10 June 2008', in: *Reforming the European Convention on Human Rights. A Work in Progress*, Council of Europe (ed.), Council of Europe Publishing, 2009, 472–476.

Crawford (2002)	Crawford, James, *The International Law Commission's Articles on State Responsibility: Introduction, Text and Commentaries*, Cambridge University Press, 2002.
Crawford (2013)	Crawford, James, *State Responsibility: The General Part*, Cambridge University Press, 2013.
Cumper and Lewis (2019)	Cumper, Peter and Tom Lewis, 'Blanket Bans, Subsidiarity, and the Procedural Turn of the European Court of Human Rights', *International and Comparative Law Quarterly*, Vol. 68 (2019), 611–638.
Czerner (2008)	Czerner, Frank, 'Inter partes-versus erga omnes-Wirkung der EGMR-Judikate in den Konventionsstaaten gemäß Art. 46 EMRK. Eine Problemanalyse auch aus strafverfahrensrechtlicher Perspektive', *Archiv des Völkerrechts*, Vol. 46 (2008), 345–367.
Dahl (2000)	Dahl, Robert A., *On Democracy*, Yale University Press, 2000.
David (2014)	David, Valeska, 'Expanding Right to an Effective Remedy: Common Developments at the Human Rights Committee and the Inter-American Court', *British Journal of American Legal Studies*, Vol. 3 (2014), 259–286.
Demir-Gürsel (2021)	Demir-Gürsel, Esra, 'For the Sake of Unity: the Drafting History of the European Convention on Human Rights and its Current Relevance', in: *The European Court of Human Rights. Current Challenges in Historical Perspective*, Helmut Philipp Aust and Esra Demir-Gürsel (eds.), Edward Elgar Publishing, 2021, 109–132.
Dijk, Hoof *et al.* (2018)	van Dijk, Pieter, Fried van Hoof, Arjen van Rijn and Leo Zwaak (eds.), *Theory and Practice of the European Convention on Human Rights*, Fifth Edition, Intersentia, 2018.
Dörr, Grote and Marauhn (2013)	Dörr, O., R. Grote and T. Marauhn (eds.), *EMRK/GG Konkordanzkommentar zum europäischen und deutschen Grundrechtsschutz*, Second Edition, Mohr Siebeck, 2013.
Dothan (2019)	Dothan, Shai, 'The Three Traditional Approaches to Treaty Interpretation: A Current Application to the European Court of Human Rights', *Fordham International Law Journal*, Vol. 42 (2019), 765–794.
Douzinas and Gearty (2014)	Douzinas, Costas and Conor Gearty, 'Introduction', in: *The Meanings of Rights. The Philosophical and Social Theory of Human Rights*, Costas Douzinas and Conor Gearty (eds.), Cambridge University Press, 2014, 1–12.
Drobak and North (2008)	Drobak, John N. and Douglass C. North, 'Understanding Judicial Decision-Making: The Importance of Constraints on Non-rational Deliberations', *Washington University Journal of Law and Policy*, Vol. 26 (2008), 131–152.

Dworkin (1978)	Dworkin, Ronald, *Taking Rights Seriously*, Harvard University Press, 1978.
Dworkin (2011)	Dworkin, Ronald, *Justice for Hedgehogs*, Harvard University Press, 2011.
Dworkin (2013)	Dworkin, Ronald, 'A New Philosophy for International Law', *Philosophy & Public Affairs*, Vol. 41 (2013), 2–30.
Eborah (2014)	Eborah, Solomon T., 'Chapter 11 International Human Rights Courts', in: *The Oxford Handbook of International Adjudication*, Cesare P. R. Romano, Karen J. Alter and Yuval Shany (eds.), Oxford University Press, 2014, 225–249.
Ely (1980)	Ely, John Hart, *Democracy and Distrust: A Theory of Judicial Review*, Harvard University Press, 1980.
Emberland (2006)	Emberland, Marius, *The Human Rights of Companies: Exploring the Structure of ECHR Protection*, Oxford University Press, 2006.
Eng (2014)	Eng, Svein, 'Why Reflective Equilibrium? I: Reflexivity of Justification', *Ratio Juris*, Vol. 27 (2014), 138–154.
Eng (2014a)	Eng, Svein, 'Why Reflective Equilibrium? III: Reflective Equilibrium as a Heuristic Tool', *Ratio Juris*, Vol. 27 (2014), 440–459.
Etinson (2013)	Etinson, Adam, 'Human Rights, Claimability and the Uses of Abstraction', *Utilitas*, Vol. 25 (2013), 463–486.
Evans and Petkoff (2019)	Evans, Malcolm and Peter Petkoff, 'Marginal Neutrality – Neutrality and the Margin of Appreciation in the Jurisprudence of the European Court of Human Rights', in: *The European Convention on Human Right and the Freedom of Religion and Belief*, Jeroen Temperman, Jeremy Gunn and Malcolm Evans (eds.), Brill Academic Publishers, 128–153.
Fabbrini (2014)	Fabbrini, Federico, 'The European Court of Human Rights, Extraordinary Renditions and the Right to the Truth: Ensuring Accountability for Gross Human Rights Violations Committed in the Fight against Terrorism', *Human Rights Law Review*, Vol. 14 (2014), 85–106.
Feteris (2008)	Feteris, Eveline T., 'The Rational Reconstruction of Weighing and Balancing on the Basis of Teleological-Evaluative Considerations in the Justification of Judicial Decisions', *Ratio Juris*, Vol. 21 (2008), 481–495.
Feteris (2008a)	Feteris, Eveline T., 'Weighing and Balancing in the Justification of Judicial Decisions', *Informal Logic*, Vol. 28 (2008), 20–30.
Fikfak (2019)	Fikfak, Veronika, 'Changing State Behaviour: Damages before the European Court of Human Rights', *The European Journal of International Law*, Vol. 29 (2019), 1091–1125.

Fischborn (2010)   Fischborn, Birgit Iris, *Enteignung ohne Entschädigung nach der EMRK?: Zur Vereinbarkeit des entschädigungslosen Entzugs von Eigentum mit Artikel 1 des Zusatzprotokolls zur EMRK*, Mohr Siebeck, 2010.

Flauss (1991)   Flauss, Jean-François, 'Le droit à un recours effectif – L'article 13 de la Convention européenne de droits de l'homme', *Revue universelle des droits de l'homme*, Vol. 3 (1991), 324–336.

Flauss (2009)   Flauss, Jean-François, 'L'effectivité des arrêts de la Court européenne des droits de l'homme : du politique au juridique ou vice-versa', *Revue trimestrielle des droits de l'homme*, Vol. 20 (2009), 27–72.

Fletcher (1982)   Fletcher, William A., 'The Discretionary Constitution: Institutional Remedies and Judicial Legitimacy', *Yale Law Journal*, Vol. 91 (1982), 635–697.

Follesdal (2011)   Follesdal, Andreas, 'The Principle of Subsidiarity as a Constitutional Principle in International Law', Jean Monnet Working Papers, No. 12 (2011).

Follesdal (2016)   Follesdal, Andreas, 'Squaring the Circle at the Battle at Brighton: Is the War between Protecting Human Rights or Respecting Sovereignty Over, or Has It Just Begun?', in: *Shifting Centers of Gravity in Human Rights Protection. Rethinking Relations between the ECHR, EU, and National Legal Orders*, Oddný Mjöll Arnardóttir and Antoine Buyse (eds.), Routledge, 2016, 189–204.

Føllesdal (2016)   Føllesdal, Andreas, 'Subsidiarity and International Human Rights Courts: Respecting Self-Governance and Protecting Human Rights – Or Neither?', *Law and Contemporary Problems*, Vol. 79 (2016), 147–163.

Forowicz (2015)   Forowicz, Magdalena, 'Factors Influencing the Reception of International Law in the ECtHR's Case Law: An Overview', in: *A Farewell to Fragmentation. Reassertion and Convergence in International Law*, Mads Andenas and Eirik Bjorge (eds.), Cambridge University Press, 2015, 191–217.

Frowein (2000)   Frowein, Jochen Abr., 'Art. 13 as a Growing Pillar of Convention Law', in: *Protecting Human Rights: The European Perspective – Studies in Memory of Rolv Ryssdal*, Paul Mahoney, Franz Matscher, Herbert Petzold and Luzius Wildhaber (eds.), Carl Heymanns Verlag, 2000, 545–550.

Frowein and Peukert   Frowein Jochen Abr., and Wolfgang Peukert, *Europäische*
(2009)   *Menschenrechtskonvention: EMRK-Kommentar*, Third Edition, Norbert P. Engel Verlag, 2009.

Fyrnys (2011)	Fyrnys, Markus, 'Expanding Competences by Judicial Lawmaking: The Pilot Judgment Procedure of the European Court of Human Rights', *German Law Journal*, Vol. 12 (2011), 1231–1260.
Gadamer (1975)	Gadamer, Hans-Georg, *Truth and Method*, Revised Second Edition 2004, Bloomsbury, 1975.
Garner and Black (2009)	Garner Bryan A., and Henry Campbell Black, *Black's Law Dictionary*, Ninth Edition, West, 2009.
Gerards (2008)	Gerards, Janneke, 'Judicial Deliberations in the European Court of Human Rights', in: *The Legitimacy of the Highest Courts' Rulings*, Nick Huls, Maurice Adams and Jacco Bomhoff (eds.), T.M.C. Asser Press, 2008, 407–436.
Gerards (2011)	Gerards, Janneke, 'Pluralism, Deference and the Margin of Appreciation Doctrine', *European Law Journal*, Vol. 17 (2011), 80–120.
Gerards (2012)	Gerards, Janneke, 'The Prism of Fundamental Rights', *European Constitutional Law Review*, Vol. 8 (2012), 173–202.
Gerards (2013)	Gerards, Janneke, 'Judicial Minimalism and 'Dependency'. Interpretation of the European Convention in a Pluralist Europe', in: *Fundamental Rights and Principles. Liber Amicorum Pieter van Dijk*, Marjolein van Roosmalen, Ben Vermeulen, Fried van Hoof and Marten Oosting (eds.), Intersentia, 2013, 73–92.
Gerards (2014)	Gerards, Janneke, 'The European Court of Human Rights and the National Courts: Giving Shape to the Notion of 'Shared Responsibility'', in: *Implementation of the European Convention on Human Rights and of the Judgments of the ECtHR in National Case-Law. A Comparative Analysis*, Janneke Gerards and Joseph Fleuren (eds.), Intersentia, 2014, 13–94.
Gerards (2014a)	Gerards, Janneke, 'Inadmissibility Decisions of the European Court of Human Rights: A Critique of the Lack of Reasoning', *Human Rights Law Review*, Vol. 14 (2014), 148–158.
Gerards (2017)	Gerards, Janneke, 'Procedural Review by the ECtHR: A Typology', in: *Procedural Review in European Fundamental Rights Cases*, Janneke Gerards and Eva Brems (eds.), Cambridge University Press, 2017.
Gerards (2018)	Gerards, Janneke, 'Margin of Appreciation and Incrementalism in the Case Law of the European Court of Human Rights', *Human Rights Law Review*, Vol. 18 (2018), 495–515.
Gerards and Fleuren (2014)	Gerards, Janneke and Joseph Fleuren (eds.), *Implementation of the European Convention on Human Rights and of the Judgments of the ECtHR in National Case-Law: A Comparative Analysis*, Intersentia, 2014.

Gerards and Fleuren (2014a)
Gerards, Janneke and Joseph Fleuren, 'Comparative Analysis', in: *Implementation of the European Convention on Human Rights and of the Judgments of the ECtHR in National Case-Law. A Comparative Analysis*, Janneke Gerards and Joseph Fleuren (eds.), Intersentia, 2014, 333–374.

Gerards and Glas (2017)
Gerards, Janneke and Lize R. Glas, 'Access to Justice in the European Convention on Human Rights System', *Netherlands Quarterly of Human Rights*, Vol. 35 (2017), 11–30.

Gerards and Brems (2017)
Gerards, Janneke and Eva Brems (eds.), *Procedural Review in European Fundamental Rights Cases*, Cambridge University Press, 2017.

Gewirtz (1983)
Gewirtz, Paul, 'Remedies and Resistance', *Yale Law Journal*, Vol. 92 (1983), 585–681.

Ginsburg (2004)
Ginsburg, Tom, 'Bounded Discretion in International Judicial Lawmaking', *Virginia Journal of International Law*, Vol. 45 (2004), 631–674.

Glas (2014)
Glas, Lize R., 'Changes in the Procedural Practice of the European Court of Human Rights: Consequences for the Convention System and Lessons to be Drawn', *Human Rights Law Review*, Vol. 14 (2014), 671–699.

Glas (2019)
Glas, Lize R., 'The European Court of Human Rights Supervising the Execution of Its Judgments', *Netherlands Quarterly of Human Rights*, Vol. 37 (2019), 228–244.

Glendon (2001)
Glendon, Mary Ann, *A World Made New: Eleanore Roosevelt and the Universal Declaration of Human Rights*, Random House Trade Paperbacks, 2001.

Golsong (1958)
Golsong, Heribert, *Das Rechtsschutzsystem der Europäischen Menschenrechtskonvention*, C.F. Müller Verlag, 1958.

Golsong (1988)
Golsong, Heribert, 'The European Court of Human Rights and the National Law-Maker: Some General Reflections', in: *Protecting Human Rights: The European Dimension*, Franz Matscher and Herbert Petzold (eds.), Carl Heymans Verlag, 1988, 239–244.

Gosepath (2005)
Gosepath, Stefan, 'The Principle of Subsidiarity', in: *Real World Justice. Grounds, Principles, Human Rights, and Social Institutions*, Andreas Follesdal and Thomas Pogge (eds.), Springer, 2005, 157–170.

Grabenwarter (2008)
Grabenwarter, Christoph, 'Das Recht auf effektive Beschwerde gegen überlange Verfahrensdauer', in: *Über Struktur und Vielfalt im Öffentlichen Recht – Festgabe für Bernhard Raschauer*, Daniel Ennöckl, Nicolas Raschauer, Eva Schulev-Steindl and Wolfgang Wessely (eds.), Springer, 2008, 19–29.

Grabenwarter (2014)	Grabenwarter, Christoph, *The European Convention on Human Rights: A Commentary*, Beck/Hart/Nomos, 2014.
Grabenwarter and Pabel (2012)	Grabenwarter, Christoph and Katharina Pabel, *Europäische Menschenrechtskonvention: Ein Studienbuch*, Sixth Edition, MANZ Verlag, 2012.
Graham (2020)	Graham, Lewis, 'Strategic Admissibility Decisions in the European Court of Human Rights', *International and Comparative Law Quarterly*, Vol. 69 (2020), 79–102.
Gray (2014)	Gray, Christine, 'Chapter 40 Remedies', in: *The Oxford Handbook of International Adjudication*, Karen J. Alter, Yuval Shany and Cesare P. R. Romano (eds.), Oxford University Press, 2014, 871–897.
Greene (2010)	Greene, Jamal, 'The Rule of Law as a Law of Standards', *The Georgetown Law Journal*, Vol. 99 (2010), 1289–1299.
Greer (2004)	Greer, Steven, '"Balancing" and the European Court of Human Rights: A Contribution to the Habermas-Alexy Debate', *The Cambridge Law Journal*, Vol. 63 (2004), 412–434.
Greer (2006)	Greer, Steven, *The European Convention on Human Rights: Achievements, Problems and Prospects*, Cambridge University Press, 2006.
Greer and Wildhaber (2012)	Greer, Steven and Luzius Wildhaber, 'Revisiting the Debate about "Constitutionalising" the European Court of Human Rights', *Human Rights Law Review*, Vol. 12 (2012), 655–687.
Griffin (2010)	Griffin, James, *On Human Rights*, Oxford University Press, 2010.
Groome (2011)	Groome, Dermot, 'The Right to Truth in the Fight against Impunity', *Berkeley Journal of International Law*, Vol. 29 (2011), 175–199.
Grote and Marauhn (2006)	Grote, Rainer and Thilo Marauhn (eds.), *EMRK/GG: Konkordanzkommentar zum europäischen und deutschen Grundrechtsschutz*, Mohr Siebeck, 2006.
Gyorfi (2019)	Gyorfi, Tamas, 'The Legitimacy of the European Human Rights Regime – A View from the United Kingdom', *Global Constitutionalism*, Vol. 8 (2019), 123–156.
Schermers (1994)	Schermers, H. G., 'The Eleventh Protocol to the European Convention on Human Rights', *European Law Review*, Vol. 19 (1994), 367–384.
Habermas (1998)	Habermas, Jürgen, *Between Facts and Norms*, MIT Press, 1998.
Hampson (2010)	Hampson, Françoise, 'The Future of the European Court of Human Rights', in: *Strategic Visions for Human Rights: Essays in Honour of Professor Kevin Boyle*, Geoff Gilbert, Françoise Hampson and Clara Sandoval (eds.), Routledge, 2010, 141–166.

Harmsen (2013)　Harmsen, Robert, 'The Reform of the Convention System: Institutional Restructuring and the (Geo-) Politics of Human Rights', in: *The European Court of Human Rights between Law and Politics*, Paperback Edition, Jonas Christoffersen and Mikael Rask Madsen (eds.), Oxford University Press, 2013, 119–143.

Harris, O'Boyle *et al.* (2009)　Harris, David J., Michael O'Boyle and Colin Warbrick, *Law of the European Convention on Human Rights*, Second Edition, Oxford University Press, 2009.

Harris, O'Boyle *et al.* (2018)　Harris, David, Michael O'Boyle, Ed Bates and Carla Buckley, *Law of the European Convention on Human Rights*, Fourth Edition, Oxford University Press, 2018.

Hart (1973)　Hart, H. L. A., 'Bentham on Legal Rights', in: *Oxford Essays in Jurisprudence*, Second Series, A. W. B. Simpson (ed.), Oxford University Press, 1973, 171–201.

Hart (2012)　Hart, H. L. A., *The Concept of Law Third Edition: With a Postscript edited by Penelope A. Bulloch and Joseph Raz and with an Introduction and Notes by Leslie Green*, Oxford University Press, 2012.

Harutyunyan (2021)　Harutyunyan, Armen, 'The Future of the European Court of Human Rights in the Era of Radical Democracy', *European Convention on Human Rights Law Review*, Vol. 2 (2021), 20–26.

Hauge (1996)　Hauge, Ragnar, *Straffens begrunnelser*, Universitetsforlaget, 1996.

Helfer (1993)　Helfer, Laurence R., 'Consensus, Coherence and the European Convention on Human Rights', *Cornell International Law Journal*, Vol. 26 (1993), 133–165.

Helfer (2008)　Helfer, Laurence R., 'Redesigning the European Court of Human Rights: Embeddedness as a Deep Structural Principle of the European Human Rights Regime', *European Journal of International Law*, Vol. 19 (2008), 125–159.

Heyning (2011)　Van De Heyning, Catherine, 'No Place Like Home: Discretionary Space for the Domestic Protection of Fundamental Rights', in: *Human Rights Protection in the European Legal Order: The Interaction between the European and the National Courts*, Patricia Popelier, Catherine Van De Heyning and Piet Van Nuffel (eds.), Intersentia, 2011, 65–96.

Hioureas (2006)　Hioureas, Christina G., 'Behind the Scenes of Protocol No. 14: Politics in Reforming the European Court of Human Rights', *Berkeley Journal of International Law*, Vol. 24 (2006), 718–757.

Hirsch (2007)　Hirsch, Danielle Elyce, 'A Defense of Structural Injunctive Remedies in South African Law', *Oregon Review of International Law*, Vol. 9 (2007), 1–66.

Hodges (2015)	Hodges, Christopher, *Laws and Corporate Behaviour. Integrating Theories of Regulation, Enforcement, Compliance and Ethics*, Hart/Beck/Nomos, 2015.
Hoffman (2014)	Hoffman, Herwig C. H., 'Article 47. III Specific Provisions (Meaning)', in: *The EU Charter of Fundamental Rights*, Steve Peers, Tamara Hervey, Jeff Kenner and Angela Ward (eds.), Oxford University Press, 2014, 1211–1228.
Hohfeld and Cook (1919)	Hohfeld, Wesley Newcomb and Walter Wheeler Cook, *Fundamental Legal Conceptions as Applied in Judicial Reasoning: And Other Legal Essays*, The Lawbook Exchange Ltd, 1919.
Holoubek (1992)	Holoubek, Michael, 'Das Recht auf eine wirksame Beschwerde bei einer nationalen Instanz', *Juristische Blätter*, Vol. 114 (1992), 137–155.
Hoof (2014)	van Hoof, Fried, 'The Stubbornness of the European Court of Human Rights Margin of Appreciation Doctrine', in: *The Realisation of Human Rights: When Theory Meets Practice. Studies in Honour of Leo Zwaak*, Yves Haeck, Brianne McGonigle Leyh, Clara Burbano-Herrera and Diana Contreras-Garduño (eds.), Intersentia, 2014, 125–149.
Horsey and Rackley (2013)	Horsey, Kirsty and Erika Rackley, *Tort Law*, Third Edition, Oxford University Press, 2013.
Huijbers (2017)	Huijbers, Leonie M., 'The European Court of Human Rights' Procedural Approach in the Age of Subsidiarity', *Cambridge International Law Journal*, Vol. 6 (2017) 177–201.
Huijbers (2019)	Huijbers, Leonie M., *Process-Based Fundamental Rights Review. Practice, Concept, and Theory*, Intersentia, 2019.
Huneeus (2011)	Huneeus, Alexandra, 'Courts Resisting Courts: Lessons from the Inter-American Court's Struggle to Enforce Human Rights', *Cornell International Law Journal*, Vol. 44 (2011), 493–534.
Huneeus (2014)	Huneeus, Alexandra, 'Chapter 20 Compliance with Judgments and Decisions', in: *The Oxford Handbook of International Adjudication*, Cesare PR Romano, Karen J Alter and Yuval Shany (eds.), Oxford University Press, 2014, 437–463.
Ichim (2014)	Ichim, Octavian, *Just Satisfaction under the European Convention on Human Rights*, Cambridge University Press, 2014.

Iglesias (2009)   Iglesias, Carlos Rodríguez, 'Presentation of the Wise Persons
                               Report, Speech at the Colloquy Organized by the San
                               Marino Chairmanship of the Committee of Ministers
                               of the Council of Europe, "Future Developments of the
                               European Court of Human Rights in the Light of the
                               Wise Persons' Report", San Marino, 22–23 March 2007',
                               in: *Reforming the European Convention on Human
                               Rights. A Work in Progress*, Council of Europe (ed.),
                               Council of Europe Publishing, 2009, 233–237.
Ioannidis (2011)   Ioannidis, Michael, 'The ECtHR, National Constitutional
                               Law, and the Limits of Democracy: Sitaropoulos and
                               Others v. Greece', *European Public Law*, Vol. 17 (2011),
                               661–671.
Jacob (2011)   Jacob, Marc, 'Precedents: Lawmaking through International
                               Adjudication', *German Law Journal*, Vol. 12 (2011),
                               1005–1032.
Jacobs, White *et al.*   Jacobs, Francis G., Robin C. A. White, Clare Ovey,
(2017)   Bernadette Rainey, Elizabeth Wicks, *The European
                               Convention on Human Rights*, Seventh Edition, Oxford
                               University Press, 2017.
Jagland (2014)   Jagland, Thorbjørn, 'Opening Address at the High level
                               Conference on the Future of the European Court of
                               Human Rights, Brighton, 19–20 April 2012', in: *Reforming
                               the European Convention on Human Rights. Interlaken,
                               Izmir, Brighton and beyond*, Council of Europe (ed.),
                               Council of Europe Publishing, 2014, 74–77.
Jahn (2014)   Jahn, Jannika, 'Ruling (In)directly through Individual
                               Measures? – Effect and Legitimacy of the ECtHR's New
                               Remedial Power', *Zeitschrift für ausländisches öffentli-
                               ches Recht und Völkerrecht*, Vol. 74 (2014), 1–39.
Jareborg (2002)   Jareborg, Nils, *Scraps of Penal Theory*, Iustus, 2002.
Jötten (2010)   Jötten, Sara, *Enforced Disappearances und EMRK*,
                               Duncker & Humblot GmbH, 2010.
Kartner and Meuwese   Kartner, Fay and Anne Meuwese, 'Responsiveness towards
(2017)   Fundamental Rights Impacts in the Preparation of
                               EU Legislation', in: *Procedural Review in European
                               Fundamental Rights Cases*, Cambridge University Press,
                               2017, 95–124.
Kavanagh (2014)   Kavanagh, Aileen, 'Proportionality and Parliamentary
                               Debates: Exploring Some Forbidden Territory', *Oxford
                               Journal of Legal Studies*, Vol. 34 (2014), 443–479.
Keller and Sweet (2008)   Keller, Helen and Alec Stone Sweet, 'The Reception of the
                               ECHR in National Legal Orders', in: *A Europe of Rights:
                               The Impact of the ECHR on National Legal Systems*,
                               Helen Keller and Alec Stone Sweet (eds.), Oxford
                               University Press, 2008, 3–26.

Keller and Sweet (2008a)
Keller, Helen and Alec Stone Sweet, 'Assessing the Impact of the ECHR on National Legal Systems', in: *A Europe of Rights: The Impact of the ECHR on National Legal Systems*, Helen Keller and Alec Stone Sweet (eds.), Oxford University Press, 2008, 677–710.

Keller, Fischer *et al.* (2010)
Keller, Helen, Andreas Fischer and Daniela Kühne, 'Debating the Future of the European Court of Human Rights after the Interlaken Conference: Two Innovative Proposals', *European Journal of International Law*, Vol. 21 (2010), 1025–1048.

Keller and Marti (2015)
Keller, Helen and Cedric Marti, 'Reconceptualizing Implementation: The Judicialization of the Execution of the European Court of Human Rights' Judgments', *European Journal of International Law*, Vol. 26 (2015), 829–850.

Kilpatrick (2000)
Kilpatrick, Claire, 'The Future of Remedies in Europe', in: *The Future of Remedies in Europe*, Claire Kilpatrick, Toni Novitz and Paul Skidmore (eds.), Hart Publishing, 2000, 1–34.

Kim (2012)
Kim, Eun-Jung Katherine, 'Justifying Human Rights: Does Consensus Matter?', *Human Rights Review*, Vol. 13 (2012), 261–278.

Kinley, Sadurski *et al.* (2013)
Kinley, David, Wojciech Sadurski and Kevin Walton (eds.), *Human Rights: Old Problems, New possibilities*, Edward Elgar Publishing, 2013.

Klein (2000)
Klein, Eckart, 'Should the Binding Effect of the Judgments of the European Court of Human Rights Be Extended?', in: *Protecting Human Rights: The European Perspective – Studies in Memory of Rolv Ryssdal*, Paul Mahoney, Franz Matscher, Herbert Petzold and Luzius Wildhaber (eds.), Carl Heymanns Verlag, 2000, 705–713.

Klein (2013)
Klein, Eckart, 'Menschenrechtsinflation?', in: *Mensch und Recht: Festschrift für Eibe Riedel zum 70. Geburtstag*, Dirk Hanschel, Sebastian Graf Kielmansegg, Uwe Kischel, Christian Koenig and Ralph Alexander Lorz (eds.), Duncker & Humblot GmbH, 2013, 117–129.

Kleinlein (2019)
Kleinlein, Thomas, 'The Procedural Approach of the European Court of Human Rights: Between Subsidiarity and Dynamic Evolution', *International and Comparative Law Quarterly*, Vol. 68 (2019), 91–110.

Klinkner and Davis (2020)
Klinkner, Melanie and Howard Davis, *The Right to the Truth in International Law. Victims' Rights in Human Rights and International Criminal Law*, Routledge, 2020.

Klinkner and Smith (2015)
Klinkner, Melanie and Ellie Smith, 'The Right to Truth, Appropriate Forum and the International Criminal Court', in: *Current Issues in Transitional Justice*, Natalia Szablewska and Sascha-Dominik Bachmann (eds.), Springer, 2015, 3–29.

Koch (2013)   Koch, Ida Elisabeth, 'The Rule of Law as perceived by the European Court of Human Rights', in: *Protecting the Rights of Others: Festskrift til Jens Vedsted-Hansen*, Thomas Gammeltoft-Hansen, Ida Elisabeth Koch, Bettina Lemann Kristiansen and Sten Schaumburg-Müller (eds.), Djoef Publishing, 2013, 323–344.

David Kosař (2017) Kosař, David, 'Nudging Domestic Judicial Reforms from Strasbourg: How the European Court of Human Rights Shapes Domestic Judicial Design', *Utrecht Law Review*, Vol. 13 (2017), 112–123.

Koskenniemi (1997) Koskenniemi, Martti, 'Lauterpacht: The Victorian Tradition in International Law', *European Journal of International Law*, Vol. 8 (1997), 215–263.

Koskenniemi (2005) Koskenniemi, Martti, *From Apology to Utopia: The Structure of International Legal Argument: Reissue with New Epilogue*, Cambridge University Press, 2005.

Krisch (2008)   Krisch, Nico, 'The Open Architecture of European Human Rights Law', *The Modern Law Review*, Vol. 71 (2008), 183–216.

Krisch (2010)   Krisch, Nico, *Beyond Constitutionalism: The Pluralist Structure of Postnational Law*, Oxford University Press, 2010.

Kumm (2004)   Kumm, Mattias, 'The Legitimacy of International Law: A Constitutionalist Framework of Analysis', *European Journal of International Law*, Vol. 15 (2004), 907–931.

Kumm (2009)   Kumm, Mattias, 'The Cosmopolitan Turn in Constitutionalism: On the Relationship between Constitutionalism in and beyond the State', in: *Ruling the World? Constitutionalism, International Law, and Global Governance*, Jeffrey L. Dunoff and Joel P. Trachtman (eds.), Cambridge University Press, 2009, 258–325.

Langford (2015)   Langford, Malcolm, 'Why Judicial Review?', *Oslo Law Review*, Vol. 1 (2015), 36–85.

Lautenbach (2013) Lautenbach, Geranne, *The Concept of the Rule of Law and the European Court of Human Rights*, Oxford University Press, 2013.

Lavender (1997)   Lavender, Nicholas, 'The Problem of the Margin of Appreciation', *European Human Rights Law Review* (1997), 380–390.

Lavrysen (2016)   Lavrysen, Laurens, *Human Rights in a Positive State: Rethinking the Relationship between Positive and Negative Obligations under the European Convention on Human Rights*, Intersentia, 2016.

Law and Versteeg (2012) Law, David S. and Mila Versteeg, 'The Declining Influence of the United States Constitution', *New York University Law Review*, Vol. 87 (2012), 762–858.

Leach (2005)	Leach, Philip, 'Beyond the Bug River – A New Dawn for Redress before the European Court of Human Rights', *European Human Rights Law Review* (2005), 148–164.
Leach (2008)	Leach, Philip, 'The Chechen conflict: analysing the oversight of the European Court of Human Rights', *European Human Rights Law Review* (2008), 732–761.
Leach (2013)	Leach, Philip, 'No Longer Offering Fine Mantras to a Parched Child? The European Court's Developing Approach to Remedies', in: *Constituting Europe: The European Court of Human Rights in a National, European and Global Context*, Andreas Føllesdal, Birgit Peters and Geir Ulfstein (eds.), Cambridge University Press, 2013, 142–180.
Leach (2013a)	Leach, Philip, 'The European System and Approach', in: *Routledge Handbook of International Human Rights Law*, Scott Sheeran and Nigel Rodley (eds.), Routledge, 2013, 407–426.
Leach, Hardman *et al.* (2010)	Leach, Philip, Helen Hardman, Svetlana Stephenson and Brad K. Blitz, *Responding to Systemic Human Rights Violations: An Analysis of 'Pilot Judgments' of the European Court of Human Rights and Their Impact at National Level*, Intersentia, 2010.
Legg (2012)	Legg, Andrew, *The Margin of Appreciation in International Human Rights Law: Deference and Proportionality*, Oxford University Press, 2012.
Lester (2013)	Lester, Anthony, 'The European Court of Human Rights after 50 Years', in: *The European Court of Human Rights between Law and Politics*, Paperback Edition, Jonas Christoffersen and Mikael Rask Madsen (eds.), Oxford University Press, 2013, 98–115.
Letsas (2006)	Letsas, George, 'Two Concepts of the Margin of Appreciation', *Oxford Journal of Legal Studies*, Vol. 26 (2006), 705–732.
Letsas (2007)	Letsas, George, *A Theory of Interpretation of the European Convention on Human Rights*, Oxford University Press, 2007.
Letwin (2021)	Letwin, Jeremy, 'Why Completeness and Coherence Matter for the European Court of Human Rights', *European Convention on Human Rights Law Review*, Vol. 2 (2021), 119–154.
Lorenzen, Christoffersen *et al.* (2011)	Lorenzen, Peer, Jonas Christoffersen, Nina Holst-Christensen, Peter Vedel Kessing, Sten Scaumburg-Müller and Jens Vedsted-Hansen, *Den Europæiske Menneskerettighedskonvention*, Djøf Forlag, 2011.

Loucaides (2000)   Loucaides, Loukis G., 'The Concept of "Continuing" Violations of Human Rights', in: *Protecting Human Rights: The European Perspective – Studies in Memory of Rolv Ryssdal*, Paul Mahoney, Franz Matscher, Herbert Petzold and Luzius Wildhaber (eds.), Carl Heymanns Verlag, 2000, 803–815.

Loughlin (2009)   Loughlin, Martin, 'The rule of law in European jurisprudence', document CDL-DEM(2009)006 presented to the European Commission for Democracy through Law (Venice Commission).

Luhmann (1983)   Luhmann, Niklas, *Legitimation durch Verfahren*, Third Edition, Suhrkamp Verlag, 1983.

Luhmann (1993)   Luhmann, Niklas, *Das Recht der Gesellschaft*, Suhrkamp Verlag, 1993.

MacCormick (1977)   MacCormick, Neil, 'Rights in Legislation', in: *Law, Morality and Society: Essays in Honour of HLA Hart*, P. M. S. Hacker and Joseph Raz (eds.), Oxford University Press, 1977.

MacDonald (1993)   MacDonald, R. St. J., 'The Margin of Appreciation', in: *The European System for the Protection of Human Rights*, R. St. J. MacDonald, Franz Matscher and Herbert Petzold (eds.), M. Nijhoff, 1993, 83–124.

Madsen (2007)   Madsen, Mikael Rask, 'From Cold War Instrument to Supreme European Court: The European Court of Human Rights at the Crossroads of International and National Law and Politics', *Law & Social Inquiry*, Vol. 32 (2007), 137–159.

Madsen (2013)   Madsen, Mikael Rask, 'The Protracted Institutionalization of the Strasbourg Court: From Legal Diplomacy to Integrationist Jurisprudence', in: *The European Court of Human Rights between Law and Politics*, Paperback Edition, Jonas Christoffersen and Mikael Rask Madsen (eds.), Oxford University Press, 2013, 43–60.

Madsen (2018)   Madsen, Mikael Rask, 'Rebalancing European Human Rights: Has the Brighton Declaration Engendered a New Deal on Human Rights in Europe?', *Journal of International Dispute Settlement*, Vol. 9 (2018), 199–222.

Madsen (2021)   Madsen, Mikael Rask, 'From Boom to Backlash? The European Court of Human Rights and the Transformation of Europe', in: *The European Court of Human Rights. Current Challenges in Historical Perspective*, Helmut Phillip Aust and Esra Demir-Gürsel (eds.), Edward Elgar Publishing, 2021, 21–42.

Madsen (2021a)	Madsen, Mikael Rask, 'The Narrowing of the European Court of Human Rights? Legal Diplomacy, Situational Self-Restraint, and the New Vision for the Court', *European Convention on Human Rights Law Review*, Vol. 2 (2021), 180–208.
Maduro (2009)	Maduro, Miguel Poiares, 'Courts and Pluralism: Essay on a Theory of Judicial Adjudication in the Context of Legal and Constitutional Pluralism', in: *Ruling the World? Constitutionalism, International Law, and Global Governance*, Jeffrey L. Dunoff and Joel P. Trachtman (eds.), Cambridge University Press, 2009, 356–380.
Mahoney (1990)	Mahoney, Paul, 'Judicial Activism and Judicial Self-Restraint in the European Court of Human Rights: Two Sides of the Same Coin', *Human Rights Law Journal*, Vol. 11 (1990), 57–88.
Mahoney (1997)	Mahoney, Paul, 'Universality versus Subsidiarity in the Strasbourg Case Law on Free Speech: Explaining Some Recent Judgments', *European Human Rights Law Review* (1997), 364–379.
Mahoney (2007)	Mahoney, John, *The Challenge of Human Rights: Origin, Development, and Significance*, John Wiley & Sons, 2007.
Malinverni (1998)	Malinverni, Giorgio, 'Variations sur un thème encore méconnu : l'article 13 de la Convention européenne des droits de l'homme', *Revue trimestrielle des droits de l'homme*, Vol. 35 (1998), 647–657.
Malinverni (2009)	Malinverni, Giorgio, 'Ways and Means of Strengthening the Implementation of the European Convention on Human Rights at National Level, Speech at the Colloquy Organized under the Swedish Chairmanship of the Committee of Ministers of the Council of Europe, "Towards Stronger Implementation of the European Convention on Human Rights at National Level", Stockholm, 9–10 June 2008', in: *Reforming the European Convention on Human Rights. A Work in Progress*, Council of Europe (ed.), Council of Europe Publishing, 2009, 486–490.
Martinez (2003)	Martinez, Jenny S., 'Towards an International Judicial System', *Stanford Law Review*, Vol. 6 (2003), 429–529.
Matscher (1986)	Matscher, Franz, 'Der Rechtsmittelbegriff der EMRK', in: *Festschrift für Winfried Kralik zum 65. Geburtstag*, Walter H. Rechberger and Rudolf Wesler (eds.), MANZ Verlag, 1986, 257–271.

Matscher (1988)   Matscher, Franz, 'Zur Funktion und Tragweite der Bestimmung des Art. 13 EMRK', in: *Völkerrecht, Recht der Internationalen Organisationen, Weltwirtschaftsrecht: Festschrift für Ignaz Seidl-Hohenveldem*, Karl-Heinz Böckstiegel, Hans-Erns Folz, Jörg Manfred Mössner and Karl Zemanek (eds.), Carl Heymanns Verlag, 1988, 315–337.

Matscher (1993)   Matscher, Franz, 'Methods of Interpretation of the Convention', in: *The European System for the Protection of Human Rights*, R. St. J. Macdonald, F. Matscher and H. Petzold (eds.), M. Nijhoff, 1993, 63–82.

McGregor (2012)   McGregor, Lorna, 'The Role of Supranational Human Rights Litigation in Strengthening Remedies for Torture Nationally', *The International Journal of Human Rights*, Vol. 16 (2012), 737–754.

Mertens (1968)   Mertens, Pierre, 'Le droit à un recours effectif devant l'autorité nationale compétente dans les conventions internationales relatives à la protection des droits de l'homme', *Revue belge de droit international* (1968), 446–470.

Mertens (1973)   Mertens, Pierre, *Le droit de recours effectif devant les instances nationales en cas de violation d'un droit de l'homme: Analyse des incidences de l'article 13 de la Convention européenne de sauvegarde des droits de l'homme et des libertés fondamentales*, Éditions de l'Université de Bruxelles, 1973.

Meuwissen (2000)   Meuwissen, Damian, 'Reflections on Habermas's Legal Theory and Human Rights', in: *Protecting Human Rights: The European Perspective – Studies in Memory of Rolv Ryssdal*, Paul Mahoney, Franz Matscher, Herbert Petzold and Luzius Wildhaber (eds.), Carl Heymanns Verlag, 2000, 905–920.

Milner (2014)   Milner, David, 'Protocols no. 15 and 16 to the European Convention on Human Rights in the Context of the Perennial Process of Reform: A Long and Winding Road', *Zeitschrift für Europarechtliche Studien*, Vol. 17 (2014), 19–51.

Moravcsik (2000)   Moravcsik, Andrew, 'The Origins of Human Rights Regimes: Democratic Delegation in Postwar Europe', *International Organization*, Vol. 54 (2000), 217–252.

Mowbray (2004)   Mowbray, Alistair, *The Development of Positive Obligations under the European Convention on Human Rights by the European Court of Human Rights*, Oxford University Press, 2004.

Mowbray (2014)	Mowbray, Alastair, 'Between the Will of the Contracting Parties and the Needs of Today: Extending the Scope of the Convention Rights and Freedoms beyond What Could Have Been Foreseen by the Drafters of the ECHR', in: *Shaping Rights in the ECHR: The Role of the European Court of Human Rights in Determining the Scope of Human Rights*, Eva Brems and Janneke Gerards (eds.), Cambridge University Press, 2014, 17–37.
Mowbray (2015)	Mowbray, Alastair, 'Subsidiarity and the European Convention on Human Rights', *Human Rights Law Review*, Vol. 15 (2015), 313–341.
Müller (2003)	Müller, Jörg Paul, 'Subsidiarität und Menschenrechtsschutz', in: *Die Welt der Verfassungstates*, Martin Morlok (ed.), Nomos, 2003, 35–43.
Naqvi (2006)	Naqvi, Yasmin, 'The Right to the Truth in International Law: Fact or Fiction?', *International Review of the Red Cross*, Vol. 88 (2006), 245–273.
Neuman (2013)	Neuman, Gerald L., 'Subsidiarity', in: *The Oxford Handbook of International Human Rights Law*, Dinah Shelton (ed.), Oxford University Press, 2013, 360–378.
Neuman (2014)	Neuman, Gerald L., 'Bi-Level Remedies for Human Rights Violations', *Harvard International Law Journal*, Vol. 55 (2014), 323–483.
Neumann (2011)	Neumann, Ulfrid, 'Vorwort', in: *Menschenrechte und Volkssouveränität in Europa: Gerichte als Vormund der Demokratie?*, Gret Haller, Ulfrid Neumann and Klaus Günther (eds.), Campus, 2011, 7–10.
Nickel (2007)	Nickel, James W., *Making Sense of Human Rights*, Second Edition, Wiley-Blackwell, 2007.
Nollkaemper (2014)	Nollkaemper, André, 'Conversations among Courts', in: *The Oxford Handbook of International Adjudication*, Cesare PR Romano, Karen J Alter and Yuval Shany (eds.), Oxford University Press, 2014, 523–549.
Nonet and Selznick (1978)	Nonet, Phillippe and Philip Selznick, *Law and Society in Transition: Toward Responsive Law*, Routledge, 1978.
Nussbaum (2011)	Nussbaum, Martha C., *Creating Capabilities: The Human Development Approach*, Harvard University Press, 2011.
Nussberger (2017)	Nussberger, Angelika, 'Procedural Review by the ECtHR: View from the Court', in: *Procedural Review in European Fundamental Rights Cases*, Janneke Gerards and Eva Brems (eds.), Cambridge University Press, 2017, 161–176.

O'Boyle (2014)   O'Boyle, Michael, 'The Role of Dialogue in the Relationship
                          between the European Court of Human Rights and
                          National Courts', in: *The Realisation of Human Rights:
                          Studies in Honour of Leo Zwaak*, Yves Haeck, Brianne
                          McGonigle Leyh, Clara Burbano-Herrera and Diana
                          Contreras-Garduño (eds.), Intersentia, 2014, 91–105.

Okresek (2006)   Okresek, Wolf, 'Subsidiarität im Verfahren nach der
                          EMRK', in: *Staat und Recht in europäischer Perspektive.
                          Festschrift Heinz Schäffer*, Metin Akyürek, Gerhard
                          Baumgartner, Dietmar Jahnel, Georg Lienbacher and
                          Harald Stolzlechner (eds.), C.H. Beck, 2006, 575–594.

O'Neill (1996)   O'Neill, Onora, *Towards Justice and Virtue: A Constructive
                          Account of Practical Reasoning*, Cambridge University
                          Press, 1996.

O'Neill (2005)   O'Neill, Onora, 'The Dark Side of Human Rights',
                          International Affairs, Vol. 81 (2005), 427–439.

Papier (2006)   Papier, Hans-Jürgen, 'Execution and Effects of the
                          Judgments of the European Court of Human Rights
                          from the Perspective of German National Courts',
                          Human Rights Law Journal, Vol. 27 (2006), 1–4.

Paraskeva (2008)   Paraskeva, Costas, 'Returning the Protection of Human
                          Rights to Where They Belong, At Home', *International
                          Journal of Human Rights*, Vol. 12 (2008), 415–448.

Parish (2011)   Parish, Matthew, *Mirages of International Justice. The
                          Elusive Pursuit of a Transnational Legal Order*, Edward
                          Elgar Publishing, 2011.

Partsch (1954)   Partsch, Karl Josef, 'Die Entstehung der europäischen
                          Menschenrechtskonvention', *Zeitschrift für auslän-
                          disches öffentliches Recht und Völkerrecht*, Vol. 15 (1954),
                          631–660.

Pauwelyn (1996)   Pauwelyn, Joost, 'The Concept of a "Continuing Violation"
                          of an International Obligation: Selected Problems',
                          British Yearbook of International Law, Vol. 66 (1996),
                          415–450.

Pedersen (2016)   Pedersen, Jussi Erik, *Begrunnelse av rettsavgjørelser*,
                          Universitetsforlaget, 2016.

Pellonpää (2007)   Pellonpää, Matti, 'Continuity and Change in the Case-Law
                          of the European Court of Human Rights', in: *Promoting
                          Justice, Human Rights and Conflict Resolution through
                          International Law. Liber Amicorum Lucius Caflisch*,
                          Marcelo G. Kohen (ed.), M. Nijhoff, 2007, 409–420.

Pellonpää (2007a)   Pellonpää, Matti, *Europeiska människorättskonventionen*,
                          Alma Talent, 2007.

Pelloux (1961)   Pelloux, Robert, 'Précédents et caractères géneraux de
                          la Convention européenne', in: *La protection interna-
                          tionale des droits de l'homme dans le cadre européen*,
                          Council of Europe (ed.), Dalloz, 1961.

Petzold (1993) Petzold, Herbert, 'The Convention and the Principle of Subsidiarity', in: *The European System for the Protection of Human Rights*, Ronald St. J. Macdonald, Franz Matscher and Herbert Petzold (eds.), M. Nijhoff, 1993, 41–62.

Pfeffer (2009) Pfeffer, Robert, *Das Verhältnis von Völkerrecht und Landesrecht: Eine kritische Betrachtung alter und neuer Lehren unter besonderer Berücksichtigung der Europäischen Menchenrechtskonvention*, Mohr Siebeck, 2009.

Polakiewicz (2001) Polakiewicz, Jörg, 'The Status of the Convention in National Law', in: *Fundamental Rights in Europe: The European Convention on Human Rights and Its Member States, 1950–2000*, Robert Blackburn and Jörg Polakiewicz (eds.), Oxford University Press, 2001, 31–54.

Pollmann and Lohmann (2012) Pollmann, Arnd and Georg Lohmann, *Menschenrechte: Ein interdisziplinäres Handbuch*, J.B. Metzler, 2012.

Popelier (2012) Popelier, Patricia, 'The Court as a Regulatory Watchdog: The Procedural Approach in the Case Law of the European Court of Human Rights', in: *The Role of Constitutional Courts in Multilevel Governance*, Patricia Popelier, Armen Mazmanyan and Werner Vandenbruwaene (eds.), Intersentia, 2012, 249–267.

Popelier (2019) Popelier, Patricia, 'Procedural Rationality Review after Animal Defenders International: A Constructively Critical Approach', *European Constitutional Law Review*, Vol. 15 (2019), 272–293.

Popelier, Lambrecht et al. (2016) Popelier, Patricia, Sarah Lambrecht and Koen Lemmens (eds.), *Criticism of the European Court of Human Rights. Shifting the Convention System: Counter-Dynamics at the National and EU Level*, Intersentia, 2016.

Popelier, Heyning et al. (2011) Popelier, Patricia, Catherine Van De Heyning and Piet Van Nuffel, 'The Interaction between European and National Courts as to Human Rights Protection: The Editor's Introduction', in: *Human Rights Protection in the European Legal Order: The Interaction between the European and the National Courts*, Patricia Popelier, Catherine Van De Heyning and Piet Van Nuffel (eds.), Intersentia, 2011, 1–16.

Popelier and Van De Heyning (2013) Popelier, Patricia and Catherine Van De Heyning, 'Procedural Rationality: Giving Teeth to the Proportionality Analysis', *European Constitutional Law Review*, Vol. 9 (2013), 230–262.

Popelier and Van De Heyning (2017) Popelier, Patricia and Catherine Van De Heyning, 'Subsidiarity Post-Brighton: Procedural Rationality as Answer?', *Leiden Journal of International Law*, Vol. 30 (2017), 5–23.

328   *Bibliography*

Popovic (2008)   Popovic, Dragoljub, 'Prevailing of Judicial Activism over
                          Self-restraint in the Jurisprudence of the European
                          Court of Human Rights', *Creighton Law Review*, Vol. 42
                          (2008), 361–396.
Posner and Sykes (2011)   Posner, Eric A. and Alan O. Sykes, 'Efficient Breach of
                          International Law: Optimal Remedies, "Legalized
                          Noncompliance," and Related Issues', *Michigan Law
                          Review*, Vol. 243 (2011), 243–294.
Rawls (1971)   Rawls, John, *A Theory of Justice*, Harvard University Press,
                          1971.
Raymond (1980)   Raymond, Jean, 'A Contribution to the Interpretation of Art
                          13 of the European Convention on Human Rights', *The
                          Human Rights Review*, Vol. V (1980), 161–175.
Raz (1979)   Raz, Joseph, *The Authority of Law. Essays in Law and
                          Morality*, Oxford University Press, 1979.
Raz (1998)   Raz, Joseph, 'On the Authority of Interpretation of
                          Constitutions: Some Preliminaries', in: *Constitutionalism –
                          Philosophical Foundations*, Larry Alexander (ed.), Cam-
                          bridge University Press, 1998, 152–193.
Raz (2009)   Raz, Joseph, *The Authority of Law*, Second Edition, Oxford
                          University Press, 2009.
Reiertsen (2007)   Reiertsen, Michael, 'EMD-dommers bindingsvirkning
                          etter EMK artikkel 46(1) sett i lys av den tyske
                          Forfatningsdomstolens behandling av Görgülü-sakene',
                          Nordic Journal of Human Rights, Vol. 25 (2007), 225–244.
Reiertsen (2016)   Reiertsen, Michael, 'Norway: New Constitutionalism,
                          New Counter-Dynamics?', in: *Criticism of the European
                          Court of Human Rights. Shifting the Convention System:
                          Counter-Dynamics at the National and EU Level*,
                          Patricia Popelier, Sarah Lambrecht and Koen Lemmens
                          (eds.), Intersentia, 2016, 361–384.
Reiertsen (2017)   Reiertsen, Michael, *The European Convention on Human
                          Rights Article 13. Past, Present and Future*, Phd thesis,
                          Oslo, 2017.
Ridruejo (2005)   Ridruejo, José Antonio Pastor, 'Le principe de subsidiarité
                          dans la Convention européenne des droits de l'homme',
                          in: *Internationale Gemeinschaft und Menschenrechte:
                          Festschrift für Georg Ress zum 70. Geburtstag am 21. Januar
                          2005*, Jürgen Bröhmer, Roland Bieber, Christian Caliess,
                          Christine Langenfeld, Stefan Weber and Joachim Wolf
                          (eds.), Carl Heymanns Verlag, 2005, 1077–1084.
Rietiker (2010)   Rietiker, Daniel, 'The Principle of "Effectiveness" in the
                          Recent Jurisprudence of the European Court of Human
                          Rights: Its Different Dimensions and Its Consistency with
                          Public International Law – No Need for the Concept of
                          Treaty Sui Generis', *Nordic Journal of International Law*,
                          Vol. 79 (2010), 245–277.

Rijnhout and Emaus (2014)	Rijnhout, Rianka and Jessy M. Emaus, 'Damages in Wrongful Death Cases in the Light of European Human Rights Law: Towards a Rights-Based Approach to the Law of Damages', *Utrecht Law Review*, Vol. 10 (2014), 91–106.
Roach (2019)	Roach, Kent, 'The Disappointing Remedy? Damages as a Remedy for Violations of Human Rights', *University of Toronto Law Journal*, Vol. 69 Supplement 1 (2019), 33–63.
Roach (2021)	Roach, Kent, *Remedies for Human Rights Violations. A Two-Track Approach to Supra-National and National Law*, Cambridge University Press, 2021.
Romano (2013)	Romano, Cesare P. R., 'The Rule of Prior Exhaustion of Domestic Remedies: Theory and Practice in International Human Rights Procedures', in: *International Courts and the Development of International Law: Essays in Honour of Tullio Treves*, Nerina Boschiero, Tullio Scovazzi, Cesare Pitea and Chiara Ragni (eds.), Springer, 2013, 561–572.
Rui (2013)	Rui, Jon Petter, 'The Interlaken, Izmir and Brighton Declarations: Towards a Paradigm Shift in the Strasbourg Court's Interpretation of the European Convention of Human Rights', *Nordic Journal of Human Rights*, Vol. 31 (2013), 28–54.
Ryssdal (1993)	Ryssdal, Rolv, 'On the Road to a European Constitutional Court', in: *Collected Courses of the Academy of European Law*, Vol. II, Book 2, Springer, 1993, 7–20.
Ryssdal (1996)	Ryssdal, Rolv, 'The coming of Age of the European Convention on Human Rights', *European Human Rights Law Review* (1996), 18–29.
Sand (2008)	Sand, Inger-Johanne, 'The Interaction of Society, Politics and Law: The Legal and Communicative Theories of Habermas, Luhmann and Teubner', *Scandinavian Studies in Law*, Vol. 53 (2008), 45–75.
Sand (2012)	Sand, Inger-Johanne, 'Hybridization, Change and the Expansion of Law', in: *Hybrid Forms of Governance*, Niels Åkerstrøm Andersen and Inger-Johanne Sand (eds.), Palgrave Macmillan, 2012, 186–204.
Sandel (2009)	Sandel, Michael J., *Justice: What's the Right Thing to Do?* Farrar, Straus and Giroux, 2009.
Sandoval and Duttweiler (2011)	Sandoval, Clara and Michael Duttweiler, 'Redressing Non-pecuniary Damages of Torture Survivors: The Practice of the Inter-American Court of Human Rights', in: *The Delivery of Human Rights: Essays in Honour of Professor Sir Nigel Rodley*, Geoff Gilbert, Francoise Hampson and Clara Sandoval (eds.), Routledge, 2011, 114–136.

Sarkin (2014) Sarkin, Jeremy, 'Enforced Disappearance as Continuing Crimes and Continuing Human Rights Violations: Studies in Honour of Leo Zwaak', in: *The Realisation of Human Rights: When Theory Meets Practice*, Yves Haeck, Brianne McGonigle Leyh, Crara Burbano-Herrera and Diana Contreras-Garduño (eds.), Intersentia, 2014, 389–414.

Sathanapally (2012) Sathanapally, Aruna, *Beyond Disagreement. Open Remedies in Human Rights Adjudication*, Oxford University Press, 2012.

Saul (2015) Saul, Matthew, 'The European Court of Human Rights' Margin of Appreciation and the Processes of National Parliaments', *Human Rights Review*, Vol. 15 (2015), 745–774.

Scalia (1989) Scalia, Antonin, 'The Rule of Law as a Law of Rules', *The University of Chicago Law Review*, Vol. 56 (1989), 1175–1188.

Schauer (1995) Schauer, Frederick, 'Giving Reasons', *Stanford Law Review*, Vol. 47 (1995), 633–659.

Schauer (2006) Schauer, Frederick, 'Do Cases Make Bad Law?', *The University of Chicago Law Review*, Vol. 73 (2006), 883–918.

Scheek (2005) Scheek, Laurent, 'The Relationship between the European Courts and Integration through Human Rights', *Zeitschrift für ausländisches öffentliches Recht und Völkerrecht*, Vol. 65 (2005), 837–886.

Schermers (2000) Schermers, Henry G., 'A European Supreme Court', in: *Protecting Human Rights: The European Perspective – Studies in Memory of Rolv Ryssdal*, Paul Mahoney, Franz Matscher, Herbert Petzold and Luzius Wildhaber (eds.), Carl Heymanns Verlag, 2000, 1271–1284.

Schilling (2014) Schilling, Theodor, 'Art. 13 EMRK und der Rechtsscutz gegen den Richter / Überlegungen aus Anlass von EGMR, Dhabi./. Italien', *Europäische Grundrechte Zeitschrift*, Vol. 41 (2014), 596–601.

Schultz (2011) Schultz, Mårten, 'Skadestånd som medel för ersättning vid kränkningar av mänskliga rättigheter', in: *Förhandlingarna vid det 39:e nordiska juristmötet i Stockholm 18–19 augusti 2011, Del 1*, Kavita Bäck Mirchandani and Kristina Ståhl (eds.), Stockholm, 2011, 217–236.

Schwartz (1996–1997) Schwartz, Gary T., 'Mixed Theories of Tort Law: Affirming Both Deterrence and Corrective Justice', *Texas Law Review*, Vol. 75 (1996–1997), 1801–1834.

Schwimmer (2009) Schwimmer, Walter, 'Presentation of the Two Introductory Reports on the Sub-themes of the Ministerial Conference in Rome 3–4 November 2000', in: *Reforming the European Convention on Human Rights. A work in progress*, Council of Europe (ed.), Council of Europe Publishing, 2009, 19–23.

Sheeran and Rodley (2013) Sheeran, Scott and Nigel S. Rodley, *Routledge Handbook of International Human Rights Law*, Routledge, 2013.

Senden (2011) Senden, Hanneke, *Interpretation of Fundamental Rights in a Multilevel Legal System: An Analysis of the European Court of Human Rights and the Court of Justice of the European Union*, Intersentia, 2011.

Settem (2015) Settem, Ola Johan, *Applications of the 'Fair Hearing' Norm in ECHR Article 6(1) to Civil Proceedings: With Special Emphasis on the Balance between Procedural Safeguards and Efficiency*, Springer, 2015.

Shane (1988) Shane, Peter M., 'Rights, Remedies and Restraint', *Chicago-Kent Law Review*, Vol. 64 (1988), 531–572.

Shany (2006) Shany, Yuval, 'Toward a General Margin of Appreciation Doctrine in General International Law?', *European Journal of International Law*, Vol. 16 (2006), 907–940.

Shany (2012) Shany, Yuval, 'Assessing the Effectiveness of International Courts: A Goal-Based Approach', *American Journal of International Law*, Vol. 106 (2012), 225–270.

Shelton (2003) Shelton, Dinah, 'The Boundaries of Human Rights Jurisdiction in Europe', *Duke Journal of Comparative & International Law*, Vol. 13 (2003), 95–153.

Shelton (2005) Shelton, Dinah, *Remedies in International Human Rights Law*, Second Edition, Oxford University Press, 2005.

Shelton (2006) Shelton, Dinah, 'Subsidiarity and Human Rights Law', *Human Rights Law Journal*, Vol. 27 (2006), 4–11.

Shelton (2009) Shelton, Dinah, 'Form, Function, and the Powers of International Courts', *Chicago Journal of International Law*, Vol. 9 (2009), 537–571.

Shelton (2013) Shelton, Dinah, 'Enforcement and Remedies', in: *Routledge Handbook of International Human Rights Law*, Scott Sheeran and Nigel Rodley (eds.), Routledge, 2013, 663–682.

Shelton (2014) Shelton, Dinah, 'Sources of Article 47 Rights', in: *The EU Charter of Fundamental Rights: A Commentary*, Steeve Peers, Tamara Hervey, Jeff Kenner and Angela Ward (eds.), Hart/Beck, 2014, 1200–1211.

Shelton (2015) Shelton, Dinah, *Remedies in International Human Rights Law*, Third Edition, Oxford University Press, 2015.

Siess-Scherz (2005)   Siess-Scherz,   Ingrid,   'Die   Bedeutung   des
                          Subsidiaritätsprinzips für den Reformprozess des
                          EGMR', in: *Internationale Gerichtshöfe und natio-
                          nale Rechtsordnung. Internationales Symposium am
                          Österreichischen Institut für Menschenrechte am 28. und
                          29. November 2003 in Salzburg zu Ehren von em.o.Univ.-
                          Prof. Dr. Dr. h.c. Franz Matscher*, Wolfram Karl (ed.),
                          N.P. Engel Verlag, 2005, 83–109.

Sinkondo (2004)   Sinkondo, M., 'Le fabuleux destin de l'article 13 de la
                          C.E.D.H. et ses suites heureuses pour les garanties indi-
                          viduelles', *Revue de Droit international et de Droit com-
                          paré*, Vol. 81 (2004), 367–417.

Skoghøy (2017)   Skoghøy, Jens Edvin A., *Tvisteløsning*, Third edition,
                          Universitetsforlaget, 2017.

Slaughter and Burke-   Slaughter, Anne-Marie and William Burke-White,
White (2007)   'The Future of International Law is Domestic (or,
                          The European Way of Law)', in: *New Perspectives on
                          the Divide Between National and International Law*,
                          André Nollkaemper and Janne Elisabeth Nijman
                          (eds.), Oxford University Press, 2007, 110–133.

Smet (2017)   Smet, Stijn, 'When Human Rights Clash in 'the Age of
                          Subsidiarity': What Role for the Margin of Appreciation?',
                          in: *Human Rights Between Law and Politics: The Margin
                          of Appreciation in Post-National Contexts*, Petr Agha
                          (ed.), Bloomsbury Publishing, 2017, 55–70.

Somek (2014)   Somek, Alexander, *The Cosmopolitan Constitution*, Oxford
                          University Press, 2014.

Somers (2018)   Somers, Stefan, *The European Convention on Human
                          Rights as an Instrument of Tort Law*, Intersentia, 2018.

Spano (2014)   Spano, Robert, 'Universality or Diversity of Human Rights?
                          Strasbourg in the Age of Subsidiarity', *Human Rights
                          Law Review*, Vol. 14 (2014), 487–502.

Spano (2018)   Spano, Robert, 'The Future of the European Court of
                          Human Rights – Subsidiarity, Process-Based Review
                          and the Rule of Law', *Human Rights Law Review*, Vol.
                          18 (2018), 473–494.

Spano (2021)   Spano, Robert, 'The Rule of Law as the Lodestar of the
                          European Convention on Human Rights: The Strasbourg
                          Court and the Independence of the Judiciary', *European
                          Law Journal* (2021), Oneline Early View, 1–17.

Spielmann (2013)   Spielmann, Dean, 'Allowing the Right Margin: The
                          European Court of Human Rights and the National
                          Margin of Appreciation Doctrine: Waiver or Subsidiarity
                          of European Review?', *Speech Delivered at the Max Planck
                          Institute for Comparative Public Law and International
                          Law Heidelberg 13 December 2013*, Published on the
                          Webpage of the ECtHR, 2013.

Spielmann (2014)   Spielmann, Dean, 'Keynote Address', in: *Judgments of the European Court of Human Rights – Effects and Implementation*, Anja Seibert-Fohr and Mark E. Villiger (eds.), Nomos, 2014, 25–32.

Spielmann (2014a)   Spielmann, Dean, 'Whither the Margin of Appreciation?', *Current Legal Problems*, Vol. 67 (2014), 49–65.

Staden (2012)   von Staden, Andreas, 'The Democratic Legitimacy of Judicial Review beyond the State: Normative Subsidiarity and Judicial Standards of Review', *International journal of constitutional law*, Vol. 10 (2012), 1023–1049.

Starr (2008)   Starr, Sonja B., 'Rethinking "Effective Remedies": Remedial Deterrence in International Courts', *New York University Law Review*, Vol. 83 (2008), 693–768.

Stephens (2002)   Stephens, Beth, 'Translating Filártiga: A Comparative and International Law Analysis of Domestic Remedies for International Human Rights Violations', *The Yale Journal of International Law*, Vol. 27 (2002), 1–57.

Stoyanova (2018)   Stoyanova, Vladislava, 'The Disjunctive Structure of Positive Rights under the European Convention on Human Rights', *Nordic Journal of International Law*, Vol. 87 (2018), 344–392.

Strasser (1988)   Strasser, Wolfgang, 'The Relationship between Substantive Rights and Procedural Rights Guaranteed by the European Convention on Human Rights', in: *Protecting Human Rights: The European Dimension: Studies in Honor of Gérard J. Wiarda*, Franz Matscher and Herbert Petzold (eds.), Carl Heymanns Verlag, 1988, 595–604.

Strauss (2008)   Strauss, David A., 'On the Origin of Rules (With Apologies to Darwin): A Comment on Antonin Scalia's "The Rule of Law as a Law of Rules"', *The University of Chicago Law Review*, Vol. 75 (2008), 997–1013.

Sunstein (1996)   Sunstein, Cass R., *Legal Reasoning and Political Conflict*, Oxford University Press, 1996.

Sunstein (2015)   Sunstein, Cass R., *Constitutional Personae*, Oxford University Press, 2015.

Sweet and Brunell (2013) Sweet, Alec Stone, and Thomas L. Brunell, 'Trustee Courts and the Judicialization of International Regimes: The Politics of Majoritarian Activism in the ECHR, the EU, and the WTO', *Journal of Law and Courts*, Vol. 1 (2013), 61–88.

Tamanaha (2004)   Tamanaha, Brian Z., *On the Rule of Law: History, Politics, Theory*, Cambridge University Press, 2004.

Tasioulas (2007)   Tasioulas, John, 'The Moral Reality of Human Rights', in: *Freedom from Poverty as a Human Right: Who Owes What to the Very Poor*, Thomas Pogge (ed.), Oxford University Press, 2007, 75–101.

Teitgen (1976)   Teitgen, Pierre-Henri, 'The European Guarantee of Human Rights: A Political Assessment', in: *Proceedings of the 4th International Colloquy about the European Convention on Human Rights Organised by the Ministry of Foreign Affairs of Italy and the Secretariat General of the Council of Europe. Rome, 5–8 November 1975*, Council of Europe (ed.), Council of Europe Publishing, 1976.

Teubner (1982)   Teubner, Gunther, 'Reflexives Recht: Entwicklungsmodelle des Rechts in vergleichender Perspektive', *Archiv für Rechts- und Sozialphilosophie*, Vol. LXVIII (1982), 13–59.

Teubner (2004)   Teubner, Gunther, 'Societal Constitutionalism: Alternatives to State-Centered Constitutional Theory?', in: *Transnational Governance and Constitutionalism*, Christian Joerges, Inger-Johanne Sand and Gunther Teubner (eds.), Hart Publishing, 2004, 3–28.

Thune (1993)   Thune, Gro Hillestad, 'The Right to an Effective Remedy in Domestic Law: Article 13 of the European Convention on Human Rights', in: *Broadening the Frontiers of Human Rights: Essays in Honour of Asbjørn Eide*, Donna Gomien (ed.), Oxford University Press, 1993, 79–95.

Tomuschat (2007)   Tomuschat, Christian, 'Reparation in Favour of Individual Victims of Gross Violations of Human Rights and International Humanitarian Law', in: *Liber Amicorum Lucius Caflisch; Promoting Justice, Human Rights and Conflict Resolution through International Law*, Marcelo G. Kohen (ed.), M. Nijhoff, 2007, 569–590.

Tomuschat (2013)   Tomuschat, Christian, 'Democracy and the Rule of Law', in: *The Oxford Handbook of International Human Rights Law*, Dinah Shelton (ed.), Oxford University Press, 2013, 469–496.

Tribe (1980)   Tribe, Laurence H., 'The Puzzling Persistence of Process-Based Constitutional Theories', *Yale Law Journal*, Vol. 89 (1980), 1063–1080.

Tribe (1997)   Tribe, Laurence H., 'Comment', in: *A Matter of Interpretation*, Amy Gutmann (ed.), Princeton University Press, 1997.

Trindade (1983)   Cançado Trindade, A. A., *The Application of the Rule of Exhaustion of Local Remedies in International Law*, Cambridge University Press, 1983.

Tripkovic (2021)   Tripkovic, Bosko, 'A New Philosophy for the Margin of Appreciation and European Consensus', *Oxford Journal of Legal Studies*, Vol. 42 (2021), 207–234.

Tsereteli (2015)   Tsereteli, Nino, *Legal Validity and Legitimacy of the Pilot Judgment Procedure of the European Court of Human Rights*, PhD thesis, Oslo, 2015.

Tuori (2002)   Tuori, Kaarlo, *Critical Legal Positivism*, Routledge, 2002.

Tuori (2011)   Tuori, Kaarlo, *Ratio and Voluntas. The Tension between Reason and Will in Law*, Routledge, 2011.

Tuori (2014)   Tuori, Kaarlo, 'Transnational Law: On Legal Hybrids and Legal Perspectivism', in: *Transnational Law. Rethinking European Law and Legal Thinking*, Miguel Maduro, Kaarlo Tuori and Suvi Sankari (eds.), Cambridge University Press, 2014, 11–57.

Tushnet (2009)   Tushnet, Mark, *Weak Courts, Strong Rights: Judicial Review and Social Welfare Rights in Comparative Constitutional Law*, Princeton University Press, 2009.

Ulfstein (2009)   Ulfstein, Geir, 'The International Judiciary', in: *The Constitutionalization of International Law*, Jan Klabbers, Anne Peters and Geir Ulfstein (eds.), Oxford University Press, 2009, 126–152.

Ulfstein (2014)   Ulfstein, Geir, 'The European Court of Human Rights as a Constitutional Court', *PluriCourts Research Paper* No. 14-08 (2014).

Ulfstein (2020)   Ulfstein, Geir, 'Interpretation of the ECHR in Light of the Vienna Convention on the Law of Treaties', *The International Journal of Human Rights*, Vol. 24 (2020), 917–934.

UN Yearbook Human Rights 1948 (1949)   United Nations Yearbook on Human Rights 1948, New York, 1949.

Valentini (2011)   Valentini, Laura, 'Global Justice and Practice-Dependence: Conventionalism, Institutionalism, Functionalism', *The Journal of Political Philosophy*, Vol. 19 (2011), 399–418.

Venzke (2011)   Venzke, Ingo, 'The Role of International Courts as Interpreters and Developers of the Law: Working out the Jurisgenerative Practice of Interpretation', *Loyola of Los Angeles International and Comparative Law Review*, Vol. 34 (2011), 99–131.

Venzke (2012)   Venzke, Ingo, *How Interpretation Makes International Law: On Semantic Change and Normative Twists*, Oxford University Press, 2012.

Venzke (2012a)   Venzke, Ingo, 'Antinomies and Change in International Dispute Settlement: An Exercise in Comparative Procedural Law', in: *International Dispute Settlement: Room for Innovations?*, Rüdiger Wolfrum and Ina Gätzschmann (eds.), Springer, 2012, 235–269.

Vermeule (2004)   Vermeule, Adrian, 'The Judiciary Is a They, Not an It: Interpretive Theory and the Fallacy of Division', *Journal of Contemporary Legal Issues*, Vol. 14 (2004), 549–584.

Vila (2017)   Vila, Marisa Iglesias, 'Subsidiarity, Margin of Appreciation and International Adjudication within a Cooperative Conception of Human Rights', *International Journal of Constitutional Law*, Vol. 15 (2017), 393–413.

Villiger (2007)   Villiger, Mark E., 'The Principle of Subsidiarity in the European Convention on Human Rights', in: *Promoting Justice, Human Rights and Conflict Resolution through International Law*, Marcelo G. Cohen (ed.), M. Nijhoff, 2007, 623–637.

Voeten (2013)   Voeten, Eric, 'Politics, Judicial Behaviour, and Institutional Design', in: *The European Court of Human Rights between Law and Politics*, Paperback Edition, Jonas Christoffersen and Mikael Rask Madsen (eds.), Oxford University Press, 2013, 61–76.

Voeten (2014)   Voeten, Erik, 'International Judicial Behavior', in: *The Oxford Handbook of International Adjudication*, Cesare P. R. Romano, Karen J. Alter and Yuval Shany (eds.), Oxford University Press, 2014, 550–568.

Vogiatzis (2016)   Vogiatzis, Nikos, 'The Admissibility Criterion under Article 35(3)(b) ECHR: A "Significant Disadvantage" to Human Rights Protection?', *International & Comparative Law Quarterly*, Vol. 65 (2016), 185–211.

Vorwerk (2004)   Vorwerk, Volkert, 'Kudla gegen Polen—Was kommt danach?', *JuristenZeitung*, Vol. 59 (2004), 553–559.

Vospernik (2001)   Vospernik, Tanja, 'Das Verhältnis zwischen Art 13 und Art 6 EMRK – Absorption oder "Apfel und Birne"?', *Österreichische Juristen-Zeitung*, Vol. 56 (2001), 361–368.

Voßkuhle (2010)   Voßkuhle, Andreas, 'Multilevel Cooperation of the European Constitutional Courts: Der Europäische Verfassungsgerichtsverbund', *European Constitutional Law Review*, Vol. 6 (2010), 175–198.

Vysockiene (2002)   Vysockiene, Lyra, 'Effective Remedy in Asylum Cases with Particular Focus on Lithuania', *Baltic Yearbook of International Law*, Vol. 2 (2002), 105–126.

Wacks (2015)   Wacks, Raymond, *Understanding Jurisprudence*, Fourth Edition, Oxford University Press, 2015.

Waldron (2006)   Waldron, Jeremy, 'The Core of the Case against Judicial Review', *The Yale Law Journal* (2006), 1346–1406.

Waters (2014)   Waters, Christopher P. M., 'Introduction', in: *Adjudicating International Human Rights: Essays in Honour of Sandy Ghandhi*, J. A. Green and C. P. M. Waters (eds.), Brill Nijhoff, 2014, 1–11.

Weiler (2014)   Weiler, Joseph, 'Editorial', *European Journal of International Law*, Vol. 25 (2014), 635–644.

Wemmers (2014)   Wemmers, J. A. M., *Reparation for Victims of Crimes against Humanity: The Healing Role of Reparation*, Routledge, 2014.

White (2000)   White, Robin, 'Remedies in a Multi-Level Legal Order: The Strasbourg Court and the UK', in: *The Future of Remedies in Europe*, Claire Kilpatrick, Tonia Novitz and Paul Skidmore (eds.), Hart Publishing, 2000, 191–204.

White (2005–2006)   White, Brent T., 'Say You're Sorry: Court-Ordered Apologies as a Civil Rights Remedy', *Cornell Law Review*, Vol. 9 (2005–2006), 1261–1312.

Widmer-Schlumpf (2014)   Widmer-Schlumpf, Eveline, 'Opening Address at the Interlaken Conference', in: *Reforming the European Convention on Human Rights. Interlaken, Izmir, Brighton and beyond*, Council of Europe (ed.), Council of Europe Publishing, 2014, 12–14.

Wildhaber (2002)   Wildhaber, Luzius, 'A Constitutional Future for the European Court of Human Rights', *Human Rights Law Journal*, Vol. 23 (2002), 161–165.

Wildhaber (2004)   Wildhaber, Luzius, 'The European Court of Human Rights in action', *Ritsumeikan Law Review*, Vol. 21 (2004), 83–92.

Wildhaber (2007)   Wildhaber, Luzius, 'The European Court of Human Rights: The Past, The Present, The Future', *American University International Law Review*, Vol. 22 (2007), 521–538.

Wildhaber (2009)   Wildhaber, Luzius, 'Address Held at the Workshop "The Improvement of Domestic Remedies with Particular Emphasis on Cases of Unreasonable Length of Proceedings", Held at the Initiative of the Polish Chairmanship of the Council of Europe's Committee of Ministers, Strasbourg, 28 April 2005', in: *Reforming the European Convention on Human Rights. A work in progress*, Council of Europe (ed.), Council of Europe Publishing, 2009, 83–84.

Wildhaber (2009a)   Wildhaber, Luzius, 'Statement Made at the European Ministerial Conference on Human Rights in Rome, 3–4 November 2000', in: *Reforming the European Convention on Human Rights: A work in progress*, Council of Europe (ed.), Council of Europe Publishing, 2009, 33–34.

Wildhaber (2013)   Wildhaber, Luzius, 'Rethinking the European Court of Human Rights', in: *The European Court of Human Rights between Law and Politics*, Paperback Edition, Jonas Christoffersen and Mikael Rask Madsen (eds.), Oxford University Press, 2013, 204–229.

Index

CPSIA information can be obtained
at www.ICGtesting.com
Printed in the USA
LVHW080601270922
729370LV00005B/239